THE NATURAL CLASSROOM

A DIRECTORY OF FIELD COURSES, PROGRAMS,
AND EXPEDITIONS IN THE NATURAL SCIENCES

Jack R. Edelman, Ph.D.

NORTH AMERICAN PRESS
GOLDEN, COLORADO

This book is dedicated to my parents, Irving and Frances Edelman,
to my uncle and aunt, Irving and Pearl Rosenbach,
and to my Ph.D. mentor, Dr. Yue J. Lin,
Department of Biological Sciences, Saint John's University, New York.

Copyright © 1996 Jack R. Edelman, Ph.D.

Book design by Bill Spahr

All rights reserved. No part of this book may be reproduced or transmitted in any form or by any means, electronic or mechanical, including photocopying, recording, or by any information storage and retrieval system, without permission in writing from the publisher.

Library of Congress Cataloging-in-Publication Data

Edelman, Jack R.
    The natural classroom : a directory of field courses, programs, and expeditions in the natural sciences / Jack R. Edelman.
        p.   cm.
    ISBN 1-55591-923-5
    1. Natural history—Study and teaching—United States—Directories. 2. Natural history—Study and teaching—Directories. 3. Natural history—Research—United States—Directories. 4. Natural history—Research—Directories. I. Title.
QH50.5.E34   1996
508'.071—dc20   96-6046
                                                              CIP

Printed in the United States of America

0 9 8 7 6 5 4 3 2 1

North American Press
A division of Fulcrum Publishing
350 Indiana Street, Suite 350
Golden, Colorado 80401-5093
(800) 992-2908

TABLE OF CONTENTS

Acknowledgments	iv
Preface	v
Introduction: A New Dimension in Science Education	vi
Section One: Courses, Programs, and Expeditions in the United States	1
Section Two: International Courses, Programs, and Expeditions	209
Section Three: National Science Foundation Teacher Enhancement Program: U.S. Courses and Workshops	235
Afterword	279
About the Author	279

ACKNOWLEDGMENTS

This work could not have been completed without the help of Richard McDermott, publisher of the *New York Chronicle*. His preparation of the manuscript was crucial to the completion of this book. In addition, appreciation is extended to Marjorie McDermott for her typing and proofreading skills, and to Shirley Lambert and Daniel Forrest-Bank, Editors at Fulcrum Publishing/North American Press, for their help and expertise. I also wish to thank Elizabeth Hawkes, Marketing Director for North American Press, for her help and consideration. I would also like to thank my literary agent, Ethan Ellenberg, for his help and encouragement in completing this work.

Appreciation is also extended to each of the institutions described in this book for providing details of their operations and program offerings. Special thanks to the National Science Foundation for providing information on their teacher workshops.

PREFACE

Welcome to the world of field courses, programs, seminars, workshops, expeditions, ecotours, and educational travel!

In the early spring of 1982, I was working on my Ph.D. and teaching high school biology. On the biology department bulletin board I happened to notice a brochure describing field courses offered at the Yellowstone Institute. Several courses in the brochure caught my eye—geothermal geology, calderas and hydrothermal systems, and the geology of Yellowstone. That summer I took two courses in volcanic geology and enjoyed them so much that I returned to Yellowstone in 1984 to take the courses again!

Several years before that experience, I had taken courses in order to fulfill teacher certification requirements in earth science. One field course I had found was called "field geology of Long Island" as well as a similar course called "geology of national parks."

As the years passed, I took a number of field courses, seminars, and workshops, at numerous other institutions. I even discovered ways to travel independently and receive college (graduate or undergraduate) credit. I enjoyed these experiences so much that I couldn't understand why relatively few science teachers (or teachers in general) were not taking advantage of these courses and programs. I had discovered a new world, a world of education adventure and travel that pays off in course credits.

But it appears that very few people know such programs exist, and that is the reason for this book. Dozens upon dozens of seminars, short courses, field courses, workshops, and programs for teachers, students, naturalists, and independent scholars are listed in this book. These programs emphasize the natural sciences, including general biology, botany, zoology, ecology, marine biology, ichthyology, microbiology, natural history, geology, etc., and to a lesser extent, chemistry, physics, mathematics, and astronomy.

Many courses and programs take place during the summer vacation so that teachers and students can combine activities—vacationing, traveling, and learning. The programs described here run from several hours to several months, or even longer. They are indescribable experiences; above all, they are *fun!*

INTRODUCTION

A NEW DIMENSION IN SCIENCE EDUCATION

In recent years there has been much concern over the shortage of qualified science teachers throughout the United States. This shortage has forced many school systems to place teachers with little or no science background—sometimes without certification—in science classrooms.

Although many of these teachers attempt to take additional science courses to fulfill certification requirements and to enhance their scientific knowledge, for many the chore of going back to college during evening hours, summers, or weekends, is a difficult and time-consuming task, especially when they have families. The courses and programs described here can alleviate much of that pain because they make learning stimulating, enjoyable, and challenging. In addition, they often allow teachers and their families to combine business with pleasure, that is, combine college science courses with vacations, especially during the summer.

Studying volcanic geology at Yellowstone National Park, for example, is not exactly a burdensome return to the college classroom. During this adventure one learns about such phenomena as geysers, hot springs and fumaroles, mudposts, ash flow tuffs, obsidian and igneous petrology, the Yellowstone caldera, basaltic and rhyolitic lava flows, travertine deposition, and the biology of hot springs. Teachers who enroll in even a few of the courses listed in this book will be able to earn enough science credits to fulfill their science certification requirements.

Opportunities are also available for college students (undergraduate and graduate) to take courses that in many cases can be credited toward degree requirements at their home institutions. Of course, prior approval is always necessary for credit that will transfer and count toward a degree.

Several entries describe programs open to high school students, and a few programs admit even younger students. In many cases, new high school graduates can get a head start on their college careers by taking some of these courses during the summer.

Even if no formal academic credit is sought, the programs described here offer a world of opportunity to study and experience natural history. These programs really add a new dimension to science education.

Things to Know

There are a number of items one should be aware of when attending these field courses, seminars, workshops, expeditions, etc. I will attempt to cover them concisely.
1) Although many of the programs carry college credit (graduate or undergraduate), others do not offer formal credit. Please note, however, that almost any program described here (of at least seven days duration) offers some form of college credit if steps for earning credit through independent study or travel study are followed.

2) There are many reasons why teachers and other individuals want credit for study. Generally it is to fulfill state or local certification requirements, in-service requirements,

Introduction

or to obtain salary increments and differentials or transfer of credit to a degree program at another institution. Do not assume that any credit will automatically be approved by a school board, state education department, or other colleges or universities. Always inquire at least several months in advance of registration, and always get it in writing!

3) Certain courses or programs are quite rigorous in nature. They may involve hiking, mountain climbing, backpacking, swimming, or traveling in hot or cold climates. Participants must be in good physical shape for such programs and have enough experience in these special skills to handle them. For example, a person who has no diving experience or who cannot swim would probably not fare well in a course that involves scuba diving. Before signing up for physically demanding courses or programs, check with the institution directly to find out what skills and experiences are needed. Getting a doctor's approval for such strenuous programs is sometimes helpful.

4) Be sure to find out what equipment is needed for a particular program; the brochures that are available from the institution will explain these requirements in detail, and many are noted in the program descriptions in this book. I remember when I took a course that involved climbing up and down steep hills made of silty soil. Sturdy boots were recommended but I chose to wear ordinary sneakers. I had no problem walking down the hill, but it took five men to hoist me back up—I'm not exactly what one would call a lightweight.

If enrolling in a program abroad, find out what documents are needed (e.g., passport, visa, birth certificate, proof of immunization, etc.) and be sure to carry them on your person.

5) In most cases, I have given only a general range of costs and fees for the programs described in this book. This is not an oversight. Costs, fees, or tuition usually change from year to year. The current prices for these programs are directly available by contacting the institutions themselves.

Current, relevant information was of primary importance in preparing this book. However, readers may wonder if these courses and programs will still be relevant four years from now. Things do change; new courses and programs are developed, others are dropped. This book has taken change into consideration by choosing what materials to present. Its intent is to provide a brief introduction to the institutions that offer these programs, so that participants may contact the institutions directly and find out exactly what is available in a particular year. This work is not intended to be a schedule of classes or a precise list of what is being offered at a particular time. The idea is to introduce interested individuals to the institutions and to give them a feel for the type of programs and courses offered, so that they may contact those that sound appealing. For this reason, each entry provides only a sample of the courses or programs available.

Gaining College Credit

Most of the programs described in this book are associated with various colleges and universities. As a result, many of them carry graduate or undergraduate credit. Participants may have a choice of graduate or undergraduate credit; this information may be obtained from the institutions themselves.

Many of the ecotours, safaris, and expeditions do not offer any formal credit, but it may still be possible to obtain college credit for most of these programs anyway. There are two basic ways to obtain such credit: independent study and travel study.

Independent Study

Most colleges and universities offer independent study courses and courses that are similar to independent study. In some colleges these are simply called "independent study" courses. In other colleges they take on a variety of similar names, like "directed research," "special topics," "independent research," and so forth. Participants should contact their local college or university, alma mater, or almost any other institution, for that matter, and inquire about the possibility of getting such independent study credit for their trip. Of course, this should be done at least several months in advance of the trip, so that all the details and course requirements can be worked out between the participants and their college. Usually participants keep a daily log of their activities while on the trip, write a term paper, do additional library research, and possibly meet with professors at the college before and after the trip. The participant is responsible for working out the particulars with a member of a specific department (biology, geology, or geography, for example). This is not to imply that every college or university will agree to grant credit for a trip, but many will do so.

Travel Study

Probably an easier way to obtain credit for a trip is through travel study. There are several colleges and universities that have special correspondence programs for teachers and others who travel and wish to obtain credit for it. In general, the travel must be of at least seven days duration to obtain credit; the longer the travel, the more credit can be obtained. Also, participants must first write a proposal about their itinerary and destination, an outline of sites to be visited, and what they hope to learn. Some prior library research and keeping an academic log may be required. A term paper or lesson plan must be submitted within several months of the end of the trip. The cost is very reasonable, usually from $65 to $200 per credit. Proof of travel must also be submitted. Additional information on travel study programs can be found on pages 22, 41, and 181.

Section One

COURSES, PROGRAMS, AND EXPEDITIONS IN THE UNITED STATES

ALABAMA

AMAZON CENTER FOR ENVIRONMENTAL EDUCATION AND RESEARCH FOUNDATION
10 Environs Park
Helena, AL 35080
(205) 428-1700 or (205) 428-1712/(800) 255-8206
Contact: Staff

SAMPLE EXPEDITIONS

All expeditions travel to their facility located in the Peruvian Amazon tropical rainforest. International rainforest workshops for the general public are offered in March, rainforest workshops for educators and children are offered in the summer, rainforest workshops for pharmacists are offered in the fall, and rainforest workshops for physicians and health care professionals are offered in the winter.

CURRICULUM AND CREDITS

Workshops are offered each year to allow participants the opportunity to share ideas with and learn from the world's leading experts and researchers of the tropical rainforest. During the one-week workshops, participants spend every day in small group sessions with each session lasting about three hours and involving lectures, presentations, and hands-on field experiences. Sessions are held in the morning, afternoon, and evening. The format allows the participants to meet and exchange information with leading botanists, entomologists, biologists, herpetologists, and field researchers. Ongoing research can be observed both at the facility and on the Canopy Walkway, a quarter-mile expanse of walkways and platforms high in the rainforest canopy, offering the opportunity to study and observe this dynamic dimension of the rainforest. Since this is an extremely unexplored area of the forest, much research is being planned for the canopy.

College credits are offered through a variety of different colleges, universities, and organizations, with each having their own credit requirements. More institutions are in the process of being approved. A partial current listing includes the Texas Pharmacy Foundation in Austin, Texas, Pittsburg State University in Pittsburg, Kansas, and Huntington College in Montgomery, Alabama.

THE INSTITUTION

The Amazon Center for Environmental Education and Research Foundation (ACEER) is a 501 C-3, nonprofit foundation, with headquarters located in Alabama, and a facility in the Peruvian Amazon tropical rainforest. ACEER equips and maintains the Amazon facility as an international focal point for research scientists, educators, children, and travelers. They also establish environmental education programs for local Peruvian teachers and children, work with local inhabitants, demonstrate the positive potential of environmentally sensitive tourism as an effective conservation strategy, protect one million acres of primary rainforest, and sponsor ongoing scientific research projects.

THE ENVIRONMENT

The ACEER site is located between the Napo and the Sucasari Rivers, downriver from Iquitos, Peru. In addition to the South American facility, the Canopy Walkway allows access to this previously unexplored part of the forest. Both are situated in primary rainforest, surrounded by an incredible biodiversity of plants, animals, and local peoples and cultures.

FACILITIES

ACEER offers accommodations for travelers, researchers, educators, and schoolchildren. The facility sits on one million acres of undisturbed primary rainforest. Built on a raised wooden platform with thatched roof and open windows, it can accommodate up to 30 people at a time. Showers and sanitary toilets are provided separately from the sleeping quarters. There is a complete kitchen, and although there is no electricity, the glow of the kerosene lanterns at night adds to the jungle atmosphere. Generators provide temporary power for slide shows and emergencies. Trails are marked and cleared for ease in walking. Hammocks provide restful spots in the midday heat, and clean drinking water is available at all times.

SUPPLIES NEEDED

A complete passenger check list of required equipment is provided upon registration. Remember, the facility is located in a remote area, miles away from any stores or shops.

APPLICATIONS AND ADMISSIONS

For information about trip and workshop schedules, contact the above address. Trips to ACEER leave Miami almost weekly, although the workshops occur only on designated dates.

Financial Aid: Currently, no scholarships or grants are available, but efforts are being made to put such a system in place for the future.

Costs: The cost for the 1-week workshop is approximately $1,800 and includes the round-trip airfare from Miami, all Peruvian transportation, lodging, and food for the entire week. Items of a personal nature are not included in the cost.

INTERNATIONAL EXPEDITIONS, INC.
One Environs Park
Helena, AL 35080
(205) 428-1700, ext. 219/(800) 633-4734
Fax: (205) 428-1714
Contact: Veronica Roads or Lane Curtis

SAMPLE WORKSHOPS AND EXPEDITIONS

Specialized rainforest workshops for enthusiastic naturalists, educators, students, and pharmacists are offered to the Peruvian Amazon, Belize, and Costa Rica. Wildlife/nature/rainforest expeditions are offered to the Amazon, Alaska, Antarctica, Australia, Baja, Belize, China, Costa Rica, Ecuador, Galapagos, Hawaii, India, Kenya, Tanzania, Komodo, Malaysia, Thailand, New Guinea, New Zealand, Panama, Peru Archaeology, Peru Solstice, Tambopata, Uganda, and Venezuela. Independent Nature Travel destinations include Alaska, Argentina, Australia, Belize, Brazil, Costa Rica, Galapagos, Guatemala, Honduras, India, Kenya, Madagascar, Mexico, New Guinea, New Zealand, Peru, Tanzania, Venezuela, and Zimbabwe.

CURRICULUM AND CREDITS

International Expeditions, Inc. (IEI) workshops offer each participant the opportunity to share ideas with and to learn from the world's leading experts on rainforest environments. Rainforest "workshoppers" participate in several small group workshop sessions, each approximately three hours long and involving hands-on field experience. This format allows participants to meet and exchange ideas with rainforest botanists, zoologists, entomologists, and field researchers, who also teach the sessions.

Optional extensions are offered to almost every destination. Some destinations offer more than one extension. Graduate or undergraduate credits are available for workshops as well as their regular programs to any of the above destinations. Persons interested in obtaining college credit should contact Veronica Roads at the above address or telephone number. Credits are offered through Pittsburg State University in Pittsburg, Kansas.

THE INSTITUTION

IEI has introduced thousands of travelers to the rainforest areas of the earth. The objective of IEI's international rainforest workshops is to engender a love and respect for rainforests that will prevail not only among participants but among all those with whom they share this experience.

THE ENVIRONMENT

Workshops and expeditions offer hands-on field experience in the tropical rainforest.

FACILITIES

All facilities are fully equipped with laboratory equipment and necessary supplies for the workshops and expeditions.

SUPPLIES NEEDED

Participants generally do not need specific supplies; inquire directly with IEI.

APPLICATIONS AND ADMISSIONS

Contact IEI at the above address for forms and information on application and admission procedures.

Financial Aid: Contact IEI for specific information. At the present time, no financial aid is available.

Costs: Inquire with IEI for the latest brochures and costs of specific programs and expeditions.

MARINE ENVIRONMENTAL SCIENCES CONSORTIUM
Dauphin Island Sea Lab
P.O. Box 369-370
Dauphin Island, AL 36528
(205) 861-2141
Fax: (205) 861-7540
Contact: Associate Director for Academic Affairs

SAMPLE COURSES AND PROGRAMS

Courses and programs include Marine Botany, Marine Biology, Marine Invertebrate Zoology, Marine Geology, Marine Technical Methods, Coastal Geomorphology, Coastal Ornithology, Introduction to Oceanography, Marine Ecology, Marine Vertebrate Zoology, Marsh Ecology, Commercial Marine Fisheries of Alabama, Coastal Zone Management, and Coastal Climatology.

Graduate courses are offered in alternating years on the academic quarter calendar. Graduate courses offered biannually include Physical Oceanography, Marine Ecology, Marine Biogeochemistry, Advanced Topics in Oceanography: Global Change, Seagrass Ecosystem Ecology, Marine Resource Management, Marine Zooplankton Ecology, Biological Oceanography, Field Marine Science, Marine Animal Physiology, Oceanology of the Gulf of Mexico, Phytoplankton Ecology and Physiology, Fisheries Oceanography, and Fish Physiology.

CURRICULUM AND CREDIT

Marine Environmental Sciences Consortium (MESC) is not a degree-granting institution. Summer school courses are offered annually for both undergraduate and graduate students. Programs are conducted in support of both undergraduate and graduate degrees of the 22 member institutions. Each summer, two 5-week course sessions are held at the sea lab. These graduate and advanced undergraduate courses are conducted by resident sea lab faculty, visiting professors, and adjunct faculty from member institutions. Courses are open to students from MESC schools and out-of-state students who may register as transient students.

Enrolled students attend one of the 22 members of the consortium and utilize MESC's resources at the Dauphin Island Sea Lab as an integral part of their graduate education while they work toward their degrees. Both M.S. and Ph.D. programs are available through MESC's member institutions. Degree requirements vary among the various campus programs. Students may be required to spend a minimum residence period at the campus granting their degree. The remainder of their graduate career is spent at the sea lab taking courses and conducting original research. Resident faculty at the sea lab serve as advisors and research consultants to the students and their graduate committees.

MESC's Discovery Hall Program offers a variety of educational programs year-round for kindergarten through high school students, teachers, and the general public. Two sessions of a 4-week summer course in marine science is available for high school students who have already taken a course in general biology. All Discovery Hall programs are intended to increase understanding and appreciation for the marine environment by directly involving participants in that environment with dynamic, hands-on activities.

THE INSTITUTION

MESC is Alabama's marine research and educational institution. Founded in 1972 by the Alabama legislature to maximize the marine sciences capabilities of several Alabama institutions and minimize duplication, MESC includes 22 public and private Alabama colleges and universities. The administrative and operational base for MESC is the Dauphin Island Sea Lab, Alabama. The MESC and its faculty work toward the combined purposes of conducting pure and applied research, and sponsoring structured educational programs for individuals and organizations interested in and dependent upon the marine environment.

Courses, Programs, and Expeditions in the United States

THE ENVIRONMENT

The MESC Dauphin Island Sea Lab facility is located on 36 acres of the eastern end of Dauphin Island, a barrier island approximately 3 miles from the mainland and 40 miles south of Mobile, Alabama. The sea lab spans the island and has direct access to the Gulf of Mexico, Mississippi Sound, and Mobile Bay. A bridge connects the island to the mainland.

FACILITIES

MESC is housed in 27 buildings at the Dauphin Island Sea Lab. The four buildings located on the south campus provide over 9,000 square feet of classroom/laboratory facilities. Marine Science Hall, the main research facility at the sea lab, contains over 13,397 square feet of laboratory and office space. The campus accommodates 150 persons in residence. Two 84-person dormitories, an efficient 2-story apartment complex with 12 units, and 13 three-bedroom houses provide quarters for visiting faculty and students.

MESC maintains two research vessels in addition to several smaller boats and skiffs. Wet lab facilities, housed in a 2,160 square-foot building, including a 25-foot recirculating research flume and several environmentally controlled labs, are available for controlled experimental work on living marine organisms. Laboratories are equipped with state-of-the-art instrumentation for biochemical research, and field collection equipment is available for marine ecological and oceanographic research.

The MESC library is highly specialized in the marine sciences, particularly those areas relating to the ecology and geology of the Gulf Coast region. Its holdings include more than 5,800 bound volumes and approximately 600 periodical titles with a wide selection of current subscriptions.

SUPPLIES NEEDED

Inquire with the institution at the time of application or registration.

APPLICATIONS AND ADMISSIONS

Admission to one of the programs includes access to the programs at the sea lab campus. Transient or transfer students should inquire directly to the Associate Director for Academic Affairs. MESC curriculum information, summer school brochures, and financial aid applications are available on request from MESC. Applicants interested in marine studies in Alabama should inquire at one of the following MESC schools in Alabama: Alabama State University in Montgomery; Athens State College in Athens; Auburn University in Auburn; Auburn University in Montgomery; Birmingham Southern College in Birmingham; Huntington College in Montgomery; Jacksonville State University in Jacksonville; Judson College in Marion; Livingston State University in Livingston; Samford University in Birmingham*; Spring Hill College in Mobile; Talladega College in Talladega; Troy State University in Troy; Troy State University in Dothan; Tuskegee University in Tuskegee*; University of Alabama in Tuscaloosa*; University of Alabama in Birmingham*; University of Alabama in Huntsville*; University of Mobile in Mobile; University of Montevallo in Montevallo; University of North Alabama in Florence; University of South Alabama in Mobile*.

* Graduate Degree Programs

Financial Aid: Available for graduate work at the sea lab campus in the form of fellowships, research assistantships, and a limited number of teaching assistantships. Several undergraduate scholarships are available during the summer and limited additional part-time jobs are available. Twelve-month stipends average from $9,600 for M.S. students to $12,000 for Ph.D. students. Extramural-supported research and teaching assistants are expected to devote approximately 20 hours per week to their assigned responsibilities. Students from any MESC school may apply for assistance.

Costs: Tuition rates and fees vary depending on the university in which the student enrolls. Student efficiency apartments are available on campus at approximately $180 per month including utilities. A limited number of houses may be available for students with children at the approximate rate of $300 per month plus utilities; summer dormitory rooms and board are available at approximately $134 per week (7-day meals) and $125 per week (5-day meals). The 4-week Discovery Hall High School Program including room, board, lab fees, and tuition is $850. Discovery Hall academic year programs are available for classes (maximum 35 students) at $180 per day for tuition, $12 a night per person for dorm rooms (based on double occupancy), and $15 a day per person for meals.

ALASKA

ALASKA WILDLAND ADVENTURES
P.O. Box 389
Girdwood, AK 99587
(800) 334-8730
Fax: (907) 783-2130
Contact: Jim Wells

SAMPLE TRIPS
Trips include Natural History Safaris (7–12 days), Discovery Voyages, and Family and Senior Safaris. Trip locations include Denali National Park, Kenai Fjords National Park, Wrangell–St. Elias National Park, and Prince William Sound.

CURRICULUM AND CREDITS
Alaska Wildland Adventures (AWA) is a nationally recognized natural history/ecotourism company operating highly reputable soft-adventure packages in Alaska. Trips feature small group experiences (a maximum of 18 guests) that combine safe and fun outdoor adventuring with the security of professional tour guides, comfortable and tastefully rustic accommodations, and delicious meals. Although credit is not granted directly, it may be obtained through independent or travel study.

THE INSTITUTION
Since 1977, AWA has offered environmentally sensitive natural history trips and wilderness expeditions. Owned and operated by Kirk Hoessle and Jim Wells, AWA donates 10% of its earnings to various environmental groups.

THE ENVIRONMENT
AWA features hikes in mountain meadows, a ride on the world famous Alaska railroad, white- and calm-water rafting, and cruising for whales while viewing seacoast glaciers. Participants enjoy the beauty of Alaska's wilderness regions, from the majestic tidewater glaciers of Kenai Fjords National Park to the upland tundra and stunning high-mountain vistas of Denali National Park. Experienced naturalists lead the way, providing information about local ecology, wildlife, and conservation ethics.

FACILITIES
Nights are spent in cozy cabins, heated wilderness lodges, and cabins complete with linens and hot showers.

SUPPLIES NEEDED
Participants should bring two-piece quality raingear, lightweight and water-repellent hiking boots, wool or pile pants, shirts (one wool), a warm jacket and sweater, long underwear, wool socks, and a hat.

APPLICATIONS AND ADMISSIONS
Save $50 to $100 on early bookings. Send a $400 deposit after March 1 (50% of trip tuition is required for deposit). A cancellation fee is applied up to 60 days prior to departure. For a free, informative 24-page color brochure, contact the above address.

Financial Aid: None available.

Costs: The average cost per day for all-inclusive trips is between $250 and $350. Discounts are offered for triple and quad rooms, early- and late-season departures, and early bookings.

JOHN WENGER
6038 East 12th Avenue, # 10
Anchorage, AK 99504
(907) 337-0608
Contact: John Wenger, Instructor

SAMPLE COURSES AND EXPEDITIONS

Courses and expeditions include the Natural History of Denali Parks, Wrangell–St. Elias National Park, Delta River Rafting Expedition, Arctic National Wildlife Refuge, Yukon River, and the Gates of the Arctic.

CURRICULUM AND CREDITS

The Matanuska-Susitna School District in Alaska offers natural history classes through the Mat-Su Community School Program during the summer. The purpose of these courses is to provide the public with an opportunity to study the natural history of Alaska under professional leadership. Each summer semester different classes involving trips into remote parts of Alaska are offered to study, enjoy, and photograph the natural history of Alaska. They may be credit or noncredit, depending on the particular class. Credit is provided by the Matanuska-Susitna College of the University of Alaska.

THE INSTITUTION

All classes are taught and lead by naturalist/wildlife biologist John Wenger, an instructor for the University of Alaska. The trips originate in Anchorage, Alaska. Before arriving, students receive detailed preparation lists. The prebriefs are held in Anchorage at the University of Alaska. One day after the prebrief, the class group leaves Anchorage for the field trip. Once at the fieldsite, most of the day is spent observing and photographing natural history. A typical day is spent based in camp along an alpine lake with daily hikes scheduled to explore the nearby wilderness which require daypacks only. All field instruction is quite informal and there is ample time for personal exploration or resting.

THE ENVIRONMENT

The national parks and wilderness areas of Alaska.

FACILITIES

Inquire with Professor Wenger upon the time of registration or application.

SUPPLIES NEEDED

Students provide their own camping gear and food, transportation to and from Anchorage, and any necessary lodging. Instructions and basic information are provided as to the availability of lodging and other needs.

APPLICATIONS AND ADMISSIONS

All applicants must be in good physical condition and have no serious health problems. Past field experience in overnight camping is required. Nature lovers interested in these exciting class trips may request information and apply directly by contacting the instructor, John E. Wenger, at the above address or phone number (no collect calls accepted). For possible future changes, consult the Anchorage phone directory for a listing under his name or write to John Wenger, c/o The University of Alaska, College for Continuing and Community Education, Alaska Wilderness Studies Program, 3211 Providence Drive, Anchorage, Alaska 99508.

Financial Aid: None available.

Costs: Fees are approximately $1,000 and include all transportation in Alaska for the courses.

ARIZONA

SONORAN ARTHROPOD STUDIES INSTITUTE
P.O. Box 5624
Tucson, AZ 85703
(602) 883-3945
Fax: (602) 883-2578
Contact: Steve Prchal

SAMPLE COURSES AND PROGRAMS

Courses and programs include Blacklighting in Box Canyon, Listening in the Dark, Teacher Training Workshops, Arthropod Discovery Under the Stars (Family Program), Biology of Sonoran Desert Bees, Biology of Spiders, Outreach Programs to Schools & Children's Educational Programs, Field Research Excursions, Arthropod Ecology Workshop for Educators, and Myths and Realities of Spiders.

CURRICULUM AND CREDITS

Teacher workshops provide an overview of entomology with a focus on classroom activities and team exploration. In addition to basic observation and collecting tools, husbandry techniques and classification, poems, songs, and skits are explored to encourage incorporating arthropods into the teaching of social sciences and the arts.

Daytime interpretive walks and activities are employed in both urban and desert settings. The urban "vacant" lot used for the program has many arthropods hiding under litter. Learn about ant foraging strategies and map the locations of arthropods in the lot. In contrast to exploring the natural diversity of the arthropods in the desert, the urban activities provide educators with experience that is easily incorporated into their own school setting for urban students. Interpretive walks at the institute allow participants to observe the desert's natural arthropod diversity and behaviors as well. Teacher workshops (15 hours) receive credit through University of Arizona or Prima Community College.

THE INSTITUTION

Founded in 1986, Sonoran Anthropod Studies Institute (SASI) brings together the general public and amateur and professional entomologists who share common ideas and goals in environmental education and conservation. Based in Tucson, Arizona, this nonprofit organization is the only one of its kind, devoted exclusively to public education about the arthropods and their relationships with plants, other animals, and humans. Through a variety of educational programs, field activities, and special exhibitions, SASI encourages its members and visitors to visit the area to take a close look at the fascinating world of arthropods.

THE ENVIRONMENT

SASI's new Arthropod Discovery Center in Tucson Mountain Park is nestled high in the biologically diverse Tucson Mountains. Still under construction, nature trails, foodplant and attractant gardens and exhibits are planned. To date, more than 530 plant species and 1,000 insect species have been recorded from this biotic community. A small collection from the site is maintained for use in SASI's programs.

The site is currently utilized by research entomologists and graduate students. A recording weather station provides data on environmental conditions, and honey bees are being used to monitor flowering phenology. Researchers are encouraged to share their experiences and findings as speakers at SASI's monthly public program held at the Tucson Botanical Gardens or in specific workshops focusing on their projects.

FACILITIES
Facilities include classrooms, laboratories, and collections.

SUPPLIES NEEDED
Supplies depend upon the particular workshop. Contact the institute at the above address for more information.

APPLICATIONS AND ADMISSIONS
None of SASI's offerings are regular. Application forms are included with announcements.

Financial Aid: None available.

Costs: Costs for courses and workshops vary from approximately $15 to $75.

SOUTHWESTERN RESEARCH STATION
The American Museum of Natural History
Portal, AZ 85632
(602) 558-2396
Fax: same as telephone
Contact: Staff

SAMPLE COURSES
Courses include research and volunteer programs.

CURRICULUM AND CREDITS
The station welcomes scientists and advanced students from all parts of the United States and from abroad to carry out their research projects. No formal courses for credit are offered, but credit might be awarded through travel or independent study.

The volunteer programs provide students interested in careers in biology and related fields with opportunities to meet, visit, and work with scientists of various biological disciplines. Volunteers are assigned to routine work chores for half of the working time; the balance is devoted to assisting scientists with research projects in the field or laboratory, or approved personal scientific projects.

THE INSTITUTION
The Southwestern Research Station (SRS) is a year-round field station owned and operated by the American Museum of Natural History in New York City. Since 1955, SRS has served biologists and geologists interested in researching the diverse environments and biota of the Chiricahua Mountains in southeastern Arizona.

Research at the station is carried on by curators from the American Museum of Natural History, scientists from universities, other museums, and government agencies around the country and from foreign countries, and by the resident director.

The station is located five miles west of Portal, by paved road, in Cave Creek Canyon, Cochise County, Arizona. Tour groups (participants of official organizations) are welcome to stay at the station by prior arrangement.

THE ENVIRONMENT

SRS is located in riparian habitat at an elevation of 5,400 feet, surrounded by oak, juniper, and piñon pine woodlands. Within a short drive up or down the Chiricahua Mountains, which reach nearly 9,800 feet, five separate ecological zones exist: Lower Sonoran, Upper Sonoran, Transition, Canadian, and Hudsonian. Biogeographically, the Chiricahua Mountains are located at a crossroads between distinct desert and mountain biota. At lower elevations, some species are derived from the Sonoran Desert to the west, whereas other species are from the Chihuahuan Desert to the east and south. At higher elevations, there is a mixing of plants and animals from the Rocky Mountains to the north, and the Sierra Madre Occidental Mountains of Mexico. The uniqueness and diversity of the biota make this one of the top birding locations in the United States.

FACILITIES

Facilities in the spacious Osborn Memorial Laboratory include a library, insect collection, herbarium, vertebrate collections, and photography laboratory. Classes from colleges and universities use the station. Amateur naturalists are accommodated when space is available (mostly in spring and fall).

The station is open year-round but visits by nonscientists are not encouraged from the end of November through early March. Participants live in comfortable cabins provided with linens and blankets, and take their meals, cafeteria style, in a common dining room. The main house contains a dining room, library, lounge with fireplace, recreation room, and laundry room. A large swimming pool, volleyball court, and horseshoe pit are located outside. The area is laced with trails for hiking and climbing.

SUPPLIES NEEDED

Bring personal belongings only.

APPLICATIONS AND ADMISSIONS

Applications for volunteers may be obtained by contacting the station at the above address.

Financial Aid: Food and lodging are provided without cost to volunteers in exchange for 24 hours of work chores a week.

Costs: No costs are applied to volunteers. Others must contact the station for fees.

CALIFORNIA

AFRICAN TRAVEL, INC.
The Safari Building
1100 East Broadway
Glendale, CA 91205
(800) 421-8907
Fax: (818) 507-5802
Contact: Jennifer Cesmat

SAMPLE TOURS AND SAFARIS
Tours and safaris are offered to Kenya (with an optional Tanzania Extension), South Africa, Botswana, Zambia, Zimbabwe, Tanzania, Namibia, and Egypt.

CURRICULUM AND CREDITS
Credit may be available through independent or travel study.

THE INSTITUTION
African Travel, Inc. is a wholesale tour operator specializing in tours to south and east Africa.

THE ENVIRONMENT
From the forest of the Aberdares where elephants slip silently into the bush before one's very eyes to the tranquil beauty of the Samburu region with its graceful people and towering giraffes, a safari in Kenya is truly the trip of a lifetime. The highlight of the trip will be the incomparable Masai Mara Game Reserve, scene of the annual migration of zebra and wildebeest. Extend the exciting stay in East Africa and spend additional days viewing game in Tanzania—the Land of Kilimanjaro and the Serengeti Plains. This special program allows participants to visit this intriguing and unspoiled country with visits to Lake Manyara National Park, the magical Ngorongoro Crater, and the fabulous Serengeti National Park.

FACILITIES
Scheduled flights to Africa via wide-body jets and luxury accommodations are provided, as well as all meals while on safari, experienced wildlife guides, all park entrance fees, and a specially equipped safari mini-van with guaranteed window seat.

SUPPLIES NEEDED
Some necessary supplies include a camera and plenty of film, lightweight cotton clothing, light raincoat, walking shoes, swimsuit, sunglasses, sunscreen protection lotion, binoculars, and small flashlight.

APPLICATIONS AND ADMISSIONS
To make reservations contact your travel agent or call the above toll-free number.

Financial Aid: None available.

Costs: Approximate costs—land and air from New York, $5,000; land and air from New York (June–October), $5,400, land and air from New York (April, May, and November), $5,200.

ASTRONOMICAL SOCIETY OF THE PACIFIC
390 Ashton Avenue
San Francisco, CA 94112
(415) 337-2126
Fax: (415) 337-5205
Contact: Robert Havlen

SAMPLE WORKSHOPS

Workshops include The Universe in the Classroom—A Workshop on Teaching Astronomy in Grades 3-12; A Grand Tour of the Universe (using color slides from recent space probes and observatories around the world); First Results from the Hubble Telescope; Making a Comet in Your Classroom; Observing the Sun, Moon, and Stars Using Inexpensive Materials; Black Holes—Spacewarps, Time Machines, and the Excruciating Death of Stars; The Cosmos on Computer—Software for Teaching and Learning Astronomy; Fostering Awareness in Math and Science Among Young Women, Their Parents, and Teachers.

CURRICULUM AND CREDITS

Designed for teachers, school librarians, curriculum specialists, and other educators at the elementary and secondary level, this workshop is part of a week-long international meeting on astronomy held at the University of Wyoming.

Workshops take place at a different universtiy each summer. Separate sessions are offered for teachers who have had little background in astronomy and for seasoned science teachers who would like to hear about new developments and teaching resources in the field. Thus, teachers with various skill levels and backgrounds are encouraged to attend.

Contact Astronomical Society of the Pacific (ASP) for more information about obtaining credit.

THE INSTITUTION

Contact ASP for the specifics on each year's workshop site.

THE ENVIRONMENT

The campus environment consists of lecture halls, cafeterias, and dormitories.

FACILITIES

The facilities available each year depend upon the institution that hosts the workshop.

SUPPLIES NEEDED

None.

APPLICATIONS AND ADMISSIONS

Entry to ASP is given on a first-come, first-served basis, and space is limited to 200 participants.

Courses, Programs, and Expeditions in the United States

Financial Aid: Teachers should check with their districts about the availability of Title 11 Eisenhower Funds for attending this workshop.

Costs: The workshop in Flagstaff includes approximately $80 for registration, $55 for double-occupancy dormitory and meals, $75 for single-occupancy, and $15 for continuing education credit.

BAJA EXPEDITIONS
2625 Garnet Avenue
San Diego, CA 92109
(619) 581-3311/(800) 843-6967
Fax: (619) 581-6542
Contact: Jeanne Prentice

SAMPLE EXPEDITIONS
Expeditions include whale watching, sea kayaking, Sea of Cortez natural history cruises, scuba diving, and Hawaiian coastline and tropical jungle adventure travel.

CURRICULUM AND CREDITS
Baja Expeditions have an expedition to meet every interest, activity level, and schedule. The staff is able to answer questions about each trip, send detailed descriptions of the traveler's choice of trip, make airline reservations, and insure that the trip is all the traveler expected it would be.

Whatever mode of travel or time of year the trip is taken, whether the participant is a whale watcher, a kayaker, a diver, or just an observer of sunsets, the staff welcomes all to their home. Credit may be available through independent or travel study.

THE INSTITUTION
Not applicable.

THE ENVIRONMENT
Expeditions take place in Baja California (Mexico) and the Sea of Cortez including Magdalena Bay, Isla Espiritu Santo (a volcanic island), the Loreto to La Paz coastline, Isla Pardito, the village of Timbabichi, Isla Santa Catalina, San Ignacio, and Cabo San Lucas.

FACILITIES
Comfortable cabins and knowledgeable guides are provided on each of the three ships: the 16-passenger *Don Jose*, the 8-passenger *Copper Sky*, or the 28-passenger *Searcher*. Superb food and an itinerary designed to take advantage of seasonal attractions such as whale migrations, bird nesting season, and the desert in bloom are also provided. On a given day, participants have the option to whale watch, snorkel, beachcomb, or hike, all in the company of a trained naturalist. Evening slide and video presentations offer an in-depth view of the Baja coast.

SUPPLIES NEEDED
Contact the institution for information on necessary supplies.

APPLICATIONS AND ADMISSIONS
Contact the institution at the above address for reservations.

Financial Aid: None available.

Costs: Prices range from approximately $695 for a 5-day expedition to about $1,995 for an 11-day expedition.

BIOLOGICAL JOURNEYS
1696 Ocean Drive
Mckinleyville, CA 95521
(707) 839-0178/(800) 548-7555
Fax: (707) 839-4656
Contact: Nora Winge, Trip Coordinator

SAMPLE EXPEDITIONS
Expeditions are offered to Baja, California—Whale Watching; Galapagos Islands—Whales, Birds, Photography, Amazon Jungle Camp; Alaska & British Columbia—Whales, Bears, and Glaciers; Australia—Great Barrier Reef, Rainforest, Outback.

CURRICULUM AND CREDITS
Biological Journeys (BJ) offers both marine and land wilderness natural-history tours with solid educational foundations that feature close encounters with wildlife. The small group sizes allow you to travel to the marine and land wilderness areas where you can experience outstanding wildlife viewing—whales, dolphins, bears, and marine birds—in comfort and security. Naturalist guides are knowledgeable and enthusiastic. Credit is available for some programs through Humboldt State University.

THE INSTITUTION
Not applicable.

THE ENVIRONMENT
The Alaska–British Columbia trips visit Friday Harbor, where orcas are encountered, as well as Frederick Sound, where humpbacks and grizzly bears are plentiful. These trips also visit Glacier bay, Misty Fjords, and Kootznahoo Island. The Central and South America trips visit the Galapagos Islands to study the flora and fauna, with special emphasis on birds and sperm whales. In Ecuador, the main attraction is La Selva Jungle Camp. In Baja, blue whales are studied in the Sea of Cortez, while gray whales are observed in San Ignacio Lagoon. The Australia trips feature the Great Barrier Reef.

FACILITIES
Most of the boats have private or semiprivate cabins. Food is prepared by gourmet chefs, and many of the boat captains are wildlife specialists in their own right.

SUPPLIES NEEDED
Binoculars and a collapsible duffle bag are a must. Clothing is casual. An equipment and clothing list is provided upon enrollment.

APPLICATIONS AND ADMISSIONS
A $500 deposit is required at the time of enrollment. Contact BJ at the above address for more information on application and admission procedures.

Financial Aid: None available.

Costs: Inquire with the institution. Costs are listed in their most recent brochures. The following are some approximate sample costs:

Baja, California—Best of Coastal Baja (12 days), $2,995; Baja's Whale Lagoons (9 days), $1,750; Whales, Whales, Whales (6 days), $1,995.
Alaska—Frederick Sound Whales, Bears, and Glaciers (7–10 days), $2,495–$3,295.
British Columbia—Johnstone Straits Orca Society (7 days), $2,195.
Galapagos Islands—Two Week Discovery (18 days), $3,995.
Australia—Great Barrier Reef, Rainforest, Outback (4–21 days), $600–$5,195.

CABRILLO MARINE AQUARIUM
3720 Stephen White Drive
San Pedro, CA 90731
(310) 548-7563
Fax: (310) 548-2649
Contact: Larry Fukuhara or John Eells

SAMPLE PROGRAMS

Programs include Marine Biology Workshop/Sea Search, Traveling Teacher/Ocean Outreach, School Field Trips/Exhibit Tours, and Outdoor Classroom. Programs for adults and families include Whalewatch Boat Trips, Tidepool Tours, Discovery Center Workshops, Evening Grunion Programs, and an annual 8-day Baja Whale Adventure.

CURRICULUM AND CREDITS

Programs are offered for elementary and secondary students. Credit may be obtained through either independent or travel study.

THE INSTITUTION

Cabrillo Marine Aquarium (CMA) is an educational, recreational and research facility dedicated to providing rich and varied opportunities that educate the general public about the marine environment.

THE ENVIRONMENT

Viewing Baja's wealth of marine life and its pristine coastal environments are also objectives of the aquarium. Exploration landings on the islands of Todos Santos, San Benito, Cedros, and Cabo San Quentin will allow participants to enjoy diverse geological formations and native vegetation at each location. Participants come within close camera range of hundreds of elephant seals, sea lions, and marine birds.

Meet the Friendly Whales of Baja (8-day boat trip; yearly in early March). Every year Pacific gray whales congregate in San Ignacio Lagoon, Baja California, to give birth and to mate. Adventurous persons can join Cabrillo Marine Aquarium's experienced naturalists on their annual expedition to encounter these magnificent giants up close. In the spring a limited number of boats are permitted by the Mexican government to enter San Ignacio Lagoon on special tours. Here passengers may come within an arm's reach of a whale mother with her calf pairs.

FACILITIES
The 105-foot *Royal Polaris*, a floating hotel out of San Diego, provides delicious meals and warm, clean cabins that offer comfortable accommodations for 30 passengers. The experienced crew and CMA's naturalists ensure exciting, informative, and enjoyable experiences every day.

SUPPLIES NEEDED
Adventure participants receive a "what-to-bring" list upon making their reservations. A pretrip meeting is held two months before the trip.

APPLICATIONS AND ADMISSIONS
Call or write to CMA for a brochure containing information and reservation coupon. Mail in the coupon with a $300 deposit.

Financial Aid: None available.

Costs: An 8-day trip costs approximately $1,895 per person.

CALIFORNIA DESERT STUDIES CONSORTIUM
California State University–Fullerton
c/o Department of Biology
P.O. Box 34080
Fullerton, CA 92634-9480
(714) 773-2428
Fax: (714) 773-2428
Contact: Dr. William Presch

SAMPLE COURSES
Course topics include Flowering Plants of Death Valley, Exploring the Mojave Desert—Shoshone and Tecopah Hot Springs, Insects of the Mojave Desert, Birds of the Mojave Desert, Reptiles of the Mojave Desert, and The Desert Sky in Spring.

CURRICULUM AND CREDITS
Most of those who use the center are either enrolled in college or university courses that involve some aspect of the desert—such as courses in archaeology, biology, geography, geology, and history—or are engaged in research related to the desert. However, school groups and organized community groups whose activities are desert related may also be accommodated.

THE INSTITUTION
The studies center, a field station of California State University (CSU), provides opportunity for individuals and groups to conduct research, receive instruction, and experience the desert environment. Established in 1976 under a cooperative management agreement with the Bureau of Land Management, the center is operated for CSU by the California Desert Studies Consortium, an organization of seven southern CSU campuses: Dominguez Hills, Fullerton, Long Beach, Los Angeles, Northridge, Pomona, and San Bernardino.

THE ENVIRONMENT

The center is situated at Soda Springs on the shore of Soda Dry Lake at an elevation of 938 feet and at the western edge of the East Mojave National Scenic Area. It serves as a convenient departure site for groups visiting the Death Valley National Monument, the Kelso Dunes, the Afton Canyon riparian areas, the Cima Dome and Volcanic area, the historic Mojave Road, the Early Man Site at Calico, and the Clark Mountains. Soda Springs itself is of great interest to archaeologists, biologists, and historians. Evidence of prehistoric and historic activity are readily seen, including prehistoric quarry sites and ancient human artifacts, such as projectile points and rock art.

The rich variety of wildlife results from the diverse habitats and plant communities located near the center, including halophytic vegetation, marsh communities, ponds and springs with pondweed, cattail, and sedges, extensive creosote bush scrub and saltbush scrub stands, sand dunes with sand-adapted vegetation, and plants of rocky slopes.

FACILITIES

The center accommodates approximately 75 individuals in dormitory-style rooms that can hold two to ten persons each with single, double, or bunk beds. A multi-station kitchen, a washhouse with hot showers, and indoor and outdoor eating areas are also provided. Although no camping facilities are provided at the center, camping is permitted in the Razor Open Area approximately 4 miles south of the facility.

In addition to living accommodations, the center maintains a laboratory for both individual and group use, a modest library, and two classrooms, the largest of which can accommodate 70 persons. Most facilities at the center are wheelchair accessible.

Kitchen facilities include stoves, refrigerators, and some cookingware. Although most individuals and groups prepare their own meals, the center can arrange for meal service for groups of 15 or larger. Recreation facilities include a campfire circle, a basketball hoop, horseshoe pits, and a soaking pool.

SUPPLIES NEEDED

Necessary supplies are directly dependent on the course requirements. Desert survival equipment, however, is strongly recommended with consideration of the time of the year.

APPLICATIONS AND ADMISSIONS

All public education courses are administered through the Extended Education Office, California State University, San Bernardino, California. College and university groups should contact the above address directly.

Financial Aid: None available.

Costs: Costs are approximately $9 a night per person.

CHEESEMAN'S ECOLOGY SAFARIS
20800 Kittredge Road
Saratoga, CA 95070
(408) 741-5330 or (408) 867-1371/(800) 527-5330
Fax: (408) 741-0358
Contact: Doug or Gail Cheeseman

SAMPLE TOURS

Tours on wildlife photography and excellent bird and mammal watching are led to the following destinations: Antarctica, Kenya, Tanzania, Uganda, Botswana, Namibia, Costa Rica, Belize, Alaska, Australia, Bhutan, and Nepal. Pelagic trips are taken to Monterey Bay in January for viewing marine mammals and seabirds.

CURRICULUM AND CREDITS

Wildlife Safaris are offerd for nonsmokers with a strong interest in learning about natural history from enthusiastic and knowledgeable guides. Small groups average one naturalist per six participants. Most tours are led by Doug and Gail Cheeseman and resident naturalists. Credit is available through independent or travel study.

THE INSTITUTION

Cheesman's Ecology Safaris (CES) is owned and operated by Doug and Gail Cheesman. Doug is a biology professor and wildlife photographer, and Gail is a naturalist and birder.

THE ENVIRONMENT

Each destination visits a particular environment. Tours are frequently led in the field to see as much interaction of animals with their environment as possible. Participants learn from nature and gain a strong interest in saving the precious plant and animal habitats that deserve to exist on this fragile planet.

FACILITIES

Facilities vary with each different destination. Contact the institution for specific information on the facilities available for a particular safari.

SUPPLIES NEEDED

Inquire with CES for information about any special supplies needed for a particular destination.

APPLICATIONS AND ADMISSIONS

Contact the institution at the above address for brochures listing dates of specific safaris and reservation information.

Financial Aid: None available.

Costs: The average cost of trips is between $200 and $250 per day, depending on the length of the trip, logistics, and location. Trips range from 10 to 30 days. A deposit of $300 is required to reserve space.

CULTURAL AWARENESS THROUGH TRAVEL
University of the Pacific Enhancement Courses
440 West First Street, #102
Tustin, CA 92680
(800) 484-1081, ext. 7775 (9A.M.–9P.M. PST)
Fax: (714) 552-0740
E-mail: TASH_S@a1.SCCD.CC.CA.US
Contact: Steve Tash, Instructor
P.O. Box 16501
Irvine, CA 92713-6501

Courses, Programs, and Expeditions in the United States

SAMPLE COURSES

Educators identify curriculum goals and develop multicultural activities and materials for instructional use based on their domestic and/or foreign travels. American and/or international cultural resources are used to develop thematic units, learning stories, instructional activities in writing, art, music, science, history, social sciences, and other disciplines.

CURRICULUM AND CREDITS

Courses can be taken for one to six credits and are granted as post-baccalaureate semester credits offered through the Office of Lifelong Learning and provided exclusively to educators for professional upgrading and salary advancement credit only; they are not applicable to a degree program. A letter grade is given based on the evaluation of a "Critical Thinking" paper and the "Classroom Learning Activities" assignments.

THE INSTITUTION

The University of the Pacific is fully accredited by the Western Association of Schools and Colleges. Independent research and development of multicultural activities and materials for instructional use are among the goals of this program. Each participant selects, develops, and reports on five learning-center activities, worksheets, instructional games, kits, bulletin board patterns, media programs, folders, and other such materials prepared for use in the classroom or program. Participants may use travel experiences gained from visits to various historic sites, ethnic neighborhoods, business areas, art and historical museums, cultural exhibits or shows, theatres, and governmental agencies. Participants may use library resources or materials from commercial outlets in order to enable the student to better understand the many social, ethnic, economic, educational, and "daily" problems encountered by various cultural groups, both within the United States and abroad.

THE ENVIRONMENT

Not applicable.

FACILITIES

Teachers share their learning experiences in their classroom or program setting by the use of slides, videos, bulletin boards, learning centers, games and activities, or through other formats they may devise and deem proper.

The teacher gains more insight into the factors facing students from various cultural and ethnic backgrounds and develops lessons that accomodate these children in a more positive learning environment. The teacher studies the rationale for cultural diversity in the classroom and comments on its usefulness to their particular classroom or program setting.

SUPPLIES NEEDED

Not applicable.

APPLICATIONS AND ADMISSIONS

Educators interested in enrolling in this travel study program should contact Professor Steve Tash at the above address.

Financial Aid: None available.

Costs: Costs are approximately $65 per credit, which may be paid upon registration by check, money order, Visa, or Mastercard.

EAGLE LAKE BIOLOGICAL FIELD STATION
Department of Biological Sciences
California State University–Chico
Chico, CA 95929-0515
(916) 898-4490 or (916) 898-5356 (voice mail)
Fax: (916) 898-4363
Contact: Raymond J. Bogiatto, Director

SAMPLE COURSES
Courses include Field Biology, Field Botany, Zooarchaeology and Field Ecology, Studies in Natural History, Field Studies in Fisheries Biology, and Archaeological Site Survey.

CURRICULUM AND CREDITS
The station may be utilized by any public or private group whose primary purpose is academic and whose activities are consonant with the natural environment. Various groups from high schools, the Boy Scouts, consulting firms, as well as from state agencies such as the California Department of Forestry have used the field station in the past, but the vast majority of its use has been by university courses in the natural and behavioral sciences. Field biology, ecology, anthropology (archaeology), and geology courses from California State University–Chico, University of California–Davis, and other institutions are offered regularly during the summer session at Eagle Lake. In addition, NSF teacher workshops, seminars, and the like are offered for periods of one day to six weeks.

THE INSTITUTION
The Eagle Lake Biological Field Station (ELBFS) is located 26 miles northwest of Susanville, Lassen County, California. California Routes 36 and 44 from the west and 395 from the north and south lead to Susanville. Eagle Lake can be reached by paved road (County Road A-1), but the field station is at the end of 10 miles of dirt roads. The recommended route is Route 139 north from Susanville for 16 miles, turn left at the field station sign and follow the ELBFS signs. The dirt roads are rough and rocky; a four-wheel-drive vehicle is not necessary but a vehicle with high-clearance is recommended.

The field station itself is sited on 62 acres on the middle eastern shore of the lake. The land accessible to students and faculty is much greater—literally thousands of acres. The station property lies within a basin sage/western juniper ecosystem, but a variety of habitats (e.g., marshlands, lakes, streams, high desert, playa lakes, and Montana coniferous forest) are very close by. Temperatures are typical for the Modoc Plateau with highs in the 90s and lows in the 50s during the summer months. Winters are cold, reaching zero degrees, and the lake freezes over regularly.

THE ENVIRONMENT
Eagle Lake, the second largest freshwater lake in California, lies in an isolated valley on the eastern side of the Cascade Range. The lake covers about 30,000 acres and is nearly 14 miles long. Located at the juncture of four major geologic provinces, it is bordered to the west by the forested slopes of the Cascades, to the south by the Sierra Nevadas, to the east by the arid Great Basin, and to the north and northeast by the volcanic Modoc Plateau.

Located in the northeastern corner of California, Eagle Lake is relatively undeveloped and undisturbed. The nearest permanent residents live 7 miles from the field station. The lake's geologic isolation provides a unique set of biological communities. Forests become interspersed with western juniper, basin sage, and mountain mahogany, eventually giving way to sage, juniper, and rabbit brush to the north and east of the field station. The alkaline waters of Eagle Lake allow only five native species of fish to thrive, including the endemic Eagle Lake rainbow trout. Nevertheless, the lake is moderately productive with large populations of invertebrates and fish-eating birds. Volcanic ice caves on the west side of the lake are home to cave crickets and other cave life.

FACILITIES
There are several buildings including cabins, dormitories, a dining hall, a library, and a five-room laboratory. Some scientific equipment is available at the station, but much more is available from the main campus and transported up as needed. Several boats are available for scientific use. The station has no public phone, but a radio phone is available in case of emergency. Groups of up to 30 people can be accommodated comfortably.

SUPPLIES NEEDED
Information is provided upon registration.

APPLICATIONS AND ADMISSIONS
Contact the institution at the above address for information on admission and application procedures.

Financial Aid: Contact the instution for information.

Costs: Approximate station and room fees—cabins, $14 per night per person; dormitory, $9 per night per person; facilities usage fee, $3 per day per person; meal service, $14 per person (3 meals per day).

F AND H TRAVEL CONSULTING/ BRAZIL TOURISM OFFICE
2441 Janin Way
Solvang, CA 93463
(212) 490-9350 (New York City direct number)
or (805) 688-8646/(800) 544-5503
Fax: (805) 688-1021
Contact: Claudio Heckmann, Director (U.S. and Canada);
Robert Falkenburg II, Sales Director

SAMPLE TOURS AND EXPEDITIONS
Special scientific and education tours and expeditions to the Amazon are offered for tourists, ornithologists, biologists, botanists, and geologists.

CURRICULUM AND CREDITS
Participants are exposed to the peculiarities of the highlands concerning fauna and flora, combining leisure, adventure, ecology, and environmental education. Credit is available through independent or travel study.

THE INSTITUTION

The company does marketing and sales promotion through ecological and environmental associations in the United States. All projects promote environmental awareness.

THE ENVIRONMENT

This tourism project introduces the visitor to the highlands of the Brazilian Amazon, where one can find colossal trees and wildlife in large areas of native jungle.

FACILITIES

The Floresta Amazonica Hotel is a four-star hotel that has a native jungle with pathways, a swimming pool, a football field, volleyball court, and game rooms. There is also a bar and restaurant, a meeting room for 50 people, and 42 rooms and 4 suites, each equipped with an air conditioner, color TV, VCR, music, mini-refrigerator, and private veranda.

The Cristalino Jungle Lodge in Cristalino Forest Reservation offers accommodations in bungalows with private toilets or in two large rooms with four toilets and four showers in each. There is a dining room, an equipped kitchen, barbecue pit, floating deck, motor boats, and canoes. Fishing rods are also available.

SUPPLIES NEEDED

Contact the institution at the above address for information on necessary supplies.

APPLICATIONS AND ADMISSIONS

Contact the institution at the above address for information about programs and reservations.

Financial Aid: None available.

Costs: Prices vary depending on tour length and destination. Contact the institution for brochures and most current rates.

FIELD STUDIES IN NATURAL HISTORY
San Jose State University
College of Science
One Washington Square
San Jose, CA 95192-0099
(408) 924-2625
Fax: (408) 924-5037
Contact: Phyllis Swanson

SAMPLE COURSES

Field study courses include Lassen Volcanic National Park, Death Valley, Calaveras Big Trees, and the Grand Canyon. Courses for dogsleds or RVs include Alaska the Beautiful, the Other California, Lava Beds National Monument, and Henry Cowell's Lime Kilns.

Courses vary each summer. Some courses have junior programs available for children ages 5 to 16. International travel study programs are also offered. For more information, call the San Jose State University Travel Programs office at (408) 924-2680.

CURRICULUM AND CREDITS

Field studies programs are offered through the Department of Continuing Education. Instructors are drawn from experts in several disciplines and departments, and the format for the programs is an educational vacation for families, students, teachers, and children, at sites of scientific, historical interest, and natural beauty. Most of the programs are located in California, but they have ventured to such places as Alaska and Hawaii. They offer programs for college students and family members and junior programs for children and young teens. All the programs are taught by highly qualified instructors.

Field studies programs are designed for teachers who require in-service teacher training credit for step increases, promotional advancement, and educational background training in specific field-related life and physical science areas.

THE INSTITUTION

San Jose State University is an urban college with a student body of 25,000 located in the heart of Silicon Valley.

THE ENVIRONMENT

Field study courses are off-campus natural history experiences. Scenic parks throughout the West become the base camps for studies in geology, botany, ecology, and zoology. Accommodations for the Death Valley trip are at an abandoned borax mining camp.

FACILITIES

Facilities are often primitive, depending upon the park that is used as the base camp. Day classes are spent hiking; the classrooms have no walls with only the sky for a roof. There are no accommodations for wheelchairs.

SUPPLIES NEEDED

Participants provide their own camping gear and food as well as transportation to and from the study sites. Car pooling is encouraged.

APPLICATIONS AND ADMISSIONS

Classes are open to any interested adult. Registration forms are available by calling or writing to the institution at the above address.

Financial Aid: None available at this time.

Costs: Costs vary from approximately $100 (Almaden Quicksilver Mines, the Other California) and $175 (Death Valley) to $200 (Lava Beds National Monument, Henry Cowell State Park, the Pacific Northwest, Trinity Alps, and Lassen National Park) and $1,700 (Grand Canyon, Alaska, and Hawaii).

GALAPAGOS TRAVEL
P.O. Box 1220
San Juan Bautista, CA 95045-1220
(408) 623-2920/(800) 969-9014
Fax: (408) 623-2923
Contact: Barry Boyce

SAMPLE PROGRAMS

Galapagos Travel (GT) conducts several 11-day and 2-week natural history and photography workshops. Basic orientation involves cruising around the Galapagos Islands in a chartered 16-passenger yacht. Each day, participants go ashore twice (led by a licensed guide, trained at the Charles Darwin Research Station), observing and photographing the unique wildlife—the plants and animals that led Darwin to his theory of evolution when he visited the Galapagos in 1835. There are also two snorkeling sessions per day. Evenings are devoted to informal discussions ranging from Galapagos natural history to the type of photographic situations expected on the following day.

CURRICULUM AND CREDITS

Credit may be available through independent study, arranged through the student's educational institution. GT also offers National Science Teachers Association–sponsored workshops for teachers. Graduate credits are available for these workshops.

THE INSTITUTION

GT has been operating professionally led Galapagos natural history workshops since 1990. They also publish and distribute Galapagos-related literature.

THE ENVIRONMENT

The Galapagos archipelago consists of 13 islands, each with its own unique flora and fauna. There are 45 visitor sites; only 2 sites can be visited per day. Participants are allowed enough time to visit all the islands, including the significant outer islands, and increased opportunities for viewing and photographing wildlife.

FACILITIES

Passengers travel on board the 80-foot yacht *San Jacinto*. Built in Ecuador in 1989 specifically for Galapagos Island service, the *San Jacinto* carries 16 passengers with a crew of 9, including a university-level naturalist guide. Eight comfortably sized double cabins are on board, each containing a private bathroom with shower and an electrically actuated flush toilet.

SUPPLIES NEEDED

Each participant receives a copy of *A Traveler's Guide to the Galapagos Islands*, written by GT owner, Barry Boyce. This serves as a complete reference and trip-planning guide. Passengers must provide their own snorkeling gear and cameras.

APPLICATIONS AND ADMISSIONS

A $300 deposit (payable by check or credit card) is required. Contact the office at the above address for a trip application form.

Financial Aid: None available.

Costs: Approximately $2,650 for 11 days in the Galapagos (not including airfare), or approximately $3,250 for 2 full weeks (18 days total trip length).

HOPKINS MARINE STATION OF STANFORD UNIVERSITY
Ocean View Boulevard
Pacific Grove, CA 93950
(408) 655-6200
Fax: (408) 375-0793
Contact: Staff

SAMPLE COURSES
Courses include Subtidal Communities, Introduction to Oceanic Biology, Cell Biology of Early Development, Biomechanics of Intertidal Organisms, Problems in Marine Ecology, and Molecular Approaches to Ion Channels.

CURRICULUM AND CREDITS
Five-week courses are offered each summer. The summer program is open to all advanced undergraduate, graduate, and postdoctoral students, and teachers whose biological backgrounds, or teaching or research activities can benefit from a summer's study of marine life.

THE INSTITUTION
Hopkins Marine Station is a division of Stanford University located on Monterey Bay in Pacific Grove, California.

THE ENVIRONMENT
The marine station is ideally situated for the study of marine life. Monterey Bay has rich and diverse marine fauna and flora. Many of the plants and animals reproduce during the summer and their development can be investigated. Various habitats include open ocean, kelp forest, granite rocks, tide pools, sandy beaches, mud flats, estuaries, and brine pools.

FACILITIES
The station has no residences or dormitories. All students find rooms, apartments, or houses in the adjacent towns, which are seaside resorts, full of tourists in summer, but with adequate living quarters available. Sometimes the station can help to bring students in contact with homeowners and apartment house managers, but it cannot be responsible for engaging quarters. It is recommended that students arrive a few days early to arrange for housing. Motels abound in the region.

SUPPLIES NEEDED
Contact the institution at time of application for information on necessary supplies.

APPLICATIONS AND ADMISSIONS
Application forms and information may be obtained by writing to Hopkins Marine Station at the above address. Completed applications should be received by March 31. Applicants will be notified of admission in mid-April. Late applications will be considered and applicants accommodated if space is still available.

Financial Aid: Partial tuition fellowships are available to students.

Costs: Approximate course costs are—for 6 units, $2,577, and for 12 units, $4,809. For noncredit students, a fee of approximately $1,460 for each 6-unit course is charged.

INNERASIA EXPEDITIONS
2627 Lombard Street
San Francisco, CA 94123
(415) 922-0448/(800) 777-8183
Fax: (415) 346-5535
E-mail: innerasia.path.net
Contact: Reservations Department

SAMPLE TOURS AND EXPEDITIONS
Tours and expeditions are offered to China, Tibet, Mongolia, Russia, Bhutan, Nepal, India, Sri Lanka, Burma, Cambodia, Laos, Vietnam, Pakistan, Iran, Turkmenistan, Siberia, Kazakhstan, Tajikistan, Uzbekistan, Kyrgyzstan, Japan, Thailand, Tannu Tuva, Italy, France, Switzerland, Greece, Austria, Turkey, Chile, Argentina, Bolivia, Costa Rica, the Galapagos Islands, Alaska, the Falkland Islands, and Antarctica.

CURRICULUM AND CREDITS
Credit may be available through independent or travel study.

THE INSTITUTION
InnerAsia is a professional travel management corporation that provides a broad range of travel services for agents and individuals, as well as location and marketing support for corporations, nonprofit organizations, and government tourism offices. The company specializes in remote locations and complicated logistical situations.

InnerAsia's current client list consists of transnational corporations, museums, academic institutions, travel agencies, and well-traveled individuals. Some of its current and past clients include the British Broadcasting Corporation, the American Broadcasting Corporation, Fox Broadcasting Corporation, ESPN, the Society for Asian Art, American Museum of Natural History, Stanford University, the Audubon Society, the Nature Conservancy, Smith College, Boston Symphony Orchestra, the California Culinary Academy, California Academy of Sciences, and the University of Chicago.

THE ENVIRONMENT
On tour, participants fly, drive, sail, or perhaps take an overnight train to the next overnight destination. Participants tour museums and walk around villages and towns, but on the whole InnerAsia's tours are physically nondemanding, and many compare in comfort level with classic European tours. InnerAsia's treks are essentially backpacking trips without the backpack (participants carry only a light daypack) and the hassles of cooking, setting up tents, cleaning up, etc. Porters or pack animals carry all baggage, food, and tents, and staff prepares all meals, washes all dishes, puts up and takes down camp, and takes care of almost everything but the walking.

FACILITIES
InnerAsia is not a youth-hosteling, low-budget company and it strives to offer the highest quality service in some of the world's most challenging destinations. Participants should pick trips that are suited to their own comfort needs, educational goals, and which aren't physically overstraining.

SUPPLIES NEEDED

InnerAsia endeavors to be extremely diligent by telling participants just what conditions they are likely to encounter and by providing extensive predeparture materials. Detailed itineraries cover history, lore, and current conditions, and the company often sends related articles and excerpts from hard-to-find books, in addition to carefully screened reading lists. Participants also receive a series of informational bulletins, covering everything from medical preparations to clothing and equipment lists.

APPLICATIONS AND ADMISSIONS

Participants must submit a detailed trip application, deposit, medical questionnaire, and other materials as indicated in the detailed trip itinerary. Contact the reservations department at the above address for forms and additional information on application and admission procedures.

Financial Aid: None available.

Costs: Sample costs range from approximately $5,000 to $7,000 on the particular tour, based on double occupancy. Singles may be available at a supplemental cost. Contact InnerAsia Expeditions at the above address for additional information.

LOST WORLD TRADING COMPANY
P.O. Box 365
Oakdale, CA 95361
(209) 847-5393
Fax: (209) 847-6383
Contact: Thomas J. Banks or Staff

SAMPLE PROGRAMS AND EXPEDITIONS

Summer Archaeological Field Schools are offered in the Caribbean and West Africa. Programs and expeditions include Shipwrecks of the Caribbean, Foot Safari into West Africa (Liberia), and Winged Safari over Mali (Timbuktu).

CURRICULUM AND CREDITS

The archaeology programs offer the opportunity to study excavation techniques, identify and catalog artifacts, map sites, and survey for new sites. Mapping, photography, and artifact identification are taught on the underwater projects. Shipwreck archaeology programs involve areas off the coasts of Grenada, Saint Vincent, and the archipelago of Los Roques off the coast of Venezuela. West African expeditions involve the study of the Liberian rainforest and its fauna. The Winged Safari Over Mali program involves working out of Timbuktu (as a base), and then flying out to the desert in search of various wildlife such as elephant, giraffe, antelope, hyena, lion, ostrich, and hippopotamus.

In order to obtain credit, participants must arrange a special independent study class with the college, university, or high school in which they are currently enrolled. The on-staff archaeologist on staff will cooperate with the special study class teacher. Credit may also be available through travel study.

THE INSTITUTION

Lost World Trading Company (LWTC) is replacing the programs that had previously been offered by the Foundation for Field Research.

THE ENVIRONMENT

Each program takes place in an exotic environment. Contact the institution at the above address for specific information.

FACILITIES

Facilities and accommodations vary considerably depending upon the program chosen, but usually consists of rented houses or guest houses. Contact the institution for more information.

SUPPLIES NEEDED

Contact LWTC at the above address for necessary equipment and supply lists for a particular program. Participants in the shipwreck archaeology programs must be certified scuba divers.

APPLICATIONS AND ADMISSIONS

Contact the institution at the above address for brochures and application materials. Dates for each program vary but at least six to eight departures are offered per year for each program.

Financial Aid: None available.

Costs: Prices vary depending on the program and departure date, but the general price ranges are as follows—Archaeology Programs/Liberia, $2,225 to $4,450; St. Vincent, $1,109; Grenada, $805 to $905; Shipwreck Archaeology Programs/Grenada, $902 to $1,054; St. Vincent, $1,110 to $1,155; Los Roques, $1,255 to $1,280; Foot Safari (Liberia) Program, $2,225 to $4,875; Winged Safari (Mali/Timbuktu) Program, $2,295 to $4,725.

MOUNTAIN TRAVEL/SOBEK
6420 Fairmount Avenue
El Cerrito, CA 94530-3606
(510) 527-8100/(800) 227-2384
Fax: (510) 525-7710
E-mail: MTSobek@aol.com
Contact: Susan Pritchard, Travel Consultant

SAMPLE PROGRAMS AND EXPEDITIONS

Programs and expeditions are offered to various remote areas of the world. Wilderness medical seminars (primarily for physicians, nurses, and other health professionals) take place in Alaska, the Alps, Tanzania, Switzerland, Chile, Bolivia, Brazil, Argentina, New Guinea, Spain, and Vietnam.

CURRICULUM AND CREDITS

Mountain Travel, founded in 1969, and Sobek, established in 1973, have joined forces to become the undisputed leader in adventure travel. Just as Mountain Travel/Sobek makes a strong team, the combined academic and field experience of the faculty makes their seminars absolutely unmatched in the field of wilderness medicine. They have brought together an outstanding group of instructors to teach field seminars in wilderness and mountain medicine and tropical and travel medicine. They have continued successful programs from previous years and have added exciting new ones, including a seminar on tropical medicine and traditional plant use in the Brazilian Amazon, cosponsored by the Dear Rainforest Alliance.

Programs are accredited for up to 16 hours of Category I C.M.E. credit for physicians and the equivalent for nurses. (Alaska and Wyoming courses are approved for 12 hours of Category I C.M.E. credit.) Each itinerary has been designed to allow direct participation in an environment relevant to the content of the seminar. Group size is limited to maximize faculty contact. Credit is offered through either independent or travel study.

THE INSTITUTION

A full-service travel agency, Mountain Travel handles every detail, from air reservations to ticketing to booking extra hotel accommodations. Many people like to arrive in the meeting city a bit earlier for a some personal leisure time and touring on their own, or wait until after their tour to do this. Those who are making a long journey (e.g., to Nairobi), may wish to make a stopover in Europe. Whatever the preference, Mountain Travel accommodates the needs of the participant.

THE ENVIRONMENT

The environment varies with the location of the expedition or seminar. Contact the institution for more information.

FACILITIES

While trekking on a river trip or safari, camping is the order of the day. Mountain Travel's camping arrangements are exceptional. Campsites are scenically situated and participants are provided with spacious sleeping tents, a dining tent, and a "toilet" tent. On most mountain treks, shower tents aren't possible, but participants are provided with hot water each morning to use for taking a sponge bath inside their tent or for washing clothes. On river trips, the river is generally the bath of choice.

The food on camping trips is as varied as the trips themselves, but always excellent. The camp cooks are experienced professionals who prepare delightful culinary treats.

SUPPLIES NEEDED

Contact the institution for specific information on supplies needed for a particular expedition or seminar.

APPLICATIONS AND ADMISSIONS

Reservations may be made by contacting the institution directly.

Financial Aid: None available.

Costs: Prices range from approximately $2,290 for a 10-day seminar to about $3,990 for an 18-day trip. These are land costs and cover tuition, accommodations, local transportation, most meals, group camping and commissary, river equipment on river trips, equipment on tented trips, and the services of a Mountain Travel/Sobek leader.

OCEANIC SOCIETY EXPEDITIONS
Fort Mason Center, Building E, Second Floor
San Francisco, CA 94123
(415) 441-1106/(800) 326-7491
Fax: (415) 474-3395
Contact: Expeditions Department (different expeditions are managed by various staff members)
Media Contact: Mary Jane Schramm, Public Information Manager

SAMPLE TOURS AND EXPEDITIONS

The following is a sampling of the various tours and expeditions that Oceanic Society offers in both the research and natural history categories.

Research Expeditions: Amazon Dolphin Research—river dolphins and manatees research in the Amazon rainforest; Bahamas Project Dolphin—spotted dolphin research on social structure and dolphin communication; Belize Primates—howler monkey abundance and distribution research; Hawaii Whale Research—documenting humpback whales, vessel interactions, and whale responses.

Natural History Expeditions: Amazon Odyssey—rainforest and river dolphins; Baja West Coast and the Sea of Cortez—gray whale close encounters, plus whale-watching with a wide variety of other whale species and snorkeling with sea lions; Belize Getaway—reef snorkeling, rainforest exploration, and Mayan ruins; Florida Manatees—snorkeling with and learning about endangered manatees; Galapagos—close-up encounters with unique wildlife endemic to these isolated islands; Honduras Snorkel—snorkel in the Caribbean's most diverse coral reef ecosystem; Patagonia, Iguassu, and Tierra Del Fuego—right whales, penguins, giant seals, waterfalls, rainforest environments, and the South American wilderness; Russia/Lake Baikal—freshwater seals and taiga forest in Siberia; San Juan Gulf Islands—marine mammals, forest, and tidepooling in the Pacific Northwest.

CURRICULUM AND CREDITS

All expeditions are conducted to minimize adverse impact. According to the code of ecotourism ethics, research expeditions involve only noncaptive, free-ranging wildlife, using noninvasive techniques. All research expeditions are conducted with untamed, free-ranging wildlife. No captive animals or invasive research techniques are used. Research certification is available for some scuba projects; however, no credit is available except through the participant's educational institution. Credit may be available through independent or travel study.

THE INSTITUTION

Oceanic Society Expeditions (OSE) is a nonprofit environmental education and research organization founded in 1972, with a mission to undertake action research to protect aquatic habitats and to promote environmental education. OSE approaches environmental protection issues by working closely with indigenous populations and by taking into account different cultural and economic conditions. OSE is the travel affiliate of Friends of the Earth, a global environmental advocacy organization. Participants in research expeditions learn hands-on research methods and work as teams with field biologists; program fees help underwrite the costs of research. Information is shared with various governmental and nongovernmental institutions to promote conservation efforts.

THE ENVIRONMENT

Programs are focused in prime breeding and feeding habitats for most wildlife, or ecosystems of unusual biological interest.

FACILITIES

Means of travel and accommodations vary, but are designed to be enjoyed by anyone in general good health with a shared interest in the natural world. In major cities, first-class hotels are provided for accomodations, while in outdoor habitats the best available facilities (generally lodges) are used in proximity to the wildlife being observed. Accommodations are based on shared occupancy, and vessel head facilities are generally shared.

SUPPLIES NEEDED

Participants receive pretrip educational materials. For vessel-based expeditions, basic swimming skills are recommended. Research trip participants also receive reference materials, research plans, data sheets, information on tasks, and on-site training. No research experience is needed; participants need adventurous spirit, patience, respect for wildlife, and an ability to follow instructions. Basic snorkeling skills are required for the Bahamas and Belize dolphin programs. For photo-identification work, participants must provide their own camera equipment. Previous scuba certification is required for the scuba programs.

APPLICATIONS AND ADMISSIONS

Contact the institution at the above address for information on application and admission procedures.

Financial Aid: None available.

Costs: Costs range from $250 to $2,850. A group international airfare is included in some programs.

PACIFIC EXPLORATION COMPANY
Box 3042
Santa Barbara, CA 93130
(805) 687-7282
Fax: (805) 569-0722
Contact: Ronald Richardson, Director

SAMPLE TOUR PROGRAMS

"Walkabout" Tours of Australia and New Zealand are offered with personalized itineraries, featuring Australian safaris (hiking, camping), the Great Barrier Reef (sailing, kayaking, camping, hiking, scuba diving), Australian mountain biking, Australian river rafting, Australian wildlife tours and sanctuaries, New Zealand hiking and treking safaris, New Zealand national parks and wilderness areas, tours of Fiji and Tahiti, and custom-designed South Pacific tours.

CURRICULUM AND CREDITS

Since 1977, Pacific Exploration Company has been designing tour programs to Australia and New Zealand for individuals, groups, and families—any and all active travelers—who enjoy nature, hiking, and the outdoors.

These itineraries emphasize stimulating outdoor activities at outstanding destinations, and feature a variety of hiking and camping safaris, lodge stays, and island resorts in the scenic national parks and wilderness areas of these countries. Each participant can be assured of dependable, personalized service, worry-free travel arrangements, and a South Pacific adventure to always remember. Credit may be obtained through independent or travel study.

THE INSTITUTION
Not applicable.

THE ENVIRONMENT
Every tour is different. The environment depends upon the particular tour locations.

FACILITIES
Information about facilities may be obtained by contacting the institution at the above address.

SUPPLIES NEEDED
Information is provided upon making reservations.

APPLICATIONS AND ADMISSIONS
Contact the institution at the above address for application and admission procedures.

Financial Aid: None available.

Costs: Costs vary for each tour. A typical 3-week tour has a land/air rate of approximately $4,000 to $5,000.

QUAIL RIDGE WILDERNESS CONSERVANCY
and
ENVIRONMENTAL EDUCATION FARM FOUNDATION
25344 County Road 95
Davis, CA 95616-9735
(916) 758-1387
Fax: (916) 758-1316
Contact: Frank W. Maurer, Executive Director

SAMPLE PROGRAMS
The Quail Ridge Wilderness Conservancy (QRWC) offers monthly field trips to Quail Ridge Ecological Reserve which consists of over 1,800 acres of near-pristine oak woodland-savannah habitat in California's Inner Coast Range; the conservancy also sponsors a variety of additional educational programs aimed at increasing public awareness about habitat destruction, the need for maintaining biological diversity, and instilling in adults and children alike a sense of environmental stewardship.

The Environmental Education Farm Foundation (EEFF), formerly known as the Research Farm, is also educational in purpose, sponsoring a variety of programs and projects for the greater Sacramento area. Some representative activities include the bat project, which teaches participants about the poorly understood bat and provides instruction about bat roosting tubes to encourage natural control of mosquitos, gnats, and flies; nightwalks to expand people's (especially children's) knowledge of nighttime sounds and to help allay any fear of the dark; photography and sketching lessons led by artists specializing in natural and rural subjects; presentations about organic farming and sustainable agriculture in classrooms and on the farm; demonstrations of solar cooking; plant identification and foot/paw print identification. Teacher workshops are available upon request.

CURRICULUM AND CREDITS

This is not a degree-granting organization, but students already enrolled in a college or university may be able to work out credits for internships of three months or more. Teachers, similarly, may be able to arrange for in-service credit for workshops completed under the aegis of one or both organizations.

EEFF can supplement a teacher's curriculum with field observations and practical experiences for the students. Teachers are invited to help design a farm tour and/or arrange for teacher workshops. QRWC is the fundraising and educational arm of Quail Ridge Ecological Reserve, which is located about 30 miles west of the farm. Morning, afternoon, or overnight guided tours are available for small groups of four persons minimum.

Mini summer camps for children aged 8–15 are available and consist of four days of activities at both the farm and the reserve. Children partake in the regular rounds of farm life, assisting in the care of farm plants and animals, and they learn how to prepare their own meals around a campfire. Principles underlying the ecologically sound use of land and resources are presented and discussed.

THE INSTITUTION

QRWC and EEFF are environmental organizations with nonprofit status. As noted above, EEFF's activities are based on the 37-acre, working family farm, which serves as a backdrop for such topics as raising domestic livestock, establishing commercial fish ponds, biology and ecology, running a small farm, career planning, community studies. It features working models of plant-animal interactions, live demonstrations, observational studies, analyses, and discussions.

THE ENVIRONMENT

EEFF is located in the Central Valley of the greater Sacramento area where much of the terrain is flat and devoted to large-scale agriculture. This farm is unique in the region (and probably in the state) with its intensive, small-scale polyculture approach to farming, which includes 14 human-made fish ponds of 1/4 to 3/4 acre each. The climate is essentially Mediterranean, with hot, dry summers, and cool, rainy winters. Freezing temperatures are rare, and ephemeral snowfalls occur once a decade or so.

The reserve managed by QRWC is located in the inner part of California's Coast Range where elevations rise to about 1,200 feet. The climate is similar to that in the valley with the exception of notably less fog in the months of December and January due to the reserve's higher elevations. The reserve overlooks Lake Berryessa, an extensive and very deep artificial body of water created in 1957 by the construction of a dam. While not without some undesirable side-effects, the creation of this lake helped ensure the isolation and hence the near-pristine quality of the habitat and an impressive range of local wildlife on the reserve.

FACILITIES

EEFF has, for resident interns, a rustic, remodeled school with most modern conveniences installed. For one-day visitors, the farm has places to picnic, two chemical toilets, and two gazebos in which to relax in the shade.

Quail Ridge Ecological Reserve is basically wilderness, and access is available only through guided walks. Overnight camping, however, may also be arranged. The conservancy is currently acquiring a property with several structures on it near a key roadway around the lake that will be eventually transformed into a visitor's center and museum.

SUPPLIES NEEDED

Supplies needed depend on each program or project. Comfortable walking gear, a hat, and other sun protection is necessary during the hot months. Campers will need camping gear. Interns who are resident for longer periods of time will need to inquire about what they should bring.

APPLICATIONS AND ADMISSIONS

Apart from the internship program, which is selective, the programs are open to virtually everyone. For walks or tours, sign-ups must be made 24 hours in advance. For summer camps and teacher workshops, arrangements must be made several weeks in advance. Those persons interested in an internship should write or contact the above address for further information.

Financial Aid: Inapplicable in most cases. Interns are provided complete room and board and are given a small weekly stipend for personal expenses.

Costs: Walks, tours, and demonstrations are either free or request a nominal donation of approxiamtely $5 per person.

REDWOOD NATIONAL AND STATE FIELD SEMINARS
Redwood National Park
1111 Second Street
Crescent City, CA 95531
(707) 464-6101
Fax: (707) 464-1812
Contact: Field Seminar Coordinator

SAMPLE SEMINARS

Seminars include Bear Facts; Outdoor Cooking; Marine Mammals; Watershed Rehabilitation; Seabird Cruise; Smith River Basin Geology; Lake Earl Natural History; Crossroad in Geology; Bats; Predators; American Indian Culture; Birds of Redwood National Park; Redwood Creek Backpack; A Day Exploring the Redwood Forest; Forestry Perspectives; Flora of Redwood National Park; Spring Wildflowers; Frogs, Snakes and Salamanders; Whales, Seals, and Sea Lions; Tidepools for the Whole Family.

CURRICULUM AND CREDITS

Redwood National Park offers in-depth outdoor seminars April through September. The instructors are accomplished park staff members, university professors, and local experts from the community, each one dedicated to excellence in their fields. Most field seminars are for adults; however, interested, young people comfortable in an adult class are encouraged to attend with an adult. Class size is limited to 12–20 participants, and fees are calculated to cover instructors' fees and materials.

Some seminars, though not all, carry college credit. Many seminars are approved for credit with Humboldt State University. Arrangements for credit and tuition are made after registration.

THE INSTITUTION

Redwood National and State Parks include Prairie Creek Redwoods, Jedediah Smith, and Del Norte Coast Redwoods Parks. Redwood National Park is administered through a cooperative effort of the National Park Service and the California Department of Parks and Recreation.

THE ENVIRONMENT

The parks are located along a 50-mile corridor of Highway 101 and Highway 199 in northern California near the Oregon border. Towering groves of ancient redwoods, oak woodlands, prairies, and spectacular coastlines make up these parks.

FACILITIES

Seminars are conducted in the field with meeting places at park information centers and outdoor education schools.

SUPPLIES NEEDED

Upon registration, seminar participants are sent a listing of personal items to bring recommended by the instructor.

APPLICATIONS AND ADMISSIONS

Contact the above address for a catalog with seminar listings and registration materials.

Financial Aid: None available.

Costs: Seminars range from $10 to $90 per person. Fees are based on instructor fees and supplies required. There are also concession fees for such things as horseback trips.

SEQUOIA NATURAL HISTORY ASSOCIATION
Sequoia and Kings Canyon National Parks
HCR 89–Box 10
Three Rivers, CA 93271
(209) 565-3756
Fax: (209) 565-3728
Contact: E. Tyler Conrad, Executive Director

SAMPLE SEMINARS

Seminars include Birds of the Sierra, Outdoor Photography, Beginning Backpacking for Women, Grant Grove Wildflowers, Natural History of the Giant Sequoias, Drawing and Painting Giant Forest, Earth & Stars: the Magic of Physics in Nature, Exploring Mineral King, and Project WILD in the Sequoias.

CURRICULUM AND CREDITS

A number of seminars are available for credit through Fresno Pacific College. Credit is designed primarily for students who have baccalaureate degrees and appropriate teaching credentials. Many school districts accept these professional credits for the purpose of teacher salary scale advancement and continuing education credit.

THE INSTITUTION

A nonprofit organization, the Sequoia Natural History Association (SNHA) has been working in conjunction with Sequoia and Kings Canyon National Parks for over fifty years to help make quality educational programs available to all park visitors. In the last decade SNHA has donated over $800,000 to Sequoia and Kings Canyon National Parks. SNHA has been offering outdoor courses in Sequoia and Kings Canyon since 1983.

THE ENVIRONMENT

Participants in field seminars have the opportunity for adventure while enjoying some of the finest scenery in North America. The field seminars use the parks as natural laboratories and are led by experienced naturalists and experts in a number of subject areas.

FACILITIES

Two buildings within the beautiful Giant Forest area of Sequoia National Park are available for those seminars requiring a classroom environment. Campgrounds, rustic cabins, and motels are available throughout the parks and in nearby areas. Participants are responsible for making their own arrangements for lodging and transportation during the seminars.

Specific meeting locations and information on accommodations including campgrounds will be described in the material sent upon registration. A checklist of any equipment that will be useful and necessary during the seminar is sent with this material.

SUPPLIES NEEDED

Participants are expected to provide their own food and equipment for each seminar unless specified in the course itinerary.

APPLICATIONS AND ADMISSIONS

For information on registration, call or write to the Sequoia Natural History Association at the above address. A seminar brochure detailing courses and registration requirements is sent upon request. Participants may pay with a check, VISA, or MasterCard, by either mail or phone.

Financial Aid: None available; however, members of SNHA receive a $10 discount on most seminars. Membership is available upon enrollment for those that are interested.

Costs: Registration fees vary from approximately $35 for 1-day seminars to $125 for 5-day seminars. Tuition for college credit costs an extra $36 for each unit of credit. One to three units of credit requires 15 hours of instruction.

SUE'S SAFARIS, INC.
P.O. Box 2171
Rancho Palos Verdes, CA 90274-8171
(310) 541-2011/(800) 541-2011
Fax: (310) 544-1502
Contact: Dr. Sue Soldoff

SAMPLE EXPEDITIONS AND SAFARIS

Wildlife expeditions and safaris offered throughout Africa include Kenya, Tanzania, Rwanda, Seychelles, Egypt, South Africa, Namibia, Uganda, Zimbabwe, Botswana, and Zambia.

CURRICULUM AND CREDITS

Sue's Safaris (SS) designs and operates deluxe custom safaris to the most desirable destinations in Africa. SS has a philosophy and a policy of conservation. They provide their clients with information and behavioral guidelines to make them more aware of the world around them and more responsive to the need for appropriate behavior when traveling in environmentally sensitive areas, in order to minimize any impact on that environment and its wildlife. While credit is not offered directly, it can be obtained through independent or travel study.

THE INSTITUTION

SS is happy to work with any academic institution to design a program to meet that institution's requirements.

THE ENVIRONMENT

A safari in Africa can be accomplished with a maximum of comfort and a minimum of inconvenience. It is their intention to provide the ultimate safari experience for their clients, one that will be cherished in the years to come. Participants will find their brochure to be different from others they have seen. The purpose is to describe the destinations in Africa that are offered with details about the parks and reserves and the accommodations that are recommended. Participants can then decide what appeals to them the most. An insert can be found inside the back cover of the company's brochure which briefly lists some sample popular itineraries with the current prices that one can use as a guideline.

FACILITIES

Facilities vary depending on the particular safari. Contact SS for their brochure. Included is free insurance and a 24-hour worldwide toll-free telephone center for emergency assistance.

SUPPLIES NEEDED

Contact SS for information on necessary supplies.

APPLICATIONS AND ADMISSIONS

Contact SS for reservations and brochures. A 25% deposit is required when booking a safari.

Financial Aid: None available.

Costs: Prices vary depending on the length of the safari and the number of participants. Inquire with SS at the above address for specific rates.

TRAVEL STUDY PROGRAM—UNIVERSITY EXTENSION
University of California
Santa Barbara, CA 93106
(800) 484-1081, ext. 7775 (9A.M.–9P.M. PST)
Fax: (714) 552-0740
E-mail: TASH_S@a1.SCCD.CC.CA.US
Contact: Steve Tash, Instructor
P.O. Box 16501
Irvine, CA 92713-6501

SAMPLE COURSES

The University of California Santa Barbara Extenşion courses (X300 series) are postgraduate credit programs presented through the extension program only and offer continuing education for professional educators. These courses serve a dual purpose: 1) they provide an opportunity for professional advancement and an opportunity for dissemination of results of current research and development, centering around innovations in the educational field, and 2) they meet the needs of school districts and to satisfy the credential requirements established by the California State Legislature and the State Board of Education.

CURRICULUM AND CREDITS

A professional postgraduate education course credit may be earned during any quarter of the year. Participants must enroll for a minimum of two quarter units at any one time (ten days or more). Thereafter, one quarter unit may be earned for each five full days of travel study, up to a maximum of five quarter units per quarter. This course may be repeated for up to a maximum of ten quarter units under the following conditions: 1) a maximum of five units of credit per three-month period will be granted; 2) travel study must be in a different area of the world; 3) a new travel idea, daily log, and unit of instruction must be completed.

Students pursuing credit toward their master's or doctoral degrees should request approval for credit from the appropriate institution prior to enrolling in this program. Students are also advised to seek approval from their school district in order to count these credits for tuition reimbursement or columnar compensation prior to enrolling in this program.

Each quarter unit of credit converts to 2/3 of a semester unit. The dates for the quarters are—summer 6/1–8/15, fall 8/16–11/30, winter 12/1–2/30, and spring 3/1–5/30.

THE INSTITUTION

The travel study program is designed to provide classroom enrichment opportunities and staff development possibilities to educators who undertake either domestic or foreign travel. It offers participants the opportunity to learn outside the classroom and to take advantage of materials and locations that are available only through travel. Participants are expected to describe how they will use the material developed or apply the knowledge gained.

The program is open to teachers, librarians, administrators, and others who work with children. Course requirements include the following:

1) Participants must submit a typed, one-page proposal (the "Travel Study Idea"), along with the study contract, enrollment application, and payment prior to travel. The "Idea" proposal must contain the basic educational objective of the travel study program. Include departure and return dates and a list of people, places, and things that will be seen or studied during the travel period. The "Travel Study Idea" should also mention what aspects of American or foreign culture will be studied or observed. Briefly describe the materials and realizations that hope to be procured during the travel study period.

2) A daily log must be maintained during the travel study period. It must contain notes on places visited, personal contacts or interviews, geographical points of interest, observations of specific cultural traits (e.g., costumes, eating habits, etc.), and a list of educational materials obtained. The instructional experience that has been gained from each day of travel should also be noted.

Courses, Programs, and Expeditions in the United States

3) A unit of instruction must be submitted containing, in outline form, at least two 20-minute lessons for each unit of travel study. The outline for the lessons should contain the title of the unit, an outline of the lesson, a list of teaching materials collected (e.g., slides, books, coins, stamps, costumes, etc.), and a statement of how they will be incorporated into the lessons.

4) Other assignments are arranged for those who are not classroom teachers. Some examples of nonclassroom projects would be study reports, development of a library resource file, a report on a special conference, etc. A paper must be submitted explaining how the material developed will be used or how the knowledge gained will be applied.

5) Evidence of travel (i.e., photocopies of receipts) is required.

Grading is on a pass/no pass basis, but a letter grade may be requested at time of enrollment. Grades are based on the material described above, which must be submitted to the instructor within five days of the end of the school quarter. Participants should also note that all materials submitted for evaluation will become the property of University of California extension. Grade reports are mailed to participants, and official transcripts may be requested.

THE ENVIRONMENT
Not applicable.

FACILITIES
Not applicable.

SUPPLIES NEEDED
None.

APPLICATIONS AND ADMISSIONS
Contact the above address for information of application and admission procedures.

Financial Aid: None available.

Costs: Approximately $100 for a minimum of two quarter units per quarter and $250 for a maximum of five quarter units per quarter ($50 per quarter unit of credit). Payment must accompany the registration form. No refunds are given for courses not completed. Enrollment may be cancelled prior to departure, in which case a $5 per unit service charge is deducted from the refund. Written notice of cancellation is required.

UNIVERSITY RESEARCH EXPEDITIONS PROGRAM
University of California–Berkeley
Berkeley, CA 94720
(510) 642-6586
Fax: (510) 642-6791
E-mail: urep a uclink.berkley.edu
Contact: Jean Colvin, Director

SAMPLE COURSES AND EXPEDITIONS
Various courses include Animal Behavior, Environmental Studies, Archaeology/Paleontology, Marine Studies, and Arts/Culture. Expeditions take place in the Galapagos Islands, Bali, California, Columbia, Baja, Portugal, Pakistan, Indonesia, East Africa, Bolivia,

Mongolia, Montana, Costa Rica, Belize, Ecuador, New Mexico, Hawaii, Germany, Ireland, Uganda, India, Ethiopia, Turkey, Colorado, Micronesia, Siberia, Utah, and Montana.

CURRICULUM AND CREDITS

University Research Expeditions Program (UREP) has enabled nearly 4,000 members of the public to spend two to three weeks (as volunteers) sharing the challenges and rewards of scientific discovery as active members of University of California research teams. The expedition teams usually include six to ten participants and leave for destinations all over the world throughout the year. Research projects span a variety of disciplines, from archaeology to zoology. Many projects emphasize research that improves peoples' lives and helps preserve the earth's resources. These projects are conducted with scientists from developing countries as part of a UREP program called SHARE (Science Serving Humanity and Research for the Environment).

Volunteer participants help excavate archaeological remains for ancient civilizations, conduct interviews in sociological studies, document with photography and video, observe animal behavior, collect botanical specimens, survey wildlife and study different ecological habitats, and dive and collect marine specimens.

THE INSTITUTION

The University of California encompasses nine different campuses from San Diego to Berkeley.

THE ENVIRONMENT

The expeditions are worldwide. Contact UREP for more information.

FACILITIES

Contact UREP with questions about facilities.

SUPPLIES NEEDED

Appropriate clothing and personal needs are required depending on the region and season. Each participant receives a packet with detailed information prior to their expedition.

APPLICATIONS AND ADMISSIONS

Contact the institution at the above address for information on application and admission procedures.

Financial Aid: UREP offers scholarships and grants to K–12th-grade teachers through the Teacher Research Participation Program. This program is supported by foundation grants and individual donors, and underwrites a major portion of the costs for teachers who join UREP field expeditions. UREP then works with these teachers during the academic year to integrate their experiences and new knowledge into the school curriculum.

Each year UREP supports graduate students either as independent project investigators on thesis research projects or as assistants on faculty research projects. In addition, UREP provides scholarships to undergraduates who participate in field research projects.

Costs: Participants in all UREP projects make a charitable contribution to cover their expenses and help make the research possible. A special program for educators enables K–12th-grade teachers to apply for grants and receive help in integrating their field experience into curriculum and classroom activities. The average cost per expedition is between $1,200 and $1,400.

WORLD EXPLORER CRUISES/S.S. UNIVERSE
555 Montgomery Street
San Francisco, CA 94111-2544
(800) 854-3835
Fax: (415) 391-1145
Contact: Steve Barber

SAMPLE PROGRAMS AND COURSES
Fourteen-day cruises are offered to Alaska, beginning and ending in Vancouver, British Columbia. Courses on board include geology, oceanography, anthropology, and history.

CURRICULUM AND CREDITS
Each course grants one credit from Chapman University in California.

THE INSTITUTION
Chapman University is a 130-year-old independent institution of liberal arts and professional training. The university is composed of the Wilkinson College of Arts and Sciences, the School of Business and Economics, the School of Natural and Applied Sciences, the School of Communication Arts, the Graduate School of Education, and the School of Music.

THE ENVIRONMENT
There are 14 places to visit and 42 shore excursions to choose from. Retrace the steps of prospectors and pan for nuggets in Skagway, the gold boomtown. Examine intricately carved totem poles near Ketchikan. See Tlingit Indian finery and detailed walrus tusk scrimshaw. Explore the old Russian trading outpost of Sitka. Hover by helicopter over the blue chasms of vast Mendenhall Glacier. Spot big game on the slopes of forested mountain ranges. Ride in charter catamarans, floatplanes, motor rafts, and lake canoes along picturesque inlets.

FACILITIES
The *S.S. Universe* is a cruise ship that offers 12,000 volumes in the largest library afloat. The Marine Dining Room serves delicious cuisine, featuring fresh seafood from the ports visited, Asian specialties, and country and cosmopolitan favorites from across the United States.

SUPPLIES NEEDED
All supplies are provided on board.

APPLICATIONS AND ADMISSIONS
No preregistration is required for the courses; simply sign up upon boarding the ship. (Of course, advance cruise reservations are required. Early booking is advisable.)

Financial Aid: None available.

Costs: Cost of cruise is approximately $45 per each CEU credit. Each course is worth one unit. Contact the institution at the above address for more information on costs.

COLORADO

BOLDER ADVENTURES, INC.
P.O. Box 1279
Boulder, CO 80306
(303) 443-6789/(800) 642-2742
Fax: (303) 443-7078
Contact: Marilyn Downing or Staff

SAMPLE PROGRAMS
Programs include natural history, wildlife, and culture tours/expeditions operated in Thailand, Indonesia, Vietnam, Burma (Myanmar), Laos, Malaysia, and Papua New Guinea.

CURRICULUM AND CREDITS
These expeditions encompass migratory tribal cultures, megalithic cultures, matriarchal societies, stone-age cultures, ancient cultures of Java, Bali, Thailand, Cambodia, Burma, and other nations. The study options are almost limitless. Bolder Adventures, Inc. (BAI) advises what programs may be most applicable to the interests of the traveler/student. Credit is available through independent or travel study.

THE INSTITUTION
BAI was founded in 1987 by Marilyn Downing Staff and Rusty Staff and specializes exclusively in arranging travel programs to Southeast Asia. Prior to establishing the company, they had lived for years in Southeast Asia, and bring real first-hand knowledge of the region to their business. Their intimate knowledge of the region, attention to detail, and highly qualified and experienced staff make BAI an excellent resource for educational or recreational travel programs. They have attracted some of the most knowledgeable tour leaders in the business including Bill Dalton, author of the venerable *Indonesia Handbook;* Joe Cummings, linguist, author, and Southeast Asian scholar; Dr. Birute Galdikas, the world's foremost authority on the orangutan and cofounder (with Dr. L. S. B. Leakey) of the Camp Leakey Orangutan Preserve in Indonesia; Dr. Jeff Petry, an anthropologist who has done extensive work with the indigenous tribal people of the region; and others.

THE ENVIRONMENT
Southeast Asia is a intricate patchwork of diverse cultural groups set in a wonderland of natural beauty.

FACILITIES
Accommodations range from luxury hotels to private teak villas to tents or simple huts in the jungle depending on availability and the requirements of each particular tour. Transportation can include motorized yacht, train, plane, car/bus, elephant, or foot travel.

SUPPLIES NEEDED
Necessary supplies vary depending upon the program. Most programs require no special equipment or supplies, while some require sleeping bag/pad, snorkeling gear, etc. Contact the institution at the above address for more information.

APPLICATIONS AND ADMISSIONS
Contact BAI at the above address to make reservations.

Financial Aid: None available.

Costs: Sample land costs range from approximately $125 to $200 per person, per day. Private or small-group custom-designed programs also available.

COLORADO OUTWARD BOUND SCHOOL®
945 Pennsylvania Street
Denver, CO 80203-3198
(303) 837-0880/(800) 477-COBS
Fax: (303) 831-6987
Contact: Rory Donaldson

SAMPLE COURSES

Courses include Alpine Mountaineering, Rock Climbing, Whitewater River Courses, Canyonlands Courses, Horsetrailing Courses, Women's Nepal Trek, Ski Mountaineering, Cross-Country Skiing, Arizona Horsetrailing, Multienvironment Courses, Alaska/Brooks Range Courses, High School Leadership Course, U.S./USSR Exchange Courses, and Professional Development Courses (for individuals and groups).

CURRICULUM AND CREDITS

Founded in 1961, the Colorado Outward Bound School (COBS) is a nonprofit, educational organization which engages participants in dramatic wilderness settings and exciting activities as a means of enhancing their skills, self-confidence, and compassion for others. Courses vary in length, location, age level, and focus, but all are designed to assure safety and a high level of skills acquisition.

Each course is different, maximizing the challenges of the environment to provide a variety of learning experiences for every student. Some courses are short and intensive; others range up to 23 days or more in length. A number of courses are designed to serve special populations, but most are open to the public on a first-come, first-served basis.

Graduate and undergraduate credit is available for some courses from the University of Colorado at Denver. Credit for other courses may be obtained through independent or travel study.

THE INSTITUTION

COBS is the nation's oldest wilderness adventure school. With programs throughout the American West and in three foreign countries, COBS promotes education, service, and personal growth through wilderness experience.

COBS conducts more than 200 courses each year, serving over 6,000 people through a wide variety of programs. While not a "survival" school in the literal sense, it provides students with the tools necessary for success in the outdoors.

THE ENVIRONMENT

COBS offers courses in a variety of locations including the canyons, rivers, and mountains of Colorado and the West. Course participants fully share in all the day-to-day aspects of outdoor living. The wilderness serves as the setting for a way of life that's simpler and more exciting—a metaphor for the complexities and challenges of the modern world.

FACILITIES

On alpine mountaineering, canyonlands, multienvironment, and wilderness leadership courses, the food is simple, filling, and nourishing. Participants learn to prepare tasty meals with staples such as flour, grain, rice, cocoa, and cheese. Fresh fruit and vegetables are occasionally available as well. Hot pan bread, donuts, and pizza are usually on the menu. These items are supplemented with meat during winter courses. River course meals include fresh foods transported in coolers in the rafts and prepared on stoves or over fires.

SUPPLIES NEEDED

A complete list of necessary supplies is included in the enrollment materials that are sent to participants upon receipt of the enrollment application and application fee. All necessary equipment—sleeping bag, ensolite pad, tarp, backpack, water bottle, compass, eating utensils, and other specialized gear—is provided for all courses except the international courses and the Alaska course. Depending on where one shops (and what one may already own), expect to spend between $150 and $300 on these items.

APPLICATIONS AND ADMISSIONS

Contact the institution directly for information on application and admission procedures.

Financial Aid: Some aid is available.

Costs: Prices range from approximately $1,300 for a 10-day course to $7,000 for an 83-day semester course.

DINAMATION INTERNATIONAL SOCIETY
and
DEVILS CANYON SCIENCE & LEARNING CENTER
550 Crossroads Court
Fruita, CO 81521
(800) 344-3466 (or DIG-DINO)
Fax: (303) 858-3532
Contact: Jonathan Cooley, Expedition Coordinator

SAMPLE EXPEDITIONS

Dinosaur Discovery Expeditions offer domestic expeditions in the Colorado Canyons (Grand Junction, Colorado), Wyoming High Plains (Medicine Bow, Wyoming), and a Dinosaur Diamond Safari in Colorado and Utah. International expeditions are offered in Argentina, Saltillo, Indonesia, Mexico, and Baja.

CURRICULUM AND CREDITS

Participants come face-to-face with the area's prehistoric creatures with exciting and interactive hands-on exhibits at this new science and learning center.

Graduate credit is offered on certain expeditions. Interested participants can receive one unit of graduate credit for an additional fee through Northern Arizona University. Contact Dr. Dale Nations at (602) 523-7180, or write to Northern Arizona University, Summer Sessions, P.O. Box 4117, Flagstaff, Arizona 86011-4117.

THE INSTITUTION

Dinamation International Society (DIS) is a nonprofit organization that promotes education, research, and preservation in the biological, earth, and physical sciences with emphasis on dinosaur paleontology. DIS believes that by being a part of a dino-dig expedition, participants will gain a new understanding of dinosaur paleontology and the fascinating geology of the Grand Valley.

THE ENVIRONMENT

Dinamation's Devils Canyon Science and Learning center is located in the heart of dinosaur country in Fruita, Colorado, off Interstate 70 and 340 South. Located 4,500 feet above sea level, the Grand Valley is framed by the Book Cliffs to the north, the Grand Mesa (largest flat-top mountain in the world) to the east, and the red rock canyons of Colorado National Monument to the south. Grand Junction is the largest community between Denver & Salt Lake City. The valley's high-desert altitude and mild climate provide sunshine on an average of 284 days a year.

FACILITIES

DIS operates Devils Canyon Science & Learning Center, one of only a few science centers in North America dedicated to the study of dinosaurs.

SUPPLIES NEEDED

Contact the institution at the above address for a copy of the catalog, which indicates the necessary supplies to bring.

APPLICATIONS AND ADMISSIONS

The registration form can be found in the catalog, or call the above phone number to sign up with a credit card. A $100 deposit will hold a spot, and the final balance is due 30 days prior to an expedition.

Financial Aid: None available.

Costs: Approximate costs are as follows—Colorado Canyons Expedition, $775; Family Dino Camp, $775 per adult and $550 per child; Wyoming High Plains, $1,050; Baja/Whales Past and Present, $1,150; Saltillo, Mexico, $1,250; Dinosaur Diamond Safari, $850; Colorado Advanced, $995.

LARRY/DARLENE FRIEDRICHS
3473 Amador Circle
Colorado Springs, CO 80918
(719) 598-1291 or (719) 520-2538
Contact: Larry or Darlene Friedrichs

SAMPLE COURSES AND PROGRAMS

Courses and programs include Grand Canyon Ecology and Geology, and Rocks and Rapids in the Grand Canyon.

CURRICULUM AND CREDITS

Graduate credit is granted by the Colorado School of Mines. These 6-day and 12-day whitewater raft trips include hikes which acquaint participants with the geology, ecology, and culture of the Grand Canyon.

THE INSTITUTION
Not applicable.

THE ENVIRONMENT
These rafting trips are taken through the Grand Canyon on the Colorado River. Trips begin at Lee's Ferry, Arizona, and end 183 miles downriver just past the famous Lava Falls. There are numerous short side-canyon hikes. On the final day, a helicopter picks the participants up below Lava Falls for an exciting flight out of the canyon, and a small plane returns them to Lee's Ferry. The trip is chartered with a professional rafting company.

FACILITIES
Contact the institution at the above address for more information about facilities and accommodations.

SUPPLIES NEEDED
A list of necessary supplies is sent to participants after a deposit is received.

APPLICATIONS AND ADMISSIONS
Contact Larry or Darlene Friedrichs at the address above for information on application and admission procedures.

Financial Aid: None available.

Costs: Fees for graduate credit are approximately $60 for two semester hours for the 6-day trip and $120 for four and a half semester hours for the 12-day trip. The 6-day trip costs approximately $1,300, while the 12-day trip costs about $1,875. A $250 deposit is required upon registration. The price includes all camping equipment, three meals a day, the helicopter and plane rides. Participants will need to provide their own transportation to and from Lee's Ferry.

MOUNTAIN RESEARCH STATION
University of Colorado
818 County Road 116
Nederland, CO 80466
(303) 492-8841/8842
Contact: Staff

SAMPLE COURSES
Courses include Arctic Field Research, Exploration in Arctic Geography, Field Techniques in Environmental Sciences, Mountain Geomorphology, Grasslands to Glaciers: Biogeography of the Intermountain West, summer workshops for teachers, Forest Ecology, Rocky Mountain Climatology, Rocky Mountain Flora, Alpine Ecology, Dendrochronology, Comparative Ecology of Alpine and Desert Ecosystems, Alpine Insect Ecology, Field Botany, Field Ecology, Limonology Field Techniques, Paleoenvironmental Field Techniques, Conservation Biology in the Rocky Mountain Region, Geologic Field Techniques in the Colorado Front Range, and Directed Research.

CURRICULUM AND CREDITS

The University of Colorado's Mountain Research Station (MRS) invites students to spend an exciting summer studying in the Rocky Mountains of Colorado, where they will gain first-hand research or field experience through the courses offered at the station. They may choose from undergraduate or graduate credit for most courses and the credit may be readily transferred to other institutions.

THE INSTITUTION

One of the nation's outstanding field facilities, MRS has been offering courses and support for research for more than sixty years. Course schedules make it easy to enroll in more than one course and the fees make this program a cost-effective alternative to a regular semester. Courses are offered at the same cost for Colorado residents and nonresidents.

THE ENVIRONMENT

Located 25 miles west of Boulder, Colorado, at an altitude of 9,500 feet and only a short distance from the Continental Divide, the station is situated on land owned by the University of Colorado and is surrounded by Roosevelt National Forest. Much of the research and many course trips take place in the Niwot Ridge Biosphere Reserve, which was a site of U.S. contribution to the International Biological Program and is now a long-term ecological research site of the National Science Foundation. Nearby study areas include the Indian Peaks Wilderness Area and the Bunker Hill Preserve, which the station leases from the Nature Conservancy. The area is also an experimental ecological reserve as well as the site for ongoing atmospheric research conducted by the National Oceanic and Atmospheric Administration. The summer climate at the station is pleasant with warm days, cool to cold nights, and short afternoon thunderstorms, particularly in July and August.

FACILITIES

Facilities include the John Marr Alpine Laboratory, the Columbine Bookshop, Mountain Climate Program Office, Dendrochronology Laboratory, classrooms, laboratories, and microcomputers. A herbarium and library are located in the Marr Lab.

A 15-meal plan (Monday through Friday) and a 7-day, 20-meal plan are available. Nutritious and ample meals are served in the station's dining hall. Rooms are double occupancy in student cabins or in one of the station's hostels for larger groups.

Opportunities for recreation in the immediate area include backpacking, hiking, fishing, and mountain biking. At a greater distance, horseback riding and rafting are other possibilities.

SUPPLIES NEEDED

Supplies vary depending upon the courses taken; inquire with the station upon registration.

APPLICATIONS AND ADMISSIONS

Contact the institution at the above address for a catalog/class schedule; registration forms are included in the catalog.

Financial Aid: Work-study opportunities are sometimes available for qualified students needing help to pay for their room and board. Submit a résumé and a letter of interest with your application.

Costs: Fees vary from approximately $495 for a two-credit course to about $2,495 for a six-credit course, with most three-credit courses costing $520. Room and board fees range from approximately $100 to $130 per week, depending on the option chosen.

NATURAL HABITAT ADVENTURES
2945 Center Green Court South, Suite H
Boulder, CO 80301
(303) 449-3711/(800) 543-8917
Fax: (303) 449-3712
Contact: Ben Bressler, Director

SAMPLE PROGRAMS AND EXPEDITIONS

Programs and expeditions include Alaska Brown Bears; Kodiak Bears of Alaska; Antarctic Wildlife Arctic Watch—Beluga whale migration; Australia Wildlife; Baja Whale Camp—gray whales; Borneo Wildlife and Rainforest (orangutan, sea turtle, and proboscis monkeys); Botswana Wildlife; Zimbabwe Wildlife; Churchill Summer Wildlife; Costa Rica Rainforest and Wildlife; Galapagos Islands Wildlife; Kenya Wildlife; Tanzania Wildlife; Namibia Wildlife, Primate Watch—Uganda (lowland and mountain gorillas and chimpanzees); and Harp Seal Watch.

Research adventures include Azores Sperm Whale Watch, Caribbean Humpback Whales, Atlantic Spotted Dolphins, Polar Bear Watch, Puffin Watch and Shetland Wildlife, and Wolf Watch.

CURRICULUM AND CREDITS

Credit may be arranged for independent or travel study. Programs vary in length and program leaders have different backgrounds in science and the environment. The participant's institution will have to evaluate the tour itinerary to establish its credit value. Studies are observational and educational more than hands-on training.

THE INSTITUTION

Natural Habitat Adventures (NHA), a Colorado-based tour company in operation since 1985, is dedicated to guiding travelers to the natural habitats of some of the world's most astounding animal life. Ben Bressler, the company's founder, claims that more people are choosing these camera safaris over typical beach or resort vacations.

Ecotourism helps to protect the animals and their habitats by providing revenue for local economies. Some destinations, such as the Galapagos Islands in Ecuador, are established tourist attractions and owe their protection to years of income from ecotourism. Animal watching is not reserved for those high adventurers with seemingly limitless physical capabilities. Many of these nature vacations cater especially to either senior citizens or those searching for a "soft" adventure.

NHA arranges private group adventures for families, museums, universities, and conservation-related organizations. These adventures offer the same quality tour itineraries and leaders but can also be customized to suit the special needs of the group.

THE ENVIRONMENT

Through group travel, participants are able to share nature's experiences. Groups are small and personal, designed to cover nature through intimate close-up wildlife encounters such as visits to see baby harp seals in Eastern Canada, orangutans in Borneo, and dolphins in the Bahamas. Most travelers are not full-time adventurers, but rather animal lovers, photographers, and people of all ages with a desire to view wildlife in its own environment.

Once a reservation is received, NHA sends a 15–40 page predeparture briefing that includes information on the animals, the region, what to bring, necessary vaccinations, necessary documents, etc. It is designed to educate and prepare the participant about the wildlife and the region of their particular trip to ensure that the trip runs as smoothly as possible. For more information on NHA's 23 animal-watching destinations and a free color catalog, contact the intitution at the above address.

FACILITIES

In keeping with the philosophy that one does not have to "really rough-it" to experience nature, the accommodations provided on these programs usually include the finest and most interesting hotels or lodges available in the visited areas, with each one specially chosen to bring the participant closer to nature and to offer an intimate look at the area without sacrificing comfort. Facilities vary with each tour destination. Contact NHA at the above address for more information on facilities and accommodations.

SUPPLIES NEEDED

Contact Natural Habitat Adventures for information on necessary supplies for each specific expedition.

APPLICATIONS AND ADMISSIONS

Contact the reservation department at the above address for information on application and admission procedures.

Financial Aid: None available.

Costs: Tour costs range from approximately $1,400 for a 5-day tour to $6,500 for a 15-day tour. Some departures include air fare from a meeting point.

OKLAHOMA CITY UNIVERSITY
2190 Bluebell
Boulder, CO 80302
(303) 444-2555
Fax: (303) 444-2555
Contact: Dr. Lois Kruschwitz

SAMPLE COURSES

Courses include Natural History of Belize, Natural History of the Hawaiian Islands, and Introduction to Alpine Ecosystems.

CURRICULUM AND CREDITS

Participants are encouraged to do some preliminary reading, make their own observations on location, and interview local experts. Master-level students are required to submit a proposal and to complete a natural history project of their own design. To receive credit for the courses, participants are also required to answer written discussion questions.

The Natural Classroom

THE INSTITUTION
Courses and tours are sponsored by Oklahoma City University, Baker University, and Valparaiso University.

THE ENVIRONMENT
The environment for each tour is "on location." Activities such as hiking, snorkeling, and canoeing are available.

The course on Belize deals with aspects of the country's natural history and includes visits to the reefs, ruins, and rainforests of southern Belize. Important aspects of Mayan archeology and contemporary Belizean culture are examined.

The course on the Hawaiian Islands deals with aspects of natural history during a tour of the Island of Hawaii. The most active volcanic islands in the world provide unique opportunities for studying ecological succession, biological evolution, and volcanism. This course also offers unusual experiences in the areas of archeology, cultural anthropology, and marine biology.

The course on alpine ecosystems discusses the observation and management of ecosystems in the Colorado Rockies. Grand County affords unusual opportunities for studying diverse environments and geological processes.

FACILITIES
Participants are housed at small hotels and lodges in the specific areas.

SUPPLIES NEEDED
Information on necessary supplies is provided upon registration.

APPLICATIONS AND ADMISSIONS
Contact the institution directly for application materials.

Financial Aid: Some financial assistance for tuition may only be available from the sponsoring universities listed above. For further information, send inquiries to Dr. Kruschwitz.

Costs: Hawaii—approximately $850 plus air fare, 10 days; Colorado—$250 without transportation, 8 days; Belize—$1,350 from Houston to Miami, 8 days.

OUTDOOR LEADERSHIP TRAINING SEMINARS
P.O. Box 20281
Denver, CO 80220
(303) 333-7831/(800) 331-7238
Contact: Dr. Rick Medrick, Executive Director

SAMPLE COURSES AND PROGRAMS
Courses and programs include San Juan Mountain Adventure, Rekindling the Fire I, Breaking Through/Deep Ecology, The Wilderness Warrior, Rekindling the Fire II, Mountain Quest, Summer Outdoor Leadership Intensive, Centered Rock Climbing Workshop, The Eagle Rising Institute, Leadership Training Institute, Colorado Outdoor Adventure Course, Arkansas River Tours, Spring Canyon Quest, Women's Canyon Quest, River Gods and Goddesses, Autumn Canyon Quest, Rocky Mountain Adventures, and Lawyers in the Wilderness.

Courses, Programs, and Expeditions in the United States

CURRICULUM AND CREDITS

Outdoor Leadership Training Seminars (OLTS) draw upon a wide range of contemporary psychological, philosophical, and educational strategies to bring insight and appreciation of the outdoor lifestyle to the personal and professional lives of participants.

Their primary commitment is the training and preparation of instructors and guides schooled in a transformational approach to outdoor learning which they call New Age Wilderness Leadership. Credit is offered for some courses through various Colorado institutions and may be obtained for other courses through independent or travel study.

THE INSTITUTION

Since 1973, OLTS has been offering quality programs with emphasis on personal growth, leadership training, and ecological consciousness through such activities as whitewater rafting, rock climbing, mountaineering, backcountry skiing, and general wilderness travel. OLTS is dedicated to personal and organizational transformation through experiences in nature. They are concerned with the survival of our planet, the health of our communities, and the personal development of all who respect and desire harmony with the earth.

THE ENVIRONMENT

The environment includes the Rocky Mountain region of the United States (Colorado, Wyoming, and New Mexico) and the canyon/desert country of Utah and Arizona.

FACILITIES

Inquire with OLTS directly for information about accommodations and facilities.

SUPPLIES NEEDED

Participants provide personal gear. Group gear and food is provided on most programs. Contact OLTS at the above address for information on specific supplies needed for specific courses or programs.

APPLICATIONS AND ADMISSIONS

Reservations with a deposit are required for short courses. Written applications are required for longer programs.

Financial Aid: Some limited scholarships are available for short workshops. Payment plans are available for longer programs.

Costs: The tuition for programs ranges from $575 to $750 for week-long courses to approximately $1,850 for 5-week intensives, and between $3,500 and $4,500 for the 5- and 8-month training programs.

ROCKY MOUNTAIN BIOLOGICAL LABORATORY
P.O. Box 519
Crested Butte, CO 81224
(303) 349-7231
Fax: (303) 349-7231
Contact: Susan Lohr

SAMPLE COURSES

Courses include Rocky Mountain Flora, Field Ornithology, Restoration Ecology, Independent Research, Introduction to Field Ecology, Behavioral Ecology, and Drawing and Painting from Nature.

CURRICULUM AND CREDITS

Six semester credits are available for the 8-week summer session.

THE INSTITUTION

For more then 67 years the Rocky Mountain Biological Laboratory (RMBL) has grown and thrived as a facility for field biologists, attracting researchers and students from around the world. RMBL is a private, nonprofit field station located in Gothic, Colorado. Widely known as one of the leading field stations in North America, RMBL offers facilities for research and study. During the summer nearly 750 research scientists, students, and staff take up residence and once again Gothic becomes an active community, with a local newspaper, seminars, educational programs, and social events. Researchers arrive annually to conduct both long- and short-term studies.

THE ENVIRONMENT

Situated high in the Elk Mountains at 9,500 feet, Gothic was once a thriving mining community during the 1880s. Surrounding Gothic are forests, rocky streams bordered by willows, and open alpine meadows known for some of the most beautiful wildflower displays in Colorado. Adjacent to RMBL are the Gunnison and White River National Forests, the Elk Mountain Wilderness Area, the Gothic Research Natural Area, and the Maroon Bells–Snowmass Wilderness Area. Crested Butte, an historic and meticulously preserved mining town, lies eight miles to the south. Within hiking distance are pristine alpine lakes, expansive tundra vistas, and high mountain passes leading between 14,000-foot peaks. Residents at RMBL use their spare time to hike, fish, raft, mountain-bike, swim, bird watch, and simply enjoy the outdoors.

FACILITIES

The laboratory owns 245 acres with more than 50 buildings, including research laboratories, offices, cabins, a library, dormitories, a dining hall, classrooms, a store, and a visitor's center.

SUPPLIES NEEDED

Special supplies are not required and depend solely on the individual.

APPLICATIONS AND ADMISSIONS

Contact the institution for application forms. Admission is highly competitive. More than 200 applicants usually apply for 35 student positions.

Financial Aid: Some financial aid may be available. The amount varies from year to year.

Costs: Room, board, and tuition for the 8-week course session costs approximately $2,000. Costs for researchers vary with their individual needs.

CONNECTICUT

TAFT EDUCATIONAL CENTER
110 Woodbury Road
Watertown, CT 06795
(203) 274-2516, ext. 275 or (203) 274-7815/(800) 274-7815
Fax: (203) 274-7815
Contact: John L. Wynne

SAMPLE COURSES AND WORKSHOPS

Various Advanced Placement (A.P.) courses are offered in Biology, Chemistry, and Physics. Courses and workshops include A.P. Math, Computer Science, Statistics, Probability, Geometry Graphics Calculators, Library Science, History/Social Studies, Foreign Language, and English.

CURRICULUM AND CREDITS

Many teachers interested in starting an A.P. program, or in improving an existing program, have found the A.P. workshops exciting and useful.

The Taft Educational Center (TEC) is associated with the University of Hartford as the granting institution for graduate credit. Participants who successfully complete workshops at Taft may elect to earn two graduate credits for each week's workshop. All participants are graded for their work at TEC, whether they choose to earn graduate credit or not. The University of Hartford issues this credit at an additional fee of $50 per credit hour. Since the program's inception, over 7,000 graduate credits have been earned.

Continuing Education Units (CEUs) may be earned by successful completion of Taft workshops, since TEC is an approved provider of Continuing Education Units by the Connecticut State Department of Education. For each week of successful work, the center grants 25 Connecticut CEUs.

THE INSTITUTION

Since 1975 TEC has offered a small number of science workshops, but in a short period the demand for a wide variety of workshops has produced a diverse offering of workshops in every discipline. TEC now hosts public and private school teachers from over 40 states and a dozen countries each summer.

THE ENVIRONMENT

TEC is located on the campus of the Taft School (founded in 1890) in Watertown, Connecticut. The cosmopolitan mix of the summer community adds a special quality to the learning experience.

FACILITIES

The facilities used by the center include the Science Center (modern laboratories, classrooms, computer laboratory), the Hulbert Taft Jr. Library (52,000 volumes and 250 periodicals), a large lecture hall, classrooms, dormitories, and dining rooms. The campus includes over 200 acres, numerous playing fields, 12 tennis courts, and extensive athletic facilities. Contact TEC at the above address for specific information on accommodations and facilities.

SUPPLIES NEEDED

Contact TEC for specific information about necessary supplies.

APPLICATION AND ADMISSIONS

Forms to apply for graduate credit are sent by TEC on request or they may be picked up during the summer at the main office. Write to the institution for their 16-page catalog of course descriptions.

Financial Aid: None available.

Costs: Tuition is approximately $525 per week and includes accommodations and meals; for commuting participants, tutition is $425 per week, including lunch. There is no extra charge for accommodations for boarding participants who remain at Taft during the weekend between workshops. Room and board costs for nontuition spouses is approximately $175; children are $125 and children-in-arms are free.

FLORIDA

BILL THOMAS NATURE PHOTOGRAPHIC SEMINARS
Box 194
Lowell, FL 32663
(904) 867-0463
Contact: Bill Thomas

SAMPLE SEMINARS
Nature photography seminars are offered in the Everglades—10,000 Islands, Ocala, Florida Eagle Country, Okefenokee Swamp, and Suwannee River—Great Smoky Mountains, Olympic Rain Forest, the San Juan Islands, Southwest Indian Country, Valley of the Cataract (Indiana), Southeast Alaska, East Africa, the Amazon Rainforest, and the Galapagos Islands. Adventure safaris are available to Australia, New Zealand, and Africa. Writing workshops for photographers are also available.

CURRICULUM AND CREDITS
These seminars introduce participants to the world of nature photojournalism and help students develop the techniques and professional skills necessary to publish their work through a combination of on-location supervised shooting and sessions on business management/photo marketing. Weekend sessions include two half-days of lecture on composition, subject selection, lighting, equipment, film, and taxes and business management, plus comprehensive discussions on marketing one's work. Two half-days of supervised shooting are spent in the field plus a Friday night session on specialized photography.

Week-long workshops offer the serious student intensive training in photography and sessions on building rapport with wildlife, stalking, and an appreciation of other lifeforms in some of America's most unique ecosystems. Credit may be available through independent or travel study.

THE INSTITUTION
Not applicable.

THE ENVIRONMENT
Each seminar takes place in a different environment. Contact the above address for information.

FACILITIES
All food, lodging, and local transportation is provided. Field work is balanced out by ongoing lectures on composition, working with wildlife, lighting, subject selection, marketing, and business management. Some film is developed when the week and group critique sessions are held.

SUPPLIES NEEDED
Camera, film, tripod, field clothes, and rain gear.

APPLICATIONS AND ADMISSIONS
Information on registration is sent with the brochure.

Financial Aid: None available.

Costs: Approxiumately $295 for weekend seminars and $895 for week-long seminars. Safaris in Botswana and East Africa generally run about $4,500 for 15 days, and includes all provisions plus air fare from New York.

BIMINI BIOLOGICAL FIELD STATION
RSMAS University of Miami
9300 SW 99th Street
Miami, FL 33176-2050
(305) 274-0628; (305) 361-4146 (voice mail)
Fax: (305) 274-0628; (305) 361-4600
E-mail: sgruber @rsmas.miami.edu.
Contact: Samuel H. Gruber

SAMPLE COURSES AND PROGRAMS

MBF 514, Tropical Marine Biology—a 10-day intensive field course open to upper-level undergraduates and graduates (anyone with a college degree). Students participate in daily field trips visiting seven marine habitats to collect and identify topical marine plants and animals. Two formal lectures are held each day. Evenings are spent in the laboratory observing the living specimens and keying out organisms.

MBF 571, Tropical Marine Communities—a shorter, 5-day version of MBF 514. This course is designed to acquaint educators with various marine communities such as rocky shore, mud flats, seagrass meadow, mangrove forest, and coral and artificial reefs.

MBF 572, Elasmobranch Biology—a new, 10-day field course on the biology of skates and rays. This team-taught course features lectures by several researchers who actively work on the biology of sharks. Lectures include taxonomy, life histories, physiology, biochemistry, and behavior of select species. Fieldwork includes the capture, tag, and release of large sharks, telemetry tracking of sharks previously marked with ultrasonic transmitters, and observing several species of free-swimming sharks baited into a special reef area. Laboratory work involves identification and dissection of preserved specimens and observation of captive sharks.

CURRICULUM AND CREDITS

Days typically begin at 7 a.m. and end at 11 p.m. Undergraduate and graduate students, as well as interested persons, are invited to participate in a shark-tracking project that was initiated in winter of 1992. MBF 514 and MBF 572 are worth 3 credits each, and MBF 571 is worth 2 credits.

THE INSTITUTION

Bimini Biological Field Station (BBFS) is an independently owned research station, chartered by the government of the Bahamas under a permit for the purpose of research and education. The station is subsumed under the administration of the Rosenstiel School of Marine and Atmospheric Sciences, a division of Marine Biology and Fisheries, whenever university-sponsored activities (e.g., academic courses, grant research, etc.) take place.

THE ENVIRONMENT

The focus of BBFS is on marine biology and the marine environment. The Island of Bimini is ecologically unique in many ways. Twice each day, the island's waters are tidally exchanged with pristine stream waters. Consequently, pollution is virtually nonexistent, making the marine flora and fauna abundant, diverse, and accessible. All marine habitats (i.e., sandy beaches, rocky shores, mud flats, seagrass beds, mangrove shore lines, coral reefs, artificial reefs, and the pelagic zone) can be reached in a matter of minutes.

FACILITIES

The station is located 43 nautical miles east of Miami, Florida, on the South Island of Bimini in the Bahamas. Excellent air service is provided to the island by commercial flights from Miami and Ft. Lauderdale. The station sits on two acres of isolated shoreline. The physical plant is a wood-frame structure with a dry laboratory/lecture room, kitchen and dining room, two baths, and five bedrooms. The station sleeps 21 people in relative comfort. The building is air-conditioned and electric power is reliable. The laboratory is located on a small lagoon with immediate access to the gulfstream. The BBFS fleet consists of 11 fiberglass outboards from 16 to 24 feet each.

SUPPLIES NEEDED

The station provides all necessary amenities. They do recommend a list of personal supplies based on each participant's potential physical discomforts (i.e., intense sun, wind, and rain, biting insects, etc.). Passports are required for all non-U.S. or Commonwealth Citizens.

APPLICATIONS AND ADMISSIONS

For information on application and admission procedures, contact Dr. Samuel H. Gruber at the above address.

Financial Aid: None available.

Costs: Living expenses for volunteer researchers is approximately $375 per month. Contact Earthwatch at (800) 776-0188, ext. 179, for volunteers' share of summer field expeditions. Tuition for University of Miami courses is approximately $670 per credit ($470 for summer); laboratory fee, room, and board $250 ($25/day). U.S. airfare, Bahamas taxes, and transfer is approximately $150.

BOTTOM TIME ADVENTURES
P.O. Box 11919
Ft. Lauderdale, FL 33339-1919
(305) 921-7798/(800) 234-8464
Fax: (305) 920-5578
Contact: Elizabeth Longtin

SAMPLE TOURS

Tours are offered in the Bahamas (Bimini, Cat Cay, Cay Sal Bank, Grand Bahamas, Eluthera, Nassau), including coral reef ecology surveys, historical research, underwater videos, dolphin and diving experiences, biking on Eleuthera, and kayaking in the Bahamas.

CURRICULUM AND CREDITS

Bottom Time Adventures (BTA) specializes in live-aboard diving at remote locations in the Bahamas seldom visited by other operators. Most of the islands are remote and not available except by a specialized live-aboard vessel. One must be a certified scuba diver and in good physical condition in order to participate in the scuba program. Resort courses are available. Although credit is not granted directly, it can be obtained through independent or travel study.

THE INSTITUTION

BTA has operated its current charter groups for 15 years, traveling to remote parts of the Bahamas. The *M.V. Bottom Time II* operated by BTA is a state-of-the-art power catamaran, capable of providing live-aboard support for 28 adventure travelers. BTA specializes in remote destinations and out-of-the-ordinary adventure themes.

THE ENVIRONMENT

The Bahamas represent a chain of approximately 1,000 islands spread over hundreds of miles from Florida to Cuba and the Dominican Republic.

The Exumas, a chain of islands that begins 35 miles southeast of Nassau, are remote and for the most part uninhabited. The people who do live there receive no visitors on a regular basis except by the *Bottom Time II*. Past participants have remarked that diving in the Exumas is an experience equal to diving in the Red Sea.

The near Bahamas, the group of islands closest to Florida, represent many different itineraries. Wall diving is good here because the gulf stream offers some of the best clarity in the Bahamas with visibility levels of 100 to 200 feet possible.

Cay Sal is a group of islands located 40 miles north of Cuba and represents another world-class destination. Cay Sal is known for its blue-hole walls and its lobster, conch, and wreck diving. A blue hole is a result of ancient volcanic activity that created a dome or bubble beneath the earth's surface. As the oceans covered and eroded the domes away, holes were created. In Cay Sal there are nine known holes in existence with each one ranging from 200 to 2,000 yards in diameter and several hundred feet in depth. Coral reef covers the edges of the holes making for a unique mixing of both shallow reef and larger species of marine life normally found in deeper water.

FACILITIES

The *M.V. Bottom Time II* has all the amenities of a land-based facility with the mobility of a live-aboard vessel. It is air-conditioned with 14 double passenger cabins, 8 heads and showers, and a large common area (salon) with television, VCR, stereo, and CD player. The vessel has the ability of filtering 3,600 gallons of salt water into fresh drinking and bathing water. It can travel the waters with a cruise speed near 30 mph, thus making traveling the distance to the Bahamas quick, stable, and comfortable.

SUPPLIES NEEDED

BTA supplies tanks and weights, meals, beverages (with meals), and accommodations aboard the vessel. Rental scuba equipment is available for a charge (contact the office for prices and details). Necessary supplies to bring include personal diving equipment (e.g., masks, fins, snorkel, back pack, regulator, etc.), personal hygiene supplies (e.g., towels, soap, etc.), a passport or another form of identification, and anything else that the participants feel are necessary to sustain them for the duration of their adventure.

APPLICATIONS AND ADMISSIONS

There are many different ways of securing passage on a BTA tour—through a personal travel agent, local dive shops, independent instructors, and directly through the BTA office.

Financial Aid: BTA does not supply any form of financial aid, but it may be possible to obtain some through the participant's school or institution.

Costs: Costs vary depending upon the length and itinerary of the adventure. One-week, live-aboard charters cost from approxiamtely $1,100 to $1,300 for passage aboard the *M.V. Bottom Time II.*

BUTTERFLY WORLD
Tradewinds Park
3600 West Sample Road
Coconut Creek, FL 33073
(305) 977-4434
Fax: (305) 977-4501
Contact: Paula Lee

SAMPLE WORKSHOPS AND TOURS

Field trips are offered for all school grades, Boy Scouts, Girl Scouts, and camps. Guided tours are available for all ages. Education workshops such as Butterfly Gardening and Breeding are given to elementary and advanced children throughout the year.

CURRICULUM AND CREDITS

All workshops are short, and no formal credit is available. Guided tours for all ages are available by reservation and parties of ten or more any be eligible for group rates.

In addition to tours, Butterfly World (BW) offers a series of how-to educational workshops throughout the year. Highlights include Butterfly Gardening and Breeding classes, both for beginners and advanced butterfly enthusiasts. If you would like information on future workshops, contact BW at the above address.

THE INSTITUTION

BW is proud to be a member of the Lepidopterists' Society, a nonprofit organization dedicated to the study and preservation of butterflies and moths. Both amateur and professional butterfly enthusiasts are encouraged to join.

BW is the first exhibit of its kind in the Western Hemisphere and the largest in the world. Careful planning and control create the right conditions for thousands of butterflies to fly, court, feed, and bask in the sunlight. In fact, most of the butterfly species are bred at the farm, allowing one to marvel at an assortment of unusual caterpillars and pupa.

Plants are essential for the survival of these creatures. The expert horticultural department propagates thousands of specialized plants that feed caterpillars and a montage of blossoms that provide nectar for the butterflies. Consequently, the tropical gardens are as beautiful as they are functional.

THE ENVIRONMENT

One of the main goals of BW is to encourage visitors to take an interest in their environment and the natural world. Toward this end, there are a number of ways in which people of all ages can use BW as an educational resource.

According to the breeding program, the number of butterflies fluctuates throughout the season. A minimum of 2,000 butterflies are on display at all times. Although bright and sunny days are most conducive to butterfly flight, some species will still perform well on cloudy days. Up to 50 species can be seen at any one time. Over the course of a year, approximately 150 species from five continents are housed in the aviary.

FACILITIES

The park is composed of a butterfly farm, an aviary, a museum, and gardens.

SUPPLIES NEEDED
None.

APPLICATIONS AND ADMISSIONS
Interested parties may sign up for workshops by contacting BW at the above address. Information pamphlets and membership applications are available at the Butterfly World admissions desk or by contacting BW directly.

Financial Aid: None available.

Costs: Workshop fees are approximately $10 per person.

CARIBBEAN WILDLIFE SURVEYS
2321 State Road 580, Suite 5
Clearwater, FL 34723
(813) 797-0466/(800) 897-0466
Fax: (813) 797-0466
Contact: Dr. Tom Turner

SAMPLE PROGRAMS
Caribbean Wildlife Surveys (CWS) arranges wildlife surveys to wilderness areas in and around the Caribbean for professionals, students, and amateurs. Emphasis is on photography of specimens. Voucher specimens are taken only as needed for scientific documentation; permits are obtained as needed. CWS offers full compliance with all host countries and international wildlife regulations. Surveys usually last 7–11 days.

CURRICULUM AND CREDITS
Group sizes range from 1 to 36 participants, including individual scientists (specialists), small groups of amateurs or professionals (e.g., birders, botanists, entomologists, etc.), or larger undergraduate student groups accompanied by their professor (ecology courses for credits). Scuba diving and spelunking are offered by special arrangement only. Classwork includes initial orientation presentations (including cultural/historical/biological aspects of the host country), nightly workshops (record of daily progress), and an optional closing workshop (review of achievements).

THE INSTITUTION
CWS provides interested participants with an opportunity to see and photograph wildlife in some of the last remaining unspoiled habitats of the Caribbean. Participants spend time examining and learning about the history, current cultural practices, and customs of the various people encountered. Sites visited may be already designated as wildlife preserves or research centers; they may be totally unoccupied, or well-known tourist attractions selected for spectacular scenery or unusual wildlife.

THE ENVIRONMENT
Rainforest, riverine, semidesert, high mountain, or coastal habitats on Caribbean islands or countries bordering the Caribbean—sites and programs are selected with applicants/institutions to meet their interests. Some sites can be driven to; others require short hikes or overnight camping in rugged terrain.

FACILITIES

All land-based activities in the host country/countries are fully covered. Exceptions are personal expenses, alcoholic beverages, medical expenses, airport departure taxes, etc. Participants are also responsible for comprehensive travel insurance (mandatory) and air fares to and from the host country. CWS assists with securing optimum rates and coordination of flights.

SUPPLIES NEEDED

Details of required clothing, travel documents, medications, inoculations, currency, equipment, etc. are sent to each applicant. Applicants must bring their own photographic and collecting equipment. Precise requirements vary depending on the localities to be visited; CWS provides customized lists.

APPLICATIONS AND ADMISSIONS

Specialized surveys are arranged by direct contact with individuals or groups. Call the above phone number for more information. A minimum of six months advance notice is required.

Financial Aid: None available.

Costs: Excluding international air fares, costs usually range between $75 and $150 per person per day. All inclusive costs average $100 per person per day. Costs for single applicants are necessarily higher—up to $200 per day.

EXPLORATIONS, INC.
27655 Kent Road
Bonita Springs, FL 33923
(813) 992-9660/(800) 446-9660
Fax: (813) 992-7666
Contact: Charlie Strader, President

SAMPLE TOURS AND EXPEDITIONS

Educational, natural history, and archaeology tours are offered to Latin America. Some of the more popular programs include a scholar-escorted jungle safari into the Peruvian Amazon and its Treetop Canopy Walkway. Amazon River boat cruises are also available, as are cultural tours to study Incan and Mayan Archeology. Multiple packages to Costa Rica and Ecuador are available.

CURRICULUM AND CREDITS

Information is provided to assist participants in securing independent study research credits.

THE INSTITUTION

Explorations, Inc. is a bonded and registered seller of travel with the state of Florida. Dedicated to providing affordable, well-paced travel experiences, the company promotes informal education and facilitates a better understanding of the natural world and foreign cultures.

THE ENVIRONMENT

Tours take place in various regions of Central and South America, including the Amazon River and jungle.

FACILITIES

Contact Explorations, Inc. for specific information.

SUPPLIES NEEDED

Explorations, Inc. prides itself on providing quality, personalized service. Educational handouts and ample pretrip information are given to enhance the travel and learning experience. Resident professional guides also provide a wealth of information. Packing lists and suggestions for each trip are supplied. Specialized equipment is not required.

APPLICATIONS AND ADMISSIONS

Most programs are open to the public. Contact Explorations, Inc. at the above address regarding group discounts, custom trip planning, trip brochures, and registration requirements.

Financial Aid: No aid is available beyond group discounts and reasonable trip prices.

Costs: Most programs are all-inclusive (i.e., air fare, lodging, meals, and tours/excursions). A typical 8-day Latin American program ranges from $1,300 to $1,900, and includes international air. Low-cost domestic air fare is available.

INTERNATIONAL JOURNEYS, INC.
17849 San Carlos Boulevard
Fort Myers Beach, FL 33931
(813) 466-6525/(800) 622-6525
Fax: (813) 466-7685
Contact: Patrice M. Hart

SAMPLE TOURS

Tours include Journey to the Amazon aboard *El Arca*, the only research vessel on the Amazon, which travels through Peru to Brazil, Columbia and back.

CURRICULUM AND CREDITS

Participants adventure 650 miles by riverboat on the Amazon River for eight days and seven nights. They participate in hands-on research projects to include a pink dolphin census, plant life, and bird and insect studies. Daily side trips include jungle walks through the Emerald Forest, small boat excursions up remote tributaries, and visits with local native villages. A trained biologist and local guides conduct the trip. Credit is available through independent or travel study.

THE INSTITUTION

A bonded and registered organization with the state of Florida as a seller of travel, International Journeys, Inc. is committed to providing quality international experiences that enhance international understanding through informal education.

THE ENVIRONMENT
The rainforest is the classroom. Tours are led out from the riverboat each day. The group travels up narrow tributaries via small motorized launches. Stops are made at jungle paths and small villages, giving participants a closer view of Amazon life.

FACILITIES
Travel on a 90-foot, 3-deck riverboat, completely renovated in 1982 with a lounge area on the top deck. Cabins are air-conditioned, clean, and comfortable, with each one containing two bunk beds. Sheets are changed daily. The food is good and served buffet-style; it is best described as Amazon ranch-style. Coffee and purified water are available 24 hours a day.

SUPPLIES NEEDED
A current passport may be obtained within two weeks for emergencies, but it is best to plan four weeks ahead. Contact your local post office for an application. Visas are not required.

APPLICATIONS AND ADMISSIONS
Call the above toll-free number for a brochure or to make a reservation.

Financial Aid: None available.

Costs: Approximately $1,695, all-inclusive from Miami.

MARINE RESOURCES DEVELOPMENT FOUNDATION
MarineLab Environmental Education Program
Tugaloo Environmental Education Center
P.O. Box 787
Key Largo, FL 33037
(305) 451-1139/(800) 741-1139
Fax: (305) 451-3909
Contact at MarineLab: Ginette Hughes, Coordinator
Contact at Tugaloo Environmental Education Center: JoAnn Smenda, Coordinator

SAMPLE COURSES AND PROGRAMS
Courses and programs include MarineLab—Introduction to Coastal Marine Ecology (1-week teacher workshop); Environments of the Florida Keys (Elderhostel); extended 3-day, 2-night environmental program (4th grade through high school). Tugaloo Environmental Education Center (TEEC): Introduction to Forest and Freshwater Ecology (1-week teacher workshop) and various student programs. Custom programs are also available at both facilities.

CURRICULUM AND CREDITS
MarineLab offers programs in student marine ecology (from 1 to 12 days) for elementary to college students, 1-week summer workshops for teachers, and Elderhostel programs. Tugaloo Environmental Education Center offers programs in forest and freshwater ecology for elementary to high school students and summer workshops for teachers. TEEC also has an outreach program. Both facilities customize programs to meet specific group needs.

All programs are residential. Fees include meals, accommodations, field trips, evening presentations, and snorkel gear. Optional activities are available. Graduate, recertification, and/or in-service credits are available for teacher workshops.

THE INSTITUTION

Marine Resources Development Foundation, a 24-year-old organization that has developed an international reputation as a pioneer of undersea science and technology resource utilization, provides undersea research and environmental education through its two centers, MarineLab in Key Largo and the Tugaloo Environmental Education Center in Oconee County.

The foundation moved to its present location in Key Largo in 1984. Since then, it has developed the MarineLab education program, which hosts 5,000 students a year, and furthered its commitment to environmental education by opening TEEC in 1992.

Located directly on Largo Sound, Key Largo, Florida, the MarineLab is uniquely situated among the fragile coral reef, seagrass, and mangrove communities protected by the John Pennekamp Coral Reef State Park, Everglades National Park, and the Florida Keys National Marine Sanctuary. The natural habitats preserved within these parks serve as the setting for an exciting and constructive educational experience.

TEEC is located in a privately owned 150-acre valley bordered by the Sumter National Forest, the Tugaloo River, and the Chatahoochee National Forest, in the southwest corner of South Carolina on the southernmost end of the Appalachian chain, and offers students and teachers the opportunity to study the singular ecology of North America's only temperate rainforest. The mixed deciduous forests of the southern Appalachians provide refuge for a rich diversity of plant and animal life.

FACILITIES

MarineLab operates six open-water 24-foot field/research boats, each carrying 13 students, one chaperone, and a boat operator, for safe and comfortable exploration of nearby ecosystems. To supplement the field instruction, large outdoor meeting areas and a floating theater/lecture hall are used for orientation and discussions associated with the field trips. The labs contain microscopes, a collection of marine specimens, and identification manuals, in addition to the newest addition of a video microscope. Dormitory accommodations can hold up to 90 people in air-conditioned, carpeted rooms. Cafeteria services are included.

TEEC operates two 28-foot pontoon boats which are used as floating laboratories for the exploration of nearby river and lake ecosystems. To supplement the field instruction, a large outdoor area, an indoor classroom, and an indoor theater/lecture area are used for discussions associated with the day's activities. The main lodge contains a library, cafeteria facilities, and a large stone fireplace. Dorms are carpeted, with heated/air-conditioned rooms and a total sleeping capacity of 88 people.

SUPPLIES NEEDED

Students must provide their own bed linens, towels, and personal supplies for both facilities.

APPLICATIONS AND ADMISSIONS

Contact the institution at the above address for application and admission procedures.

Financial Aid: Limited scholarships are available for individuals within a group.

Costs: A 1-week introduction course to coastal marine ecology or forest and freshwater ecology is approximately $464 per person (including room and board). A 5-day MarineLab program is approximately $425 per person, and a 5-day TEEC program, $250 per person.

SHELLS OF THE SEAS, INC./LIVING WORLD TOURS
P.O. Box 1418
Fort Lauderdale, FL 33302
(305) 763-7516/(800) 253-9255
Fax: (305) 763-9506
Contact: Peter Bright

SAMPLE TOURS

Tours specializing in the study and collection of seashells and the study of marine life in general are offered in the following countries: Costa Rica, Thailand, Philippines, Fiji, Dominican Republic, Venezuela, Solomon Island, Vanuatu, and the Grenadines.

CURRICULUM AND CREDITS

Shells of the Seas, Inc./Living World Tours offers the best in group shelling and sightseeing tours. All tours are personally escorted by knowledgeable guides and are carefully previewed so that no surprises occur when traveling. Small groups of 15–20 people enjoy traveling, sightseeing, and nature, and have a common interest in seashells and marine life in general. Whether one is a serious shell collector or just enjoys traveling, sightseeing, and having a great time, Shells of the Seas, Inc. has a tour for every individual. While credit is not offered directly, it can be obtained through independent or travel study.

THE INSTITUTION

Shells of the Seas, Inc./Living World Tours is a privately owned tour operator. The two owners are also the tour guides—Peter Bright and Glen Duffy—and have extensive field knowledge of marine environments on a worldwide level.

THE ENVIRONMENT

The environment varies with the itinerary of each individual tour.

FACILITIES

Tour accommodations while include hotels and resorts available on-site. These vary depending on the locale, and are always mid- to upper-grade.

SUPPLIES NEEDED

Supplies vary depending on the types of collecting available. Details of necessary supplies to bring, along with a day-by-day itinerary and other information, are sent to tour participants.

APPLICATIONS AND ADMISSIONS

Reservations can be made by phone, fax, or mail request.

Financial Aid: None available.

Costs: Shells of the Seas, Inc./Living World Tours attempts to include all basic costs in their tour rates (i.e., air fare, hotels, transportation, guides, taxes, I.D., clinics, shells, marine life, etc.), and some meals where possible. Tour costs range from approximatley $840 for a 6-day tour to $3,450 for an 18-day tour.

STUDY ABROAD FOR THE EARTH
Saint Thomas University
16400 Northwest 32nd Avenue
Miami, FL 33054
(800) 367-9010, ext. 6650
In Florida call, (800) 367-9000, ext. 6650
Fax: (305) 626-2950
Contact: Professor Elisabetta Ferrero

SAMPLE PROGRAMS
Programs include "Study Abroad for the Earth" in Assisi, Italy, which combines travel with ecological studies. Courses are offered in art, communication, education, English, history, Italian, Italian literature in translation, philosophy, and science.

CURRICULUM AND CREDITS
Saint Thomas University's Study Abroad for the Earth offers a summer program of study. The 3- and 8-week programs offer (for full academic credit or for continuing education) a variety of courses on the undergraduate level. These programs provide a challenging opportunity for the serious student who wishes to combine travel with ecological studies. Students have the opportunity to study three weeks in Assisi and earn nine academic credits.

THE ENVIRONMENT
The birthplace of Saint Francis, Assisi is recognized as the European capital of all environmentalists. A city rich in spirituality and culture, it has one of the most interesting bioregions in Umbria.

FACILITIES
Accommodations are available in a fine hotel in the heart of the city, with double-room occupancy and a private bath. A vegetarian diet with pasta, legumes, fresh vegetables, and fruits is offered.

SUPPLIES NEEDED
None.

APPLICATIONS AND ADMISSIONS
Students must submit an essay and two letters of recommendation with their application form. Call of write to the above address and phone number for the appropriate forms.

Financial Aid: Partial scholarships are given based on financial need and grades.

Costs: The total cost of the 3-week program is approximately $2,800 and includes accomodations, three meals a day, motor coach to and from Assisi upon arrival and departure, and various field trips to nearby cities.

TARA TOURS, INC.
6595 N.W. 36th Street, #306A
Miami Springs, FL 33166
(305) 871-1246/(800) 327-0080
Fax: (305) 871-0417
Contact: Daniel Taramona

SAMPLE TOURS AND EXPEDITIONS

Tours and expeditions include: Argentina—Bariloche/Puerto Montt Lake Crossing and Iguassu Falls; Belize—Mayan Ruins and Panti Medicinal Trail; Bolivia—Lake Titicaca; Brazil—Brazilian Amazon and the Pantanal; Chile—Easter Island, Atacama Desert, and Torres del Paine National Park; Columbia—Amazon River; Costa Rica—Volcanoes and Forests, Marenco Biological Station, Underwater Safari, and National Parks; Ecuador—Galapagos Islands, Machalilla National Park, and the Ecuadorian Amazon; El Salvador—Volcanoes, Mayan Ruins, and Montecristo Forest; Guatemala—Mayan Ruins; Honduras—Ruins of Copan and Jungle Islands; Nicaragua—Volcanoes and Selva Negra Cloud Forest; Panama—Darien Jungle; Paraguay—Ypacarai Lake; Peru—Inca Ruins, Peruvian Amazon, Manu National Park, and the Amazon Center for Environmental Education and Research; and Venezuela—Amazon Jungle and the Orinoca River.

CURRICULUM AND CREDITS

Participants will venture into virgin forests, meet with indigenous Indians, enjoy viewing wildlife, flora, and fauna in all of Central and South America's National Parks and Reserves. Credit may be available through independent study or travel study.

THE INSTITUTION

Since 1980 Tara Tours, Inc. (TTI) has been a wholesale tour operator specializing in Central and South America, and is experienced in working closely together with educational facilities and museums.

THE ENVIRONMENT

A wide diversity of environments are encountered, ranging from hot and humid to dry and frigid.

FACILITIES

A wide variety of accomodations are available, from hotel to camping. Meals are either included or excluded depending on choice. Transportation ranges from airplanes, ships, boats, and buses as well as trekking.

SUPPLIES NEEDED

Depending on the particular tour itinerary chosen, necessary supplies range from personal clothing to camping gear.

APPLICATIONS AND ADMISSIONS

One can reserve directly through a retail travel agent, educational facility as a group, or with TTI.

Financial Aid: None available unless extended by private sponsorship or educational institution.

Costs: Vary greatly depending upon itinerary selections. Check directly with TTI at the above address for specific tour prices.

GEORGIA

WILDERNESS SOUTHEAST
711 Sandtown Road
Savannah, GA 31410
(912) 897-5108
Fax: (912) 897-5116
Contact: Kelly Cichy, Director

SAMPLE COURSES, TRIPS, AND EXPEDITIONS

Courses, trips, and expeditions include Okefenokee Swamp Courses/Canoe; Costa Rica Jungle/Backpacking; Belize–Tikal/Hike; Amazon Riverboat/Lodge; Seaturtle Watch (Georgia/South Carolina Coast); Everglades Paddle/Hike; Houseboat/Canoe; Teens' Marine Science Camp/ Backpacking; Wilderness Camp for Junior High Students; Smokies Backpack/Hike; Big Bend/Hike and Raft; Coastal Georgia/Sea Kayak; Georgia Barrier Island Ecology; Florida Springs Basecamp/Canoe.

CURRICULUM AND CREDITS

Although courses do not carry formal college credit, credit may be granted through travel study institutions or independent study. Programs can be custom designed for one's school, club, church, museum, or family group. The customized learning experiences offer a variety of trip locations and program emphases. Program options are listed in the catalog.

THE INSTITUTION

Wilderness Southeast (WSE) is a nonprofit school which offers outdoor programs for those who find nature not an adversary to conquer or destroy, but a storehouse of infinite knowledge and experience linking people to all things past and present. Each program minimizes the use of natural resources and human impact on these wilderness areas. Groups are purposely kept small (16 or less) to assure a close sense of togetherness and to satisfy the policy of minimal-impact camping. People are encouraged to lend a hand with camp chores and to take ample time for quiet relaxation and personal reflection.

THE ENVIRONMENT

A typical group is made up of both men and women whose ages range from 20 to 80. The eldest participant celebrated his 89th birthday in the Okefenokee Swamp. Many people come alone and many are complete novices in the outdoors. The instructors describe the ecosystems, plants, wildlife, and their interactions. The goals is to train one's eyes and ears to observe more closely.

FACILITIES

The institution does not have facilities per se, since travel is to wilderness areas. WSE handles the logistics by taking participants to the best places during the best times. Their programs are field-tested before being offered to the public.

SUPPLIES NEEDED

WSE provides comfortable tents or cabins, food, safety equipment, other travel gear, and all necessary arrangements and permits. The pace for each trip is leisurely, itineraries fairly flexible, and many optional activities are available.

APPLICATIONS AND ADMISSIONS

Contact the institution at the above address for a catalog.

Financial Aid: Scholarships are available but limited. Inquire directly to WSE for more information.

Costs: Contact WSE for information on current costs.

HAWAII

EYE OF THE WHALE
Marine/Wilderness Adventures
P.O. Box 1269
Kapa'au, HI 96755
(808) 889-0227/(800) 657-7730
Fax (808) 889-0227
Contact: Mark or Beth Goodoni

SAMPLE TOURS AND EXPEDITIONS
Tours and expeditions include a 6-day Earth, Fire & Sea—Natural History & Environment; a 10-day Hawaiian Hiking Odyssey—Natural History & Island Discovery.

CURRICULUM AND CREDITS
Credit is available through either independent or travel study.

THE INSTITUTION
Eye of the Whale (EOW) is a family-run organization that operates in the field. There is no "institution" as such.

THE ENVIRONMENT
Hawaii is a land of great diversity containing 11 of the world's 13 climate types. The environment consists of rainforests, coral reefs, volcanos, coastal areas—in essence, all of Hawaii. Temperatures range from 90°F to near freezing, and rainfall is between 10 to 500 inches a year. During the trip participants spend most of their time in temperatures ranging from 70°F to 80°F. One should be prepared, however, for cooler weather—40°F to 50°F—especially at night and during rain showers.

FACILITIES
Facilities consist of various bed-and-breakfast lodgings.

SUPPLIES NEEDED
Upon reservation or inquiry, EOW provides participants with an extensive clothing and equipment list.

APPLICATIONS AND ADMISSIONS
Reservations can be made by contacting EOW directly.

Financial Aid: None available.

Costs: Approximate per person costs for the 6-day Earth, Fire, & Sea trip is $975, and for the 10-day Hawaii Hiking Odyssey, $1,485.

HAWAII 2000
Educational and Cultural Programs
76-6304 Mahuahua Place
Kailua-kona, HI 96740
(808) 329-0715/(800) 844-2008
Fax: (808) 329-0803
Contact: Trudi Zelko

SAMPLE TOURS
Tours of Hawaii, Kenya, Siberia/Mongolia/Far East Russia, Australia/New Zealand/Indonesia, Alaska, Thailand, and Burma are offered with possible additional tours of Papua New Guinea and Irian Jaya.

CURRICULUM AND CREDITS
Hawaii 2000 invites participants to share one of their exciting adventure and learning experiences, which includes visits to families, schools, and religious and cultural centers. Continuing Education Credits are offered for some tours. Credit may be obtained through independent or travel study.

THE INSTITUTION
Small, congenial groups of 15 to 30 people go on tours with knowledgeable guides. Some tours are offered in association with the University of Hawaii.

THE ENVIRONMENT
Each tour visits a particular geographic environment. Inquire with Hawaii 2000 for information on specific tours.

FACILITIES
Information on facilities for a particular tour is provided by Hawaii 2000 on request.

SUPPLIES NEEDED
Information on necessary supplies is provided at the time of reservations or by inquiry in advance.

APPLICATIONS AND ADMISSIONS
Contact the institution at the above address for information on application and admission procedures.

Financial Aid: None available.

Costs: Tours range from $1,500 and up. Contact Hawaii 2000 for more information.

IDAHO

TAYLOR RANCH WILDERNESS FIELD STATION
Wilderness Research Center
University of Idaho
Moscow, ID 83844-1144
(208) 885-5779
Fax: (208) 885-2268
Contact: Dr. Jeffrey J. Yeo

SAMPLE COURSES
Courses include Field Research in Wilderness Ecology—hands-on field research in ecology of natural ecosystems and in conservation biology for college students and teachers; Wilderness Internships—currently limited to University of Idaho undergraduates; and National Science Foundation–sponsored Research Experience for Undergraduates—ten weeks of independent, student-initiated field research in ecology and conservation biology for undergraduate students nationwide (proposed).

CURRICULUM AND CREDITS
Credit is offered through the University of Idaho (e.g., 3 semester credits for Field Research in Wilderness Ecology and 3 semester credits for Research Experience for Undergraduates).

THE INSTITUTION
Taylor Ranch Wilderness Field Station (TRWFS) is the only university-owned field station within designated wilderness areas in the United States. TRWFS is administered by the University of Idaho Wilderness Research Center and is dedicated to facilitating wilderness-dependent research and education. Research has been conducted from the field station for the past 30 years beginning with the well-known studies on cougars by Dr. Maurice Hornocker, which spanned 20 years. TRWFS can be reached by trail (37 miles inside the wilderness boundary) or by bush plane.

THE ENVIRONMENT
TRWFS lies in the heart of the 2.4-million-acre Frank Church River of No Return Wilderness in central Idaho, one of the largest wilderness areas in the United States. The topography is rugged with deep canyons along the Middle Fork and main stem of the Salmon River (the "River of No Return") and high mountain peaks above 10,000 feet. Vegetation transitions range from dry bunchgrass rangeland at lower elevations to coniferous forest to alpine.

FACILITIES
The field station has rustic living quarters—most with bathrooms and showers—for up to 18 people. Three kitchens with cookware, utensils, stove, oven, and refrigerators are available for students and scientists to prepare individual or group meals. A large laboratory/classroom provides simple laboratory facilities, herbarium and animal collections, a small library, field research equipment, and a few computers. Limited electrical power is supplied by solar panels.

SUPPLIES NEEDED

Clothing and equipment lists are supplied well in advance of course initiation to all registered participants.

APPLICATIONS AND ADMISSIONS

Application for courses or internships should be made to the above address. Admission is through the University of Idaho Registrar's Office. A summer catalog is available on request.

Financial Aid: For the National Science Foundation–sponsored Research Exploration for Undergraduates program, funding for stipend (approximately $2,500 per ten weeks) plus travel, food, and lodging expenses is provided.

Costs: For Field Research in Wilderness Ecology, travel expenses to and from the trailhead, summer registration (3 credits) plus course fee ($150) are the responsibility of each participant.

ILLINOIS

ALICE L. KIBBE LIFE SCIENCE STATION
Department of Biological Sciences
Western Illinois University
Macomb, IL 61455
(309) 298-1553 or (309) 298-1546
Fax: (309) 298-2270
Contact: Dr. Richard V. Anderson

SAMPLE COURSES
Courses include Ornithology, Ichthyology, Ecological Techniques, Plant Systematic, Plant Ecology, Streams Ecology, Field Study in Biology (for teachers), Field Mycology, Mammalogy, Animal Ecology, Environmental Microbiology, Bryology, Entomology, Freshwater Biology, Herpetology, and Bird Identification.

CURRICULUM AND CREDITS
Admission is open to students with graduate, senior, junior, or sophomore standing. Some courses may be taken for either graduate or undergraduate credit. Students from universities other than Western Illinois University who want to transfer credit should secure approval in advance from their home institutions.

THE INSTITUTION
Established in 1964, the Alice L. Kibbe Life Science Station is a scientific research and instructional unit of Western Illinois University. It is a permanent field installation designed to offer opportunities for special study to qualified scientists, students, and other persons interested in all branches of science. The university operates the station as a nature preserve to protect unique natural features from unnecessary human disturbance.

THE ENVIRONMENT
The station consists of approximately 215 acres. The Nature Conservancy owns the 734 acres adjacent to the station and provides a sanctuary for a wintering population of eagles. The Illinois Department of Conservation owns a 206-acre nature preserve and floodplain forest in the immediate vicinity of the station, which is readily available for use by the station's students and staff.

The many diversified habitats at Kibbe Station and in the vicinity offer excellent opportunities for studies in aquatic and terrestrial field biology. The sandbars, islands, and sloughs of the Mississippi River, as well as the sand hills located occasionally along the banks, are easily accessible.

Floodplain forests along the station's shoreline contrast sharply with the upland timber regions located on the sides and tops of the bluffs. Limestone outcroppings are common. Hill prairies are also found on the bluffs and temporary streams are found in the ravines. An established tallgrass prairie is another feature of the station.

FACILITIES
The physical plant of Kibbe Station includes several buildings. The station herbarium, insect collection, vertebrate animal collection, laboratories, dining room, kitchen,

staff room, station office, and living areas are all located in the Frank House. The resident manager and family have living quarters in the Miltner House.

Students are not required to live at the station and no accommodations exist for families of married students. Those who do not live at the station will be responsible for their own transportation. Students living at the station must provide their own bedding and prepare their own food in the kitchen or they may eat in area restaurants. No fees are assessed for accommodations.

SUPPLIES NEEDED

Required books and supplies are available at bookstores in Macomb. Microscopes, collecting nets, animal traps, binoculars, specimen bottles, glassware, plant presses, and chemicals are provided at the station for use by students and staff. Aquatic and terrestrial transportation is available. Students must bring their own personal items of bedding, clothing, and food. Cooking utensils are available at the field station.

APPLICATIONS AND ADMISSIONS

Students must register at the Admissions Office of Western Illinois University at the above address.

Financial Aid: For more information, contact the Financial Aid Office of Western Illinois University at the above address.

Costs: In-state undergraduate students pay approximately $77 per semester hour, and graduate students, $81 per semester hour. These rates are for students taking 1–11 semester hours. For those taking 12–18 semester hours, the flat fees are $924 for undergraduates and $972 for graduate students. Out-of-state student rates are approximately three times higher than in-state student rates.

WHEATON COLLEGE SCIENCE STATION
Biology Department
Wheaton College
Wheaton, IL 60187-9937
Contact: Dr. David S. Bruce, Director, or Staff

SAMPLE COURSES

Courses include Stellar Astronomy, Field Zoology, Plant Taxonomy, General Ecology, Environmental Chemistry, Introductory Geology in the Field, Field Geology, and Geology Field Methods.

CURRICULUM AND CREDITS

Available credits range from 2 credits for a 2-week program to 10 credits for a 9-week program.

THE INSTITUTION

The Wheaton College Science Station (WCSS) has had a program in continuous operation since 1934. The campus is located nine miles west of Rapid City, South Dakota's second largest city, where modern shopping centers and other conveniences are available.

THE ENVIRONMENT

Wheaton's western campus offers students outstanding opportunities for study. The 50-acre park-like campus is situated at a 4,300-foot elevation near the middle of the Black Hills in western South Dakota, surrounded by ponderosa pines of the Black Hills National Forest. To the west lies the rugged terrain of the Black Hills, and beyond that, the Rocky Mountains. The Great Plains spread eastward, introduced by the desolate but beautiful Badlands National Park.

The area is a unique outdoor classroom for biology and geology students. Plants and animals of both eastern and western ranges are found. Rocks, minerals, and geologic structures abound too, presenting students unparalleled access to field learning experiences.

For recreation there are many sporting and leisure activities on campus and nearby, including volleyball, softball, trout fishing, swimming, boating, and horseback riding.

FACILITIES

WCSS has student dormitories, study facilities, classroom buildings, a modern dining hall, a lodge, outdoor swimming pool, faculty cabins, and service buildings.

SUPPLIES NEEDED

Contact the institution for information.

APPLICATIONS AND ADMISSIONS

Contact the institution at the above address for information on application and admission procedures.

Financial Aid: Financial aid is available for qualified students. Some work scholarships are available. Contact the institution for more information.

Costs: Costs range from approximately $895 for a 2-credit program to $3,150 for a 10-credit program.

IOWA

IOWA LAKESIDE LABORATORY
University of Iowa
R.R. 2, P.O. Box 305
Milford, IA 51351
(712) 337-3669
E-mail: lakeside@aol.com
Contact: Director

SAMPLE COURSES

Courses include Aquatic Ecology, Vertebrate Zoology, Quaternary Studies (Geology), Developmental Biology of Freshwater Invertebrates, Prairie Ecology, Field Ornithology, Ecology and Systematics of Diatoms, Field Natural History, Field Botany, Plant Taxonomy, and Field Entomology.

CURRICULUM AND CREDITS

The Iowa Lakeside Laboratory (ILL) provides an opportunity for the serious biology student, undergraduate or graduate, to investigate plants and animals in their natural habitats. The summer program provides highly concentrated instruction in specific areas. Maximum credit is five semester hours per term for one course; all courses carry undergraduate or graduate credit. Although the Lakeside Laboratory does not grant degrees, the credits earned may be applied toward a degree program. Any teacher unable to meet the starting date may consult the instructor for special accommodation. Classes meet all day every day and are taught at the upperclass/graduate level.

THE INSTITUTION

ILL is one of Iowa's educational institutions controlled by the State Board of Regents. It seeks to serve the scholars of Iowa and elsewhere through the cooperative efforts of Iowa State University, the University of Northern Iowa, and the University of Iowa. Students and scholars from other institutions are welcome.

THE ENVIRONMENT

ILL is located in the lakes region of northwest Iowa. The campus, a tract of about 140 acres of grassland and gallery forest, is adjacent to Miller's Bay on the west shore of West Okoboji Lake. It provides material for classes, as well as a place to execute experiments in a natural setting. In addition to the campus, students and other researchers have access to local wetlands, prairies, and woods. Facilities and space are available for long-range or short-term studies.

FACILITIES

Research and instruction are done in eight laboratories, a library, and a lecture hall, arranged in an arc from the waterfront around the crest of a grassy hill. The cottages, dormitories, and large mess hall where all the meals are served are located across a wooded ravine.

Final registration assures dormitory space for each student. The dining hall accommodates the entire student body, faculty, and families; there are no facilities for separate cooking. Sanitary facilities are located in central bathhouses. A few rooms and cottages are available for student spouses or small families.

SUPPLIES NEEDED
Sturdy outdoor clothing, hiking boots, rain gear, and hip boots for aquatic courses.

APPLICATIONS AND ADMISSIONS
Contact the institution at the above address for information on application and admission procedures.

Financial Aid: Fellowships of $2,000 are available to predoctoral and postdoctoral scholars. Part-time kitchen jobs are available for a few students to earn room and board. The Graduate College of the University of Iowa provides a number of tuition scholarships for undergraduate and graduate students from any school. These are the Thomas H. Macbride Scholarships in Natural Science.

Costs: Tuition fee, including lab expenses, is approximately $453 per term, with room and board being $510. There are additional charges for the cottages.

LOUISIANA

LOUISIANA UNIVERSITIES MARINE CONSORTIUM
Marine Research and Education Center
8124 Highway 56
Chauvin, LA 70344-2124
(504) 851-2800
Fax: (504) 851-2874
E-mail: jcaruso@smtpgw.lumon.edu
Contact: Dr. Paul W. Sammarco, Executive Director;
Dr. John H. Caruso, University Education Coordinator;
Mr. Clayton A. Harpold, K-12 Teacher and Public Education

SAMPLE COURSES
Summer courses include Costal Habitat Loss, Introduction to Marine Science, Introduction to Marine Zoology, Mariculture, Marine Ecology, Marine Invertebrate Zoology, Marine Vertebrate Zoology, Marine Science for Teachers, Sedimentary Geochemistry, Major River/Ocean Mixing Zones, Wetland Biogeochemistry, and Wetland Vegetation. Internships and directed research projects are also available during the summer and academic year.

CURRICULUM AND CREDITS
The Louisiana Universities Marine Consortium (LUMCON) is active throughout the calendar year for research and educational purposes. During the summer, an array of field courses are offered, many of which take advantage of the unique opportunities available with LUMCON. Directed research courses and internships under the supervision of LUMCON's resident research faculty are also available on a year-round basis. In order to receive credit for LUMCON courses, students must register at one of the 18 Consortium member universities. Students not currently enrolled in a member university should contact the University Education Coordinator for assistance. Field trips and workshops for grades K-12, teachers, and public education groups are also available with LUMCON.

THE INSTITUTION
LUMCON was formed to provide centralized facilities for research and education in the marine sciences for the 13 universities in the Louisiana State University System. Four additional private universities in Louisiana are affiliate members of LUMCON. The consortium arrangement avoids unnecessary duplication and provides facilities that are beyond the means of individual universities.

THE ENVIRONMENT
LUMCON Marine Center is located approximately 85 miles southwest of New Orleans in the small coastal community of Cocodrie, situated between the two active deltas of the Mississippi River and within the nation's greatest expanse of coastal wetlands (40% of U.S. coastal wetlands are in Louisiana). Within a short distance are extensive salt, brackish, intermediate, and freshwater marshes, as well as the Gulf of Mexico and the

fertile, highly productive waters of the Timbalier/Terrebone Bay system, one of the most productive estuaries on Earth. The towns of Chauvin and Dulac, which together rank as the nation's seventh most productive fishing port, are close by. With LUMCON's larger research vessels, even the offshore waters, including the deep-sea environment of the Mississippi Canyon, are accessible.

FACILITIES

LUMCON operates three coastal laboratories: its main facility, the Marine Center in Cocodrie, and two smaller satellite laboratories (one to the east near Barataria Bay and the other to the west near Vermilion Bay). The Marine Center consists of one large, 75,000-square-foot building that houses well-equipped laboratories and classrooms, an auditorium, library, cafeteria, apartments, and dormitory rooms. A seawater system carries filtered, high- and low-salinity water to teaching and research laboratories, and a nutrient analyzer, racetrack flume, and weather station are available for research purposes. A fleet of small boats and two large research vessels, the 58-foot *Acadiana* the 105-foot *Pelican*, are based at the Marine Center. Available on board the *R/V Pelican* are a depth profiler, an acoustic Doppler current profiler, and MIDAS (Multiple Interface Data Acquisition System), an on-board soft- and hardware computer system for continuous real-time monitoring of numerous biological, chemical, and physical parameters of seawater.

SUPPLIES NEEDED

Students attending summer courses should bring clothing appropriate for fieldwork, including shoes suitable for wading, and protection against rain, sun, and biting insects. LUMCON provides all necessary linens, and meals are available Monday through Friday. A student lounge provides cooking facilities for use on weekends.

APPLICATIONS AND ADMISSIONS

Applications for admission to the summer program may be obtained by contacting the University Education Coordinator at the above address. The application form, official transcripts, and nonrefundable application fee (applicable toward the cost of room and board) should be sent to the University Education Coordinator. Enrollment is usually limited, so early application is advised (applications will be accepted at any time depending upon available space).

Financial Aid: Highly qualified summer students and interns may request financial support in the form of LUMCON Foundation, Inc. fellowships to help defray the cost of room and board. Applications for financial assistance should be requested from the University Education Coordinator.

Costs: Room and board costs are approximately $125 per week. Applicable tuition and fees are paid to the university through which the student registers.

MAINE

AMERICAN INSTITUTE FOR CREATIVE EDUCATION
23 University Drive
Augusta, ME 04330
(207) 622-5662/(800) 448-5343
Fax: (207) 626-3276
Contact: Dr. Barbara A. Pullen or Gail A. Towns

SAMPLE COURSES

Some science courses offered include Ocean and Children's Literature (K–8), Critical and Creative Thinking Approach to Elementary Science (K–6), Ocean as a Classroom Resource (K–12), Teaching Science Using Everyday Household Materials (K–8), Elementary Science in the Classroom (K–8), and Science Through Children's Literature (Pre K–6).

In addition to the science courses listed above, the following courses are also offered: Anger and Conflict Recognition and Management (K–12), Getting Started with Portfolios (K–6), Making the Transition to Literature-Based Instruction (4–6), School Success for the Attention-Deficit Disordered Child (K–8), Teaching the Exceptional Child in the Regular Classroom (K–12), and What's New in Children's Literature (K–6).

CURRICULUM AND CREDITS

As each course offers a specific field of study, interested participants should contact the American Institute for Creative Education (AICE) for information about material covered in specific courses. Graduate credit and/or Continuing Education Credits (CEUs) are also available; contact AICE for more information.

THE INSTITUTION

The American Institute for Creative Education was founded on January 10, 1970, on the belief that education is a continuous process that should be exciting, valuable, and challenging. AICE has presented practical seminars in an atmosphere that stresses the human qualities of the professional participants, encourages active group participation, and focuses on classroom application of the seminar materials. In AICE's Professional Advancement Seminars and in-service training, participants acquire new, useful, and stimulating information, guided through the process by seminar leaders selected for their subject expertise and also for their ability to communicate effectively with participants.

THE ENVIRONMENT

AICE is located in Augusta, Maine, and is surrounded by a pond, pines, and rolling terraces.

FACILITIES

Courses are held at the AICE facility, a traditional brick structure with modern flexibility. Other courses are held in New Hampshire, Massachusetts, Connecticut, Vermont, New York, and New Jersey. Arrangements can be made to offer courses at any school or motel in the United States.

SUPPLIES NEEDED

Information regarding necessary supplies for specific courses is provided by AICE upon registration.

APPLICATIONS AND ADMISSIONS

Contact AICE directly at the above address for application materials, course schedules, etc.

Financial Aid: Contact AICE for information.

Costs: Contact AICE for the most current information on tuition and fees.

EAGLE HILL WILDLIFE RESEARCH STATION
P.O. Box 99
Steuben, ME 04680
(718) 622-0452 (before April 1); (207) 546-2821 (after April 1)
Fax: (207) 546-3042
Contact: Joerg-Henner Lotze, Station Director

SAMPLE COURSES

Courses include Ecological Zoogeography, Forest Entomology, Lichens, Spiders, Field Ethnobotany, Late Glacial History of Eastern Maine, Peatland Ecology, Reclamation and Restoration, Intertidal Marine Invertebrates, Bryophytes of Maine, Reproduction and Development of Marine Invertebrates, Terrestrial and Wetland Plant Communities of Coastal Maine, Ornithology, and Soils.

CURRICULUM AND CREDITS

Seminars may be taken for two or more graduate or undergraduate university credits through the University of Maine. Continuing Education Units and teacher recertification credits are also available.

THE INSTITUTION

Eagle Hill Wildlife Research Station (EHWRS) is an independent field station open to individuals interested in educational programs and research activities on the Maine coast. It is best known for its week-long educational programs taught by leading authorities on natural history.

Course participants come from across the United States and are primarily well-established professionals like teachers, consulting field biologists, independent scholars, professors, and amateur naturalists, but some university students are also included. Others come from various state and federal agencies. The natural history seminars at EHWRS are intensive workshops on a wide variety of classical terrestrial freshwater and marine natural history subjects.

THE ENVIRONMENT

The station overlooks the rocky evergreen coast of Maine from Acadia National Park to Petit Manan National Wildlife Refuge and beyond. It lies on the highest point (235 feet) on one of a series of granite peninsulas that extend far into the Atlantic Ocean.

Much of coastal Maine in this area is still relatively uninhabited, and to the north the land is still essentially wilderness. An unusually rich variety of habitats can be found within a short distance of the station. Marine habitats include mud and sand flats, cobble and boulder beaches, and exposed granite ledges, as well as coastal marshes. Terrestrial habitats include bogs and heaths, blueberry barrens, lakes and ponds of all kinds, as well as a rich variety of forested lands.

FACILITIES

The station includes eight buildings on about 150 acres on the summit of Eagle Hill. There is a general-purpose classroom for teaching purposes and a separate research laboratory for use by individuals. Residential facilities include cabins with woodstoves, as well as simpler cabins with common washrooms. The facilities are generally open from early summer though late fall for both individual and group visits.

SUPPLIES NEEDED

All supplies are provided, other than general field equipment like binoculars.

APPLICATIONS AND ADMISSIONS

Contact the institution at the above adress for information on application and admission procedures.

Financial Aid: Discounts and general scholarships are available.

Costs: Tuition is approxiamtely $295 per week, with room and board being $30–$160 per week.

HURRICANE ISLAND OUTWARD BOUND®
P.O. Box 429
Rockland, ME 04841
(207) 594-5548/(800) 341-1744
Fax: (207) 594-9425
Contact: Admissions Office

SAMPLE COURSES

Outward Bound offers courses in sailing, ecology/natural history, canoeing, youth at risk, rock climbing, wilderness first-aid training, snorkeling, backpacking, semester internship, sea kayaking, winter backpacking, and dog sledding. Courses are available in Florida, Maryland, New Hampshire, Maine, and Virginia for individuals of all age groups and abilities, individuals, families, teachers, education administrators, and corporate executives/managers. Individuals may also custom design their own programs.

CURRICULUM AND CREDITS

Courses range in length from 8 to 22 days and longer. Course participants range from 14 to 60 years and older. Students 18 years and older may elect to earn up to 12 college credits for their Outward Bound experience. These credits may be applied to satisfy requirements in both major and elective course options. College credits for Outward Bound courses are available through the University of Southern Maine.

The 68-day Outward Bound Wilderness Leadership Semester Internship combines action-learning with academics and awards up to 12 college credits. These internship courses are taught by several university professors and Outward Bound instructors. Each participant is expected to engage in a multitude of experiences that require full physical, emotional, and intellectual commitment. These courses will encompass four general study areas that include Autobiographical/Reflective Thinking, Brain and Learning, Environmental Science, and Learning and Communication. Each study area includes a theoretical review, a demonstration, and a practicum.

Professors from the University of Maine present workshops on leadership, communication, environmental science, and reflective writing. Programs, seminars, and workshops can also be designed on a contractual basis for school and university systems and faculty groups. Working with school board members, school superintendents, teachers, principals, and counselors, team building and leadership skills essential for school improvement are developed. A diversity of Outward Bound learning experience courses are also available for the personal and professional development of educators.

Graduate college credit for recertification is available through the University of Southern Maine. Three credits are granted upon the completion of the university's Leadership Training in Experiential Education & Learning course in conjunction with an Outward Bound Educators course. For more information on college credit, call (207) 780-5139.

THE INSTITUTION

Outward Bound is the oldest and largest adventure-based education program in the world. A nonprofit, tax-exempt educational institution that has celebrated more than 50 years of educational excellence in 50 schools and 20 countries, Outward Bound provides experiences that enhance self-esteem and leadership skills, while building teamwork, positive values, compassion for others, perseverance, good citizenship, and respect for the environment.

THE ENVIRONMENT

The goal in the area of environmental responsibility is to improve how individuals relate to and care for the natural environment. The focus is on becoming a role model for environmental responsibility, while encouraging students to become familiar with, appreciate, and learn from the environment.

Sailing, backpacking, and canoeing open-enrollment courses provide a dynamic learning environment for professional educators, increasing interpersonal effectiveness and personal renewal. Courses are particularly suitable for teachers, guidance counselors, school psychologists, and school and university administrators.

FACILITIES

Hurricane Island Outward Bound has operation bases in Maine, Maryland, and Florida, specifically in Newry, Greenville, Rockland, and Hurricane Island, Maine. Bases are also located in Baltimore, Maryland, and Scottsmoor and Big Pine Key, Florida.

SUPPLIES NEEDED

Life jackets, sleeping bags, foul weather gear, backpack, duffel, tents, tarps, cook stoves, pots, and other specialized gear appropriate for each course are provided. Participants should bring only those items listed on the clothing and equipment lists they send.

Courses, Programs, and Expeditions in the United States

APPLICATIONS AND ADMISSIONS

To register for a course, send a nonrefundable $60 application processing fee and $100 registration deposit.

Financial Aid: Outward Bound as an organization offers a limited amount of financial aid which is based on need. For an Outward Bound financial aid form contact the above address.

Costs: Approximately $100 a day, ranging from about $795 for an 8-day course to $5,195 for 68-day semester courses.

SUMMER FIELD STUDIES FOR TEACHERS
College of the Atlantic
Bar Harbor, ME 04609-1105
(207) 288-5015, ext. 238 or 239
Fax: (207) 288-4126
Contact: Brenda Horton (ext. 238) or Ted Koffman (ext. 239)

SAMPLE COURSES

Courses include Resource Conservation Education, Earth Science for Elementary Teachers, Marine Biology, Marine Science for Elementary Teachers, Meteorological Lab and Field Techniques, Field Botany, Geological Foundations, Evolutionary Biology for Teachers, Environmental Chemistry, Human Ecology—Field and Classroom Methods, Life Science Workshop for the Elementary and Middle School Teacher, Intermediate Cetacean Biology, Biology of Birds, Educational Strategies in Health Education, Teaching Biology Through Sports Activities, Biology of Whales, Porpoises, and Seals, and Introduction to Teaching Geography.

CURRICULUM AND CREDITS

Established in 1981, the Field Studies by the Sea Program provides introductory through advanced summer courses in the life sciences and environmental subjects for elementary and secondary school teachers. The curriculum stimulates fresh perspectives and provides opportunities for elementary and secondary school teachers to learn new subject material and teaching techniques for use in their classrooms. Courses emphasize field trips which take advantage of the varied and picturesque habitat of Acadia National Park. Graduate credit is awarded by the University of Maine, College of Education.

THE INSTITUTION

Small classes assure close interaction among students and faculty. Courses emphasize a balance of field trips, laboratory exercises, and seminar/lecture periods. Some courses take place aboard the 95-foot schooner *Harvey Gamage*.

THE ENVIRONMENT

Situated on 150 square miles of coastal mountains, forests, fields, and wetlands, the surrounding bays, estuaries, beaches, open ocean, and the college's waterfront campus provide excellent resources for marine study.

FACILITIES

Participants are accommodated in single or shared rooms in college houses. Bathrooms are shared. Single rooms are available on a first-requested, first-provided basis. Students who intend to commute should notify the Summer Program Office as early as possible. Commuting students can deduct the $188-per-week campus room and board charges from the comprehensive course fee.

Three meals are served on weekdays, continental breakfast on Saturday, and dinner on Sunday night. Box lunches are provided for students during field trips. All students housed on campus are expected to participate in the summer program meal plan.

SUPPLIES NEEDED

Students should bring their own bed linens and towels. Pillows and blankets are provided.

APPLICATIONS AND ADMISSIONS

Completed applications are reviewed on a rolling admissions basis and applicants are informed of an admission decision within two weeks. A $15 application fee must accompany the application. Accepted applicants are required to forward a $150 nonrefundable deposit which is applied toward the tuition.

Financial Aid: Although the college does not provide scholarship aid, nearly 60% of the field studies students receive partial or full financial support from their school, school districts, or from private foundations.

Costs: Contact the institution for specific information.

MASSACHUSETTS

DEPARTMENT OF BIOLOGY
University of Massachusetts–Boston
Harbor Campus
Boston, MA 02125-3393
(617) 287-6600
Fax: (617) 287-6650
E-mail: biology@umbsky.cc.umb.edu
Contact: Dr. Michael Shiaris, Ms. Jan MacLeod

SAMPLE COURSES
Courses include coastal ecology and maritime ecology research. Program and schedule information vary slightly each year.

CURRICULUM AND CREDITS
The University of Massachusetts at Boston offers courses in marine biology during the summer at UMass/Boston's Marine Field Station at Quaise, Nantucket.

The coastal ecology course offers investigations into the natural history and community dynamics of salt marshes, seagrass beds, mud flats, and beaches. Field and laboratory exercises on the adaptations and interactions of marine organisms are emphasized as well. This course awards 5 credits. Prerequisites include one year of college biology and permission from the instructor.

The maritime ecology research course offers supervised research into the adaptations and interactions of marine organisms of the beaches, salt marshes, sand dunes, and embayments of Nantucket. This course awards 5 credits. Prerequisites include courses in genetics, physiology, college algebra, and permission from the instructor.

THE INSTITUTION
The field station is administered by the University of Massachusetts at Boston.

THE ENVIRONMENT
The UMass Nantucket Field Station is a biologist's paradise. The station's 115-acre property consists of a pristine 45-acre salt marsh, a freshwater pond, and a half-mile of private beach and dunes on Nantucket harbor. The station also embraces upland habitat, including a blueberry forest, and is located within walking distance of rare heathlands preserved by the Nantucket Conservation Foundation.

The field station salt marsh and harbor are rich with finfish, shellfish, and all manner of marine invertebrates. Birding is superlative. Raptors, waders, shorebirds, ducks, and owls abound. The station has whitetail deer, cottontail rabbits, mice, rats, voles, snakes, and turtles. Nearby habitats support rare wildflowers, and the station itself has colorful insect fauna.

FACILITIES
The field station property is home to a small but well-equipped laboratory. Lab exercises in support of field research are an important and required component of course work. IBM-compatible personal computers and a variety of software are provided for student use, while small boats and a photographic darkroom can be made available with the director's permission.

Summer ecology students are provided with free housing at the field station. Course participants share a large bunkhouse on the property, prepare their own meals in a fully outfitted community kitchen, and attend classes in a comfortable living area with pond and harbor views. Nantucket's beaches and bicycle paths furnish delightful opportunities for after-class recreation.

SUPPLIES NEEDED
Students are advised to bring a bathing suit, snorkeling gear, sunglasses, binoculars, camera, calculator, portable computer (if available), rain and cold-weather gear, protective clothing against ticks, insects, and the sun, a sleeping bag or bed linen, towel and beach blanket, bicycle, and rubber boots or throw-away sneakers.

APPLICATIONS AND ADMISSIONS
Contact the above adress for information on application and admission procedures.

Financial Aid: None available.

Costs: Each course for the summer costs approximately $650 ($130 per credit), including laboratory, registration, and fees. Housing is free and students provide their own meals.

EARTHWATCH
680 Mount Auburn Street
Box 403EB
Watertown, MA 02272
(617) 926-8200/(800) 776-0188
Telex: (510) 600-6452
Fax: (617) 926-8532
Contact: Staff

SAMPLE EXPEDITIONS
Participants join 2-week research expeditions helping scientists on projects ranging from preserving endangered sea turtles in St. Croix, to building solar ovens in Indonesia, to excavating a castle in Wales. Scientific disciplines include ornithology, public health, marine ecology, paleontology, and wildlife management. Projects run year-round.

CURRICULUM AND CREDITS
Graduate credit for teachers earning master's degrees in education is available through Bank Street College in New York City. Working in teams of five to ten people, they receive all training necessary for working in the field.

THE INSTITUTION
Founded in 1972, Earthwatch, a nonprofit membership organization and a leader in experiential education, offers unique opportunities to work side-by-side with renowned scientists and scholars on 155 research projects in 60 countries and across the United States. Over 3,000 high school students and 3,000 teachers have participated in Earthwatch expeditions.

THE ENVIRONMENT
Each expedition takes place in a unique environment. For specific information on the locations of these expeditions, contact Earthwatch at the above address.

FACILITIES
Facilities and accomodations vary with each expedition. Contact Earthwatch for more information.

SUPPLIES NEEDED
Participants are advised at the time of project sign-up about what supplies and/or equipment they need to bring.

APPLICATIONS AND ADMISSIONS
Earthwatch projects are offered on a first-come, first-served basis to anyone age 16 and over. No special skills are required, although membership in Earthwatch is necessary for participation.

Financial Aid: Limited fellowships and scholarships are available for K–12 teachers and high school students over 16.

Costs: Tax-deductible contributions ranging from $800 to $2,400 support research and cover food and lodging expenses.

ECOTOUR EXPEDITIONS, INC.
P.O. Box 381066
Cambridge, MA 02238
(617) 876-5817/(800) 688-1822
Fax: (617) 876-3638
Contact: Mark Baker

SAMPLE PROGRAMS AND EXPEDITIONS
All programs and wilderness expeditions are offered in the Amazon rainforest areas of Brazil, including the Igapo Flooded Forest, an expedition that explores the many natural environments of the least-inhabited place on earth, the Rio Negro. The expedition also explores the Amazon River itself. The focus is on tropical ecology in addition to the specialties of the research scientists that accompany every expedition (e.g., ornithology, botany, entomology).

CURRICULUM AND CREDITS
Expeditions offer students and participating instructors the opportunity to study the ecology of the rainforest in an academic setting as well as through actual field exploration. The guides on all expeditions are scientists who conduct narratives on the ecology of the Amazon. Credit may be obtained through independent or travel study.

THE INSTITUTION
Ecotour Expeditions, Inc. (EEI) operates field expeditions in the central Amazon rainforest of Brazil. They provide field equipment and expertise for groups visiting wilderness areas. All of the scientists are field researchers in the region and are drawn from the research facilities located in the Amazon.

THE ENVIRONMENT
Because the expeditions are based on a research vessel, groups are able to visit and observe a great variety of Amazon environments, including Igapo black-water-flooded forest, Varzea white-water-flooded forest, and terre firme, the tall forest above the annual high-flood mark.

FACILITIES

EEI owns and operates an 80-foot research vessel outfitted for scientific study. There are a large classroom space, small laboratory, and field equipment sufficient to set up temporary field stations for groups to observe inland environments.

SUPPLIES NEEDED

Participants should bring clothing suitable for warm weather, along with long-sleeve shirts and long trousers. Binoculars are highly recommended, as well as any specialized laboratory equipment that participants may want with them.

APPLICATIONS AND ADMISSIONS

Contact EEI by telephone or mail to receive departure schedules and applications. EEI works in conjunction with group leaders to establish a unique schedule and expedition plan for group departures.

Financial Aid: Most costs of instructors accompanying student groups can be compensated in the form of grants.

Costs: Two-week expeditions vary in cost from $1,700 to $2,000 per participant, and includes air fare from the United States to Brazil, all meals, field equipment, accommodations, and the services of scientists and staff members.

JAMES A. KAUFMAN & ASSOCIATES
Laboratory Safety Consultants
101 Oak Street
Wellesley, MA 02181
(617) 237-1335
Fax: (617) 239-1457
Contact: James Kaufman

SAMPLE COURSES AND PROGRAMS

Laboratory Safety Training Seminars are short courses for teachers, students, and employers and employees of industrial, academic, and governmental laboratories in the chemical, biological, and medical fields. Course topics include Asbestos, Biological and Animal Hazards, Disposal of Chemicals, Effective Safety Programs, Handling Chemical Reagents, Emergency Planning, and Safety Information Resources.

CURRICULUM AND CREDITS

As laboratory safety consultants, Kaufman & Associates (K&A) provide training programs, conduct audits and inspections, and assist in program development and regulatory compliance at schools, collleges, universities, and industrial organizations. They run private seminars and workshops around the country with open enrollment.

Training programs vary in length from one hour to several days depending on the number of topics covered and the depth to which these topics are discussed. The program content can be tailored to meet the specific needs of a particular staff, and sessions can accommodate almost any number of participants. These presentations are suitable for groups as small as a half-dozen or as large as several hundred. In all cases, group participation is fully encouraged.

THE INSTITUTION

K&A is a health, safety, and environmental affairs consulting company that provides services to academic institutions, industries, medical facilities, and goverment agencies. Although they specialize in laboratory issues, their services extend to general industry and workplace safety. Their goal is to assist clients in protecting the health and safety of the people they care about.

THE ENVIRONMENT

Programs are usually held regionally at hotel/conference centers or on-site for the sponsoring institution.

FACILITIES

Not applicable.

SUPPLIES NEEDED

All necessary materials are provided.

APPLICATIONS AND ADMISSIONS

Applications are accepted throughout the year as sessions are scheduled.

Financial Aid: Requests for assistance are considered on an individual basis.

Costs: Registration fees for seminars and short courses vary from approximately $50 to $595, depending on the length of the session.

MANOMET OBSERVATORY
P.O. Box 1770
Manomet, MA 02345-1770
(508) 224-6521
Fax: (508) 224-9220
Contact: Mark Kasprzyk

SAMPLE COURSES

Courses include Field Biology Training Program, Tropical Forest Ecology and Bird Communities, Migration Ecology of Landbirds, and Tropical Wetlands and Shorebird Ecology (courses for each program include student research, ecology seminar, field techniques, research seminar, and research statistics). Four-week programs include Introduction to Field Biology, Landbird Migration and Introduction to Field Biology, Shorebird Migration (courses for each program include migration research and field study methods).

CURRICULUM AND CREDITS

The Field Biology Training Program (FBTP) at the Manomet Observatory (MO) offers students the opportunity to earn college credits while participating in ongoing field research and conservation. Students gain training in every phase of biological research from hypothesis generation to field work to analysis and presentation of results for research and conservation use. The program is informal but intense. Enrollment is small; students interested in attending are urged to apply early. No previous research experience is required.

Academic credit (graduate and undergraduate) for the field biology training program is granted by many colleges for semester courses (16 credits) and 4-week courses (2 credits).

THE INSTITUTION

MO conducts scientific research to facilitate environmental decision making and natural resource management. Through collaborations with government agencies, conservation organizations, colleges and universities, and industries, MO works to improve the conservation of natural resources for the benefit of wildlife and human populations throughout the Americas.

MO's programs focus on five goals:
- Conserving birds of the Americas and their habitats.
- Improving management of fisheries, marine mammals, and seabirds in the northwest Atlantic.
- Promoting improved stewardship of coastal and wetland habitats.
- Fostering sustainable use of tropical and temperate forests.
- Providing courses and other learning opportunities in ecology and conservation biology for environmental resource managers, science teachers, and college students.

THE ENVIRONMENT

MO is located on approximately 18 acres of coastal woodland, pond, and shrub habitat. Mist nets, scattered throughout the property, have been used to monitor migrant and resident bird populations for over 25 years. Just to the west is Miles Standish State Forest, 20,000 acres of pine/oak forest that is visited on field trips. Approximately one hour to the north lie the activities of Boston, and the dunes and beaches of scenic Cape Cod are a half-hour to the south.

FACILITIES

MO has several shorefront properties overlooking Cape Cod Bay near Plymouth, Massachusetts. The facilities include offices and laboratory and residential space. MO's excellent ornithological library may be supplemented with extensive libraries in Cambridge and Woods Hole. Students learn to run programs for statistical analysis on IBM personal computers, a valuable tool for graduate students and career biologists. Despite intensive research activity, students enjoy a relaxed communal atmosphere. There is no room fee but students are expected to help maintain the facility by contributing two hours of housework each week. Students at MO buy their own food (a grocery story is within walking distance), which they can store and prepare in a communal kitchen. Groups often cooperate on planning and preparing meals. There are also inexpensive restaurants nearby.

SUPPLIES NEEDED

Bring clothes suitable for a variety of weather conditions and temperatures, depending on which FBTP course you are attending. Bring binoculars and a telescope (both may be loaned to students, depending upon availability). Students will receive a list of required readings and supplies following acceptance to FBTP.

APPLICATIONS AND ADMISSIONS

Prospective students should: 1) complete an FBTP application form and return it to MO with a $20 nonrefundable processing fee, 2) have official college and graduate school transcripts sent to MO, and 3) request recommendations from two references (with at least one being a college biology professor).

Financial Aid: Financial assistance in the form of scholarships is available on an "as needed" basis. Interested persons should request a financial aid application when applying for admission.

Costs: The cost per field semester is between $5,500 and $6,500; the cost for the 4-week program is approximately $1,570. These fees include tuition, room at MO, and a registration charge. Air and land travel expenses to out-of-state field sites as well as board fees are not included.

MUSEUM OF SCIENCE
Courses & Travel
Boston, MA 02114-1099
(617) 589-0340
Fax: (617) 589-0454
Contact: Staff

SAMPLE COURSES AND PROGRAMS

The museum offers courses, programs, and services for teachers and their students, grades K–12. These include:

1) Programs for school groups, grades K–12. Topics in a given year may include Birds of a Feather, DNA Fingerprinting, Getting Close to Bugs, Secrets of the Sky, Dinosaurs and Early Life, and Rocks & Minerals All programs require a small museum admission and a program charge of approximately $125.

2) Teacher workshops are offered both in the museum and at school sites. Topics include Tropical Rainforests, Earth Sciences, and Green Planet. Call (617) 723-2511 for additional information on workshops and fees.

3) Science Kits for rental: 16 kit topics are offered for 3- to 5-week rentals currently at $63–$105 per rental. Kits feature a teacher's guide, and sufficient materials for a class of 30 students to explore a topic. Call 1-800-772-5487 for more information.

The museum regularly offers a variety of in-museum courses on natural history topics for children and adults. All require individual tuition and preregistration. Examples include Snails for grades 1–4 (total of 4 contact hours, $35); Discover! Animals Big and Small for first and second grades (15 hours, $174); The Sun & The Stars for second and third grades (2 contact hours, $35); a series of astronomy courses including Naked Eye Astronomy and Telescopic Astronomy (12 hours each, $88); Astronomy mini-courses for adults including How to Choose a Telescope and the Universe from Here to There (2 hours each, $35).

The museum also offers field experiences including:

1) One-week field program Marine Field Experience for students in grades 6–9 each summer. The program is held at the Suffolk University Marine Field Station on the Bay of Fundy, Maine. Approximate cost: $720.

2) Long weekend programs for adults—Marine Science for Adults—at the Shoals Marine Laboratory, Maine. Approximate cost: $290.

3) A variety of half- or full-day trips: Downtown Geology, Palermo Mine, and Edible Wild Plants. Day programs are for adults and kids eight years and older. Costs range from $25 to $59.

4) Expeditions currently offered include Family Safari to Tanzania, two weeks for $4,500; and Solar Eclipse in Chile, eight days for $3,800.

CURRICULUM AND CREDITS

No credit is offered by the museum for any programs listed. However, credit for some programs may be available for independent or travel study.

THE INSTITUTION

The Museum of Science (MS) was founded in 1830 as the New England Society of Natural History. After the Civil War, it evolved into the New England Museum of Natural History and moved to a new site as the Museum of Science in the late 1940s. Today it is a large science museum with exhibits and programs in the natural and physical sciences, health, transportation, technology, and astronomy. More than 400 exhibits are currently on display with temporary exhibitions offered regularly. The Charles Hayden Planetarium and the Mugar Omni Theater offer a variety of programs annually. The mission of the MS is education, not research. In all the exhibits and programs, the museum seeks opportunities for members and visitors to have direct, interesting, and useful access to all aspects of scientific fact and inquiry.

THE ENVIRONMENT

Courses and programs are conducted in museum classrooms and laboratories.

FACILITIES

Field experiences are held in facilities that are directly contracted for specific activities.

SUPPLIES NEEDED

Programs provide all necessary materials with few exceptions. Field programs may require field glasses, work gloves, sleeping bags, etc.

APPLICATIONS AND ADMISSIONS

Applications and admission are on a rolling basis. New programs are announced more than three times each year and registrations are accepted on a first-come, first-served basis.

Financial Aid: Some financial aid is available for in-museum courses. Contact the institution at the above address for further details.

Costs: Sample course and program costs are indicated above.

THE SCHOOL FOR FIELD STUDIES
16 Broadway
Beverly, MA 01915-4499
(508) 927-7777
Fax: (508) 927-5127
Contact: Andrea Walgren

SAMPLE COURSES AND PROGRAMS

Courses and programs include Australia—Rainforest Studies; Caribbean—Marine Resource Management; Kenya—Wildlife Management Studies; Costa Rica—Studies in

Sustainable Development; Palau—Island Management Studies; and British Columbia—Coastal Studies.

CURRICULUM AND CREDITS

The School for Field Studies (SFS) semester programs incorporate four courses and carry a total of 16 semester credits in biology, economics, anthropology, and independent study from Boston University. SFS summer programs carry 4 semester credits in environmental studies.

THE INSTITUTION

SFS is the country's oldest and largest educational institution exclusively dedicated to offering undergraduate environmental field courses throughout the world. Since its founding in 1980, more than 6,000 college and high school students, with a variety of academic interests, have had the unique opportunity of hands-on field work that addresses some of the earth's most critical environmental issues.

THE ENVIRONMENT

Environments vary with the location of each particular course.

FACILITIES

Facilities also vary by location. The Center for Wildlife Management in Kenya is based at Game Ranching, Ltd. with a 40-minute drive to Nairobi. The Center for Marine Resource Studies in the Caribbean is based in a former hotel on the southern edge of South Caicos Island. The Center for Rainforest Studies lies at an elevation of 800 meters in the northern foothills of the Atherton Tableland; half of the property's 153 acres are primary rainforest. The Center for Sustainable Development Studies is located in Barrio Los Angeles, a small town on the outskirts of Atenas. The Center for Coastal Studies is located on the west coast of Vancouver Island near the small coastal town of Tofino. The Center for Island Management Studies is in a small village on the island of Babeldaob.

SUPPLIES NEEDED

Necessary supplies vary according to each center. Some general supplies required include, binoculars, a sleeping bag and ground pad, a flashlight, calculator, backpack, and a water resistant watch.

APPLICATIONS AND ADMISSIONS

SFS works on a rolling admissions system. A $35 application fee is required. Applicants must be 18 years of age and have completed at least one semester of college-level ecology or biology for semester programs. For summer programs, applicants must be 16 years of age and have completed their junior year in high school.

Financial Aid: Financial assistance totaling more than $450,000 in the form of scholarships and/or interest-free loans is available to qualified students based on need.

Costs: The cost of a semester program is approximately $10,350. The cost of a summer program ranges from approximatley $2,450 to $3,980. Costs include tuition, room and board, and ground transportation during the course. It also covers group equipment, medical supplies, scientific instruments, and materials (transportation to and from the departure point is not included in the cost).

MICHIGAN

BIOLOGICAL STATION
The University of Michigan
1111 Natural Sciences Building
Ann Arbor, MI 48109-1048
(313) 763-4461 or (616) 539-8408
Fax: (313) 747-1952 or (616) 539-8785
Contact: Associate Director

SAMPLE COURSES
Courses include Biology of Birds, Natural History of Invertebrates, General Ecology, Biology of Insects, Freshwater Phycology, Bryology, Biology and Ecology of Fish, Behavioral Ecology, Boreal Flora, Plant Population Biology, Ecology of Streams and Rivers, Photography for Field Biologists, Aquatic Vascular Plants, Conservation Biology, and Research Experience for Undergraduates.

CURRICULUM AND CREDITS
University of Michigan credit is offered for advanced undergraduate- and graduate-level courses each summer. Strong emphasis is placed on ecology and field biology. Research opportunities are available for promising undergraduates and graduate students.

THE INSTITUTION
Located on the south shore of Douglas Lake at the northern tip of the lower peninsula of Michigan, the University of Michigan Biological Station was established in 1909 and has served as a major instructional and research center for students and scientists throughout the United States and other countries.

THE ENVIRONMENT
Situated in the northern hardwood ecosystem, the climate of the area is modified by the nearby Upper Great Lakes of Michigan, Huron, and Superior. Consequently, summers are cooler and winters milder. The station's property consists of beech-maple forests and successional stages of aspen, oak, and pine on the better-drained soils. Moister habitats contain spruce, fir, and cedar forests. Wetlands are comprised of bogs, fens, swamps, and marshes. Lakes are especially numerous in the region, including access to the upper Great Lakes and St. Mary's River. The station's property contains a river, streams, and eight miles of undeveloped natural lake shoreline. Dunelands found near the shores of the Great Lakes are unique regional environments.

FACILITIES
There are 150 buildings, including the Lakeside Laboratory (a modern research building), a new auditorium, a large library, a dining center, 16 classrooms, 3 small winterized dormitories, 10 winterized homes, 90 cabins used for summer housing, and maintenance and storage facilities. About 280 students, faculty, staff, scientists, and families can be accommodated in the summer and 40 in the winter.

SUPPLIES NEEDED

Clothing and personal supplies are needed for the type of work and the particular season involved.

APPLICATIONS AND ADMISSIONS

Contact the institution at the above address for information on application and admission procedures.

Financial Aid: Limited financial aid is available to select graduate investigators. Generous student financial aid is available.

Costs: For Michigan residents, an 8-week summer session worth 10 credits is approximately $1,400; nonresidents, $3,000; student fees, $100; dining and housing, $800; research fee (graduate student investigators only), $240.

CENTRAL MICHIGAN UNIVERSITY BIOLOGICAL STATION
Department of Biology
Central Michigan University
Mt. Pleasant, MI 48859
(517) 774-3173
Fax: (517) 774-3462
Contact: Dr. James C. Gillingham

SAMPLE COURSES

Courses include Introduction to Field Biology, Animal Behavior, Behavioral Ecology, Limnological Methods, Water Chemistry, Vertebrate Field Zoology, Field Botany, Biostatistics, and Independent Research.

CURRICULUM AND CREDITS

The academic program at Central Michigan University Biological Station (CMUBS) is designed to meet the needs of both undergraduate and graduate students in biology as well as students in a variety of other disciplines. Credit may be counted as on-campus credit toward baccalaureate or graduate degrees at Central Michigan University or may be transferred to other institutions.

Because of the brevity of the sessions, courses are full-time endeavors and may be taken sequentially but not concurrently. Courses at CMUBS are offered either as university-registered or College of Extended Learning–registered courses. Although these registration procedures are different, all courses have equal transferability and are recorded on transcripts in the same manner.

THE INSTITUTION

CMUBS is located on Beaver Island in northern Lake Michigan. The island is about 13 miles long and 6.5 miles wide with an area of about 55 square miles. Established in 1966, the station offers a diversity of academic courses during the spring and summer months and provides research facilities throughout the year.

THE ENVIRONMENT

CMUBS is located on 45 acres of pristine habitat on the sandy eastern shore of Beaver Island. The greatest resource available to CMUBS is the abundant natural habitat on Beaver Island and on the islands of the surrounding archipelago. The ecosystems on the islands are pristine in comparison to similar systems on the mainland or at similar latitudes elsewhere in the Midwest.

There are abundant cedar swamps, upland and lowland coniferous forests, beech-maple climax forest associations, sand dunes, marshes, and beaver dams. Such habitats are conducive to biological research on a variety of significant and relevant problems. Abandoned attempts at agriculture dating from the early 19th century have created extensive old field successional areas of varied age and vegetational composition. The island boasts seven largely undeveloped inland lakes, each being biologically unique from the others. The majority of Beaver Island's aquatic and terrestrial ecological associations are largely untouched by human development and are readily accessible for study.

Located approximately 32 miles northwest of Charlevoix, Michigan, the island is served by ferry out of Charlevoix (operating annually from mid-April to December) and by a small, year-round commercial air taxi service from the Charlevoix Airport. Beaver Island is inhabited by about 400 year-round residents, most of whom live on a beautiful natural harbor at the north end of the island in the town of St. James. This community has restaurants, grocery stores, a public library, taverns, a medical center, a K-12 school, churches, and service facilities. Although the island supports a modest lumbering industry and a small fishery, its economic base is largely derived from summertime tourism, during which time the island's population swells substantially.

FACILITIES

Four teaching laboratory/classrooms are utilized for larger academic classes and are equipped to accommodate courses that rely on both laboratory and field experiences. Standard light microscopes, chemical laboratory glassware, an autoclave, and a variety of state-of-the-art environmental monitoring gear support the academic course work.

A recently constructed research building is convieniently located adjacent to the classroom facilities and contains four individual research laboratories. The same building also houses two classrooms for seminars and graduate classes and a natural history museum.

Both research and coursework are supported by a library containing more than a thousand reference volumes, over two dozen periodicals spanning several decades, and more than ten thousand scientific reprints. For retrieval purposes, most of these reprints are catalogued on database, and the CENTRA index at CMU's library on the main campus may be accessed by modem. A variety of microcomputers are available to faculty, students, and researchers.

A new research building on the shores of Lake Michigan provides four comfortable laboratories, a seminar room, and a natural history museum. The latter contains plant and animal holdings representative of Beaver Island that have been subjected to a systematic inventory which is stored on a retrievable database. A recently constructed greenhouse provides facilities for plant studies and a computer room is available for analysis.

SUPPLIES NEEDED

The weather in the upper Great Lakes is unpredictable; so both warm- and cool-weather clothing should be brought along. In addition, a flashlight, rain gear, and insect repellent should be included. All students at CMUBS must provide their own linens (or sleeping bags), soap, and towels. Pillows, mattress pads, and blankets are available on request as needed. Coin-operated washers and dryers are conveniently located near the dormitories. The CMUBS bookstore sells textbooks and reference books, general classroom supplies, snacks, and clothing.

APPLICATIONS AND ADMISSIONS

Contact the institution at the above address for application and admission procedures.

Financial Aid: Each year a limited number of CMUBS Tuition Scholarships are awarded to qualified and deserving students who are enrolled in courses during the regular summer sessions (Sessions I, IIa, and IIb). Awards are made for one course only and either partially or totally cover the tuition for that course. Application forms are available on request. Contact the above address for further information on application deadlines. *Nonresident Tuition Reduction*—All nonresident (out-of-state) students, undergraduate or graduate, taking any course at CMUBS can register through the College of Extended Learning at resident rates (see rate schedule below).

Costs: Students enrolling in CMUBS course work must submit an application along with a $50 nonrefundable residence deposit in order to guarantee housing space at CMUBS. All housing assignments are made on a first-come, first-served basis. The residence deposit is deducted from room and board charges, all of which are due and payable upon course completion.

Full meal plan—(Dormitory, campground) room and board (per person, weekly) is approximately $105.

Camper plan—(Campground residency and cooking; occasional cafeteria meals). The camping fee (per person, weekly) is approximately $30. Meals (daily rate, per person) are breakfast, $3.50; lunch, $5.50; and dinner, $7.00.

University-registered courses—Michigan resident undergraduate, approximately $90 per semester hour; Michigan resident graduate, approximately $123 per semester hour. An approximate registration fee of $50 is assessed for each session enrolled (up to 6 semester hours). (*Note:* All nonresident students may register for any CMUBS course at resident rates through the College of Extended Learning registration [see below]).

College of Extended Learning-registered courses—Michigan resident and nonresident undergraduate, approximately $125 per semester hour; Michigan resident and nonresident graduate, $137 per semester hour. (*Note:* No registration fee is charged for College of Extended Learning-registered courses.)

JOURNEYS INTERNATIONAL, INC.
4011 Jackson Road
Ann Arbor, MI 48103
(800) 255-8735
Fax: (313) 665-2945
Contact: Florine Herendeen

SAMPLE EXPEDITIONS

Worldwide nature and culture expeditions are offered to Nepal, Tibet, India, Burma, Bhutan, Sikkim, Laos, Thailand, Indonesia, Borneo, Papua New Guinea, New Zealand, Kenya, Tanzania, Madagascar, Botswana, Zimbabwe, Namibia, Ethiopia, Jordan, Egypt,

Turkey, South and Central America, and Hawaii. All trips are actively guided and nature- and culture-oriented.

CURRICULUM AND CREDITS
Credit may be available through independent or travel study.

THE INSTITUTION
Journeys International, Inc. (JI) has been offering educational nature and culture travel since 1978. Local affiliations with colleges, monasteries, research stations, hospitals, or other projects can lead to extended internships or residential involvement. Credit may be obtained through independent study or by participation on trips cosponsored by academic institutions. Many guides and company directors have an association with Michigan colleges and universities.

THE ENVIRONMENT
Each environment is dependent upon the particular tour. Contact the institution for more information.

FACILITIES
JI has six branch offices around the world. Accommodations include hotels, lodges, guest houses, local homes, or campsites.

SUPPLIES NEEDED
Participants are supplied with a complete checklist of required equipment and supplies prior to each trip.

APPLICATIONS AND ADMISSIONS
Participation is open to individuals and families. A trip reservation and traveler information form is available on request. Initial deposit is $300 by check or credit card with the balance of land cost due 60 days before departure.

Financial Aid: Not available.

Costs: Approximately $50–$250 per day on trips ranging in length from 8 to 35 days.

OUTER EDGE EXPEDITIONS
45500 Pontiac Trail
Walled Lake, MI 48390
(810) 624-5140/(800) 322-5235
Fax: (810) 624-6744
Contact: Brian Obrecht, Director and Founder

SAMPLE EXPEDITIONS
Expeditions include Patagonia (Chile and Argentina)—kayaking and hiking for scenery and wildlife viewing; Peru and the Amazon Jungle—wildlife viewing in remote wilderness like Manu National Park; Canada—dog sledding, kayaking with killer whales, skiing, and trekking trips; Australia—camel safaris, diving, trekking, mountain bike riding, white-water rafting, and kayaking trips; New Zealand—mountain bike trips; Indonesia and Irian Jaya—cultural exploration to areas never before visited by westerners; Russia—kayaking in Lake Baikal.

CURRICULUM AND CREDITS

Outer Edge Expeditions (OEE) allows participants to experience a destination rather than to watch it through a bus window. Learn from local guides about the environment and wildlife that inhabits the area. Spend time conversing and living with unusual cultures to learn how they live. Credit may be obtained through independent or travel study.

THE INSTITUTION

OEE specializes in offering small group (one to ten people) educational expeditions to remote wilderness and cultural destinations worldwide. Keeping groups small allows a maximum level of interaction with the guide and the environment, enabling participants to see wildlife and interact with local cultures in a way that would be impossible with a large number of people. OEE offers personal experience to every one of its destinations.

THE ENVIRONMENT

In all cases the natural environment is used as a classroom. An example of a wilderness expedition is to Manu National Park in the Amazon, the most pristine piece of rainforest left in the world. Since one of their guides is the foremost ornithologist in South America, it is possible to educate participants about the unique environment. An example of a cultural expedition is one to the lowlands of Irian Jaya in western New Guinea, where participants stay overnight in the tree-house homes of the locals. A range of other less-extreme environments are also available.

FACILITIES

Facilities differ for each trip.

SUPPLIES NEEDED

Supplies required differ for each trip. A detailed packing list is sent to all participants along with a comprehensive, 70-page predeparture packet.

APPLICATIONS AND ADMISSIONS

Call OEE to obtain reservation forms. A $400 deposit secures one's space on the desired departure.

Financial Aid: None available.

Costs: Costs range from $90 to $200 per day. A 5-day dog-sledding trip in the Canadian Rockies costs approximately $790 per person, while a 22-day trip trekking in Irian Jaya costs about $3,565 per person.

WHITEFISH POINT BIRD OBSERVATORY
Highway Contract 48
Box 115
Paradise, MI 49768
(906) 492-3596
Contact: Director

SAMPLE PROGRAMS AND WORKSHOPS

Programs and field workshops include Bird Identification, Bird Walks, Birding Excursions, Bird Banding Demonstration, Raptors Up-Close, Grouse Tour Package, Spying on

Spruce Grouse, Searching for Sharp-Tailed Grouse, Winter Raptor Tours, Seney National Wildlife Refuge Adventure, Watching Wood Warblers, Waterbird Identification Workshop, Owl Identification/Natural History Workshop, and a Hawk Identification Workshop.

CURRICULUM AND CREDITS

If one's hobby is bird watching, then Whitefish Point Bird Observatory (WPBO) is definitely the place to go. Through observations and banding studies conducted over the past three decades, it has been determined that approximately 309 bird species, both the rare and common, have visited the point. Spring migration activity begins in late March, builds dramatically through April and May, and continues into mid-June. By autumn, the process is reversed.

Educational programs have become a key element at WPBO. Three arenas of educational programming are offered: General Public Programs, Environmental Education Programs, and Adult Educational Enrichment Programs. This format is designed to give educators, tour operators, and individuals a feeling for what is available at WPBO.

WPBO offers internships in the spring and fall to qualified individuals studying natural resources. Internships have included Owl Banding, Passerine Banding, Field Ornithology, and Interpretive/Naturalist. Credit may be available through independent or travel study.

THE INSTITUTION

WPBO is a nonprofit membership organization established in 1978 to document and study the birds in the Great Lakes region, with special emphasis on migration. Through a unique blend of research, education, and conservation programs, WPBO is working to preserve bird populations and the environment. Located at the northeastern tip of Michigan's Upper Peninsula, Whitefish Point is a phenomenal concentration spot for migrating birds. The surrounding land and water features create a natural corridor, funneling thousands of birds directly to the point as they travel through the Great Lakes region. This makes for spectacular bird watching and provides tremendous opportunities to study and monitor bird populations.

THE ENVIRONMENT

WPBO is located on the southeast shore of Lake Superior just north of the small Upper Peninsula community of Paradise. Only a short distance separates WPBO from Canada's mainland, a fact that helps to make the observatory one of the best spots in Michigan for witnessing the annual spring migration of a wide variety of birds as they head north. Hawks, waterfowl, owls, and songbirds of all types regularly pass the point on their travels.

FACILITIES

Limited facilities are available at Whitefish Point because of its remote location. The Great Lakes Shipwreck Museum next to the observatory has bathroom facilities. Paradise (11 miles south of Whitefish Point) offers numerous motels, cabins, campgrounds, and restaurants. For a listing of these services contact WPBO or the Paradise Area Chamber of Commerce at (906) 492-3219 or 492-3560.

SUPPLIES NEEDED

Lake Superior has a tremendous affect on local weather conditions. Temperatures are much cooler than interior locations and the wind can be relentless. Even in late spring and early fall warm clothing is a must. Participants should bring binoculars, spotting scopes, and bird identification guides.

APPLICATIONS AND ADMISSIONS

Intern applicants should submit a letter of interest, résumé, and 3 references to Director WPBO, Highway Contract 48, Box 48a, Paradise, Michigan 49768. Information regarding tours and workshops may be obtained by writing or calling the observatory directly.

Financial Aid: None available. Interns and volunteers are provided housing and a small stipend for purchasing food.

Costs: Winter Raptor Tours—nonmembers $75, members $65; Sharp-Tailed Grouse Tour—nonmembers $35, members $25; Seney National Wildlife Adventure—nonmembers $30, members $20. Free programs include Spruce Grouse Tours, Morning Bird Walk, Morning Bird-Banding Talk, and Raptors Up-Close. Bird-identification workshop fees are arranged on an individual basis.

W. K. KELLOGG BIOLOGICAL STATION
Michigan State University
3700 East Gull Lake Drive
Hickory Corners, MI 49060-9516
(616) 671-2355
Fax: (616) 671-2104
E-mail: adams@kbs.msu.edu
Contact: Char Adams

SAMPLE COURSES

Courses include Ecology, Plant Systematics, Comparative Limnology, Biology of Birds, Biology of Mammals, Biogeochemistry, Current Topics in Ecological Research, Advanced Field Ecology and Evolution, Topics in Conservation Biology, Science Education Classes for Teachers, Habitats and Organisms (a 2-week summer science institute for selected high school students), and Youth Exploring Science—the Yes! program.

CURRICULUM AND CREDITS

The W. K. Kellogg Biological Station (WKKBS) of Michigan State University transforms into a community of scholars during the summer. Visiting and resident research scientists and highly motivated students all become participants in this dynamic scientific community.

Each summer, a diverse array of field-oriented undergraduate and graduate courses are offered to students interested in botany, crop and soil sciences, entomology, fisheries and wildlife, microbiology, zoology, and other related areas in the biological sciences. In addition to the summer session course offerings, students are encouraged to pursue independent research projects with the resident research faculty at the station.

"Special Problems" courses (student-initiated research) can be taken for either full or half terms. Students must make arrangements with a specific faculty member to sponsor their project prior to the beginning of the summer session.

THE INSTITUTION

WKKBS has developed an international reputation for limnological and ecological research on both natural and managed systems. The station is located on the eastern shore of Gull Lake in southwestern Michigan, 15 miles northeast of Kalamazoo and 12 miles northwest of Battle Creek. It is comprised of an education center, research laboratories, a bird sanctuary, farm, forest, and a conference center. Students attending summer courses at WKKBS join an active and distinguished group of resident faculty members, postdoctoral biologists, and graduate students.

THE ENVIRONMENT

Within the station's boundaries are approximately 3,836 acres of forest, wetlands, streams, lakes, and farmland, some of which has recently been designated a Long-Term Ecological Research site in agricultural ecology.

The country surrounding the station is varied and includes glacial terrain and a range of draining conditions, slopes, and soils. Many nearby swamps support a diversity of wildlife, including a great blue heron colony. The area is ideal for both aquatic and terrestrial studies. The 200-acre Sherriffs Marsh nearby contains a bog, lake, small stream, and tamarack swamp. Twelve miles north, the Barry County State Game Area and Yankee Springs Recreational Area provide additional habitats including several tracts of remnant prairie, while Lake Michigan and its famous sand dunes are only 40 miles to the west.

FACILITIES

A new academic complex, including auditoriums, classrooms, and research and teaching laboratories is located on the premises. There are also excellent computing facilities and the W. Morofsky Memorial Library, a branch of the MSU library, houses an extensive research collection in ecology, limnology, and related sciences. Students live in roomy new dormitories near the main classroom building or in apartments overlooking Gull Lake. Excellent meals are served in the cafeteria, and all facilities are handicapped accessible.

There are private swimming areas, tennis courts, basketball courts, a softball and Frisbee area, and rowboats are available after class hours for use on the lake. The Kellogg Bird Sanctuary, the Kellogg Forest, and other natural areas provide quiet walking trails. For cultural events, Kalamazoo and Battle Creek both provide a wide array of entertainment including art, theater, music, and nightlife.

SUPPLIES NEEDED

The clothing style is practical and varies from boots and cutoffs to old clothes and old shoes depending on the particular course and day. In general, one should be prepared for a moderate number of insects, hot weather, and sudden rains. It is advisable to bring any special biological study equipment (e.g., insect nets, binoculars, etc.), although some minor equipment, supplies, and textbooks may be purchased at the station's bookstore.

APPLICATIONS AND ADMISSIONS

Students must be admitted to Michigan State University. Students working toward a degree in another institution will be admitted to MSU for the summer semester only as unclassified students by using a Lifelong Education (LE) application. Requirements for admission to the university (degree and nondegree) are stated in the MSU catalog. The

MSU catalog and LE application forms for unclassified students are available from the Registrar's Office, Room 150, Administration Building, Michigan State University, East Lansing, Michigan 48824-1046. Please specify registration for WKKBS.

Domestic undergraduate applications for admission should be filed at least 30 days prior to the beginning of the semester desired. International graduate and undergraduate applications for admission should be filed at least 90 days prior to the beginning of the semester desired. Admission for any semester is subject to earlier closing without notice. To ensure full consideration, domestic graduate applications should be received by the admissions office at least two months prior to the first expected enrollment. Individual departments may have an earlier deadline.

Financial Aid: A number of part-time jobs may be available for the WKKBS summer term, ranging from dishwasher to field assistant. MSU students who qualify for the work-study program should apply for WKKBS positions at student services on campus. A list of potential jobs for WKKBS summer students is available upon request.

Qualified undergraduate and graduate students may apply for the George H. Lauff tuition and research scholarships. Students pay tuition on the basis of their residence, class level, and credit hours carried per semester. Students working toward a degree in another institution will be admitted to MSU for the summer semester only as unclassified students by using a LE application.

Costs: Besides the following tuition per credit hour, there is a registration fee of approximately $157 for MSU students enrolling for 4 credits or less and approximately $196 for more than 4 credits, plus a lab fee of $15 per class for appropriate classes. LE students (non-MSU) are not required to pay registration fees or taxes for summer classes at KBS.

	Tuition/Per Credit		
	Undergraduate Lower Division	Undergraduate Upper Division	Graduate
Michigan Resident:	$125	$139	$190
Out-of-State Resident:	$337	$349	$384

Other approximate costs include—
Lifelong Education students: $190 per credit hour; $15 lab fee (for both in-state and out-of-state residents).
Housing fees: Application deadline April 1.
    Dormitory cost for 6.5 weeks: $338 per person (double occupancy); $513 per person (single occupancy).
    Apartments cost for 6.5 weeks: $373 per person (double occupancy); $618 per person (single occupancy).
Meal plan: 20 meals per week for 6.5 weeks, $505.
Meal ticket (only breakfast and/or lunch): $38 per 10 meals. (*Note:* The meal plan is offered only if at least 20 people sign up. Anything less than this number and the participant's money will be refunded. Lunch is available in any case.)

MINNESOTA

HAMLINE UNIVERSITY
Graduate Continuing Studies
1536 Hewitt Avenue
St. Paul, MN 55104
(612) 641-2900
Fax: (612) 641-2987
Contact: Jennifer Gasperini, Director,
Center for Global Environmental Education

SAMPLE COURSES
Summer institutes focus on global environmental topics, such as Antarctica, rainforests, and oceans, and feature leading experts, field trips, etc. Often, classes for children (ages 9–12) are offered simultaneously on the same topic at the Hamline University campus through the Science Museum of Minnesota.

CURRICULUM AND CREDITS
The institute program, awarded the most innovative and creative summer program by the North American Association of Summer Sessions in 1989, provides an extraordinary opportunity to meet with and learn from leading scientists and environmental and policy specialists from around the globe. Teachers, supervisors, principals, superintendents, and education consultants come from across the country.

These courses are graduate-level courses offered by the Graduate Continuing Studies Program of Hamline University for three graduate quarter credits (40 hours of contact time).

THE INSTITUTION
Founded in 1854, Hamline University is the oldest university in Minnesota. A liberal arts university, it has a longstanding tradition in teacher education and today provides graduate continuing studies course work to over 8,000 educators annually. Hamline University is fully accredited at the master's and first professional degree levels by the North Central Association of Colleges and Universities. The institutes are managed by the Center for Global Environmental Education, which also produces supplemental materials for K–12 educators focused on adventure learning and the global environment.

THE ENVIRONMENT
The Hamline University campus is situated between Minneapolis and St. Paul on a small, picturesque campus serving 2,000 undergraduate students and over 1,000 graduate students.

FACILITIES
Osborn Residence Hall has been set aside for the exclusive use of summer adult students. Room and board fees are by the week and include the room, linens, and telephone. The Sorin Hall Cafeteria, a modern, air-conditioned facility, is open throughout the summer for all meal periods except Sunday evening.

SUPPLIES NEEDED
No specific supplies are required.

Courses, Programs, and Expeditions in the United States

APPLICATIONS AND ADMISSIONS

Contact the institution at the above address for information on application and admission procedures.

Financial Aid: None available.

Costs: Between $195 and $300 per course, plus an additional $37 per graduate quarter credit.

ITASCA BIOLOGY PROGRAM
University of Minnesota
Ecology Building
1987 Upper Buford Circle
St. Paul, MN 55108
(612) 624-6743
Fax: (612) 624-6777
Contact: Dr. Donald B. Siniff, Director

SAMPLE COURSES

Courses include Botany, General Ecology, Genetics, Mycology, Entomology, Geology, Vertebrate Ecology, Ornithology, Conservation Biology, Field Biology, Photography, Aquatic Ecology, and Behavior/Telemetry.

CURRICULUM AND CREDITS

Three- to five-week courses are offered each summer. Because courses are taught at an advanced level, students should have a firm foundation in the biological sciences, although this requirement can be waived for highly qualified persons trained in other academic disciplines. Classes meet daily and registration is possible for only one course during each 5-week session. Each 5-week course carries 5 credits. Graduate and undergraduate courses are available each year, as well as independent research.

THE INSTITUTION

The Itasca Biology Program (IBP) is administrated by the University of Minnesota.

THE ENVIRONMENT

The 50 square miles of Itasca State Park offer an unusual variety of aquatic and upland habitats that are unpolluted and relatively unspoiled. A great variety of mammals, birds, and other animals are indigenous to the area.

FACILITIES

The facilities and resources at IBP include 11 well-equipped laboratories and computer facilities with both IBM-compatible and Apple microcomputers. The station maintains a library, with many popular journals and books, and with good service from the main campus library system. Other resources include a fine herbarium of the region, and collections of birds, fish, reptiles, amphibians, algae, insects, and small mammals.

SUPPLIES NEEDED

Students must provide their own bed linen, towels, and blankets. Rain gear, sturdy hiking boots, outdoor clothing, swim suits, flashlights, a calculator, and sweaters and jackets are recommended.

APPLICATIONS AND ADMISSIONS
Contact the institution at the above address for information on application and admission procedures.

Financial Aid: Available for qualified students. Other assistance in the form of student employment on the station, work-study opportunities, and employment in area resorts is sometimes available.

Costs: Approximate costs are $70 per week for a cabin rental and meals; $10 laboratory fee; $30 student service fee; $81 per credit for visiting students, nondegree students, or adult special students.

VOYAGEUR OUTWARD BOUND®
Suite 120, Mill Place
111 Third Avenue South
Minneapolis, MN 55401-2551
(612) 338-0131/(800) 328-2943
Fax: (612) 338-3540
Contact: Admissions Office, Outward Bound School

SAMPLE EXPEDITIONS
Expeditions include Arctic Dog Sledding/Cross Country Skiing, White Water River and Flat Water Lake Canoe Expeditioning, Desert and Canyon Backpacking, Alpine Backpacking, Sea Kayaking, and Rock Climbing and Rappelling.

CURRICULUM AND CREDITS
The Voyageur Outward Bound School offers 8–29-day courses as well as semester expeditions in various U.S. wilderness areas. Students may obtain academic credit through independent or travel study, or through high schools and/or colleges that have acknowledged Outward Bound's commitment to experiential education.

THE INSTITUTION
Outward Bound, the oldest and largest adventure-based education organization in the United States, uses challenging activities, set primarily in wilderness areas, to inspire and develop self-esteem, self-reliance, concern for others, and care for the environment.

THE ENVIRONMENT
Spectacular wilderness areas in the United States and Canada, including Minnesota—Boundary Waters Canoe Area, Lake Superior; Montana—Beartooth Wilderness Area of the Rocky Mountains, Pioneer Mountain Range, Continental Divide; Texas—Rio Grande River and Big Bend National Park; New Mexico—Gila/Blue Mountains–Rocky Mountain Range.

FACILITIES
Not applicable.

SUPPLIES NEEDED

Outward Bound provides all instruction, food, and equipment, including backpacks, winter parkas or rain gear, cross-country skis, sleeping bags, tarps or tents, sea kayaks, canoes, and paddling gear.

APPLICATIONS AND ADMISSIONS

Contact the institution directly for admission materials. Student ages range from 14 to 70 with the average age being 16 for youth courses and 31 for adult courses.

Financial Aid: Scholarship opportunities are available based on individual need and are allocated per course on a first-come, first-served basis.

Costs: Outward Bound courses cost approximately $80–$100 per day (an 8-day Minnesota canoe course is approximately $795; a 15-day Montana backpacking course, $1,595).

MISSOURI

WORLD BIRD SANCTUARY
P.O. Box 270270
St Louis, MO 63127
(314) 938-6193
Fax: (314) 938-9464
Contact: Margaret Bogart

SAMPLE PROGRAMS
An internship program is offered for high school and college students interested in wildlife biology/ornithology careers.

CURRICULUM AND CREDITS
The internship at the World Bird Sanctuary (WBS) was developed for those individuals with a deep, abiding interest in birds of prey (raptors) and parrots (psittacines). This program provides hands-on experience in all management aspects of raptors in captivity. Participants work alongside a qualified staff of professionals who have dedicated their lives to the conservation of birds of prey and parrots.

THE INSTITUTION
A nonprofit organization that is overruled by a board of directors, a support staff, and many volunteers, WBS began in 1977 in response to growing concern for the preservation of birds of prey. Gradually, its scope broadened to include endangered raptors worldwide. More recently, it has expanded to include parrots native to this country and to shrinking rainforest areas. Today, WBS works with more than 70 species. It operates within the Washington University Tyson Research Center near Eureka, Missouri.

THE ENVIRONMENT
WBS has obtained a long-term agreement for the use of a prime parcel of heavily wooded land within Castlewood State Park in St. Louis County, Missouri. The site is located next to the heavily visited Lone Elk County Park and is easily accessible from Interstate 44.

FACILITIES
WBS currently operates from temporary structures, office trailers, and numerous chambers that house the birds at Tyson. Interns stay in a farmhouse (circa 1850) in Eureka, Missouri, on 1,000 acres of farmland.

SUPPLIES NEEDED
Housing and utilities are provided and interns are given a list of necessary items to bring when they are accepted for the position.

APPLICATIONS AND ADMISSIONS
Contact Margaret Bogart at the above address for a descriptive brochure and application. Applicants are notified at least three months prior to their intended date of arrival.

Financial Aid: None available.

Costs: Interns are responsible for their own food, laundry, transportation, and phone expenses.

MONTANA

THE GLACIER INSTITUTE
P.O. Box 7457
Kalispell, MT 59904
(406) 756-3911
Fax: (406) 756-3815
Contact: Judith Pressmar or Kristin Bruninga

SAMPLE COURSES
Courses include Glacier's Grizzlies, Nature Photography (black-and-white and advanced), Alpine Wildflowers, Rivers of Ice, Lions of Glacier, Blackfeet History, Geology and Glaciology, Astronomy, Wolves, and Wildlife Ecology. There are a number of camps for young people ages 8–18, ranging from one day to one week, as well as specially designed programs for groups.

CURRICULUM AND CREDITS
Contact the institution for specific information. Field seminars offer optional credit which is available from Flathead Valley Community College and the University of Montana. Graduate credit may be available for some courses.

THE INSTITUTION
The Glacier Institute (GI), a private, nonprofit organization founded in 1983, provides a variety of field classes, seminars, and workshops for people of all ages and from all over the world. The purpose is to study the cultural and natural resources of the area while increasing public awareness of ecosystem management and sustainability issues.

Educational programs are conducted during a seven-month season (April–October) at the Glacier Park Field Camp in Glacier National Park and the historic Big Creek Outdoor Education Center in the Flathead National Forest adjacent to Glacier Park. Programs range from multi-day, academic credit field seminars and noncredit, 1- and 2-day explorations for personal enrichment, to week-long field ecology camps for young people.

THE ENVIRONMENT
Home to the legendary gray wolf and the largest grizzly population in the lower 48 states, the Crown of the Continent Ecosystem includes Glacier National Park, the adjoining Bob Marshall Wilderness Complex, national forest land, and state, tribal, and private lands. This vast 2.5-million-acre wilderness offers a wide variety of landscapes, habitats, and rich cultural resources which provide an unparalleled learning environment.

FACILITIES
The Glacier Park Field Camp, located on the scenic Middle Fork of the Flathead River, is exclusively for enrolled students. This rustic facility includes cabins, a classroom, restrooms with hot showers, and a kitchen.

The Big Creek Center, a former Flathead National Forest ranger station, is located along the North Fork of the Flathead River adjacent to Glacier Park. The center, a candidate for the National Historic Register, provides a remote and pristine setting ideal for outdoor educational activities and is used for school groups, youth camps, Elderhostels, retreats, conferences, and specially designed group programs. The facility includes a kitchen, residence buildings to accommodate up to 38 people, and two meeting rooms.

All Big Creek Center programs have small student-to-instructor ratios to assure maximum individual attention. Participants work and play together—in the field, in the kitchen, and on the volleyball court. The richness of the Big Creek experience fosters close and long-lasting friendships among students, young and old.

SUPPLIES NEEDED

All participants receive a course letter from the instructor, as well as a local accommodations list, public transportation options, and a suggested equipment list upon enrollment.

APPLICATIONS AND ADMISSIONS

Contact the institution at the above address for information on application and admission procedures.

Financial Aid: Some scholarships are available for youth ecology camps.

Costs: Course fees range from approximately $110 to $235 per course.

PALEONTOLOGY FIELD PROGRAM OF THE MUSEUM OF THE ROCKIES
Montana State University
Bozeman, MT 59717-0040
(406) 994-5282
Fax: (406) 994-2682
Contact: Bonnie Sachatillo Sawyer, Director of Education

SAMPLE COURSES AND PROGRAMS

Courses and programs include A Brief Experience in Paleontology, Introductory Dinosaur Paleontology, Advanced Vertebrate Paleontology, Paleontology for Educators, and Extended Studies—Expedition to Dinosaur Sites in Mongolia.

CURRICULUM AND CREDITS

Enrolled students participate in the science of vertebrate paleontology and continue research on one of the world's most extraordinary and productive fossil sites. This is the dinosaur fossil site immortalized in Jack Horner's best-selling book, *Digging Dinosaurs* (Workman Press, New York, 1988), where dozens of significant dinosaur finds have revealed a detailed portrait of the late Cretaceous Period.

The Paleontology Field Program of the Museum of the Rockies (PFPMR) is open to individuals, museum trips, organized groups, educators, and researchers. It is an educational and continuing research experience available to lay people and professionals who have an abiding interest in paleontology, other sciences, and museums. If one is interested in paleontology, these week-long sessions will yield a wide range of experiences. In addition to field paleontology at Egg Mountain and a tour of the Nature Conservancy's Pine Butte Swamp Preserve, participants tour the Museum of the Rockies and the dinosaur exhibits in the Phyllis B. Berger Dinosaur Hall which are based on research at Egg Mountain.

The PFPMR season begins in mid-June and ends in mid-August. Sessions range from single days to two weeks.

THE INSTITUTION

The Paleontology Field Program is administered by the Museum of the Rockies, a department of Montana State University in Bozeman, Montana. As a regional museum interpreting the history, prehistory, and culture of the northern Rockies, the museum has achieved a national and international reputation for its paleontology and archaeology research.

THE ENVIRONMENT

The Willow Creek Anticline lies on the eastern slope of the Rocky Mountains near Choteau, Montana, just 90 miles south of Glacier National Park, and is the site of PFPMR. Fossil finds have included dinosaur eggs, embryos, nests of several species, and a massive bone-bed of *Maiasaura peeblesaurum* fossils that have revealed very significant information about dinosaur behavior and physiology. The Egg Mountain site is now owned and protected by the Nature Conservancy.

FACILITIES

Participants are housed in Blackfeet tipis. A large, main tipi is used as a dining hall and a classroom in inclement weather. Great meals are served out of the open-sided cookhouse, and electricity is provided by the camp generator. A radio-telephone, chemical toilets, and shower are available. Commercial showers are also available in town.

SUPPLIES NEEDED

Essential personal items include an airline ticket (if appropriate), money and credit cards, and personal identification including a driver's license and medical insurance cards. Other items of clothing participants may find necessary to bring include a hat (to provide protection for face, ears, and nose), a scarf (to protect the neck from the sun), sunblock lotion, good sunglasses with 100% UV light protection, insect repellant, work gloves (cotton or soft leather), a raincoat or water-repellent long jacket with hood, a sleeping bag rated for temperatures of 0–10°F or lower, plenty of clothing for variable temperatures (e.g., work pants, T-shirts, heavy sweater, swimsuit, thick socks, shorts), hiking boots, a flashlight and spare batteries, personal toiletry articles (e.g., toothbrush, tissues, towel, washcloth), any prescriptions and/or medications, a camera and plenty of film, a water bottle, and day pack.

Optional items include binoculars, hand lens, knee pads, a rock hammer, pillow, and books.

APPLICATIONS AND ADMISSIONS

PFPMR is held for only a short time during the summer and class sizes are limited. Contact the above address for detailed information regarding the program and registration materials. Interest is already very high. Book early by contacting Bonnie Sachatillo Sawyer at the above address.

Financial Aid: None available.

Costs: Costs vary according to the type of program. Week-long sessions average $900 and include meals, lodging, transportation in Montana, and instructor fees. Teachers may be able to obtain Eisenhower Science Education Funds to help with their expenses.

SEVEN LAZY P GUEST RANCH
P.O. Box 178
Choteau, Montana 59422
(406) 466-2044
Contact: Chuck or Sharon Blixrud

SAMPLE WORKSHOPS

One workshop offered is the Rocky Mountain Front Exploratory—an educational vacation in Montana.

CURRICULUM AND CREDITS

Seven Lazy P Guest Ranch (SLPGR) invites participants to share the beauty of the mountains near the ranch itself, or on pack trips into the remote wilderness nearby.

For a number of years SLPGR has conducted pack trips into the Bob Marshall Wilderness, where over a million acres of unspoiled mountain country is available to foot and horseback explorations. All-day trips, such as a ride to Hidden Lake to fish for rainbow trout, or a trip up Clary Coulee in search of some big buck deer and mountain goats, are offered. For those who like to fish, the North Fork offers a challenge to the experienced while the beaver ponds contain some of the easier-to-catch rainbows and brookies.

Participants visit sections of the summer range of the nationally known Sun River elk herd, and may also be treated to glimpses of mule and white-tailed deer, Rocky Mountain goats, bighorn sheep, moose, black bear, and perhaps the rare silvertip. Golden eagles, grouse, and a variety of songbirds add greatly to the pleasurable surroundings. Two quarter-hours of graduate credit are available from the University of Montana.

THE INSTITUTION

Since 1965 SLPGR has functioned as a guest ranch that offers various wilderness pack trips. The ranch is also used for seminars and other group functions.

THE ENVIRONMENT

SPLGR is located in the Teton River Canyon on the eastern slope of the Rockies in Western Montana, south of Glacier National Park and just a few miles from the Continental Divide. It can be reached by road 30 miles west of the nearest town of Choteau and by airlines into Great Falls.

SLPGR rests on the valley of the North Fork of the Tetons surrounded by majestic peaks, some of which tower over 2,000 feet above the buildings. Directly behind the ranch lies the one-million-acre Bob Marshall Wildlife Area, which spreads 90 miles north to south, and 60 miles east to west.

Variety is especially striking, from flower-strewn meadows along the rivers and the shady woods of side canyons to the snowbanks and high tundra lands of the Continental Divide. Three lovely wild rivers have their sources among the peaks of this beautiful, secluded area. Those who enjoy fishing will find a special thrill in being a part of such an unchanged natural environment.

FACILITIES

Meals are served family style in the ranch's rustic lodge, which is made out of native logs and has a huge stone fireplace, a roomy lobby and porch, and the finest in kitchen and dining equipment. Six comfortable guest cabins are pleasantly spaced among the nearby pines (five with private baths and two with fireplaces). A central bathhouse serves the other cabins, and laundry facilities are available. There is also a fine tack room and packing shed where all the gear is stored and made ready for mountain trips.

Guided tours on horseback are taken on the many trails leading out from the ranch. SLPGR has approximately 50 horses and mules, and the riding equipment is top quality (25 riding saddles and 30 Decker pack saddles). Most gear is packed on mules—the freight train of the Rockies.

SUPPLIES NEEDED

Necessary supplies include binoculars, a camera, plenty of film, a sleeping bag, warm boots, a small magnifier for plant exploration, gloves, good hiking and riding shoes, a mattress pad for horse trips, a day pack, flashlight, coat, hat, and rain gear for the feet and the body during hiking and riding trips. Optional textbooks are available for purchase at the ranch.

APPLICATIONS AND ADMISSIONS

Contact the institution at the above adress for application materials.

Financial Aid: None available.

Costs: Approximately $1,200 per person.

NEVADA

DESERT RESEARCH INSTITUTE
University of Nevada System
P.O. Box 60220
Reno, NV 89506-0220
(702) 673-7325
Fax: (702) 673-7597
Contact: Susan Sawatzky

SAMPLE COURSES AND PROGRAMS

Courses and programs include Desert Research Institute Summer Fellowship Program; Long-Term Climate Studies; Global Climate Change and Great Basin Ecosystems; Dendrochronology and Great Basin Forest Ecology; Spectral Studies of Vegetation; Climate History of Northern Nevada; and Greenland Field Assistant.

CURRICULUM AND CREDITS

The Desert Research Institute (DRI) Summer Fellowship Program is open to Nevada teachers only. A maximum of three Continuing Education Credits are awarded.

Summer Fellows remain under the supervision of a DRI faculty member and are expected to work an eight-hour day, five days a week for eight weeks unless the project requires a different schedule. By working with your faculty advisor, the fellow can arrange the exact dates of the eight weeks of service to accommodate vacations or other commitments. The fellowship position should be regarded as any other job. One should arrive to work on time, avoid excessive absences, and complete assignments. All applicants must possess a valid Nevada driver's license and be able to commit to a 40-hour work week for the duration of the fellowship.

An additional requirement of the fellowship program is the development of a specified number of lesson plans based on the fellow's work during the summer. This is an especially important aspect of the fellowship, as it provides the means for transferring personal experiences to the students. Half of the lesson plans are geared toward the underserved student, while the other half are designed to interest and challenge unusually talented students.

Two consultants from the University of Nevada at Reno (UNR) are available to assist in the development of the fellow's lesson plans. Once developed, these plans are compiled into a single volume and distributed to the science departments of all of Nevada's secondary schools for use by all instructors.

THE INSTITUTION

A nonprofit, statewide division of the University and Community College System of Nevada, DRI pursues a full-time program of basic and applied environmental research on a local, national, and international scale. DRI's 400 scientists, technicians, and support staff conduct approximately 100 research projects annually.

THE ENVIRONMENT

DRI offices and laboratories for field or laboratory work are located in Las Vegas and Reno.

FACILITIES
Contact DRI for information about facilities.

SUPPLIES NEEDED
None.

APPLICATIONS AND ADMISSIONS
In early spring, DRI circulates a detailed announcement to Nevada secondary teachers describing the program and 15 to 20 different research positions available. Applications from all interested science teachers are invited. If participants do not receive the announcement by the end of March they should contact Susan Sawatzky at the above address.

Applicants must apply for specific positions, explaining their interest and qualifications. Applications are divided into Clark, Washoe, and rural counties, as DRI announces the awards in late spring.

Financial Aid: Approximately $1,700 a month. Rural fellows may be eligible to receive a $500-per-month relocation expense.

Costs: Fellows obtaining UNR graduate credit may be charged credit fees of approximately $200.

NEW JERSEY

COLLEGE BEFORE COLLEGE
University of Maryland–College Park
P.O. Box 120
Short Hills, NJ 07078
(201) 467-1770
Fax: (201) 376-5793
Contact: Dr. Clifton A. Steere,
Manager of Enrollment Services

SAMPLE COURSES AND PROGRAMS
A variety of courses and programs is offered for students entering grades 9–12. In addition to credit and noncredit courses in the traditional high school sciences (e.g., Biology, Chemistry, Physics), courses are offered in Astronomy, Anthropology, Human Heredity, Plants and Humanity, and Pollution and the Environment. The Science Research Program is designed to permit students to join science and math professors in active, current research, leading to the development of proposals for submission to national competitions such as Westinghouse.

CURRICULUM AND CREDITS
College Before College (CBC) is a highly academic program. All students must be actively involved with academics for four hours daily and for an additional one and one-half hours daily with their faculty mentor. Students elect courses that meet for various times from a vast listing. These courses are very intensive and have lectures, discussions, and laboratories. Laboratories are not included in determining the 4-hour time requirement. These courses may be taken for advanced high school credit or college credit. CBC employs only certified teachers and university staff as instructors and does not rely upon undergraduates.

THE INSTITUTION
The University of Maryland at College Park (UMCP) is the seventh largest campus in the nation that provides students with an opportunity to experience college life on a large university campus with the benefits of intimate living patterns. The National Academy of Sciences ranked five UMCP departments among the top ten in public institutions in the United States. UMCP is located 9 miles from Washington, D.C. During the academic year 20,000 students interact with a superb faculty of more than 200 academicians.

THE ENVIRONMENT
Not applicable.

FACILITIES
With more than 350 buildings located on a 1,538-acre campus, CBC is an internationally known research university which offers excellent computer facilities. Students may bring a computer from home or rent one for their personal use.

SUPPLIES NEEDED
A supply of computer disks is essential for use in the university's computer centers.

APPLICATIONS AND ADMISSIONS
Applications are processed and reviewed on a "rolling basis"; that is, as soon as the file is totally complete. Acceptance is based upon character, integrity, and the ability to succeed in courses chosen. The recommendation of a counselor and subject teacher for Science Research Program applicants is required, as is a copy of the transcript and latest report card. SATs/ACTs are not required, but must be submitted if they have been taken. A parent endorsement/contract, student contract, and application form complete the file. All materials are included in the catalog.

Financial Aid: A limited number of scholarships are available to students on the basis of need, ethnic diversity, and on the basis of extraordinary talent and skill. To qualify for a need-based award (up to $1,000), a photocopy of the student's parent/guardian's latest 1040 form and a letter stating why the student deserves such aid must be submitted with the application. To qualify for any other award (up to $725), evidence of extraordinary talent/skills and a letter must be submitted.

Costs: The nonrefundable application fee is approximately $45, the comprehensive fee about $3,130, and the damage deposit $25.

NEW JERSEY MARINE SCIENCES CONSORTIUM
Sandy Hook Field Station
Fort Hancock, NJ 07732
(908) 872-1300
Fax: (908) 291-4483
Contact: Joan A. Sheridan

or

Seaville Field Station
Box 549
Marmora, NJ 08223
(609) 390-3320
Contact: Sue Slotterback

SAMPLE COURSES
Courses include Introduction to Marine Biology, Introduction to the Marine Sciences, Independent Study in Marine Sciences, Basic SCUBA-PADI/NAUI Certification, Field Methods in the Marine Sciences, Toxic Substances in the Marine Environment, Marine Invertebrates, Marine Science Education, Marine Fossils of the New Jersey Coast, and Biology of Marine Fishes.

CURRICULUM AND CREDITS
The New Jersey Marine Sciences Consortium (NJMSC) offers a wide variety of water-oriented summer courses for credit. These outdoor experiences will help partici-

pants understand, appreciate, and see more of the marine environment, and include field trips along the beaches, bays, and marshes of New Jersey as well as on-water excursions aboard one of the 35–60-foot research vessels or a Boston whaler. While a variety of subjects and disciplines are included, all are sea related and use the shore as a classroom.

THE INSTITUTION

The programs take place along New Jersey's seacoast, from Sandy Hook in the north to Seaville in the south. Some are taught by consortium faculty or visiting professors, while others are offered by member or associate institutions.

THE ENVIRONMENT

The courses utilize the shoreline and waters of New Jersey.

FACILITIES

The consortium's 40-acre Seaville Field Station in Cape May County includes dormitories, classrooms, laboratories, and a main dining hall. Sandy Hook Field Station in Monmouth County is a scenic peninsula managed by the National Park Service and includes dorms, classrooms, and labs. Certain courses may require an overnight field trip to the other station. In such cases, commuting students are welcome to board at the station.

SUPPLIES NEEDED

Residents students must bring swimsuits, flashlights, insect repellent, clothing suitable for all weather conditions, desk or study lamps, and linens, blankets, and pillows. Textbooks and some laboratory supplies are available for purchase at the field stations.

APPLICATIONS AND ADMISSIONS

Contact the institution for information on application and admission procedures.

Financial Aid: A limited scholarship fund is available.

Costs: Approximate costs per credit—member institutions, undergraduate $75, graduate $125; out-of-state, undergraduate $100, graduate $155. Administrative/lab fees are $25 per credit, the basic scuba fee is approximately $210 (includes all equipment), and the room fee is $7 per day (rooms contain cooking equipment and utensils).

THE WOODROW WILSON NATIONAL FELLOWSHIP FOUNDATION
CN 5281
Princeton, NJ 08543
(609) 452-7007
Fax: (609) 452-0066
Contact: Teacher OutReaCH (TORCH) Program

SAMPLE PROGRAMS

The Woodrow Wilson National Fellowship Foundation (WWNFF) administers one-week (5-day) summer TORCH programs in science, mathematics, and history for middle and secondary school teachers throughout the country. In biology, TORCH institutes at all

Courses, Programs, and Expeditions in the United States

levels have been developed on the topics of human ecology, bioethics, biotechnology, human evolution and heredity, chemistry of water, and chemistry of the environment.

CURRICULUM AND CREDITS

TORCH presents techniques and approaches proven successful in teaching students. Teams of teachers who attended WWNFF 4-week institutes held in Princeton, New Jersey, conduct the 1-week institutes. TORCH programs present a wealth of ideas, exercises, and approaches to involve students in their own learning for immediate use back in the classroom. The philosophy of the program is "Teachers Teaching Teachers." In repeated evaluations, more than 85% of the 2,500 annual participants have valued this approach for major criteria over other in-service experiences not led by teachers.

THE INSTITUTION

WWNFF is a nonprofit foundation dedicated to the encouragement of excellence in education through the identification of critical needs and development of effective programs to address them.

FACILITIES

In 1994, 108 TORCH programs took place at 70 different colleges, universities, and other educational entities in 28 states. They are administered through the cooperation and support of the host organizations.

SUPPLIES NEEDED

Supplies vary by institute topic. All participants receive a notebook of materials—papers on content and technique, lab demonstrations, computer software—initially compiled by the teachers at the month-long Princeton institutes. Emphasis is on low-cost, readily available materials.

APPLICATIONS AND ADMISSIONS

WWNFF issues a flyer announcing specific dates and locations in late winter. Interested persons must contact the local host coordinator for a brochure and registration form. Participants must be assured of a teaching position in the succeeding academic year.

Financial Aid: Participants are encouraged to contact their local Title II (Eisenhower Program) in-service coordinator for aid to defer the fee and/or other costs.

Costs: A registration fee of approximately $150 is typically required.

NEW YORK

ADIRONDACK WILDLIFE PROGRAM
Route 28 North
Newcomb, NY 12852
(518) 582-4551
Fax: (518) 582-2181
Contact: Richard W. Sage, Associate Director

SAMPLE COURSES AND WORKSHOPS
Courses and workshops include an Introduction to Adirondack Herbivores, Stalking Science Education in the Adirondacks, Adirondack Adventures in Science, Adirondack Ecological Weekends for High School Biology Teachers, Introductions to the Adirondack Ecosystem, and Field Systems Ecology.

CURRICULUM AND CREDITS
The Adirondack Wildlife Program links research with education. This unique effort focuses on the wildlife and ecology of the Adirondack Park, including human relationships with all facets of the ecosystem. This program, funded by the state legislature, closely integrates research and education components.

These workshops are intended primarily for New York State Teachers of Regents Biology. Class size is limited. Graduate credit is available through SUNY College of Environmental Science and Forestry in Syracuse.

THE ENVIRONMENT
The Adirondack Park of New York State—the second wild area to be preserved in the United States after Yellowstone National Park—is within a few hours driving distance from the major population centers of the Northeast. For millions of residents, the Adirondack Park means remoteness, relaxation, and natural beauty—a white-tailed deer browsing in the forest, a beaver swimming in a woodland pond, loons calling at dusk from a mountain lake. Wilderness and villages, wild rivers and developed lake shores, public lands and private forests—all exist side by side in the six-million-acre Adirondack Park.

FACILITIES
Bunkhouses are provided and a cafeteria accommodates 70 people.

SUPPLIES NEEDED
Participants should bring a sleeping bag, towels, personal field gear, and clothing.

APPLICATIONS AND ADMISSIONS
For information on application and admission procedures write to the Office of Continuing Education, State University of New York, College of Environmental Science and Forestry, 1 Forestry Drive, Syracuse, New York 13210.

Financial Aid: None available.

Costs: Approximately $200 per week (varies with each course).

CONSERVATION EDUCATION WORKSHOP
The New York State Conservation Council
8 East Main Street
Ilion, NY 13357
(315) 894-3302
Fax: (315) 894-2893
Contact: Linda Coffin

SAMPLE COURSES

The workshop is designed for educators who want to integrate information about ecology, natural resources, and environmental quality into their classroom lessons. Various courses are offered, including sessions in general ecological principles, modern natural resources issues, current environmental management challenges, and methods of infusing these topics into education programs. Activities include classroom sessions, field trips, simulation projects, data collecting, and discussion of the outdoors in an Adirondack setting.

CURRICULUM AND CREDITS

The New York State Conservation Council Conservation Education Workshop (CEW) is completed with special cooperation with the New York State Department of Environmental Conservation and SUNY College at Cortland. The program is held at SUNY College at Cortland's Outdoor Education Center located in the beautiful Adirondacks at Raquette Lake, New York. Two graduate or undergraduate credits in the educational field are available through SUNY College at Cortland. The workshop is offered for two 1-week sessions at the Outdoor Center. Participants may choose which week they wish to attend the resident program. Recommendations for in-service credit are also available. A letter recommending in-service credit includes details on hours spent on particular topics, and a copy of the program agenda is also attached.

THE INSTITUTION

The New York State Conservation Council (NYSCC) was formed in 1933 as a private nonprofit organization to represent the sportsmen-conservationists of the state. In 1936 leaders of the NYSCC, along with other state leaders, met to form the American Wildlife Federation. These concerned leaders felt that there was a need for national interest in wildlife and the environment. The group later became the National Wildlife Federation.

The center is located approximately one mile north of the Raquette Lake Village via Route 28, two to three hours from Albany, and one to two hours from Utica. The NYSCC is active in all phases of outdoor and field recreation. It has interests in conservation education principles, ethical hunting, fishing, and trapping, as well as air and water pollution, and the wise use and management of our resources. Members of the NYSCC have consistently worked for better habitat for all game and nongame species. For 47 years the NYSCC has sponsored this workshop, held first in cooperation with Cornell University, and in recent years the cooperation has been with the New York State Department of Environmental Conservation. In 1983 the workshop was awarded a Gulf Oil award for excellence for helping others better understand and be aware of their environment.

THE ENVIRONMENT

SUNY College at Cortland's Outdoor Education Center at Raquette Lake is nestled in the Adirondacks. The buildings and facilities at Cortland's Outdoor Education Center are historically unique. Many of the buildings are from the Adirondack "great camp" style of architecture. Lodging consists of multiple housing units for 43 people; however, the workshop number is 30. The program accepts any individual involved in teaching others about the outdoors. Participants need not be involved in the formal side of education (i.e., schools). Through the programs, participants develop an attitude of appreciation for natural resources worldwide.

FACILITIES

An extensive library in the form of pamphlets, books, and audio materials is available for the use of the participants. Food service operates in the dining hall with meals prepared at appointed times.

SUPPLIES NEEDED

Participants are sent a listing of necessary materials. Besides personal items and sleeping materials, participants can bring a favorite identification book, binoculars, camera, tape recorder, etc. They should also bring an assortment of outdoor clothes for the various weather changes and should be prepared for a fair share of insects. Because of tight scheduling they should bring a watch and alarm clock (sessions start at 8:00 a.m. and often go until 9:00 p.m.).

APPLICATIONS AND ADMISSIONS

The workshop can take up to 30 participants a week. Application forms may be secured from the NYSCC office located at the above address. Applications are accepted on a first-come, first-served basis, and the deadline is usually the first of June.

Financial Aid: Scholarships are available in many areas of the state. These scholarships may be for the entire amount or a portion of the cost and do not include aid toward credit costs.

Costs: Program costs are approximately $225. Contact the institution at the above address for current information on tuition and fees.

HOFSTRA UNIVERSITY MARINE LABORATORY
Hofstra University
Biology Department
Gittleson Hall, Room 130
Hempstead, NY 11550
(516) 560-5520
Fax: (516) 463-6010
Contact: Dr. Eugene Kaplan

SAMPLE COURSES

Courses include Marine Biology for Teachers and Nature Lovers (Jamaica, West Indies).

CURRICULUM AND CREDITS

A staff of marine biologists is led by Dr. Eugene Kaplan, author of Peterson's *Field Guide to Coral Reefs of the Caribbean and Florida* and Peterson's *Field Guide to Southern and Caribbean Seashores*. A UNESCO expert in science teaching, Dr. Kaplan helps teachers create lesson plans useful in their own classrooms, such as making slide and seashell collections.

The course may be taken for graduate credit or as a continuing education course (no tests required). A certificate of completion will be sent to all successful participants. Dates never vary more than a few days each summer. This is a professional course for elementary, secondary, and college teachers which may be considered tax deductible by the IRS This course has been sponsored by the New York State Science Teacher's Association, and the New York State Marine Education Association.

THE INSTITUTION

The Hofstra University Marine Laboratory is used by over 35 college classes and 8 Elderhostels each year. In its 15th year, this fully equipped field station contains three labs, a library, and a complete set of field equipment.

THE ENVIRONMENT

A fleet of boats deliver the students to the calm, sheltered coral reef that lies just offshore. Study coral reefs, rocky and sandy beaches, tide pools, mangrove swamps, and seagrass beds. Participants learn how to snorkel and to use oceanographic instruments to analyze water quality and a sextant to determine one's position as the members of their team obtain bottom samples of water and sediment. Participants are allowed to use the laboratory's underwater cameras. Scuba diving is available at a modest extra cost to certified divers (they have their own dive shop and compressors).

FACILITIES

Participants live in a waterfront hotel in airy rooms with private baths (double). Three fine Jamaican-style meals are prepared by the laboratory's chef. The laboratory is located near a small town on the north coast of Jamaica and is secluded to insure privacy. A 15-minute ride takes you to Dunn's River Falls, Jamaica's premier tourist attraction, where, led by a guide, one may climb the 600-foot falls in the water. Ocho Rios, with its many hotels and bazaar, is just eight miles away. Tennis courts, golf courses, and horseback riding are nearby. However, the course is intense, and only a few afternoons are available for tourism.

SUPPLIES NEEDED

Standard scuba or snorkel equipment.

APPLICATIONS AND ADMISSIONS

Contact Dr. Eugene Kaplan at the above address for information on application and addmission procedures.

Financial Aid: None available.

Costs: All costs include air fare from New York (adjusted for other departures), room and board, and tuition. Cost is approximately $2,075 for 3 graduate credits, $2,030 for 3 undergraduate credits, and $1,375 for full participation without credit.

HUDSONIA LTD.
Bard College Field Station
Annandale, NY 12504
(914) 758-1881
Contact: Laura Pilkington

SAMPLE COURSES
The following 1-day natural history courses are offered throughout the spring and summer: Geological Survey, Freshwater Tidal Wetlands, Wetland Delineation, Exploring an Acidic Bog, Stream Ecology Survey, Botanical Survey, Archaeological Survey, Significant Habitats Identification, and Natural History of a New York River.

CURRICULUM AND CREDITS
The Hudson River Valley and neighboring regions of New York, New Jersey, Massachusetts, and Connecticut are the focus of much of Hudsonia's project work. Data on endangered, threatened, or rare species of animals and plants are reported promptly to the appropriate agencies and institutions as required or expected.

These are noncredit courses. Credit courses are offered through the Bard College Graduate School of Environmental Studies.

THE INSTITUTION
Hudsonia Ltd. is an institute for research and education in the environmental sciences. It conducts pure and applied research on natural and social sciences aspects of the environment, produces educational publications, and offers courses and seminars. Projects are funded by a number of public and private sources.

A prospectus and an educational newsletter (*News from Hudsonia*) are available on request.

THE ENVIRONMENT
Hudsonia's base of operations is the Bard College Field Station. Home to Bard's undergraduate and graduate programs in environmental studies as well as the Hudson River National Estuarine Research Reserve of the New York State Department of Environmental Conservation, Hudsonia is the only research facility located on a Hudson River wetland.

FACILITIES
Equipment, boats, specimen collections, library, and laboratory space are available to professionals and students doing research on the Hudson River.

SUPPLIES NEEDED
Contact the institution at the above address for information on necessary supplies and materials.

APPLICATIONS AND ADMISSIONS
Contact the institution for information on application and admissions procedures.

Financial Aid: Contact the institution for information.

Costs: Approximately $40 for a 1-day course.

MICATO SAFARIS
15 West 26th Street
New York, NY 10010
(212) 545-7111/(800) MICATO-1
Contact: Reservations Department

SAMPLE SAFARIS
Twelve, fifteen, and eighteen-day safaris of Kenya and Kenya/Tanzania are offered with options and extensions. Trips include Lake Victoria and Rusinga Island, Ballooning over Kenya, the Indian Ocean/Mombasa, and the Indian Ocean/the Seychelles.

CURRICULUM AND CREDITS
The Micato Safari is customized for discerning individuals wishing to see Africa as only few have seen it before. Credit is available through independent or travel study.

THE INSTITUTION
Not applicable.

THE ENVIRONMENT
The environment consists of East African wildlife deluxe safaris.

FACILITIES
Meticulous attention to detail is evident throughout, from one's personal shopping assistant to vehicles uniquely equipped with binoculars (one pair per person) and coolers stocked with complimentary beverages and snacks. A safari library is provided, as well as a private aircraft to wing you across the more difficult terrain. Every participant is given special care and attention on each safari.

SUPPLIES NEEDED
None.

APPLICATIONS AND ADMISSIONS
Contact the reservations department at the above address for information on application and admission procedures.

Financial Aid: None available.

Costs: Approximate rates for land and air safaris begin at $4,180.

NATURE DISCOVERIES, INC.
P.O. Box 427
Rochester, NY 14603
(716) 473-1098
Contact: Peter Debes, President

SAMPLE TOURS AND EXPEDITIONS
Tours and expeditions include Southwest Canyons and Pueblos, Yellowstone and the Grand Tetons (summer and winter only), National Parks of Utah, Pacific Northwest, Death Valley, Alaska, Hawaii, Virgin Islands–St. John National Park, Russia, Iceland, the Natural History of the Galapagos, Costa Rica, Belize, and the Amazon Basin in Venezuela.

CURRICULUM AND CREDITS

Itineraries are planned to maximize the greatest variety of habitats, flora, and fauna observed. Naturalists have a broad base of expertise and instruction covers all aspects of natural history encountered, including general ecology and biology, birds, mammals, reptiles and amphibians, insects, marine life, wildflowers, ferns, trees, mushrooms, geology, and nighttime astronomy.

Nature Discoveries, Inc. (NDI) provides employers or universities with an outline of instruction. Credit may sometimes be obtained through independent or travel study.

THE INSTITUTION

Founded in 1988, NDI trips are researched and conducted by three teachers who lead expeditions during vacation periods. All have over ten years experience leading expeditions. Itineraries include famous sites while others are not likely to be found by the average traveler.

THE ENVIRONMENT

Expeditions are vacation-learning adventures. Participants are keenly interested in all aspects of natural history, enjoy moderate hiking, and range in age from 20 to over 70. Pretrip gatherings provide the opportunity to meet fellow travelers, discuss trip details, ask questions, and see a photographic preview. Post-trip reunions allow sharing of photos and renewing the camaraderie that invariably develops during the course of the trips.

FACILITIES

Lodging is provided in hotels, motels, or lodges with modern (not luxury) facilities.

SUPPLIES NEEDED

Suitable clothing and hiking boots (for some trips) are necessities while participants may bring such optional equipment as binoculars and field guides.

APPLICATIONS AND ADMISSIONS

Contact NDI at the above address for application and admission procedures.

Financial Aid: None available.

Costs: Approximately $1,400 for expeditions in the continental United States (air fare and meals not included), and up to $2,300 for the Galapagos (air fare not included).

NEW YORK BIOLOGY TEACHERS ASSOCIATION
P.O. Box 360192
Brooklyn, NY 11236-0004
Contact: Staff

SAMPLE TRIPS AND WORKSHOPS

A variety of field trips and workshops are offered to help science teachers become comfortable in the classroom and field while teaching life and earth sciences.

CURRICULUM AND CREDITS
Not applicable.

THE INSTITUTION
Founded in 1899, the New York Biology Teachers Association (NYBTA) is the oldest professional organization of its kind in the Greater New York area. The organization's primary mission is to help the science teacher become more comfortable in the ever-changing world of life and earth science. The organization has also been a voice for the science teacher in many classrooms in the Greater New York area.

THE ENVIRONMENT
Each field trip or excursion visits a particular environment. In the past, examples have been to bird sanctuaries, wetlands, salt marshes, aquariums, zoos, wildlife preserves, areas rich in fossils, ancient stream beds, and other areas of ecological interest.

FACILITIES
Facilities vary depending upon the event or activity.

SUPPLIES NEEDED
None.

APPLICATIONS AND ADMISSIONS
For information on application and admission procedures, contact the above address.

Financial Aid: None available.

Costs: Regular membership is $20. The cost for a new member the first year is $5. The rate for a full-time college student (taking 12 credits) is also $5.

NEW YORK BOTANICAL GARDEN
Continuing Education, Department BD
200th Street and Southern Boulevard
Bronx, NY 10458-5126
(718) 817-8747
Fax: (718) 220-6504
Contact: Beth Kneller, Program Specialist,
Adult Continuing Education

SAMPLE COURSES AND PROGRAMS
Certificate courses and programs include Gardening, Landscape Design, Botanical Art & Illustration, Floral Design, Commercial Horticulture, Botany and Horticultural Therapy, Crafts, and an annual symposium. Master Classes for experienced amateurs and professionals are taught by celebrated experts in floral design, horticulture, landscape design, and related botanical arts. School programs, family programs, and environmental courses for children are also offered.

Some programs include an "acoustiguide" audio tour, a tram tour, a forest ecotour, nature walks, plant and bulb sales, and festivals to celebrate spring and fall, Arbor Day, and Rose Weekend.

Day trips to nearby botanical gardens and private homes are also taken, as well as weekend excursions to outstanding horticultural collections and historic sites, overseas tours to Europe, and research field trips to exotic lands like the Amazon, French Guiana, and other tropical areas.

CURRICULUM AND CREDITS

Because the programs and courses offered are so numerous and diverse, interested individuals should contact the institution at the above address for specific information about programs that interest them. Some courses and programs may grant college credit; contact New York Botanical Garden (NYBG) for further information regarding credit availability. Research field trip participants may receive credit through independent or travel study.

THE INSTITUTION

Programs are operated by NYBG in Bronx, New York.

THE ENVIRONMENT

The Bronx is one New York City's five boroughs. Lehman College is a branch of the City University of New York. The Bronx Zoo and Yankee Stadium are nearby.

FACILITIES

Contact NYBG for information about facilities for specific courses, field trips, weekend excursions, overseas trips to Europe, and research field trips to Central and South America.

SUPPLIES NEEDED

Inquire with NYBG for specific supplies needed for particular courses, field trips, or other programs. Plants, gifts, books, and gardening supplies are sold at the shop in the garden or at NYBG's midtown Manhattan Shop at the atrium of the IBM Building on 57th Street and Madison Avenue.

APPLICATIONS AND ADMISSIONS

Contact NYBG for brochures and catalogs and application materials.

Financial Aid: Inquire with NYBG for specific information regarding financial aid.

Costs: Because programs, courses, and field trips are so diverse, costs may vary greatly. Contact NYBG at the above address for further information.

NEW YORK CITY AUDUBON SOCIETY
71 West 23rd Street
New York, NY 10010
(212) 691-7483
Fax: (212) 924-3870
Contact: Marcia Fowle, Executive Director

SAMPLE COURSES AND TRIPS

Courses are offered in nature photography and bird identification. One-day trips include Ducks in Bucks (Bucks County, Pennsylvania); Central Park Bird Walk; Jamaica

Bay (Manhattan); Wildlife Refuge—Floyd Bennett Field (Brooklyn); Jones Beach (Nassau County, New York); and Alley Pond Park (Queens).

Past weekend trips have included Montauk Point: Seals, Surf, and Seabirds (Long Island). Longer trips have included Venezuela, Arizona, Costa Rica, and Africa.

CURRICULUM AND CREDITS

Field trips are noncredit; however, credit for long trips may be available through independent or travel study. Field trips are offered to New York City Audubon Society (NYCAS) members and their guests. In many cases advance registration is required. Most field trips are just one day, but a few last up to two weeks in length. Field trips are listed in the chapter newsletter *The Urban Naturalist*.

THE ENVIRONMENT

Each field trip has its own environmental features. Contact NYCAS for additional information.

FACILITIES

Contact NYCAS for information about facilities on longer trips.

SUPPLIES NEEDED

Contact NYCAS for information about supplies for specific field trips.

APPLICATIONS AND ADMISSIONS

The NYCAS automatically grants membership into their organization. Initial fees are approximately $20.

Costs: Approximately $2 for members and $4 for guests on local trips.

NEW YORK MINERALOGICAL CLUB
American Museum of Natural History
79th Street and Central Park West
New York, NY 10024
Contact: John H. Betts, President

or

215 West 98th Street, Apt. 2–F
New York, NY 10025
(212) 678-1942
Fax: (212) 265-5839

SAMPLE TRIPS

Various field trips are offered, lasting from one to three days, to gather minerals in the field. Many field trips take place in the New England area, but the club also travels on extended trips to Montana, Arizona, and New Mexico.

CURRICULUM AND CREDITS

Monthly lectures are given on diverse subjects relating to minerals, geology, and gems. Speakers are solicited from the professional community and from the membership. Study groups for novices in mineralogy, crystallography, and gemology are conducted by professionals in the fields. The groups review minerals, view videotapes, or have discussion sessions.

A monthly newsletter is published with information about club activities, field trip maps and locations, historic reprints, a Mineral-of-the-Month column, recent articles related to gems and minerals, member classified ads, a Q&A column, minutes of previous meetings, and a calendar of events. There is a holiday banquet with a guest speaker, who is usually someone widely respected in the earth sciences. Dinners and lectures are open to members and the public at an additional fee. There is also an annual auction of gems, minerals, books, publications, and equipment donated by members. Credit for extended trips to Montana, Arizona, New Mexico, and other places is available through independent or travel study.

THE INSTITUTION

The New York Mineralogical Club (NYMC) was founded in 1886 by George Kunz, the director of gemstone acquisition for Tiffanys. The club is devoted to the exploration, understanding, and appreciation of minerals and the gems they produce. The current active membership is a mix of approximately 150 amateurs, professional geologists, mining geologists, and educators.

THE ENVIRONMENT

Participants visit mineral shows, working quarries, old prospects, road cuts, and other mineral outcrops. Emphasis is on sites where all participants can gather good mineral specimens.

FACILITIES

The club meets for its monthly lectures and study groups in lecture rooms at the American Museum of Natural History that provide plenty of space to display gem and mineral specimens.

Each member is responsible for providing their own transportation on field trips. NYMC will occasionally provide a van for members who do not have cars, but prefers to maintain the clublike atmosphere where members share rides with each other.

SUPPLIES NEEDED

No supplies are needed to attend meetings, although it is part of the essence of the club to bring in specimens to share with other members. On field trips, participants will need a construction hard hat, hard-toe work or hiking boots, some form of eye protection, a small knapsack, a 3-pound hammer and 1-inch cold chisel, insect repellent, sunscreen, water, food, and rain gear. Special required equipment is announced prior to trips.

APPLICATIONS AND ADMISSIONS

Contact the institution at the above address for information on application and admission procedures.

Financial Aid: None available.

Costs: There are no requirements for membership. Annual dues are approximately $20 per individual or $30 per family for the full calendar year. Call the above phone number for current rates. To join, mail a check to the contact person listed above or visit one of the club's meetings.

PHYSICS TEACHER INSTITUTE

SUNY at Buffalo
Department of Learning and Instruction
Graduate School of Education
593 Baldy Hall
Buffalo, NY 14260
(716) 645-3171 or (716) 645-2455
Fax: (716) 645-3161
Contact: Dr. Rodney L. Doran

SAMPLE COURSES

A 1-week institute for new Regents physics teachers in New York State.

CURRICULUM AND CREDITS

Three graduate credits are available for a fee from the State University of New York at Buffalo, and is payable by the individual participant who chooses this option.

The institute is open to high school teachers assured of a teaching position in Regents physics in the State of New York, who have not taught Regents physics before or who have only taught it for one year. Exceptions to these criteria may be made in special circumstances.

THE INSTITUTION

The institute is designed specifically for instructors new to the teaching of Regents physics. Using the concept "teachers teaching teachers," a team of four experienced physics teachers lead a statewide training institute that accomplishes the following goals:

1) To develop a yearly course plan with appropriate time allocated to the five major content areas specified in the Regents physics syllabus and the six optional areas.

2) To provide classroom instruction that accurately presents the major principles of physics in the Regents physics syllabus.

3) To plan and direct student laboratory activities that illustrate science concepts in the syllabus and develop problem-solving skills among the students.

4) To choose and use audio-visual and computer-aided instructional material for science concepts elusive to other strategies.

THE ENVIRONMENT

The environment for the institute is the University at Buffalo Amherst campus.

FACILITIES

The facilities for the instructional program include a science-teaching lab and a large general-purpose classroom. Equipment and materials for the laboratory experiences are available in Baldy Hall. Participants live in the university dormitories, and meals are provided by the campus food service. Local restaurants are available as well.

SUPPLIES NEEDED

Participants need only to bring a calculator and a copy of their expected lab book and textbook.

APPLICATIONS AND ADMISSIONS

Contact the institute at the above address for application materials.

Financial Aid: A stipend of approximately $250 is paid to each participant.

Costs: Except for travel to and from the institute, all other expenses are covered by a grant from the New York State Education Department.

QUESTERS WORLDWIDE NATURE TOURS
257 Park Avenue South
New York, NY 10010
(800) 468-8668
Fax: (212) 473-0178
Contact: Michael L. Parkin

SAMPLE TOURS

Guided nature tours are offered to Hawaii, Alaska, the Pacific Northwest, Wyoming/Montana, Arizona/New Mexico, West Texas, the Canadian Rockies, Newfoundland, Nova Scotia, Mexico/Copper Canyon, Costa Rica, Guatemala, Venezuela, the Amazon, Ecuador/Galapagos, Argentina/Chile, Iceland, Scotland, Norway, France, Austria/Switzerland, Greek Isles, Thailand, Vietnam/Laos/Cambodia, Indonesia, Morocco, Southern Africa, Tanzania/Zanzibar, Australia, and New Zealand.

CURRICULUM AND CREDITS

Drawing on their expertise as travel professionals and aided by professional naturalists, Questers Worldwide Nature Tours (QWNT) crafts itineraries that focus on the natural history of a country or region, while paying attention to cities, architecture, and other achievements of human history. They have been specializing exclusively in nature tours since 1973.

Although formal credit is not granted directly, it can be obtained through independent or travel study.

THE INSTITUTION

Founded in 1973 by Michael L. Parkin and Frederick Rappaport, with the aim of providing environmentally conscious people with first-class nature tours, QWNT offers naturalist-led tours to the national parks and reserves of the United States and other nations. It is their belief that nature-oriented tourism aids in the cause of worldwide conservation, as host countries see the economic benefits to protecting their wildlife in tourist revenues. All tours are limited to 20 participants in order to minimize any effect on the environment and maximize each person's enjoyment and learning experience.

THE ENVIRONMENT

On a nature tour, anything is possible—a Buddhist monastery in the timeless Himalayas, a column of leafcutter ants parading across the path in the rainforest surrounding the Mayan city of Tikal, a troop of coatimundis passing through the trees.

FACILITIES

Tour costs are all-inclusive, covering first-class hotels wherever available, first-class surface transportation, and all meals, sightseeing, field excursions, baggage handling, entry fees, service charges, taxes, and tips.

Courses, Programs, and Expeditions in the United States 139

SUPPLIES NEEDED
None. Binoculars and cameras are recommended.

APPLICATIONS AND ADMISSIONS
Call the above toll-free number to request QWNT's annual catalog describing 28–30 destinations with departure dates and prices, or a detailed itinerary for a particular destination. Reservations made by telephone must be reconfirmed in 10 days and a deposit of $400 per person is required, with the balance of payment due 60 days before tour departure.

Financial Aid: None available.

Costs: Tour costs range from approximately $1,810 for the 10-day West Texas/Big Bend and the Davis and Guadalupe Mountains trip to about $8,310 for the 29-day Australia and New Zealand tour (round trip from Los Angeles).

RENSSELAER FRESH WATER INSTITUTE AT LAKE GEORGE
Rensselaer Polytechnic Institute
Box 84C
State Route 9N
Bolton Landing, NY 12814
(518) 644-3541
Fax: (518) 644-3640
Contact: Bruce Wagoner, Site Manager

or

On-campus address:
FRESH WATER INSTITUTE
Rensselaer Polytechnic Institute
MRC 306
Troy, NY 12180
(518) 276-6757
Fax: (518) 276-2162
Contact: Sandra Nierzwicki-Bauer, Director

SAMPLE COURSES
Summer courses, involving both classroom and laboratory instruction as well as intensive field studies, are offered at the Lake George field station. Undergraduate and graduate classes in various aspects of limnology and freshwater ecology instill in students an appreciation for the complexity of ecosystems, providing them with an understanding of current research problems. Independent study courses, given under the guidance of summer session faculty, are available to exceptional students who wish to develop research skills in the area of environmental sciences.

The Rensselaer Fresh Water Institute (RFWI) offers high school science classes programs related to water quality and other regional environmental issues. During the summer, public evening lectures dealing with a variety of regional environmental, historical, and cultural issues are offered at Lake George. RFWI strives to educate the public both on the results of institute research and on global environmental issues.

Current research directions include chemical and biological lake monitoring, aquatic plant ecology, community ecology, microbial ecology, zebra mussel research, groundwater studies, and acid rain studies.

CURRICULUM AND CREDITS

Those wishing to take courses at Lake George during the summer must enroll at Rensselaer as nonmatriculating students. Course credits are typically transferable to their home institutions. Independent study and both graduate and undergraduate research projects are available. Students must make prior arrangements with a specific faculty member at the field research station to sponsor a particular project. In addition, visiting faculty from other institutions may bring students to the station for research activities.

THE INSTITUTION

Founded in 1967, RFWI has maintained a Lake George field station since 1968 and the present site since 1982. The institute is a member of the organization of Biological Field Stations, an affiliation of environmental research and education centers associated with colleges and universities throughout North America.

A multidisciplinary environmental research center of Rensselaer Polytechnic Institute, RFWI is dedicated to providing an understanding of the structure and function of aquatic, terrestrial, and atmospheric systems. The primary research focuses on the ecological consequences of environmental perturbations due to human activities. Researchers study basic ecological processes associated with environmental disturbances and investigate methods of ameliorating or reversing these impacts. The main Rensselaer campus is located in Troy, New York, along the upper Hudson River, seven miles north of Albany. RFWI operates analytical laboratories on the Rensselaer campus and maintains a field research station 75 miles from campus at Bolton Landing on Lake George. The institute welcomes scientists from other institutions to use its resources to pursue individual or collaborative research projects.

THE ENVIRONMENT

The glaciated Northeast provides a diversity of environments for study. The Adirondack Mountains contain a variety of low-alkaline clear-water lakes, buffered brown-water lakes, and first-order pristine streams. Many large and small lakes in various states of disturbance, ranging from pristine oligotrophic waters to highly disturbed eutrophic lakes, are available for research opportunities. Lake Champlain, the largest lake in New England, is within easy access. Major industrial rivers in various stages of degradation and rehabilitation provide valuable basic and applied research opportunities. The unique and diverse geology of these old, glaciated landscapes offers extraordinary academic and athletic facilities and opportunities.

Lake George, "Queen of North American Lakes," is of particular scientific interest. This deep, 32-mile-long, clear-water oligotrophic lake, located on the eastern periphery of the Adirondack Mountains, contains environments ranging from the undisturbed to the moderately impacted. Approximately 80% of the watershed is forested. Due to recent urbanization, parts of the lake are in the initial stages of eutrophication and are beginning to experience a proliferation of invasive aquatic plants, contamination by coliform bacteria, and pollution from runoff of deforested land.

FACILITIES

RFWI maintains administrative offices and analytical laboratories on Rensselaer's campus in Troy, New York. The campus laboratories, equipped with the latest in analytical and other scientific equipment, include a life sciences laboratory for electron microscope investigations.

The field station is located at Bolton Landing, on the western shore of Lake George. This year-round lakeside operation includes a turn-of-the-century Adirondack lodge with a meeting space for scientific workshops and seminars, adjacent cabins providing long-term housing, a new 7,500-square-foot laboratory providing facilities for research and instruction, and a boathouse. The laboratory is equipped with a variety of analytical and field equipment for both class instruction and research. The institute maintains two large research vessels, a 22-foot aluminum-hulled trawler and a 19-foot fiberglass skiff, as well as other smaller craft.

SUPPLIES NEEDED

Outdoor clothing, rain gear, and hiking equipment are necessary. During the winter, the landscape is virtually snow covered and Lake George is frozen. Summers are moderate and buggy in humid weather with frequent midsummer thunderstorms. Snorkeling gear is useful.

APPLICATIONS AND ADMISSIONS

Contact the institute at the above address for information on application and admission procedures.

Financial Aid: A limited number of summer job opportunities are available to undergraduates to assist in ongoing research projects and environmental monitoring programs. The deadline for applications is April 1.

Costs: A limited number of shared effeciency cabins on-site are available at a nominal cost to visiting researchers and students. Courses taken at the field station for Rensselaer credit are at the institute rate of approximately $500 per credit hour.

SEAMESTER
Long Island University
Southampton College
Southampton, NY 11968
(516) 283-4000, ext. 315
Fax: (516) 283-4081
Contact: Pat Dzintarnieks

SAMPLE COURSES

Courses during the Seamester program include Navigation and Seamanship, Field Work in Coastal Ecology, Ichthyology, Literature of the Sea, Maritime History, and Biological Survey of the Atlantic and Caribbean Coasts.

CURRICULUM AND CREDITS

Each fall and spring, Southampton College offers the Seamester, a 9-week sailing program that awards up to 16 academic credits. This popular and intensive program provides up to 20 students with the unique opportunity to study and live in the ocean environment. Students may earn from 12 to 16 credits while undertaking the responsibility of crewing a large gaff-rigged schooner. Seamester students sail almost 3,000 miles in nine weeks, stopping to examine unique ecosystems at various selected ports of call. Field work includes studies on the finest reefs in the Caribbean to the mudflats of North Carolina.

A full semester of accredited undergraduate courses is offered while participants act as student-sailors aboard the gaff-rigged schooner, Spirit of Massachusetts.

THE INSTITUTION

Southampton College of Long Island University is a private, four-year coeducational institution, fully accredited by the New York State Department of Education and Middle States Association.

THE ENVIRONMENT

The Seamester program takes place entirely on board the vessel from Boston to the Caribbean. The Atlantic Seaboard from New England to the Caribbean serves as the field laboratory in this practical and intensive educational adventure.

FACILITIES

The rugged *Spirit of Massachusetts* is modeled after the "fast and able" *Fredonia* which was a beautiful and successful Gloucester fishing schooner at the turn of the century. One hundred twenty-five feet long with a beam of 24 feet and a main mast that towers over 100 feet from the water, the *Spirit* is an extraordinary education platform, providing an incredible opportunity to learn traditional nautical skills.

Certified as a school training vessel by the U.S. Coast Guard, this schooner is fully operated by an experienced and licensed crew, and equipped with an impressive array of electronic navigational equipment.

SUPPLIES NEEDED

Contact Seamester for information on necessary equipment and supplies.

APPLICATIONS AND ADMISSIONS

Any student who has successfully completed at least one year of undergraduate education (with a minimum cumulative GPA of at least 2.5) is eligible for the program. There are absolutely no requirements for previous sailing experience, though seasoned sailors are welcome.

Financial Aid: Most state and federal aid may be applied to Seamester.

Costs: Tuition is approxiamtely $9,400 and includes all course costs up to 16 credits, lab fees, books, meals, and berth aboard the ship. Costs may vary; contact Seamester for current information.

SHOALS MARINE LABORATORY
Cornell University
G-14 Stimson Hall
Ithaca, NY 14853-7101
(607) 255-3717
Fax: (607) 255-0742
Contact: Staff

SAMPLE COURSES

Courses include Field Marine Science I and II, Coastal Ecology & Bioclimates, Introduction to Field Marine Science, Marine Pollution, Marine Biology for Teachers, Wetlands Resources, Ciliophorology, Marine Vertebrates, Adaptations of Marine Organisms, Coastal & Oceanic Law & Policy, Ecology of Animal Behavior, Underwater Research, Marine Coastal Geology, Underwater Archaeology, Biological Illustration, Oceanography of the Gulf of Maine, and Neurobiology of Animal Behavior.

CURRICULUM AND CREDITS

Courses at Shoals Marine Laboratory (SML) are open to current and former students at an accredited college or university, provided they meet SML admissions criteria. Interested persons not desiring college credit are welcome on a space-available basis. Although emphasis in the curriculum is primarily on biology, the diversity of SML courses draws an increasing number of students from disciplines such as political science, engineering, natural science, and education.

Credit courses at SML are full-time, intensive learning experiences. A typical day combines lecture sessions, laboratory and field work, field trips to nearby islands and the mainland, and collecting and research excursions aboard a laboratory vessel. Field experience is an integral component of all courses. A whale-watching trip to observe the region's four common cetacean species is included, at no extra charge, in all courses that are academically relevant. If time permits, students in other courses have the option of joining a whale-watching trip at an extra cost of approximately $25.

Many students choose to take only one course during a summer, but the SML curriculum is designed so that qualified students may earn a full semester's college credit in three summer months, called the "Island Semester." By taking a series of courses, usually beginning with Field Marine Science and following it up with other selections from the biological, physical, and applied marine sciences, serious students can earn up to 16 semester credits. Noncredit programs are also available.

THE INSTITUTION

Founded in 1971 as a cooperative venture of Cornell University and the University of New Hampshire, SML is the largest marine field station in North America focusing on undergraduate education. The number of program participants at any one time never exceeds 70 people.

THE ENVIRONMENT

Appledore Island is the largest of the nine Isles of Shoals, which lie six miles off the Maine and New Hampshire coasts. They have been intermittently inhabited for the past 350 years, beginning as fishing and trading outposts and even becoming a resort center of sorts during the late 19th century. The rugged granite coastline and thick low-lying vegetation typify the North Atlantic coastal environment. The island is a heron rookery with nesting black-crowned night herons, little blue herons, glossy ibis, and snowy egrets. It also has an extensive, rocky intertidal and subtidal community. The cool waters surrounding the island support the fishing industry and a rich seaweed flora. Thousands of gulls nest on the island and more than 125 species of pelagic and inland birds use the island as a migratory resting spot. A colony of harbor seals breeds in the area, and whales, porpoises, and dolphins are annual visitors.

FACILITIES

The facilities are simple, attractive, and designed for utility. SML generates its own electricity and maintains systems for sewage disposal and fresh and saltwater distribution. It operates a compressed air system for divers and a radio telephone unit for emergency communications. An operating staff of about ten people provides dining services and maintenance for 11 buildings, numerous boats, and several floats.

Program participants are housed two to a room in three modern dormitories with bathroom facilities in each dorm. SML provides towels and linens. Because fresh water is at a premium, showers are limited, but saltwater bathing is encouraged. The facilities include showers, dining and lecture halls, a darkroom, and a recreation area. The main laboratory, Palmer-Kinne Laboratory, is equipped with bench space for 60 people, both compound and dissecting microscopes, and sea tables with continuously running seawater for preserving organisms. Laboratory vessels include inflatables, Boston whalers, a 19-foot sailboat, and a 47-foot coastal research vessel.

The island is accessible through scheduled public ferry service from Portsmouth, New Hampshire. A laboratory vessel provides shuttle service between the ferry at Star Island and Appledore. Ferry services are fairly regular throughout most of the summer, but may be subject to change or cancellation depending on sea conditions.

SUPPLIES NEEDED

The terrain on Appledore is rugged and the weather is typically subject to sudden change. Therefore, all participants should have modest agility and suitable clothing. Participants help regularly, within each person's own capabilities, in transporting food and luggage from the dock to a laboratory vehicle.

APPLICATIONS AND ADMISSIONS

Applications consist of an SML application form, a letter of recommendation (preferably by one of the applicant's college science instructors), and a college transcript—this need not be an official one. Applicants with postgraduate degrees are required to submit a college transcript. Acceptance into each course is considered on an independent basis.

Interested persons who do not desire college credit (i.e., professionals and former students) must also fill out application forms. Nonstudents should feel free to contact SML for guidance.

Application packets may be obtained by writing to the admissions office at the above address. Enrollment is limited; complete applications are reviewed on a rolling basis in the spring. Applicants are notified about acceptance usually three or four weeks after the complete application, transcript, and recommendation have been received. If space is available, qualified applicants may submit completed applications for admission up until a week prior to the beginning of a course.

Financial Aid: SML attempts to provide financial aid to students accepted in credit courses who demonstrate financial need. In order to be considered for any aid, students must be enrolled for four or more credit hours. Financial aid is in the form of work opportunities and/or scholarships and may be combined with other courses. Often, a student's home institution will have aid available that may be applied to a summer program. The need for financial aid has no bearing on acceptance to SML's credit courses.

Costs: All fees, tuition costs, etc. are quoted in the credit course descriptions, which may be obtained by contacting the above address. Tuition usually ranges from approximately $950 for a 7-day, 2-credit course to between $1,600 to $1,800 for a 14-day, 4-credit course, and $2,500 to $2,800 for a 21-day, 6-credit course. Additional costs may be incurred for texts, optional souvenirs, and extra trips to the mainland (about $8–$10 round trip), off-island expenses, and optional whale watch and sportfishing trips ($15–$25 per person). All course charges must be paid in full before arriving at the laboratory.

SUNY-ONEONTA BIOLOGICAL FIELD STATION
RD #2, Box 1066
Cooperstown, NY 13326
(607) 547-8778
Fax: (607) 547-8926
Contact: Dr. Willard N. Harman, Professor and Director

SAMPLE COURSES

Courses include Aquatic Biology (Upper Susquehanna Institute for Environmental Studies), An Introduction to Ecology and Field Biology, and An Introduction to Aquatic Biology.

CURRICULUM AND CREDITS

Some courses are open to and encouraged for ecologically advanced high school students. Selected students are supported by the New York Academy of Sciences' Research Training Internships and by the Otsego County Conservation Association's F.H.V. Mecklenburg Conservation Fellowships. High school students may earn up to 3 hours of college-level credit. At the present time, two formal college-level courses are offered to high school students on an alternating basis during summers. On even-year summers, Biology 108—An Introduction to Ecology and Field Biology is offered, and Biology 184—An Introduction to Aquatic Biology is available during odd-year summers. Both courses are taught by full professors who have received awards for excellence in teaching by the Chancellor of the State University of New York. Both courses are usually offered during the first three weeks in July.

THE INSTITUTION

The State University of New York College at Oneonta invites students to take part in research at this 2000-acre Biological Field Station. The goal is to provide students with the experience of participating in activities carried on by researchers. This approach is designed to integrate research and instruction into a single coordinated effort. Whenever possible, high school students are assigned to teams of researchers.

THE ENVIRONMENT

Otsego Lake provides the setting for the program. It is the only body of water in the region that possesses a cold-water fishery (whitefish, cisco, lake trout, and Atlantic salmon), and has been called the area's greatest natural resource.

Goodyear Swamp Sanctuary, a 5-acre wetland that lies adjacent to Otsego Lake north of the lakeside site, is the only remaining habitat of its type adjoining the lake and serves as an excellent example of a unique lakeside environment. Over 2,000 feet of trails and raised walkways are maintained for public use as an environmental education center.

FACILITIES

The property consists of five parcels of land plus laboratory and teaching facilities. The main laboratory consists of a 13,314 square-foot and well-equipped two-story complex. The aquarium room is equipped with two 15-foot running water fish troughs, six 50-gallon aquaria, and many smaller tanks. All are supplied with air and incandescent lights that approximate natural sunlight. The library contains over 1,000 volumes, not including periodicals. The analytical laboratory has much of the equipment necessary for state-of-the-art limnological analysis. Boats of various sizes are rigged for scuba-based limnological research.

SUPPLIES NEEDED

None.

APPLICATIONS AND ADMISSIONS

Contact the Registrar's Office, SUNY College at Oneonta, Oneonta, New York 13820.

Financial Aid: Seven high school summer research internships are available at approximately $1,000 each. Ten tuition and fee waivers are available for those enrollees in Biology 108 and 134 (housing expenses still pertain).

Costs: Tuition and fees for formal courses are approximately $45 per credit hour. Room and board on campus is approximately $40 per day. Transportation to the station is provided.

NORTH CAROLINA

HIGHLANDS BIOLOGICAL STATION
P.O. Drawer 580
Highlands, NC 28741
(704) 526-2602
Fax: (704) 526-2797
Contact: Executive Director

SAMPLE COURSES

Courses include Amphibian Larval Biology, Taxonomy and Natural History of Southern Appalachian Mayflies, Stoneflies and Caddisflies, Fleshy Fungi of the Southern Appalachians, Biology of Spiders, Freshwater Fishes, and Ecological Research Techniques.

CURRICULUM AND CREDITS

Credit is usually offered through Western Carolina University or University of North Carolina, Chapel Hill. Courses may be taken without credit.

THE INSTITUTION

The Highlands Biological Station (HBS) is a regional field station for biological research and education in the southern Appalachian Mountains. The station is an institutional facility of the University of North Carolina and is administered by Western Carolina University, a constituent institution of the University of North Carolina. The facilities of the station are available for year-round use by qualified scientists who are engaged in research on the biota and environments of the southern Appalachian region.

Twenty-three colleges and universities support the station through institutional memberships. The research program is guided by a Board of Scientific Advisors, composed of biologists from the associated institutions.

THE ENVIRONMENT

The station is located in the town of Highlands, a summer resort in southwestern North Carolina, near the Georgia and South Carolina boundaries. It is situated on a high plateau of the Blue Ridge Mountains, just west of the main drainage divide of the eastern part of the continent. The Cowee Mountains lie to the north, and beyond them, across the Tuckasegee Valley, the Balsams. The Great Smoky Mountains lie to the northwest, with the Nantahalas to the west, across the Little Tennessee Valley. To the south and southeast is a series of gorges of spectacular rivers, punctuated by high waterfalls, that drain into the Piedmont from the escarpment of the Blue Ridge. Much of the land in the Highlands region is within Nantahala National Forest.

Opportunities for field studies in the Highlands area are superlative. The location of the station affords easy access to a great variety of communities. The area is renowned for the diversity of its plant and animal life, and few regions outside the tropics offer such opportunities as the southern Blue Ridge for analytic and experimental work in ecology, systematics, and biogeography. Through cooperation with the USDA Forest Service, large tracts of relatively undisturbed land are available for studies by investigators at the station.

FACILITIES

HBS has fully equipped laboratories and computers that are available for use by participants. The Ranch Library has an extensive reprint file, a collection of books and monographs, and subscriptions to numerous journals. A comprehensive collection of maps of the region is also maintained.

The freshwater laboratory includes six 130-gallon tanks with compressors and circulators, and two artificial stream units, for research on fishes and other stream-dwelling organisms.

The station can house approximately 40 visiting investigators and students. The nearest national forest campgrounds are at Van Hook Glade and Cliffside Lake, about four miles west of Highlands. Further information on public campgrounds in the area can be obtained from the Highlands Ranger District, Nantahala National Forest, Highlands, North Carolina 28741.

HBS does not serve meals but does provide fully equipped kitchens where investigators can store food and prepare meals. There are several grocery and convenience stores in Highlands within a half mile of the station. As a resort town, Highlands has numerous restaurants. Washers and dryers are available at the station.

SUPPLIES NEEDED

Blankets, bed linens, and towels can be supplied for a fee. For those bringing their own bedding, it is advisable to bring two blankets. Nights are cool and rain frequent in the summer months. Investigators should bring adequate rainwear and warm clothing.

APPLICATIONS AND ADMISSIONS

Contact the executive director for information on application and admission procedures.

Financial Aid: A number of grants-in-aid, scholarships, and fellowships are available. Contact the executive director before March 1.

Costs: Approximately $325 per course, plus a $15 application fee and $52 registration fee. Housing costs are approximately $30 per week.

NORTH CAROLINA OUTWARD BOUND SCHOOL®
121 North Sterling Street
Morganton, NC 28655-3443
(800) 841-0186
Fax: (704) 437-0094
Contact: Course advisors

SAMPLE COURSES

Courses include Mountain Intensive for Educators, Intensives for Health Service Professionals, and Contract Courses for college, public, and independent schools.

CURRICULUM AND CREDITS

Outward Bound offers a wide range of outdoor activity courses in backpacking, canoeing or sea kayaking, and rock climbing and rappelling. Under the guidance of skilled instructors, strangers quickly become friends, working together toward common goals. Hands-on outdoor experience courses in wilderness skills are offered for women, parents, and children. Credit is available through Appalachian State University in Boone, North Carolina.

THE INSTITUTION

North Carolina Outward Bound School (NCOBS) is a nonprofit organization that offers educational experiences to a diverse population. Their mission is to conduct safe, adventure-based courses that inspire self-reliance, concern for others, and care for the environment. NCOBS participants learn by going through a process called experiential education that not only offers excitement and adventure, but teaches new wilderness skills and provides a chance to build self-confidence. Courses emphasize teamwork and include a service project and time for personal reflection. Participants learn valuable everyday skills such as leadership, problem solving, decision making, and communication.

THE ENVIRONMENT

The magnificent wilderness areas of the Florida Everglades and Blue Ridge Mountains are the classrooms. NCOBS courses are conducted in the wilderness and great care is taken to leave the environment intact. Course areas include the Outer Banks of North Carolina, the Southern Appalachians and Blue Ridge Mountains, the Florida Everglades, and wilderness areas in Georgia and Mexico.

FACILITIES

Not applicable.

SUPPLIES NEEDED

Participants should bring supplies, clothing, and hiking boots.

APPLICATIONS AND ADMISSIONS

Contact the institution directly for information on application and admission procedures.

Financial Aid: NCOBS offers financial assistance and interest-free loans.

Costs: Tuition covers all equipment, food, and transportation relating to a course. In addition to tuition, expenses include transportation to and from the pick-up locations at the Asheville airport (North Carolina Courses) or Miami airport (Florida courses), a medical examination, and a $60 nonrefundable application fee.

Approximate sample costs: 4-day immersion, $495; 8-day adventure, $895; 9-day sea kayak, $995; 11-day Mexico, $1,495; 21-day challenge, $1,795; 50-day instructor for development, $4,095; 22-day youth, $2,245.

OHIO

BRAZIL ECOLOGY
Antioch Education Abroad
Antioch University
Yellow Springs, OH 45387
(513) 767-6366/(800) 874-7986
Fax: (513) 767-6469
Contact: JoAnn de A. Wallace

SAMPLE PROGRAMS
Programs include Brazilian Ecosystems—The Protection and Management of Diversity (September through November), and Brazilian Ecosystems—Field Research.

CURRICULUM AND CREDITS
This 3-month study semester in the southern Brazil cities of Paran and Santa Catarina focuses on a variety of tropical and subtropical ecosystems, including plateau araucarian forests, subtropical forests, the river ecology of the Tibag River, Pantanal (the world's largest wetland), marine ecology, and the Atlantic coastal rainforests.

Undergraduate credits—16 semester hours; graduate—10–12 semester hours by arrangement with the director. Narrative evaluations are provided. Letter grades may be requested.

THE INSTITUTION
Students from such schools as Stanford, the University of Wisconsin, Fort Lewis College, Harvard, Middlebury College, the University of Puget Sound, and the University of Virginia have joined Antioch students on past programs.

Students will: 1) participate in intensive seminars on the language, culture, and natural resources of Brazil; 2) travel to the Amazon, Atlantic coastal rainforest, subtropical forests, temperate araucarian forests, estuaries, and marine environments to gain in-depth understanding of the rich variety of ecosystems; 3) work independently with Brazilian researchers engaged in balancing development and preservation.

THE ENVIRONMENT
The program is based in the southern Brazilian state of Parana where a moderate climate and a broad variety of ecosystems make it the ideal laboratory for ecological studies. Parana is a progressive agricultural and industrial state which is making serious efforts to overcome indifference to environmental issues.

The program visits a number of tropical rainforests, wetlands, dunes, coastal rainforests, subtropical forests, the Amazon, estuaries, marine environments, and temperate araucarian forests.

FACILITIES
Accommodations range from small hotels to field station dormitories, as well as homestays, guest houses, and a hammock boat.

SUPPLIES NEEDED
Contact the above address for specific information on necessary supplies.

APPLICATIONS AND ADMISSIONS
The program is open to graduate students and undergraduates who have completed two years of academic study. Students should be in good academic standing with the home institution. Evidence of support and recommendation of academic advisers and home campus authorities is required. Preparation in environmental sciences or environmental studies and previous study of Portuguese or Spanish is recommended.

A complete application includes: 1) Antioch application form; 2) $35 application fee; 3) two recommendations from professors, advisers, or others capable of assessing the abilities and readiness to study abroad of the applicant; 4) an official transcript showing all college credit earned; and 5) a statement of purpose with an essay that outlines the applicant's background and interest in environmental studies and demonstrates how this experience will fit into the applicant's overall academic and personal goals. Applications must be completed around the middle of March. Accepted candidates will be notified within two weeks. Late applicants who are accepted will be placed on a waiting list and considered on a space-available basis.

Financial Aid: Students should contact the financial aid offices of their home institution for information on aid, and also inquire about aid with their institution's study-abroad office.

Costs: The comprehensive fee in 1993 was $9,200. The comprehensive fee includes round-trip air fare from Miami, travel within Brazil, tuition, and fees. Housing and food are included during the 8-week program.

Some internship positions provide accommodations. Students are responsible for any additional expenses during the internship and for personal expenses during the entire program. Students should consider their personal spending habits when budgeting for the program. The estimate of approximately $25 to $35 per week for personal expenses is adequate for most students.

F. T. STONE LABORATORY
Ohio State University
Put-in-Bay Campus, P.O. Box 119
Put-in-Bay, OH 43456
(419) 285-2391
Contact: Laboratory Secretary

SAMPLE COURSES
Courses include Great Lakes Education Workshop, Introduction to Aquatic and Terrestrial Entomology, Field Zoology, Introduction to Aquatic Biology, Field Techniques in Ornithology, Ichthyology, Plankton, Freshwater Malacology, Ecosystem Modeling, Limnology, Invertebrate Zoology, Higher Aquatic Plants, and Fish Ecology.

CURRICULUM AND CREDITS
F. T. Stone Laboratory (FTSL), Ohio's freshwater biological field station on Lake Erie, offers a summer of intensive courses in biological sciences and natural resources.

FTSL is the oldest freshwater biological field station in the United States and the only one on Lake Erie.

Courses include comprehensive studies of freshwater systems and specific information on the unique environmental attributes of Lake Erie. Courses are designed for advanced undergraduate and graduate biological science and natural resource majors, professional biologists and ecologists, and biology and general science teachers. Concurrent enrollment classes are available to precollege-level students through the introduction level.

FTSL offers courses from June to August. Conferences and custom-planned aquatic biology workshops are held from mid-April to mid-June and August through October. Research facilities are available year-round. During a summer course, students spend time in a classroom, laboratory, and in the field and can earn credit from Ohio State University or directly from participating consortium colleges.

THE INSTITUTION

FTSL is a unit of Ohio State University.

THE ENVIRONMENT

FTSL is located on Gibraltar Island across the harbor from Put-in-Bay, and the field includes much of the Western Basin of Lake Erie. Some interesting habitats include glacial grooves, abandoned limestone quarries, several acres of wet prairie, stream environments, extensive shoreline marshes, larger inhabited islands, and Lake Erie itself.

FACILITIES

The buildings at FTSL are located on Gibraltar and South Bass Islands. An instructional building on Gibraltar Island and the research lab on South Bass Island are the classroom and research facilities. The student dormitory and dining hall are located on Gibraltar Island.

The library specializes in books, journals, reprints, and maps about freshwater aquatic environments with emphasis on Lake Erie and the Great Lakes. Material from the Ohio State Library can be delivered weekly by courier. Three large boats are equipped for research and field trips. Rowboats are available for student use in the bay and near Gibraltar Island. University vehicles provide transportation for mainland field trips.

Students, faculty, and staff often relax during the evening hours by playing volleyball together, fishing, or simply watching the sun set. The town of Put-in-Bay is a 15-minute walk from FTSL and has many restaurants and an active night life.

SUPPLIES NEEDED

For summer attire bring shorts, tennis shoes, T-shirts, sunscreen, linens, towels, and other specific personal items.

APPLICATIONS AND ADMISSIONS

Applications are made through JoAnn Damon, Ohio State University, F. T. Stone Laboratory, OSU Research Center, Room 1541, 1314 Kinnear Road, Columbus, Ohio 43212.

Financial Aid: Scholarships and laboratory assistant jobs are available.

Costs: Approximately $200 per week for room and board, in addition to current quarter-hour tuition.

GEOLOGY FIELD COURSES
Miami University
Department of Geology
114 Shideler Hall
Oxford, OH 45056
(513) 529-3216
Contact: Jeanine Via or Staff

SAMPLE COURSES

Courses include Geology Field Course in Wyoming (Geology 311) and Field Geology for Teachers at Yellowstone and Grand Tetons (Geology 699).

CURRICULUM AND CREDITS

Geology 311 offers all the essentials of field geology: description of rocks in the field, interpretation of rock structures, and various forms of geologic mapping. Emphasis is on the description and interpretation of stratified rocks, but nonstratified rocks are studied also.

Students work in field parties of two or three. There is one instructor for approximately every 15 students. A brief report summarizing their interpretations of the geologic history and structure of selected areas is required at the conclusion of the course.

Geology 699, a three (semester hour) credit course for elementary, junior, or high school teachers, is conducted near the Grand Teton and Yellowstone National Parks and includes field excursions to these areas. Emphasis is on the description, identification, and interpretation of geologic features in the field. Participants learn how to identify minerals and rocks and interpret geologic history, geologic structure, and geomorphology by field observation. In addition, they learn how to use and interpret topographic maps and geologic maps. This course can be taken for three semester hours of graduate credit at Miami University or transferred to another university or college.

THE INSTITUTION

The field station is at Timberline Ranch, 71 miles southeast of the entrances to Yellowstone and Grand Teton National Parks. The closest town is Dubois, Wyoming, 15 miles to the southeast on US 287. Transportation by air is available to Jackson, Wyoming. Miami University vans will pick up students arriving in Jackson.

THE ENVIRONMENT

The Wind River Range, with peaks well over 13,000 feet in elevation, is in western Wyoming near the Teton Mountains and Yellowstone Park. Glacial and stream erosion has produced a wide variety of geomorphic features exposing a nearly complete rock section from the Precambrian Age to recent times.

Within a radius of ten miles of the field station are a variety of faults and folds, allowing the study of igneous and metamorphic rocks of the Precambrian and Cenozoic Ages, and sedimentary rocks from the Cambrian to Pleistocene Ages. Several formations are abundantly fossiliferous.

FACILITIES

The facilities are western rustic, more on the primitive side than a dude ranch. The log buildings include bunkhouses, a washhouse with showers, modern toilet facilities, and a main lodge. The main building has a large, comfortably furnished living room with a huge fireplace, kitchen, and dining room. The dining room is converted into a study hall in the evenings. There are no private rooms. Married couples who are taking the course together are accommodated separately in the men's and women's cabins.

Lectures are almost entirely in the field. Some library resources are available for student use during the evening. Breakfast and dinner are provided in the dining lodge, and sack lunches are carried to the field. Lodging and meals are provided on the Yellowstone trip, but one breakfast and one dinner on this trip are the responsibility of individual participants.

SUPPLIES NEEDED

Outdoor and hiking shoes and clothes, brimmed hat, shower sandals, swimsuit, extra socks, rain gear, sunglasses, pens, pencils, small spiral notebook, felt-tip marker, goggles, canteen, soft backpack, sleeping bag, flashlight, flexible 3-ring binder, and clipboard. Gear should be brought in a duffel bag or similar soft container.

APPLICATIONS AND ADMISSIONS

Prerequisites are physical and historical geology plus six additional credit hours in geology. Courses in structural geology and petrology are also recommended. Contact the institution at the above address for information on application and admission procedures.

Financial Aid: Contact the institution for information.

Costs: Contact the institution for information.

Courses, Programs, and Expeditions in the United States

OKLAHOMA

SOUTHERN NAZARENE UNIVERSITY
6729 NW 39th Expressway
Bethany, OK 73008
(405) 491-6316
Fax: (405) 491-6302
Contact: Wayne Murrow, Ph.D.

SAMPLE COURSES AND WORKSHOPS

A graduate summer workshop is offered for teachers and administrators, including a variety of education courses, computer courses, and a tropical science workshop in Costa Rica.

CURRICULUM AND CREDITS

Each workshop is designed as a short, in-service graduate course at a cost less than half the regular tuition. Workshops are recommended for electives in graduate programs, updating teaching certificates, postgraduate enrichment, or to earn staff development points.

Workshops are offered for graduate credit. Grading is based on completion of assignments and attendance. A "P" or "Pass" is awarded for satisfactory completion of the workshop. Those who do not complete assignments receive a "NC" or "No Credit."

If participants do not wish to receive credit for the workshop, a certificate of satisfactory completion will be awarded on the last day of the workshop. The cost remains the same even if participants elect the noncredit option.

THE INSTITUTION

Since 1899 Southern Nazarene University [formerly Bethany Nazarene College] (SNU) has offered quality higher education in a unique Christian environment. An independent liberal arts university affiliated with the Church of the Nazarene, Southern Nazarene University is accredited by and a member of the North Central Association of College and Secondary Schools, the National Council for the Accreditation of Teacher Education, and the National League for Nursing. Enrollment is approximately 1,500 students.

ENVIRONMENT

The 40-acre campus is located in Bethany, Oklahoma, and remains an integral part of the Oklahoma City Metropolitan area.

FACILITIES

Contact SNU for information.

SUPPLIES NEEDED

Contact SNU for information.

APPLICATIONS AND ADMISSIONS

Contact the Graduate Office at Southern Nazarene University at the above address for information on application and admission procedures.

Financial Aid: None available.

Costs: Special workshops for teachers cost between $80 and $100 per credit hour. Normal class tuition is approximately $220 per credit hour.

UNIVERSITY OF OKLAHOMA BIOLOGICAL STATION
730 Van Vleet Oval Room 111
Norman, OK 73019-0235
(405) 325-5391
Fax: (405) 564-2479
Contact: Staff

SAMPLE COURSES

Courses include Invertebrate Zoology, Terrestrial Sampling Procedures, Systematics and Ecology of Phytoplankton, Aquatic Entomology, Stream Ecology, Reservoir Ecology, Ecological Statistics, Field Botany, Molecular Techniques for Field Biology, and Ecology of Stream Fishes.

CURRICULUM AND CREDITS

The facilities of the University of Oklahoma Biological Station (UOBS) are available to independent investigators during the summer sessions and at all other times throughout the year. Special optical equipment and other unusual equipment must be supplied by the investigator.

Faculty members of the station are available for advice and help on research problems, and consultation with all staff members in the Departments of Botany and Microbiology may be had by correspondence or personal contact. All credits earned at the UOBS may be applied toward degrees in the same manner as credits earned at the main campus.

THE INSTITUTION

UOBS is a permanent field station designed and operated to offer opportunities for study and research in ecology and natural history, and those areas that require extensive study of organisms in their natural habitats, such as taxonomy, evolution morphology, and physiology. The station is an instructional and research unit of the University of Oklahoma and is subject to the general rules and regulations thereof.

THE ENVIRONMENT

The station lies on the north shore of the Red River arm of Lake Texoma at the mouth of Buncombe Creek, 2 miles east of Willis and 18 miles south of Madill, Oklahoma, in Marshall County.

The biotic province in which Lake Texoma and the surrounding region are located is characterized by tallgrass prairies and blackjack-post forests. Bottom land and flood plain vegetation are found along many of the tributary streams. Low limestone hills covered with sand, clay, loam, or a mixture of these are abundant, as are the plains and valleys with similar soil types. Cultivated fields of various crops, eroded areas in beginning to advanced stages, permanent and intermittent streams, farm ponds, and marginal wetlands all abound in the vicinity.

The location of UOBS—on a human-made lake where little biological investigation has occurred in an area with a variety of both aquatic and terrestrial environments—greatly enhances the opportunities for research in both botany and zoology. Since Lake Texoma is used primarily for flood control and electric power production, the areas and its shorelines are alternately inundated during periods of high water, and exposed by drawdown. The constantly changing environment created by these water fluctuations offers interesting and dynamic problems. The large and diverse fish population and the many aquatic habitats of water-hunting birds and mammals present vital problems for taxonomists and ecologists as well as a wide and relatively unexploited field for parasitologists.

FACILITIES

The physical plant of the station consists of 28 buildings. The main building includes a recreation room, a photographic darkroom, an aquarium with large outdoor and indoor concrete tanks, a kitchen and dining hall, men's and women's dormitories, and study and work rooms for advanced students. Two laboratory buildings (all laboratories are air-conditioned) are large and well qualified for most types of ecological and taxonomic research. There are also an air-conditioned library, research laboratory buildings, greenhouses, a faculty apartment building, two apartment buildings for married students, families, and research technicians, and a water filtration plant and two bathhouses.

Unmarried students and investigators live in furnished dormitories equipped with running water, electricity, and air-conditioning. The dormitory for women is divided into two- and three-room units, each with private bath. The one for men is a single large unit. Married students and investigators live in air-conditioned apartments, each with a private bath. Meals are served cafeteria-style in a large dining hall. Board is provided by the commissary. Lunches are provided for field trips.

SUPPLIES NEEDED

Bedding such as sheets, pillowcases, blankets, and toiletry articles including towels and washcloths must be provided by the occupants, and since bedding items will be needed immediately, they should arrive with or in advance of the persons attending.

Only light clothing is needed during the summer months. Because of occasional cool evenings in June, a warm sweater or jacket is desirable. Clothing should be tough and serviceable for comfort, rough wear, and hard service. Sturdy shoes, a bathing suit, and a raincoat are essential. Formal or "dress up" clothes are not needed, but may be brought if desired for church or the informal dances.

Free laundry facilities are available at the station for those who wish to use them. Laundry service can also be found in Willis, Madill, and Kingston. Textbooks and other needed school supplies may be purchased from the station bookstore. Students who own dissecting kits and field equipment should bring them.

APPLICATIONS AND ADMISSIONS

Before acceptance into UOBS, all students must first be admitted to the University of Oklahoma. Application for admission to the station may be made by students of good scholarship who have successfully completed two collegiate laboratory courses in biological sciences. Biological station admission blanks are provided on request by the director of the biological station or by the office of admissions and records. Completed admission blanks, as well as full official transcripts of all colleges attended from the registrar's office should be returned to the director of the station, who in turn will forward the transcript to the office of admissions and records. Application for admission may be made at any time, but no later than mid-May. Notifications of acceptance are mailed no later than late May.

Financial Aid: Scholarships of $150 and $250 are available.

Costs: Approximate tuition per credit hour—

	In-State	Out-of-State
4000 level	$60	$181
5000 level	$76	$225

A $1 facility usage fee per day is charged to students enrolled in all formal classes. Room and board for two weeks costs an additional $234. All fees are subject to change.

OREGON

HATFIELD MARINE SCIENCE CENTER
Oregon State University
2030 Marine Science Drive
Newport, OR 97365
(503) 867-0212
Fax: (503) 867-0138
Contact: Director of Education

SAMPLE COURSES
Courses include Field Marine Botany, History of Science, Laboratory Studies in Marine Science, Invertebrates, Field Techniques in Marine Science, Marine Mammals, Marine Environmental Issues, Evolution, Biological Oceanography, Ecology of Fishes, History of Science, Introduction to Aquaculture, and Topics in Science Education.

CURRICULUM AND CREDITS
The Hatfield Marine Science Center (HMSC) plays an integral role in ocean-related research and instruction programs, both as a laboratory facility serving resident scientists and as a base for far-ranging oceanographic studies. It has become a home to researchers throughout the university and to several state and federal agencies. Institutes, programs, regional headquarters, and national laboratories are all found in the marine science complex on Yaquina Bay.

The public education program at HMSC offers educational experiences for students, teachers, and families in the aquarium laboratories, estuary shores, and local ocean beaches. Summer workshops, films, talks and tours, and coastwide whale-watching programs provide visitors with the opportunity to learn more about the marine environment. University courses and workshops help teachers establish marine science curricula in their schools. The courses are conducted by HMSC marine educators who are assisted by a core of 60 volunteers.

THE INSTITUTION
HMSC is a research and teaching facility affiliated through Oregon State University (OSU) and located in Newport on the Yaquina Bay estuary approximately one mile from the open waters of the Pacific Ocean. The main OSU campus is located 55 miles to the east in Corvallis, and Portland is 114 miles to the north.

THE ENVIRONMENT
A variety of marine habitats in close proximity to the center offer ideal sites for ecological studies and a rich flora and fauna for laboratory investigations. The Yaquina Bay estuary provides a gradient from marine to freshwater habitats with extensive intertidal sand, mudflat, and salt marsh areas. These natural areas support a biota typical of the Pacific Northwest intertidal environment. Research vessels operated by the center provide access to open-ocean habitats.

FACILITIES
The center consists of the main HMSC building, a second building for service and ship support, a dock for oceanographic research vessels, modern teaching laboratories and research facilities, as well as on-site housing. The Newport Aquaculture Laboratory

and the Research Support Facility were built by the National Marine Fisheries Service (NMFS) in 1979 and 1981 respectively, and are operated jointly by OSU and NMFS. In 1990 the Environmental Protection Agency completed a new library and a new laboratory. The Oregon Department of Fish and Wildlife Regional Marine Research Laboratory is also nearby.

SUPPLIES NEEDED

Students should bring bedding (pillows, sheets, blankets, or sleeping bags), towels, warm clothing, and rain gear. Hip boots are recommended for marine biology.

APPLICATIONS AND ADMISSIONS

Contact the institution at the above address for application materials.

Financial Aid: Inquire with the institution directly for information on the availability of financial aid.

Costs: Estimated tuition is approximately $70 per credit for Oregon resident undergraduates and about $207 per credit for nonresident undergraduates. Credit tuition for resident graduate students is approximately $100 per credit and $170 per credit for nonresident graduate students.

THE HIGH DESERT MUSEUM
59800 South Highway 97
Bend, OR 97702-8933
(503) 382-4754
Fax: (503) 382-5256
Contact: Holly Remer

SAMPLE PROGRAMS

Public programs include on-site and off-site field courses ranging from 1 to 14 days in duration. These programs focus on a variety of topics, including Outdoor Environmental Studies, Ornithology, Animal Ecology, Field Plant Systematic Taxonomy, Forest Science, Geology, Riparian Ecology, and Aboriginal Skills. On-site Teacher Training Programs focusing on Science, History, Art, and Native Peoples topics are also offered.

CURRICULUM AND CREDITS

The High Desert Museum (HDM) has invited and attracted established experts in their respective fields to participate as facilitators of these programs. Research scientists as well as college and university instructors have lent their knowledge, talents, and names to these programs. Many of the courses take place in the field and are limited to a maximum of nine or ten participants, serving to encourage highly motivated instructor/student interaction. These courses introduce topics relating to the natural and cultural history of the region while encouraging an understanding of the region's rich and varied resources.

Programs affording credit have been offered in cooperation with Portland State University. If not offered from the program, credit may be obtained through independent or travel study programs. Programs are offered throughout the year, with the majority of the programs occurring in the spring and summer seasons.

Teacher programs are taught by the museum's staff science educator and education specialist as well as visiting instructors. These programs as well have credit opportunities offered through Portland State University.

THE INSTITUTION

HDM is a private, nonprofit educational institution, established in 1974. Its mission is to broaden the knowledge and understanding of the history and resources of the High Desert for the purpose of promoting thoughtful decision making that will sustain the region's natural and cultural heritage. Located six miles south of Bend on U.S. Highway 97, this "living," participation-oriented museum interprets the arid Intermountain West, which includes portions of eight Western U.S. states and the Canadian province of British Columbia.

THE ENVIRONMENT

From its location in Bend, Oregon, the museum's region of concern spans northward to include the Columbia Plateau, east to the Rocky Mountains, south to the Colorado Plateau, and west to the Cascade Mountains. The high, dry landscape of the expansive interior Northwest, largely publicly owned, is a diverse array of mountains, valleys, deserts, waterways, and forests with intricate interwoven life forms. For some 13,000 years these lands were the province of skilled and resourceful groups of Native peoples. The expansion of the frontier brought a host of others, from explorers to buckaroos, in pursuit of adventure and opportunity.

The museum is located on a 150-acre site bordering the Deschutes National Forest, an ideal setting for historic and environmental studies with an abundance of accessible, relevant sites and ecosystems nearby.

FACILITIES

Program facilities include camping along rivers and in wilderness areas, staying in streamside cabins, overnighting in high-quality motels and lodges, as well as booking cruise ship accommodations. Care is taken to choose accommodations that reflect the content of the program while enhancing the learning experience of the participant. Travel varies according to the particular field course and can include the use of vans, ships, river rafts, pack horses, or small buses. Most meals are provided and vary from restaurant fare to group and camp-style dining.

SUPPLIES NEEDED

Outdoor clothing is preferable, allowing protection from variable weather and insects. Participants are advised to bring any special field study equipment they may find helpful, such as binoculars, field guides, and resource books. A detailed reading and supply list is provided upon registration.

APPLICATIONS AND ADMISSIONS

Programs are offered through the museum's education department. Interested parties may contact the museum for more information.

Financial Aid: Discounts may be available for certain courses and programs. Contact the institution at the above address for additional information.

Costs: Prices vary considerably, depending on the particular course or program.

MALHEUR FIELD STATION
HC 72 Box 260
Princeton, OR 97721
(503) 493-2629
Fax: (503) 493-2025
Contact: Karen Starbuck or Staff

SAMPLE COURSES, PROGRAMS, AND EVENTS

Courses, programs, and events include volunteer work week, John Scharff Migratory Bird Festival, Desert Conference, Bird Identification, Field Techniques for Studies of Wetland Birds, Riparian Plant Identification, Lithic Technology, Botany, Geology, Astronomy, Photography, Ecology, Aboriginal Life Skills, Fibre Arts, and Birding Tours.

CURRICULUM AND CREDITS

Malheur Field Station (MFS) is a regional educational center whose primary mission is to provide education and research opportunities in the northern Great Basin and Intermountain West from mid-March to mid-October. This residential field station is dedicated to the concept that education is a life-long process. This philosophy is implemented by informal visitations, organized field trips from schools (elementary through college), program offerings of accredited college-level courses, and nonaccredited courses, lectures, and workshops for the general public, Elderhostel programs, conferences, and research. One- to three-week courses as well as weekend workshops are offered.

The field station also offers Elderhostel programs in spring, summer, and fall. Students must be at least 60 years of age to attend these week-long courses. Elderhostel, Inc. is an international nonprofit organization whose goal is to serve older adults by offering them educational programs at modest cost.

The number of credits, course listings, and level of each class is listed with each course description. Credit is listed as semester hours and is granted by Pacific University in Forest Grove, Oregon. Transcripts are sent free of charge to consortium schools or to other institutions of the participant's choice for a fee of $10.

THE INSTITUTION

MFS is administered by the Great Basin Society, Inc., a nonprofit, private corporation. Educational programs are directed by representatives of a consortium of 19 Pacific Northwest colleges and universities that have supported the field station from its beginning in 1971.

THE ENVIRONMENT

Located on Malheur National Wildlife refuge, 32 miles south of Burns, Oregon, in a diverse setting of extensive marshlands, desert basins of alkali playas, uplands of desert scrub steppe, volcanic and glacial land forms, and fault block mountains, MFS provides a rich outdoor classroom for the biologist, anthropologist, artist, environmental student, and visitors interested in the natural history of the region.

FACILITIES

Students and volunteers are assigned to dormitories. Visitors may choose between dorms (with or without kitchens), trailer homes with kitchens, or may use RV hook-ups. The field station is the perfect place for meetings. Classroom and conference space as well as a small library are located on the premises. Reservations for meals in the dining hall are essential.

SUPPLIES NEEDED

The station supplies food and equipment for overnight field trips, but students should bring their own sleeping bags, mess kits, and tents. All participants must bring their own bedding, linens, and personal items.

APPLICATIONS AND ADMISSIONS

Reservations are always strongly advised; during the spring they are *absolutely necessary*. A registration fee of $150 must be included with the application before it can be processed, even if the fees will be paid by a federal agency or work-study arrangements. The deposit is applied toward the total cost of the course. For a course catalog, contact MFS at the above address.

Financial Aid: Scholarships and work-study are available.

Costs: Course fees include tuition, room and board, supplies, and travel. Some classes, however, include a lab and/or a transportation fee. These fees are listed with individual courses. All tuition payments or federal PO numbers must be received by the first day of the course.

Two weeks before the starting date of the class, the course must have six students or more to be offered. If enrollment is less than six students, participants will be notified of any class cancellations. Please consider this possibility before purchasing a nonrefundable airline ticket. MFS reserves the right to cancel courses and refund any payments participants have made.

One-week credit courses are approximately $215; noncredit courses, $175; and room and board, $165. Individual prices are approximately $13 per night. Special rates for members and grammar and high school students are available.

OREGON INSTITUTE OF MARINE BIOLOGY
University of Oregon
Charleston, Oregon 97420
(503) 888-2581
Fax: (503) 888-3250
Contact: Jan Hodder

SAMPLE COURSES

Courses include Marine Biology, Marine Birds and Mammals, Invertebrate Zoology, Biological Illustration, Marine Biology of the Oregon Coast, Larval Ecology of Estuarine Invertebrates, Biology of Fishes, Marine Ecology, and Algae.

CURRICULUM AND CREDITS

The majority of courses are designed for upper-division biology majors and graduate students. A few courses are designed for teachers or students with a limited academic background in biology.

THE INSTITUTION

The Oregon Institute of Marine Biology (OIMB) has offered a variety of exciting courses in marine biology to undergraduate and graduate students since 1932.

The summer program provides a superb opportunity to study in detail many topics in marine biology. Courses are designed to stimulate curiosity, excitement, and exploration. Attendees live with students from a wide range of cultural backgrounds from across the United States and other countries.

THE ENVIRONMENT

The dramatic Oregon coast lies within walking distance of the OIMB laboratory, and contains an exceptionally rich, rocky intertidal shore teeming with colorful marine invertebrates, extensive near-shore kelp beds, and a fantastic variety of marine plants.

The Coos Bay Estuary, with its remarkable mud, sand, eelgrass, marsh, and piling animals and plants, is also at the front door. The South Slough National Estuarine Research Reserve is located in Charleston. Both places are close to the harbor entrance providing optimum locations for collecting ocean organisms. Within eight miles of OIMB, sea lions, elephant seals, and harbor seals can be closely observed in their native habitat. Grey whales migrating off the coast in winter and spring, plus several species of porpoises and whales, are often observed on the field trips.

FACILITIES

OIMB has 110 forested acres along the mouth of Coos Bay at Coos Head; the buildings are located on the bay side of this property, close to the post office and the small stores of the fishing village of Charleston. The modern, well-equipped laboratory is ideally located for studying marine plants and animals. The institute's buildings include an attractive dining hall and dormitories, several well-equipped teaching and research laboratories, a library, extensive holding tanks and field trip staging facilities, a boathouse, a dock, and a lecture auditorium with an impressive view of the bay. The marine laboratory has a number of boats for estuarine trips and a 43-foot boat for offshore trips to observe marine vertebrates.

New dormitories, located above the dining hall and classrooms, are open-loft areas for 10 to 15 students with individual spaces created by a bed, desk, dresser, wardrobe, and bookshelves.

SUPPLIES NEEDED

Bring rubber boots, warm clothes, and rain gear. All other supplies can be purchased at OIMB.

APPLICATIONS AND ADMISSIONS

An application may be obtained by writing to the institution at the above address. Admissions occur on a first-come, first-served basis for qualified applicants.

Financial Aid: Some aid is available. Inquire with OIMB.

Costs: Fees are approximately $1,100 for undergraduates and $1,700 for graduate students, with room and board costing about $125 per week.

PACIFIC CREST OUTWARD BOUND SCHOOL®
0110 S.W. Bancroft
Portland, OR 97201
(503) 243-1446/(800) 547-3312
Contact: Stephanie Allen, Admissions Coordinator

SAMPLE COURSES

Various courses include Mountaineering in the High Sierra of California and the North Cascades of Washington; Seamanship in the San Juan Islands, Puget Sound; Canoeing at Ross Lake, Washington; Whitewater Rafting in Central Oregon, Southern Oregon, and Idaho; Desert Trekking in Joshua Tree, California; Sea-Kayaking in Baja, Mexico. Courses are for ages 14 and older. Special adult and teenage courses are also available.

CURRICULUM AND CREDITS

Outward Bound courses are designed to offer safe wilderness courses structured to instill leadership skills, self-esteem, perseverance, and concern for others and the natural world. Courses range from 5 to 78 days.

Outward Bound is a unique educational enterprise that takes students out of familiar environments and into a setting where adventure and challenges demand perseverance, self-reliance, and teamwork. Outward Bound does not offer credit. Credit must be arranged through independent study with a university or high school, or through travel study.

THE INSTITUTION

Outward Bound is the leader in outdoor education. The Pacific Crest Outward Bound School (PCOBS) was founded in Eugene, Oregon. Today the school's headquarters are in Portland, Oregon. PCOBS maintains field offices in Mazama, Washington, Odin Falls, Oregon, Lakeshore, California, and Joshua Tree, California.

THE ENVIRONMENT

Courses are conducted in the West's most stunning wilderness areas, including Pasayten Wilderness, Sequoia/Kings Canyon National Park, Ansel Adams Wilderness, San Juan Islands, Puget Sound, Joshua Tree National Monument, and Baja, Mexico.

FACILITIES

Outward Bound courses are entirely mobile expeditions. They do not operate out of base camps. Students spend the entire course in the backcountry. The exception is the Professional Development Program, which conducts site-based programs for one or two days for companies or management teams.

SUPPLIES NEEDED

Participants need to bring only personal clothing items. Outward Bound provides all course equipment, backpacks, sleeping bags, rain gear, utensils, food, tarps, etc.

APPLICATIONS AND ADMISSIONS

Outward Bound admits students without regard to gender or race to all the rights and privileges, programs, and activities generally accorded or made available to students. Students are asked to fill out an application for enrollment on the course of their choice.

Financial Aid: PCOBS offers financial aid on a first-come, first-served basis. Aid granted is based on financial need, not the applicant's income. PCOBS grants over $300,000 in aid per year.

Costs: Approximate sample costs include 21-day mountaineering, High Sierra—$1,895; 14-day mountaineering, North Cascades—$1,695; 8-day mountaineering, High Sierra—$995; 12-day seamanship, Puget Sound—$1,395.

RICHARD DUNCAN
13240 S.W. Juanita Place
Beaverton, OR 97008
(503) 646-0794
Fax: (503) 646-0794
Contact: Richard Duncan, Tour Leader

SAMPLE PROGRAMS

Programs include a Natural History Tour of Australia and New Zealand (17–20 days). Participants travel to the South Pacific together and return to the United States, taking advantage of numerous side-trips to exciting locations such as Fiji, Tahiti, Hawaii, and Southeast Asia.

CURRICULUM AND CREDITS

Each summer, interested people from the United States travel to New Zealand and Australia. The tour is sponsored by the National Science Teachers Association, but one does not have to be a member to participate. Those who are fortunate enough to participate gain first-hand knowledge of geological history, flora, fauna, the Great Barrier Reef, settlement patterns, Maori and aboriginal culture, cave biology, rainforests, marsupials, and natural history. Those involved in the tour actively engage in field studies, tours, cruises, snorkeling, reef walking, and spotlighting nocturnal mammals, among other activities. Lectures and discussions are led by local experts, many of whom have advanced degrees in specialty areas.

THE INSTITUTION

Tour leader Richard Duncan has led tours to Australia, New Zealand, and the Great Barrier Reef for the past 13 years. He teaches science, biology, and outdoor survival, and is the recipient of several awards including Oregon's Biology Teacher of the Year, OMSI Award for Excellence in Science Teaching, and the Presidential Award for Excellence in Science Teaching. Richard has taught classes at the Oregon Museum of Science and Industry, Oregon State University Marine Science Center, Lewis & Clark College, Portland State University, and other institutions. He has traveled extensively in Asia and the South Pacific and is an avid photographer and backpacker.

THE ENVIRONMENT

Participants will be in the warm tropics of North Queensland and will need the usual summer clothing and sunburn preparations.

FACILITIES

Lodging each night is always clean and comfortable. On Fitzroy Island participants stay in beach bungalows only 50 meters from the water's edge. Many meals are included in the tour, including a Hangi—the traditional Maori feast—and a typical Aussie barbecue. Fresh fruits and baked goods are readily available.

SUPPLIES NEEDED

Bring comfortable walking shoes, a wind/rain parka, camera and film, binoculars, water gear, toiletries, sunglasses, and a day pack.

APPLICATIONS AND ADMISSIONS

Because of the tour's uniqueness and low cost, it is limited and always fills up. Applications and inquiries should be sent to Richard Duncan at the above address.

Financial Aid: None available.

Costs: The cost of the tour is approximately $2,495, including round-trip air fare from the West Coast to and throughout Australia and New Zealand on Qantas airlines, all lodging, admissions, tours, ground and ship transportation, and many meals.

PENNSYLVANIA

CURRICULUM TRAVEL OF AMERICA, INC.
5194 Hamilton Boulevard
Allentown, PA 18106
(610) 395-6606/(800) 541-6606
Fax: (610) 395-8693
Contact: Glen Fulton

SAMPLE TRIPS
Educational field trips for teachers and their classes and for independent scholars. Among the trips offered are whale watching (Cape Cod), Washington, D.C., French Canada, New England, the Poconos (natural science), Bermuda, Galapagos, Alaska, Hawaii, and the Virgin Islands.

CURRICULUM AND CREDITS
Trips are one or more days in length, and have a variety of educational purposes, including science, language, art and music, history, and government. Professional field trip directors travel with every group. These individuals have strong experience in education and have mastered the art of blending fun with learning for groups of students from diverse backgrounds. At least one field trip director is assigned to every bus. Continuing Educational Units approval is pending. Credit may also be available through independent or travel study programs.

THE INSTITUTION
Curriculum Travel Of America (CTA) provides full-service, comprehensive educational field trips to schools and organizations from the Northeastern United States. Restaurants, attractions, museums, hotels, bus companies, and theaters are prescreened in order to insure that each is appropriate for the students. Instructional learning packets are developed in advance of each trip and made available to the participants at the time of departure.

THE ENVIRONMENT
A wide variety of cultural and natural environments are offered.

FACILITIES
CTA encourages participation of groups of students together with their teachers. They will support participation in each student's field trip by providing one free chaperone position for every 20 paid students (one per 10 on trips with air transportation). CTA encourages participants to bring their spouses or a fellow teacher along who will assist in the responsibilities of chaperoning.

SUPPLIES NEEDED
Contact the institution at the above address for information on application and admission procedures.

APPLICATIONS AND ADMISSIONS
Contact CTA directly for application forms.

Financial Aid: Some public and private grants are available.

Costs: Approximate sample costs include 3-day whale watching, $150; 3-day Washington, D.C., $140; 7-day Bermuda, $725; 8-day Mexico, $795. All 3-day trips include expenses for travel, lodging, and meals; 7- and 8-day trips include expenses for lodging, meals, field trips, and all instructional fees; air fare is additional.

OUTBACK AMERICA
5194 Hamilton Boulevard
Allentown, PA 18106
(610) 395-6606/(800) 541-6606
Fax: (610) 395-8693/(800) 561-7447
Contact: Glen Fulton, President

SAMPLE TRIPS

Educationally geared environmental summer camping trips are offered for teacher/student groups or for individual students. Scheduled trips last between two weeks and one month. One counselor is provided per four to five students. Custom itineraries of various lengths are an option for preformed groups, as well as fall, winter, and spring outback trips to Florida.

Trips include Alaska Adventure (30 days; Seattle–British Columbia–Alaska–Yukon–Seattle loop), Pacific Panorama (14 days; Los Angeles–Pacific Coastline northward–Seattle), Canyon Landscapes (Denver–Pike's Peak–Black Canyon–Bryce Canyon–Zion Canyon–Grand Canyon–Arches National Park–Denver loop), and Mountain Vistas (14 days; Denver–Rocky Mountain National Park–Badlands National Park–Black Hills–Mt. Rushmore–Yellowstone National Park–Grand Teton National Park–Jackson Hole–Snake River–Dinosaur National Monument–Denver loop).

CURRICULUM AND CREDITS

Experienced biologists, paleontologists, geologists, botanists, and environmental educators direct daily activities and evening recreation. Continuing Education Units (CEU credits) are pending. In-service or graduate credit may be arranged via Temple University Independent Study.

THE INSTITUTION

Outback America (OA) arranges "Educational Travels of a Lifetime" geared for students between the ages of 11 and 17. Teachers from various backgrounds assist in the chaperone and educational duties in exchange for free travel the first year, and earn cash stipends in following years. One free trip for ten paid participants is provided for sponsoring teachers or community group leaders. A second trip is available for eight more paid participants. Husband-and-wife teams are encouraged.

THE ENVIRONMENT

The diverse habitats of Florida, the Pacific Coast, the western United States, and Alaska's marine and interior environs are explored.

FACILITIES

Not applicable.

SUPPLIES NEEDED

A "To Bring" list is provided at the time of booking. All OA equipment, such as canoes, eating and cooking utensils, sports and recreation equipment, are provided; however, individuals must bring their own sleeping bags, pillows, and toiletries. Substantial meals and healthy snacks are provided throughout all trips.

APPLICATIONS AND ADMISSIONS

Contact OA directly for application and registration forms.

Financial Aid: Some public and private grants are available.

Costs: 14-day trips (Canyon Landscapes, Pacific Panorama, and Mountain Vistas) are approximately $995 plus air*; 30-day trips (Alaska Adventure) are about $2,495 plus air. Meals, admission fees, land transportation, and all outfitting equipment are included.
*Add $100 per trip for using one's own air arrangements.

POCONO ENVIRONMENTAL EDUCATION CENTER
R.R. 2, Box 1010
Dingman's Ferry, PA 18328
(717) 828-2319
Contact: John Paladino

SAMPLE WORKSHOPS AND PROGRAMS

Teacher in-service credit workshops and special event workshops are offered in environmental education, science and technology, art and recreation, nature study, bird watching, and nature photography. The center also offers family vacation programs, Elderhostel programs, and instructor internships.

CURRICULUM AND CREDITS

In-service credit is offered by the state education department for participation in Pocono Environmental Education Center (PEEC)–sponsored workshops throughout the year. All in-service credit workshops offer a minimum of 15 contact hours of instruction. Leading naturalists and other professionals are featured in the workshops to help participants explore science and nature in unique and exciting ways.

THE INSTITUTION

PEEC, in cooperation with the National Park Service (NPS), is the largest residential center for education about the environment in the Western Hemisphere. This private nonprofit organization has formed a public-private partnership with the NPS and is committed to the education of all individuals, including minorities and people with special needs. Natural systems and the environment are emphasized through programs ranging from workshops for teachers, school field trips, and innovative enrichment programs for inner city youth-at-risk, to Elderhostel programs for senior citizens.

THE ENVIRONMENT

PEEC is located in the Pocono Mountains of northeastern Pennsylvania within the boundaries of the Delaware Water Gap National Recreation Area, 20 miles southwest of the tri-state junction of New York, Pennsylvania, and New Jersey. The Recreation Area, a unit of the National Park Service, includes land in both Pennsylvania and New Jersey along a 35-mile stretch of the Delaware River. This is a special place because of the natural scenic diversity of the area. The landscape varies from farmland to forested areas and rugged mountain terrain, from swiftly flowing waterfalls to slow-moving river currents and still ponds.

Local flora, fauna, and ecology offer excellent opportunities for study. Areas readily available for study at PEEC include the Delaware River and its banks, lowland and upland forests, scenic gorges, fields, a quarry with Devonian fossils, scrub oak barrens, ravines, and talus slopes. Aquatic habitats such as reservoirs, upland lakes, streams, ponds, and acid bogs also offer a wide variety of biotic and physiographic characteristics for study.

FACILITIES

The facilities at PEEC reflect the rustic atmosphere of a residential outdoor camp; however, each cabin has heat, electricity, and modern plumbing. Physical resources at PEEC include 54 buildings on a 38-acre tract of land. The main building where the administrative and program offices are located has spacious open areas for exhibits and displays as well as program space for groups. Two large meeting rooms, a computer lab, library, craft center, darkroom, indoor swimming pool, and the bookstore are also located in the main building complex. In addition, there is a resource cabin with materials for staff and visiting instructors, a cabin for medium-sized groups to use as a meeting room, and several other buildings which serve as meeting places and outdoor classrooms.

Program support facilities available to groups include audio-visual equipment, 14 passenger vans and a bus for field trips from the center.

SUPPLIES NEEDED

Participants should bring their own sleeping bag or bed linens and towels, or they may rent a linen packet. Recommended items to bring include comfortable footwear for hiking, casual and comfortable clothing, raincoat and umbrella, sweater or sweatshirt, and a flashlight.

In addition to these items, past participants have found binoculars, field guides, cameras, alarm clocks, reading lights, folding chairs, day packs, and radios to be helpful. Seasonal items include fan, insect repellent, cooler, fishing tackle and license, lightweight clothing, shorts, hats/sunglasses, and sunscreen for warm weather and gloves, hat, lined boots, heavy coat, layered clothing, ice skates, and thermal underclothes for the cold months.

APPLICATIONS AND ADMISSIONS

Educators, naturalists, and parents, as well as the general public, are welcome to attend the workshops. Registration is by mail and must include a check or money order for the full amount or a $25-per-person nonrefundable deposit.

Financial Aid: Teachers and other educators can apply for a Dr. Harry K. Miller–Peter De Gelleke Scholarship. This scholarship fund originated in 1990 to provide educators with an opportunity to increase knowledge and skills through minds-on/hands-on learning at PEEC.

Costs: Special events rates range from approximately $39 for a 1-day seminar to $999 for the week-long Maine Photography Workshop and Safari, with the average weekend costing between $84 and $114. Group rates range from approximately $11 per person for one day to $81 per person for two nights and six meals over a weekend.

PYMATUNING LABORATORY OF ECOLOGY
University of Pittsburgh
Route 1, Box 7
Linesville, PA 16424
(814) 683-5813
Fax: (814) 683-2302
Contact: Director

SAMPLE COURSES
Courses include Introduction to Ecology, Ornithology, Limnology, Ecology of Fish, Ecology of Aquatic Plants, Field Botany, Field Entomology, Ecology of Amphibians and Reptiles, and Teacher Training Workshops in Aquatic and Terrestrial Ecology.

CURRICULUM AND CREDITS
The Pymatuning Laboratory of Ecology (PLE) is a biological field station for environmental education and ecological research operated by the Department of Biological Sciences of the University of Pittsburgh. A variety of courses are offered to both graduate and undergraduate students each summer in three, three-week sessions. Research by graduate students is carried out year-round under the direction of members of the graduate faculty.

THE INSTITUTION
PLE is located near Linesville, in northwestern Pennsylvania, on the shores of the Pymatuning Reservoir, about 100 miles north of Pittsburgh and 45 miles southwest of Erie. The University of Pittsburgh has a cooperative program with three regional institutions of higher education. Faculty from Clarion University of Pennsylvania, Edinboro University of Pennsylvania, and Indiana University of Pennsylvania participate in the teaching program of PLE and cooperate in its research activities.

THE ENVIRONMENT
PLE's teaching and research site overlooks the Sanctuary Lake portion of the Pymatuning Reservoir, part of an 11,000-acre tract of water, wetlands, and forest managed as a wildlife refuge and propagation area by the Pennsylvania Game Commission. A warm-water fish hatchery, operated by the Pennsylvania Fish and Boat Commission, is located adjacent to the laboratory site. Many natural lakes dot the landscape, which includes two of the largest wetlands in the state: Pymatuning Swamp and Conneaut Marsh. Additional wetlands of the Erie National Wildlife Refuge are located nearby. Wooded tracts, representative of the Hemlock-White Pine-Northern Hardwoods and the Mixed Mesophytic Forest types, are also available for study.

FACILITIES
PLE facilities are open to students who are interested in developing knowledge and skills in basic and applied ecology through direct observation and hands-on experience with living organisms and complex ecosystems under field conditions. Research and classroom laboratories, instrument rooms, and other support facilities are located in a complex of buildings at the Sanctuary Lake site. The Tryon Library provides a comfortable reading room with access to a collection of ecological journals and reference books.

Housing, dining, and recreational facilities are located on a separate site outside of the wildlife refuge. Three dormitories and several cottages are available for students and faculty. Shower and toilet facilities are contained in each of the housing units. Breakfast, lunch, and dinner are served daily in the dining hall. Individuals have access to all recreational facilities including canoes, rowboats, volleyball court, and a recreation hall with Ping-Pong tables, television, and fireplace.

SUPPLIES NEEDED

Students must furnish their own sheets, blankets, or sleeping bags. Students are advised to bring rain gear, warm clothes, boots or old shoes, insect repellent, a flashlight, and an alarm clock. Laundry facilities and convenience stores are located in nearby Linesville. Required textbooks may be purchased at PLE on the first day of classes.

APPLICATIONS AND ADMISSIONS

Students enrolled at the University of Pittsburgh should register for courses at PLE through regular registration procedures on the main campus. Undergraduate and post-baccalaureate students from other institutions should contact PLE for information on registration procedures.

Financial Aid: Several awards in payment of room and board for undergraduate students will be available from the Richard T. Hartman Scholarship Fund. Contact the director about these awards before April 15.

Awards to graduate students and postdoctoral investigators for studies to be carried out at PLE are made available each year from two sources: The G. Murray Research Fund and the Leasure K. Darbaker Prize in Botany. Applications for these awards must include a description of the proposed research and a tentative budget for the year's work and should be submitted by March 25 to Grants Award Committee, Pymatuning Laboratory of Ecology, at the above address.

Costs: Approximate tuition rates for Pennsylvania residents are—undergraduate students, $174 per credit; graduate students, $279 per credit. Nonresidents are eligible for scholarships that reduce their tuition charges to amounts equal to Pennsylvania residents. All students are charged a laboratory fee of $40 per class. Student room and board for 3-week classes is approximately $240, and the laboratory bench fee is about $50 per week. Housing and meal charges for investigators vary depending on the facilities available.

SEMESTER AT SEA
Institute for Shipboard Education
University of Pittsburgh
811 William Pitt Union
Pittsburgh, PA 15260
(412) 648-7490/(800) 854-0195
Fax: (412) 648-2298
E-mail: pwatson@sas.ise.pitt.edu
Contact: Paul H. Watson, Director of Admissions

SAMPLE COURSES

Courses include Environmental Biology, Marine Biology, Oceanography, Anthropology, Business, Economics, English, Fine Arts, Geography, History, Literature, Music, Philosophy, Photography, Political Science, Psychology, Religious Studies, Sociology, and Theater Arts.

CURRICULUM AND CREDITS

Semester at Sea (SAS) combines traditional undergraduate course work with a profound opportunity for international fieldwork, plus a unique sea-going community that shares unparalleled travel opportunities around the world. The shipboard curriculum provides students with a series of insights into various societies and allows them to dissect and assess their own observations.

Conducted aboard the American-built *S.S. Universe,* SAS is designed to be a global semester in a student's undergraduate career. As academic sponsor of the program, the University of Pittsburgh grants academic credit for participation in Semester at Sea.

While at sea, classes meet daily. Most SAS classes average between 20 to 30 students and are conducted with emphasis on maximum student involvement. Students may not enroll for less than 12 semester hours and no more than 15 semester hours. Credits earned must meet the required standards, permitting transfer to other universities or colleges in the United States.

THE INSTITUTION

The Institute for Shipboard Education (ISE) is a nonprofit, tax-exempt organization that administers the SAS program. Through cooperative arrangements, the University of Pittsburgh acts as the academic sponsor for the program, and the Seawise Foundation operates the *S.S. Universe.*

The SAS voyage is available to adult passengers on a limited basis. Although the *S.S. Universe* is not a typical cruise ship, it is attractive and very comfortable. Special sections of the cabin area are reserved for adult participants.

A fully air-conditioned and stabilized ocean liner, the *S.S. Universe* is fully equipped as a small floating college. It is the heart of SAS, and quickly becomes "home" to the students, faculty, and staff.

THE ENVIRONMENT

Students develop the ability to understand new cultures and gain the intellectual tools that will allow them to relate past experiences to future situations. Similarly, they are called upon to examine such crisis issues of global concern as the environment, population, foreign policy interrelationships, and economics, in the context of the nations they visit. The ship becomes a campus on which students work in a traditional classroom setting, and the world a laboratory from which approximately 20% of the credit earned for a course is fulfilled. The integration of classroom and international fieldwork, achieved through written and oral feedback from the field, enables SAS to provide a learning environment otherwise unattainable on a traditional land-based campus.

Port stops range from 3 to 7 days, offering ample opportunity for in-depth discovery and sightseeing. The time in port permits a wide range of optional tours, not possible on other cruises.

FACILITIES

The ship serves as the students' dormitory while they experience each country visited. The shipboard campus includes classrooms, study lounges, a library, and a theater. Other facilities include a cafeteria-style dining room, student union, campus store, snack bar, swimming pool, sports and sun decks, darkrooms, and a hospital.

The library, managed by the University of Pittsburgh's Hillman Library, is a core library structured to support the itinerary and international theme of the voyage. Instructional resources, including a closed circuit television system, support the academic program. A computer lab offers personal computers and software to students and faculty.

Student cabins are available in doubles or triples, either with or without a porthole. Linens and blankets are provided and laundry facilities are available. Three meals a day are served throughout the semester, at sea and in port.

SUPPLIES NEEDED

A supply list can be found in the voyager's handbook. Contact ISE directly for more information.

APPLICATIONS AND ADMISSIONS

Students must be full-time undergraduates to enroll, be in good standing, and have completed at least one full semester. ISE operates on a rolling admissions basis without any application deadlines. In addition to the student participation, there is space for approximately 40 adults. Senior participants are often attracted to educationally based travel and become an integral part of the shipboard community.

A 16-minute VHS video tape that provides an in-depth view of SAS is available for purchase prior to admission. If you feel that a visual presentation of the SAS program would be helpful in making this important decision, interested applicants should send a check for $10 (made payable to ISE) along with mailing instructions. Credit card orders are accepted by phone. Upon application participants may deduct the $10 video purchase price from the application fee.

Financial Aid: Students who typically receive aid on campus, such as Pell Grants and Stafford Loans, may apply that aid toward SAS. Additionally, they can qualify for aid offered by the institute in the form of work grants, reduced cabin rates, and monetary grants. Assistance is awarded based on need. Grants are also available for students who do not qualify for federal or state aid, but who demonstrate a particular need in order to participate in the program.

For students who complete the Federal Student Aid application process and typically qualify for financial aid on their home campus, significantly reduced rates are available. A work-grant program provides a rate of approximately $6,295, and special inside triple cabins are available at $9,595.

Combined with transferable state and federal aid and loans, the cost of SAS can be further reduced. Additional monetary grants are often included with the inside triple rate.

Funding is available to students who do not typically qualify for financial aid on their home campus, yet who need assistance in order to meet the costs of the program. Monetary grants of $1,000 to $2,500, applied to the inside double rate, are available to eligible students. Documentation of financial status is required, but the Federal Student Aid application need not be completed. A payment plan enabling the deferral of tuition payments and financing options is also available. Individual rates include tuition, passage fare, and student fees. Travel to and from ports of embarkation and debarkation, textbooks, in-country travel, personal expenses, and incidental fees are additional.

Costs: Approximate rates without financial assistance include—Inside Double (1 upper, 1 lower berth without porthole), $12,195; Outside Triple (1 upper, 2 lower berths with porthole), $13,195; Outside Double (1 upper, 1 lower berth with porthole), $13,895; Outside Double (2 lower berths with porthole), $14,495.

TEXAS

CHAPALA ECOLOGY STATION
Baylor University and Universidad Autónoma de Guadalajara
P.O. Box 97388
Waco, TX 76798-7388
(817) 755-2911
Fax: (817) 755-2969
Contact: Laura Dávalos-Lind

SAMPLE COURSES
Courses include Limnology and the Management of Lakes and Reservoirs, Ecology and Conservation of Mammals in Latin America, Special Problems in the Environment, Aquatic Biology, Biometrics, Biology of Wetland and Aquatic Vascular Plants, Forestry Management, and Independent Research.

CURRICULUM AND CREDITS
Admission is normally limited to students of junior, senior, or graduate academic standing. A minimum of one year of college-level biology and chemistry is expected. Academic credit may be obtained through Baylor University or through Universidad Autónoma de Guadalajara. The classes enroll an equal number of students from Canada, the United States, Mexico, and Central and South America. Each course is team-taught by an American and Mexican professor. Outlines of each lecture, lab, and field trip are provided in English and Spanish while the lecturer uses his/her native language with further translation as needed. The academic program is complemented by visiting researchers, visiting speakers, and cultural trips on weekends.

THE INSTITUTION
The uniqueness of the Chapala Ecology Station (CES) program is the combined experience of field ecology, cultural exchange, and international cooperation. CES is a joint program administered by Baylor University and Universidad Autónoma de Guadalajara. CES occupies a portion of La Floresta motel, which is located on the north shore of Lake Chapala, in the village of Ajijic, approximately 30 miles south of Guadalajara, Jalisco. CES is easily reached by air, auto, or bus. Nonstop air service to the Guadalajara International airport is maintained from many U.S. cities.

THE ENVIRONMENT
CES is on the shore of Mexico's largest natural lake, Lago de Chapala, and at the foot of the mountain range on the southwestern boundary of the Mesa Central. Human-impacted and unimpacted ecosystems abound in the region. Ecosystems easily reached from the station include montane coniferous forest, desert scrubland, tropical rainforest, large and small lakes, salt lakes, reservoirs, rivers, marshes, and thermal springs. Within a half-day drive, one can reach alpine forests (Nevado de Colima), a smoking volcano (Volcán de Colima), or the Pacific Ocean. The climate at CES is one of "year-round springtime." Daytime high temperatures during July and August rarely exceed 85°F, with

night temperatures dropping into the 60s. July and August are the middle of the rainy season for this tropical region. Rains occur during the late afternoon and early evening.

FACILITIES

CES has classrooms, research and teaching laboratories, computer facilities, and a health clinic. Students, faculty, and visiting researchers live in units consisting of one or two bedrooms, each with two beds, a sitting room/kitchenette, and a bath. Special accommodation can be made for married students and families. A cafeteria-style dining room provides three meals daily (breakfast, dinner, and light supper), except Sunday when a late brunch and dinner are served. CES recreational facilities include a swimming pool, tennis courts, table tennis, and billiards. Tourist-type activities include group trips into Guadalajara city to attend the Ballet Folklorico, concerts, sightseeing, and shopping. The station has a telephone and fax machine. Money can be exchanged in the village bank, and a self-operated laundry is within walking distance.

SUPPLIES NEEDED

Clothing is casual and needs to be appropriate for the class taken. All linens are supplied. Sturdy boots, heavy pants and shirts for terrestrial courses, while T-shirts, short, wading shoes, and a towel are appropriate for the aquatic courses. A sweater or light jacket for evenings, raincoat or poncho, umbrella, and lots of suntan lotion are needed. Students receive a list of required books and supplies following acceptance to CES and are responsible for bringing them to the station.

APPLICATIONS AND ADMISSIONS

Admission to CES is by formal application. An information booklet with an application form attached is available upon request. Students should inquire about scholarships by writing to the program coordinator.

Financial Aid: None available.

Costs: Session room and board costs are approximately $550, and tuition varies by university and credit hours taken.

The Natural Classroom

UTAH

CANYONLANDS FIELD INSTITUTE
P.O. Box 68
1320 South Highway 191
Moab, UT 84532
(801) 259-7750/(800) 860-5262
Fax: (801) 259-2335
Contact: Vicki Barker

SAMPLE COURSES AND TRIPS

Land- and river-based instructional field trips and training courses are available for student groups (day camps for K–12), professional guides and outdoor educators, and adults through Elderhostel, open-enrollment hiking and river trips, and special trips and programs customized for groups of 8 or more (custom trips require three months advance notice). Children ages 8–14 can also enroll for "intergenerational" Elderhostel trips on the San Juan River.

Various adult and family programs are offered, including Eagle Float, Women over 40 Raft & Hiking Trip, Four Winds Women's Network Raft Trip, Women in Wilderness (canoe trip), "Intrigue of the Past" Teachers Workshop (archaeology), Desert Writers Workshop, American Red Cross Emergency Response, and Interpretive & River Skills (workshops). Elderhostel programs include History of the Southwest/Monument Valley Photography, Natural & Cultural History of the San Juan River, and Geology of Arches National Park. Youth programs and camps include Whitewater Academy for Teens, GeoWhiz Kids Day Camp, and GeoWhiz Explorer's Camp.

CURRICULUM AND CREDITS

Canyonlands Field Institute (CFI) offers year-round interdisciplinary base-camp programs in the Outdoor Science School for student groups (K–12) from one to six days. Land-based study at the Professor Valley Field Camp can be combined with river study to create a longer program. The science school and other youth programs for students up through college age take place in the field or on the river, providing hands-on lessons in the natural sciences and cultural history, with emphasis on basic concepts of ecology. Lessons may incorporate low-impact camping, outdoor survival, river rowing, safety and rescue, and team-building skills. Adult programs also offer instruction on the unique features of the Colorado Plateau, its plants, animals, and inhabitants.

College credit is available for the Intrigue of the Past and Desert Writers workshops and for training through CFI's Colorado Plateau Professional Guide Institute. College credit is optional for selected adult courses. Credit is awarded either by quarter (through Utah State University or the College of Eastern Utah) or by semester (Brigham Young University). Grades are either letter grade (USU and CEU) or pass/no pass (BYU) and are fully transferable. Costs for academic credit are not included in course fees and must be paid separately. Arrangements to do so can be made with CFI's registrar.

THE INSTITUTION

As a nonprofit 501(C-3) educational organization, CFI offers programs that promote understanding, appreciation, and responsible stewardship of the natural environment and cultural resources of the Colorado Plateau. Through its experiential educational field trips for youth and adults, CFI promotes informed and responsible personal action and public decision making that supports a sustainable future for the plateau and the earth as a whole. Founded in 1984, CRI is supported by tuition (65%), contributions (35%), and memberships. After taking a course, all program participants receive complimentary CFI memberships good through the following May. Participants come from all over the United States and other countries.

THE ENVIRONMENT

CFI is based in Moab, Utah, and operates a field camp adjacent to Professor Valley Ranch about 20 miles from town near the Colorado River. Students enjoy outdoor classrooms in settings that range from the red-rock desert landscapes of Arches and Canyonlands National Parks, BLM Wilderness Study Areas, and American Indian reservations to the aspen-covered, lake-studded mountains of the Manti-LaSal National Forest, and the lush canyons of the Colorado, Green, San Juan, and Dolores Rivers.

FACILITIES

The administrative offices, equipment storage, and teaching assistant quarters of CFI are in Moab, Utah. Residential day camps for youth, and seminars and retreats for nonstudent groups such as families, businesses, and clubs, are based at the Professor Valley Field Camp, two miles from the nearest paved road. CFI also utilizes ranches and cabins in nearby mountains for residential programs. A camp host/caretaker who lives on-site at the field camp prepares meals for groups and serves as a resource. The weatherproof field camp is available year-round for groups of 10 to 40 people. Two large yurts serve as kitchen and classroom or additional sleeping quarters. The camp has running water, picnic tables, vault toilets, primitive showers, and solar-powered electricity. Rental rates range from $75 a night for 1–10 people to $150 for groups up to 40 (the fourth night is always free). If three meals plus snacks are included rates are $30 a person for one night, or $25 a person for two or more nights. Write to CFI for a brochure on field camp rental rates. For information on lodging in the Moab area, call the Grand County Travel Council at (801) 259-8825.

SUPPLIES NEEDED

Most CFI programs are conducted at an elevation of 4,000–5,000 feet in a high-desert climate. The LaSal Mountains rise to 12,000 feet (subalpine climate). Clothing needs vary seasonally, with temperatures ranging from the 100s in the summer to the teens in midwinter when snow is possible. CFI provides lists of suggested clothing and gear for each program. Depending on the program, participants may need to bring their own sleeping bags (rentals are available at CFI).

APPLICATIONS AND ADMISSIONS

Contact the registrar's office at CFI for information on application and admission procedures. Contact CFI's Director of Student Programs regarding availability of the field camp for Outdoor Science School groups and to receive a brochure and video on youth programs at CFI.

Financial Aid: Partial and full scholarships are available to educators and guides, and for GeoWhiz Kids and GeoWhiz Adventure day camps. Hostelships are available from Elderhostel, Inc. six months in advance for qualifying participants in Elderhostel programs.

Costs: Tuition for adult courses ranges from $50 to $120 per day. Tuition for the Outdoor Science School ranges from $12 per student for a half day of instruction to approximately $420 per student for an all-inclusive 6-day educational Green River canoe trip. Deposits are required to hold space in a class. Full payment is due upon arrival. For tuition information on specific programs, field camp rental, gear and equipment rental, and other costs, contact CFI at the above address.

FOUR CORNERS SCHOOL OF OUTDOOR EDUCATION
P.O. Box 1029
Monticello, UT 84535
(801) 587-2156: office
(801) 587-2859: basecamp
Fax: (801) 587-2193
Contact: Janet Ross, Director

SAMPLE COURSES

Courses include Archaeology (e.g., Chaco Canyon Archaeology, Mapping Ruins of Ute Tribal Park, Rock Art Adventure on Lake Powell); Cultural Studies (e.g., Journey to Navajoland—An Immersion into Lifeways at Navajo Mountain, Utah, Native Cultures of the Southwest, Southwest Weaving); Photography and Writing (e.g., Reflections on the San Juan—A River Notebook, Desert Vision/Desert Voice—Creative Immersion in Landscape); Natural History (e.g., Stories from Navajo Mountain and Rainbow Bridge, In Pursuit of the Peregrine Falcon—A River Trip); Off the Plateau (e.g., Winter Wildlife and Geology of Yellowstone National Park, Slip Sliding with Otters, Tracking the Great Bears of North America, Wolves of the North Country); and Special Interest (e.g., Wilderness First Aid).

CURRICULUM AND CREDITS

The Four Corners School (FCS), a nonprofit organization located in Monticello, Utah, provides outdoor educational and environmental opportunities within the 160,000-square-mile region known as the Colorado Plateau. Its purpose is to increase participants' awareness and sensitivity to the physical and cultural heritage of this rich and varied environment. The school teaches outdoor skills, natural sciences, and land stewardship by creating a community of individuals who share their interest through informal and relaxed hands-on experience. Graduate or undergraduate college credit is available, but not required, for all programs run by FCS from either Prescott College, Mankato State University, or Fort Lewis College. The number of academic credits, the departments granting the credits, and the costs vary with each institution and program.

THE ENVIRONMENT

The FCS is located in the heart of canyon country on the Colorado Plateau. Depending on where the course takes place, the environment varies from high desert plateau to mountainous region to river terrain. The dry and arid climate can be very hot in the summer and quite cold in the spring and fall.

FACILITIES

FCS uses an old homestead located 19 miles southeast of Monticello, Utah, as its residential basecamp for some programs. Lodging is in the original rustic bunkhouse or you may bring your own tent. There is a shower, and meals are cooked in a communal kitchen by the staff and served in an adjacent dining room. A telephone is also available.

SUPPLIES NEEDED
Each trip necessitates different equipment. Inquire with FCS for specific information.

APPLICATIONS AND ADMISSIONS
Contact the institution for a catalog. To help applicants determine if a specific program is right for them, briefing packets are available for $12 per program. Packets include full program details, travel information, maps, logistics, detailed itineraries, an equipment list, a reading list, and staff. The cost of the briefing packet is deducted from the tuition of the FCS program the participant chooses.

Financial Aid: Scholarships are usually available to teachers and members of the Southern Utah Wilderness Alliance. Contact the above address for an application, information, and deadlines; write after January 1, 1996 (SUWA members) or after February 1, 1996 (teachers).

Costs: FCS provides supplies, staff, fees, group equipment, instruction, food (except optional alcoholic beverages, and soft drinks), lodging (unless otherwise specified), and transportation from program start to end location. Trip prices vary according to the area and other descriptions; please refer to the catalog.

NSTA TOURS
702 Hilltop Road
Salt Lake City, UT 84103
(801) 359-3389
Contact: Ivan Dyreng

SAMPLE TOURS
Tours include Alaska Curise, the Wild West Tour, and Canyon Spectacular Tour.

CURRICULUM AND CREDITS
Credit is available from Brigham Young University in Provo, Utah. Three graduate credits are awarded for each of the above tours.

INSTITUTION
Not applicable.

THE ENVIRONMENT
The national parks, selected monuments, and state parks of the West serve as the classrooms and laboratories.

FACILITIES
For the canyon and Wild West tours the bus is a classroom on wheels. In addition, there is boat and mule transportation as well as hikes on the Colorado River and the Grand Canyon. The Alaska cruise features on-deck instruction by naturalists, and additional instruction can be obtained from television in the cabins.

SUPPLIES NEEDED

Participants should bring notebook, camera, good walking shoes, and a love of adventure.

APPLICATIONS AND ADMISSIONS

Contact the institution at the above address for information on application and admission procedures.

Financial Aid: None available.

Costs: Canyon Tour—13 days, $1,095 per person, double occupancy; Wild West Tour—13 days, $1,175 per person, double occupancy; Alaska Cruise—7 nights, $1,199 per person, plus air fare; Alaska Cruise/Tour—11 days, $2,379 per person, plus air fare.

VERMONT

TRAVEL FOR ACADEMIC GROWTH
Goddard College
Plainfield, VT 05667
(802) 454-7835 or 454-8311/(800) 468-4888 (for application forms)
Fax: (802) 454-8017
Contact: James Galloway

SAMPLE COURSES
Courses include Travel for Academic Growth. Participants may propose an individual academic study plan in the area of their own professional interests.

CURRICULUM AND CREDITS
The Travel for Academic Growth program is an opportunity for participants to earn undergraduate or graduate-level credit while traveling in the United States or overseas. This program allows educators to combine travel with independent study while on any tour or while traveling independently. Participants may earn up to 15 semester hours of graduate credit annually by completing all requirements. Prior approval from the faculty director is necessary before qualifying for more than 6 credits.

The first credit for each enrollment requires seven days of travel study. Subsequent credit hours call for five days each (i.e., 2 hours credit for 12 days, etc.). The credits may be applied to undergraduate programs, in graduate and credential programs, for salary increments, and for professional growth. The decision to accept credits is always within the control of the receiving institutions.

THE INSTITUTION
Goddard College is fully accredited by the New England Association of Schools and Colleges. Educators, university students, or other professionals pursue an academic program of their own choice and design, after consultation with and approval by Goddard's campus-based faculty director. Since participants may enroll for travel study at any time during the year, there is essentially a rolling enrollment that changes daily during the year, as some students complete their studies and others register.

A major strength of this program is that participants are encouraged to create a final product that will be practical in their classrooms and, therefore, be valuable to their students. The two most common projects are the unit of study and a summary paper. Individuals should decide what will work best in their classroom and design a program based on that decision. Other examples of successful projects include a video or slide presentation, the outline for an in-service course, or a workbook or guidebook to local museums and historic sites. Perhaps bits and pieces of knowledge and insight may be added to existing units of study. Some teachers choose the standard 5- or 10-day classroom unit because these slots simply work best for them. Whatever the decision, it should make sense for the participant's educational and professional goals.

Work is judged as either successfully completed at the graduate or undergraduate level, or not completed. Work judged not completed is equivalent to withdrawal without academic penalty. Goddard evaluates by individual learning objectives, not group norms, so no letter grades are issued. Minimum standards for completion, however, are at least the equivalent in norm-referenced systems of "B" for graduate work and "C" for undergraduate work. Contact the faculty director for more information about various options not mentioned here.

THE ENVIRONMENT

Not applicable.

FACILITIES

Not applicable.

SUPPLIES NEEDED

None.

APPLICATIONS AND ADMISSIONS

This program is open to college and university students, classroom teachers, and other educators. The participant develops an academic plan and submits it to the college for approval. Course participants must register before departure and pay in advance for the number of hours they expect to earn. A typed copy of all the required materials must be submitted and accepted before credits are authorized.

Before travel, a student must submit a study plan, detailing the exact nature of the study to be undertaken; included in the plan are the itinerary, a bibliography of books and articles to be read in preparation for travel, learning objectives, and proposed back-home application. While traveling, the student must keep a daily log, including activities, academic applications, and academic materials obtained. Upon completing the travel (within 60 days), the student must submit a reflective evaluation, proof of travel, a copy of the daily log, and either a summary paper (for the undergraduate or nonclassroom educator) or a unit of study (for the classroom teacher).

Depending on the number of credits applied for and the manner of the proposed study, the faculty director may suggest either several registrations or a single study plan encompassing the entire proposed study. Contact the above address for details and advice. It is not necessary to matriculate at Goddard in order to participate in this course.

Financial Aid: None available.

Cost: Tuition is approximately $115 per semester credit hour. There are no other registration or tuition fees. A senior discount is available; for information, contact the above address. Refunds are not given for courses completed in an unsatisfactory manner, but an enrollment may be canceled before departure for a $10 processing charge. Costs are subject to change. Contact the institution at the above address for current rates.

VIRGINIA

MOUNTAIN LAKE BIOLOGICAL STATION
University of Virginia
Gilmer Hall
Charlottesville, VA 22903-2477
(804) 982-5486
Fax: (804) 982-5626
Contact: Dr. Henry Wilbur

SAMPLE COURSES
Courses include Biology Research, Mammalogy, Animal Behavior, Ecological Genetics, Plant Taxonomy Ecology, Molecular Techniques for Population Genetics, Ecology of Fungi, Ornithology, Conservation Biology, and Evolutionary Biology.

CURRICULUM AND CREDITS
Courses at Mountain Lake are part of the summer session of the University of Virginia. Courses may be taken for graduate or undergraduate credit. Students may pursue a master's degree in biology by summer study, a program particularly suitable for teachers in secondary education. For the master's degree in biology students must maintain residence at the station for at least three full summer sessions. A vigorous research program is offered that includes research assistantships for undergraduates.

THE INSTITUTION
The Mountain Lake Biological Station (MLBS) is located in the Allegheny Mountains of southwestern Virginia at an elevation of nearly 4,000 feet. A branch of the University of Virginia established in 1929, the station serves as an inland field station for research and advanced training in field biology.

THE ENVIRONMENT
Many rich and diversified habitats near the station afford excellent opportunities for studies in aquatic and terrestrial field biology. Mountain streams, a large natural lake, mixed deciduous forests, rocky ridges, a sphagnum bog, and stands of red spruce, Canadian hemlock, and white pine are among the habitats located within walking distance of the station.

Adjoining the station property is the Jefferson National Forest, where over 100,000 acres of woodland are available for study. In addition, 10,500 acres adjacent to the station have been set aside as a wilderness area kept entirely in its natural state.

FACILITIES
The main laboratory building is a stone structure containing fully equipped laboratories, classrooms, a library, photographic rooms, computers, an auditorium, and private research rooms. The station also has a fine herbarium and good collections of insects, bird skins, and small mammal skins. A modest wood and metal workshop is also available for use in preparing special equipment. A small laboratory containing an integral efficiency apartment provides an opportunity to carry out research at MLBS throughout

the entire year. A new winterized facility has a community kitchen and dining room, three two-room apartments, and eight single rooms.

Dormitory rooms for men and women, and cottages for families are available. Meals are served in the common dining room. Housekeeping facilities are not available in the summer and cooking is not allowed in the dormitories. Laundry facilities are available at the station.

SUPPLIES NEEDED

Students are responsible for supplying their own blankets, bed linen, towels, and toilet articles. The chilly nights require warm covering. It is advisable to bring two or three blankets.

Essential personal equipment includes outdoor clothing, rainwear, and a flashlight. Good hiking boots are recommended for field trips in the mountains. Tennis shoes or hip boots are the best type of footwear for aquatic work. Individual courses may require a hand lens, field glasses, dissecting kits, and pocket field guides. Some basic supplies may be purchased at the supply store. Some overnight trips may be taken, in which case a sleeping bag is useful.

APPLICATIONS AND ADMISSIONS

Admission is open to men and women of good standing who have a minimum of eight semester hours of college credit in biology. To apply, students should submit the application accompanying the bulletin. An advance registration fee of $50 is required. Applicants not previously enrolled at the station must submit full official transcripts. Students from other universities who plan to transfer credit course study at Mountain Lake should secure approval in advance from their home institutions.

Financial Aid: Numerous work scholarships are available which provide for room and board. Duties involve waiting on tables, cleaning the laboratory, and assisting with the opening and closing of the station.

The Walton Scholarship—$750 or $1,000—is awarded competitively to students demonstrating high academic qualifications and financial need. Other scholarships that provide financial assistance are available .

The Pratt Fellowships provide support of up to $2,000 for pre- and postdoctoral research at Mountain Lake.

Applications for awards should be sent to the Director, Mountain Lake Biological Station, at the address above.

Costs: Approximate costs are listed below:

	Virginia students	Out-of-state students
Tuition Fee (per credit hour)	$128	$410
Lab & Field Trip Fee (per course)	$67	$67
Rent per term (5 weeks)	$93	$93
Board per term (5 weeks)	$390	$390
Group insurance	$9	$9

NATIONAL SCIENCE TEACHERS ASSOCIATION/ UPJOHN "SCIENCE GRASP" PROGRAM
1840 Wilson Boulevard
Arlington, VA 22201-3000
(703) 243-7100
Fax: (703) 243-7177
Contact: Eric Crossley or Monica Snipes

SAMPLE PROGRAMS

Programs include Science Grasp!—It's Elementary, a hands-on science education summer workshop for elementary teachers (sponsored by Upjohn and the National Science Teachers Association).

CURRICULUM AND CREDITS

The National Science Teachers Association (NSTA) and the Upjohn Company invite elementary teachers grades K–5 to apply for the annual Science Grasp program. Teachers should have a strong desire to teach science and be committed to the profession of teaching and willing to conduct an in-service activity based upon what they learn in the Science Grasp program for their colleagues.

Science Grasp consists of several elements designed to foster the teaching of hands-on science in the elementary grades. The program enhances participants' backgrounds in science and their awareness of hands-on science techniques. Participants may elect to receive continuing education credits or graduate credits for the program.

THE INSTITUTION

Not applicable.

THE ENVIRONMENT

The program begins with an intensive 10-day summer workshop at Kalamazoo College and the Kalamazoo Area Mathematics and Science Center in Kalamazoo, Michigan. Workshop presenters, experts, and practitioners in elementary hands-on science education demonstrate creative applications of science guaranteed to excite students and to involve them in the learning process. The workshop ends with a practice session in which participants conduct a hands-on science activity with a group of local elementary students. The activity is based on concepts and demonstrations learned during the week.

FACILITIES

Not applicable.

SUPPLIES NEEDED

None.

APPLICATIONS AND ADMISSIONS

Contact the institution at the above address for information on application and admission procedures.

Financial Aid: The Upjohn Company provides a grant to each participant and his/her school to help purchase the supplies necessary for hands-on science activities.

Costs: The Upjohn Company pays all travel and lodging expenses for participants in the summer session.

WASHINGTON

ARCTIC ODYSSEYS
2000 McGilvra Boulevard East
Seattle, WA 98112
(206) 325-1977
Fax: (206) 726-8488
Contact: Robin Duberow, President

SAMPLE TOURS AND EXPEDITIONS
Tours and expeditions include Dog Sledding, North Pole and Greenland, Polar Bears in Wager Bay, Discover the Worlds of the High Arctic, Baffin Island Summer Wildlife & Culture, Siberia/Lena River, and the Russian Far East.

CURRICULUM AND CREDITS
Arctic Odysseys (AO) are real adventures in the northernmost parts of the world that have a special allure even to the most seasoned traveler. The Arctic displays an awesome vastness and breathtaking beauty to those who visit and experience the land's "other world" mystique. Legends and solitude wrap every part of the rolling tundra, frozen seas, soaring peaks, and sparkling glaciers.

Credit for independent or travel study may be obtained through the participant's college or university. Consult your academic advisor for the specific requirements of your individual college or university.

THE INSTITUTION
AO began in 1976 by creating exciting tour alternatives to the commonplace, and features such diverse alternatives as dog sledding in the Yukon and a working cattle ranch in Wyoming. With over 17 years experience, AO pioneered the high Arctic as a viable destination for formal tours. Over the years, the company's primary mission has been to maintain its standards of quality in Arctic regions. (Through an affiliate, itineraries are also offered to Antarctica as well.) This experience is the single most critical element in achieving success, if not learning basic safety in Arctic travel. AO's trip leaders are recognized authorities in their respective areas of interest, and because of the experienced leadership and unique destinations, the odysseys offered appeal to affinity group interests in wildlife, ornithology, photography, and Native cultures.

THE ENVIRONMENT
Environments vary with the tour destinations.

FACILITIES
AO's facilities include the natural and cultural environments and the modes of travel by which participants visit them, such as by DeHaviland Twin Otter airplane (the workhorse of the Arctic), dog sled, or small boats. The small group format affords intimate and unique experiences not available from high-volume operators. Going on its 18th year of operation, AO has made a point never to be intrusive of either the host culture's privacy or the natural environment. The only influence extant upon a group's departure has been a benign one, and the fact that AO participants are so thoroughly

briefed prior to their arrival in the Arctic, they have gained a sensitivity to the nuances of behavior and are welcomed as friends by the local hosts.

SUPPLIES NEEDED

Specialized equipment or clothing are typically not required of AO participants. A weight limit of 30 pounds, however, is typically required, and winter (sub-zero) clothing is necessary on spring odysseys. Dog sled participants are provided with the traditional caribou clothing on loan. Each participant is provided with orientation materials and an equipment list. Age is not as much of a factor as good health and a flexible attitude which becomes essential when coping with such variables as weather changes and the elements.

APPLICATIONS AND ADMISSIONS

Tour applications may be obtained directly through AO at the above address. All applicants must complete a registration agreement and standard liability release. A telephone interview is required of each applicant. AO provides additional information on specific trips as necessary, including background study material, reading lists, and trip leader résumés.

Financial Aid: None available.

Costs: Approximate tour and expedition costs include—Dog Sledding ($3,080–$3,600); North Pole(s) and Greenland ($11,500); Polar Bears in Wager Bay ($4,450); Discover the Worlds of the High Arctic ($4,980); Baffin Island Summer Wildlife and Cultural ($3,080–$3,600); the Russian Far East and Siberia ($4,800).

JOSEPH VAN OS PHOTO SAFARIS
P.O. Box 655
Vashon, WA 98070
(206) 463-5383
Fax: (206) 463-5484

and

TRAVELWILD INTERNATIONAL
(formerly DBA as Joseph Van Os Nature Tours)
P.O. Box 1637
Vashon, WA 98070
(800) 368-0077
Fax: (206) 463-5484
Contact: Mary Toth

SAMPLE EXPEDITIONS

Nature and photo expeditions are offered to exotic places such as Kenya/East Africa/Great Rift; Churchill, Manitoba, for the Polar Bear gathering on Hudson Bay; Namibia, the Namib Desert and Etosha National Park; Botswana; Australia; Michoacan, Mexico; North Pole expedition aboard a Russian Icebreaker; and Beijing to Hanoi train tours.

In the United States, photo workshops and tours are offered to the following National Parks: Yellowstone, Acadia, Washington's Olympic, Alaska's Katmai and Denali National Parks, California's Joshua Tree National Park, and Utah's Capitol Reef.

CURRICULUM AND CREDITS

Trips embrace a holistic approach to nature, discussing everything from mammals and birds to plate tectonics and the continuing impact of humans on the landscape. Credit may be available through independent or travel study.

THE INSTITUTION

For 15 years, Joseph Van Os Tours has been an outstanding operator of worldwide natural history, wildlife, and photo travel tours. Among the pioneers of many exceptional nature travel destinations, they maintain an ongoing commitment to discover new ways of seeing familiar places by seeking out fresh and exciting locations. Joseph Van Os Photo Safaris and TravelWild International have skilled leaders who offer a wealth of naturalist information. From tropical rainforest to frozen tundra, African savanna to the world's living deserts, they sweat the details of a trip while the participant stays in comfortable accommodations and travels with a congenial group of kindred spirits.

THE ENVIRONMENT

Photo Safaris travel to some of the world's finest wildlife and scenic locations with the main purpose of making great photographs. They design their photo safaris to be near many wildlife and natural spectacles and to get participants to the right places at the right time for photography. Since participants are photographing right alongside some of America's top outdoor photographers, expert help is always nearby for advice on how to take the best picture possible. Tours are conducted with the least amount of disturbance to the natural environment.

FACILITIES

Most photo safaris are lodged in comfortable hotels or tented camps. For a more intensive hands-on photo technique learning experience, they recommend participants begin their photo travels with a photography workshop.

SUPPLIES NEEDED

Practical information sheets are available for each tour. Photo tours require a working knowledge of a 35mm camera with long-range photo lenses and macro lenses.

Financial Aid: None available.

Costs: Advanced Photo Workshop including instruction and van transportation is $675. Photo and TravelWild Tours range in cost from approximately $1,400 to $15,000 (North Pole).

NORTHWEST TRAVEL AND STUDY
6034 Butterball Cove NE
Olympia, WA 98506
(206) 456-1854
Contact: Susan Wertz

SAMPLE COURSES AND PROGRAMS
Courses and programs have been to the Virgin Islands, Andros Island in the Bahamas, Cabo San Lucas in Baja, the island of Kauai in Hawaii, and the Bay Islands of Honduras and Belize.

CURRICULUM AND CREDITS
Credit offered through Antioch University in Seattle. Continuing education and graduate credit are offered at upper course levels. A maximum of 12 credits can be earned during a 2-week trip. Course subjects include tropical reef ecology, rainforest biology, or desert ecology. These are primarily ecotourism adventures with a strong academic component. Each summer, at least one course is offered in the tropics.

THE INSTITUTION
Northwest Travel and Study, a small corporation owned and staffed by teachers, offers courses associated with field studies in natural history. The institution, environment, and facilities are on location.

THE ENVIRONMENT
The environment varies with the particular program.

FACILITIES
Facilities range from established field stations to small hostels or luxury condos and dive resorts.

SUPPLIES NEEDED
Necessary supplies vary depending on the particular trip. An extensive list is provided upon registration.

APPLICATIONS AND ADMISSIONS
Information and applications are sent upon request. A complete 200-page book of information about the field sites, plus videos and other references are sent prior to the trip.

Financial Aid: None available.

Costs: A 13-day trip to the rainforests, reefs, and ruins of Belize costs approximately $1,100.

OLYMPIC PARK INSTITUTE
111 Barnes Point Road
Port Angeles, WA 98363
(206) 928-3720
Fax: (206) 928-3046
Contact: Program Director of Field Seminars

SAMPLE PROGRAMS AND COURSES

Programs offered include Olympic field seminars, general interest classes, continuing education courses for credit, and weekend classes offered for adults and families during the spring, summer, and fall.

Course offerings include: Tracking in the Olympics, Fly Fishing/Aquatic Ecology of the Olympics, Seabirds by Kayak, Geology of Olympic National Park, Birds of the Olympics, Illustrating the Natural World, Marine Mammals of the Puget Sound, Photographing the Olympic Landscape, Intertidal Life of the Olympics, Mountain Flowers and High Country Ecology, Glacial Legacy, Wild Olympic Salmon, and Archeology of the Olympic Peninsula.

CURRICULUM AND CREDITS

Graduate-level academic credit is offered at Western Washington University, Bellingham, Washington. Many field seminar classes are offered for 1 credit. Olympic Park Institute (OPI) is an authorized provider of teacher Continuing Education Units (CEUs), by the Office of the Superintendent of Public Instruction, Olympia, Washington.

THE INSTITUTION

OPI is a private, nonprofit educational organization whose mission is to inspire environmental stewardship through education. Incorporated in the state of Washington in 1987, the institute established its residential campus at Rosemary Inn on Lake Crescent through a cooperative agreement with the National Park Service. The institute provides 85,000 hours of programming on an annual basis, representing about 45% of the interpretive services in Olympic National Park. OPI is the newest campus of Yosemite National Institutes, a nationally recognized environmental education organization that has been in operation since 1971 and is based in Yosemite National Park and Golden Gate National Recreation Area.

THE ENVIRONMENT

OPI programs emphasize direct observation experiences in the majestic setting of the Olympic Peninsula. Participants have access to wilderness, ecological preserves, and public and private managed lands, such as sub-alpine and alpine communities, a classic old-growth rainforest, coastal tidepools and beaches, tree farms and experimental forests, local Native American cultures, and state and federal forests.

Five-day, five-night residential field science curriculum programs for students and teachers (K–12) introduce the natural and human systems of the Olympics. Participants directly observe temperate old-growth rainforest, alpine, and intertidal/coastal habitats as they begin to understand the ecology of these communities and the continuum of natural resource management strategies in this area.

Elderhostel, for people 60 years and older, extends for a 25-week period offering 5-day, 5-night courses. It offers field walks, workshops, and lecture/facilitated discussion about the natural and cultural history of the region, the natural resource issues related to its protection, its sustainable development, and adaptive management.

Week-long teacher-training and educational conferences discuss environmental education and natural resource management.

FACILITIES

The institute's one-million-dollar campus lies on Lake Crescent, Olympic National Park, and includes a science lab for vertebrate and plant collection, lab, and library and field equipment. Rosemary Inn, a historic building on the National Registry of Historic Sites, is located three hours from Seattle. The institute facilities offer outstanding meals and an informal, friendly atmosphere in which to learn. One hundred participants can be housed in the new section of simple cabins with central bathhouses.

SUPPLIES NEEDED

Equipment lists and bibliographies are provided in preclass registration packets for each course. Participants are generally responsible for their own personal gear, including a sleeping bag, a day pack, and toiletries.

APPLICATIONS AND ADMISSIONS

Enrollment is available based on a space-available reservation system. A course catalog for the Olympic Field Seminar program is available every March. Reservations made six months to a year in advance for residential field science programs are recommended. Registration for Elderhostel programs at Olympic Park Institute can be made by calling (617) 426-8056.

Financial Aid: Partial scholarships are available for needy students. Contact the institute office.

Costs: Field seminars are approximately $50 per person for 1-day classes and $170 per person for weekend classes, Friday through Sunday afternoon. Prices include instruction, meals, and lodging.

The residential field science programs (K–12) student cost is approximately $171 per person for 5-day, 4-night programs and $111 per person for a 3-day, 2-night program. Price includes instruction, meals, evening programs, and overnight lodging (field trip transportation is additional). Conference service fees, $41 per person for three meals and overnight lodging (linens and conference room additional); Elderhostel, $330 per person for the 5-day, 5-night programs. Price also includes instruction, field trip transportation, and all meals.

THOMAS B. CROWLEY LABORATORY
Seattle Pacific University
P.O. Box 1273
Blakely Island, WA 98222
(206) 375-6721
Fax: (206) 281-2882
Contact: Dr. Ross F. Shaw, Director

SAMPLE COURSES

Courses include Aquatic Ecology, Marine Invertebrate Zoology, Marine Plants of Puget Sound, Independent Study in Biology, Forest Ecology, and Ecomorphology.

CURRICULUM AND CREDITS

Seattle Pacific University and Seattle University jointly sponsor the Thomas B. Crowley Laboratory program. The field study classes, designed for undergraduate students and educators, are taught by professors of both institutions. The classes are self-contained, 11-day units offered during June and July, of which students can take one unit or all three. Qualified students may also sign up for a maximum of 5 credits of independent study under the guidance of summer faculty. Students may register for credit at either university.

THE INSTITUTION

The Thomas B. Crowley Laboratory is located on Blakely Island, one of the San Juan Islands in northern Puget Sound, Washington. The field station is located on the shore of Spencer Lake near the center of the island.

THE ENVIRONMENT

Blakely Island and the surrounding rich, intertidal marine waters provide a diverse environmental setting in which to study. Two freshwater lakes contain representative fish, invertebrates, and plant communities. Island vegetation reflects the plant communities of northern coastal areas with grassland, marshes, and second-growth timberland. The island is home to blacktail deer, raccoons, river otters, bats, and various small mammals. Several families of bald eagles nest on the island each year. A variety of birds are permanent residents, while others are spring and fall migrants. Reptiles and amphibians typical of the Pacific coast region inhabit the island.

FACILITIES

The physical plant includes a dormitory that houses 20 students with apartments for the residential director and the teaching faculty, a dining hall/library classroom building that can accommodate up to 24 students and staff, and a dive shop building equipped with an air compressor for scuba, showers, and a dressing room. Small boats are available for use on the lake, as well as a 17-foot "whaler" for use on Puget Sound. The laboratory is equipped for work in freshwater and marine biology environments.

SUPPLIES NEEDED

Participants are encouraged to bring warm clothing, waders, and scuba gear (if certified).

APPLICATIONS AND ADMISSIONS

Contact the above address and phone number for information on application and admission procedures.

Financial Aid: Some work-study grants are available.

Costs: Tuition per class is approximatley $750. Room, board, and transportation to the island from Anacortes are included for an extra $350 per class.

WASHINGTON, D.C.

NASA
NASA Headquarters
Elementary and Secondary Branch
Education Division
Mail Code FEE
Washington, D.C. 20546-0001
(202) 358-1518
Fax: (202) 358-3048
Contact: Dr. Eddie Anderson

SAMPLE PROGRAMS AND WORKSHOPS
Programs and workshops include NASA Education Workshop for Math, Science, Technology Teachers (NEWMAST); NASA Education Workshops for Elementary School Teachers (NEWEST); Teacher Workshops on Astronomy, Aeronautics, Life in Space, Principles of Rocketry, Earth Science, and Remote Sensing; Urban Community Enrichment Program—Science and Math; and Technology Summer Workshops for Teachers in the Norfolk-Hampton, Virginia, area.

CURRICULUM AND CREDITS
NEWMAST and NEWEST are administered by NASA in cooperation with the National Science Teachers Association, the National Council of Teachers of Mathematics, and the International Technology Education Association. NEWMAST makes awards to mathematics, science, and technology teachers in grades 7–12 with a 2-week, expense-paid workshop at a NASA field center each year. NEWEST, modeled after NEWMAST, is for elementary school teachers (grades K–6) in all disciplines.

Selected teachers are awarded a 2-week, expense-paid workshop at a NASA field center, with each center hosting about 25 Aerospace Education Services Program (AESP) specialists who conduct workshops for teachers each summer at NASA field centers, elementary and secondary schools, and on college campuses. Workshops cover astronomy aeronautics, life in space, principles of rocketry, Earth sciences and remote sensing.

A typical workshop includes how-to and hands-on activities to help teachers incorporate what they learned into classroom activities and programs to supplement existing curricula. Credit may be available through independent or travel study.

THE INSTITUTION
Instruction is given by NASA scientists, engineers, technicians, and aerospace specialists.

THE ENVIRONMENT
Workshops are conducted at U.S. Government laboratories.

FACILITIES
Facilities consist of NASA field centers. Housing is available in nearby hotels.

SUPPLIES NEEDED
None. NASA supplies all necessary materials.

APPLICATIONS AND ADMISSIONS
Contact the nearest NASA field center for application materials.

Financial Aid: None available.

Costs: No specific costs exist for these programs.

NATIONAL WILDLIFE FEDERATION EXPEDITIONS
National Wildlife Federation
1400 16th Street, N.W.
Washington, D.C. 20036-2266
(800) 606-9563
Fax: (603) 445-2289
Contact: Staff

SAMPLE PROGRAMS AND EXPEDITIONS
Programs and expeditions include the Amazon Rainforest; Classic Kenya Safari; the Wildlife of Borneo; Reefs, Rainforests, and Ruins of Belize; and a Grand Safari to Botswana and Zimbabwe. Various shipboard expeditions include Amazon by Riverboat, Alaska Odyssey, High Canadian Arctic, Antarctica and the Falkland Islands, Polynesia, and the Galapagos Islands.

CURRICULUM AND CREDITS
National Wildlife Federation Expeditions (NWFE) are guided by experienced naturalists with several trips led by world-famous field and marine biologists. Each expedition is designed to delight, fascinate, and educate participants. Credit is available through independent or travel study.

THE INSTITUTION
For over 56 years, the National Wildlife Federation (NWF) has been recognized as one of the world's largest and most active private nonprofit conservation education organizations. Founded in 1936 with the primary objective of promoting the conservation and sustainable use of natural resources through education programs, publications, research activities, cooperation with legislators, government agencies, and private groups, NWF publishes four award-winning magazines: *National Wildlife, International Wildlife, Ranger Rick,* and *Your Big Backyard.*

THE ENVIRONMENT
NWF Expeditions are conducted in various ecosystems and habitats from exotic rainforests to polar glaciers. Contact the institution at the above address for information on a specific destination.

FACILITIES
A variety of facilities are used for each expedition from small ships to tented safaris. NWFE offers a level of comfort to fit everyone's travel needs.

SUPPLIES NEEDED

Necessary supplies vary based on the destination. Contact the institution at the above address for details.

APPLICATIONS AND ADMISSIONS

NWFE provides itineraries and reservation forms for any of their destinations upon request.

Financial Aid: None available.

Costs: Expedition costs range from $2,000 to $6,000 depending on the destination. Call or write NWFE for more information. Prices and destinations are subject to change.

SCIENCE AND ENGINEERING RESEARCH SEMESTER
U.S. Department of Energy
Office of Energy Research
P.O. Box 23575
Washington, D.C. 20026-3575
(202) 488-2426 or (202) 586-4570
Fax: (202) 488-2444
Contact: Donna Procop

SAMPLE PROGRAMS

Science and Engineering Research Semester (SERS) programs are offered to undergraduate students who are assigned to one of the following seven national research laboratories operated by the U.S. Department of Energy: Argonne National Laboratory near Chicago, Illinois; Brookhaven National Laboratory on Long Island, New York; Lawrence Berkeley Laboratory in Berkeley, California; Los Alamos National Laboratory in Los Alamos, New Mexico; Oak Ridge National Laboratory in Oak Ridge, Tennessee; Pacific Northwest Laboratory in Richland, Washington; and Lawrence Livermore National Laboratory in Livermore, California.

CURRICULUM AND CREDITS

SERS promotes training in science and engineering research and allows access to facilities and state-of-the-art equipment and instrumentation unavailable on most campuses. It allows participation in an ongoing research project at the cutting edge of science and provides training and experience in the operation of sophisticated equipment. SERS helps students focus on a particular field by integrating hands-on laboratory research within the student's chosen area of study. The experience also provides valuable contact with the scientific research community. Student appointments are normally for one academic term. An extension of appointments through the summer is encouraged, however, and participants are encouraged to arrange for academic credit by their home institutions for the research performed during the appointment period.

THE INSTITUTION

Contact SERS at the above address for a listing of the seven participating U.S. Department of Energy laboratories used for the SERS program.

THE ENVIRONMENT
The environment is dependent upon the particular laboratory location (see above).

FACILITIES
Contact the individual laboratory for information on facilities.

SUPPLIES NEEDED
Contact the individual laboratory for information on necessary supplies.

APPLICATIONS AND ADMISSIONS
Contact SERS at the above address for a program description booklet which contains an application form. Approximately 400 vacancies become available every year (this number varies depending on the laboratory). Application deadlines are March 15 for the fall semester and October 20 for the spring semester.

Financial Aid: A stipend of approximately $225 a week is provided, in addition to complimentary housing and round-trip transportation to the laboratory.

Costs: Tuition and fees are levied for credit by the home institution and are the responsibility of the student.

SMITHSONIAN STUDY TOURS AND SEMINARS
Smithsonian National Associate Program
Smithsonian Institution
1100 Jefferson Drive, S.W.
Room 3045, MRC 702
Washington, D.C. 20560
(202) 357-4700
Fax: (202) 633-9250
Contact: Amy Kotkin Warner, Program Manager

SAMPLE TOURS AND SEMINARS
Tours and seminars include Birds of the Chesapeake Bay, Everglades—River of Grass, Grand Canyon Adventure, Chinese Art Seminar, The Legacy of Florence, Folk Art and Celebrations of Mexico, Alpine Snow Trains, Southwestern Culture and Cuisine, British Isles Cruise, and Hidden France Countryside.

CURRICULUM AND CREDITS
The goal of Smithsonian Study Tours and Seminars (SSTS) is to present short courses that mirror the interests and concerns of the Smithsonian Institution. Domestic seminars highlight a broad range of topics that relate to permanent collections and special exhibitions at Smithsonian museums. All seminars are designed with an emphasis on classroom experience of the highest quality, enhanced by tours and field trips to related sites.

More than 300 study tours and seminars are offered each year. Smithsonian Seminars are unlike any other educational experience, offering the opportunity to add significantly to one's knowledge of a favorite subject (be it in the arts, humanities, or sciences). SSTS makes the most remarkable array of Smithsonian resources directly available to participants. Credit may be available through independent or travel study.

THE INSTITUTION
SSTS is operated by the Smithsonian Associates, a division of the Smithsonian Institution.

THE ENVIRONMENT
Each study tour and seminar visits a particular region. Contact the institution for specific information and brochures.

FACILITIES
Moderately priced accommodations at well-located hotels are available for all seminars. These accommodations, however, are usually optional. Most seminar fees are available with and without hotel accomodations.

Three to six days of lectures, tours, and field trips are provided with transportation between the designated hotel and seminar site specified in the catalog. The faculty of experts are chosen for their knowledge and classroom experience, and a Smithsonian representative accompanies each seminar.

SUPPLIES NEEDED
Information is provided at time of reservation. Interested participants should consult SSTS catalog.

APPLICATIONS AND ADMISSIONS
Contact the institution at the above address for information on application and admission procedures.

Financial Aid: None available.

Costs: Interested applicants should contact the institution at the above address for cost information on the seminars and study tours.

WISCONSIN

MILWAUKEE FIELD STATION
University of Wisconsin–Milwaukee
3095 Blue Goose Road
Saukville, WI 53080
(414) 675-6844
Fax: (414) 675-6844
Contact: Dr. Millicent S. Ficken

SAMPLE COURSES
Courses include Wetland Delineation, Butterfly Identification and Ecology, and Bird Banding.

CURRICULUM AND CREDITS
No formal credit courses are offered, but numerous 1- and 2-day workshops are given each summer on a variety of topics. The station includes a diverse group of high-quality habitats available year-round for research and special courses.

THE INSTITUTION
The field station of the University of Wisconsin–Milwaukee (UWM) invites researchers and instructors to use its research and educational facilities in Saukville in southeastern Wisconsin (Ozaukee County). The station is located 30 miles north of Milwaukee, about 45 minutes from downtown, and 90 minutes from Madison. The university owns 300 acres of fields, upland forests, and wetland habitats. These areas are adjacent to the 1,500-acre Cedarburg Bog Natural Area managed by the Department of Natural Resources, which is open to research and classroom use.

THE ENVIRONMENT
Cedarburg Bog is the largest undisturbed bog in southern Wisconsin, containing 2,000 acres of deep and shallow bog lakes, submergent and emergent aquatic communities, a small stream, cattail stands, sedge communities, shrub carrs, swamp hardwoods, and large expanses of cedar-tamarack swamp forest. Access into the heart of the bog is provided by a boardwalk.

Open-field habitats maintained in various stages of succession, including almost 20 acres still being cropped, are available for experimental research. The field station has an undisturbed upland forest of about 50 acres, dominated by beech, maple, ash, basswood, and hickory trees. Old-growth beech-maple forests are rare in southeastern Wisconsin.

The uniqueness of the bog and upland forest areas have been included as part of the Wisconsin Scientific Area System, and both are registered as National Natural Landmarks by the Department of Interior. The Cedarburg Bog Scientific Area is also an experimental ecological reserve and part of the National Experimental Ecological Reserve Network.

FACILITIES
Laboratory and teaching facilities as well as overnight accommodations are located within these natural areas. The laboratory building houses a small library, meeting room, offices, and three laboratories. A well-equipped shop is located in the service building. A

fully equipped sound lab with a Kay Sonagraph, tape recorders and microphones, a portable video recorder, cameras, and a night-vision scope are provided for studies of animal behavior. The station has equipment for trapping and marking animals, and maintains a complete weather station with meteorological equipment.

A small greenhouse and gardens are maintained for experimental work, and farm and cultivating machinery are available. The field station herbarium contains most of the plants found in the area and species lists have been prepared for plants and vertebrates. Computer services can be obtained via a telephone hookup to the UWM campus computer center. For soils and hydrologic work, a permanent lysimeter pit in the beech-maple woods exists, as well as a system of peizometers running from the upland into the bog and a gaging station on the bog outlet.

The old farmhouse accommodates about 15 visiting investigators and students. The station does not serve meals but provides kitchen space where visitors can store food and prepare meals.

SUPPLIES NEEDED

Supplies for specific studies are to be provided by the investigator.

APPLICATIONS AND ADMISSIONS

For information on application and admission procedures, contact Dr. Millicent S. Ficken at the above address.

Financial Aid: None available.

Costs: The field station currently does not impose charges for its workshops.

INSTITUTE FOR CHEMICAL EDUCATION
University of Wisconsin–Madison
Department of Chemistry
1101 University Avenue
Madison, WI 53706-1396
(608) 262-3033
Fax: (608) 262-0381
Contact: Staff

SAMPLE WORKSHOPS

Summer workshops are offered at eight different universities: Catholic University of America (Washington, D.C.), Miami University (Oxford, Ohio), Mount San Antonio College (Walnut, California), Sacred Heart University (Fairfield, Connecticut), the University of Arizona (Tucson), the University of California (Berkeley), the University of Northern Colorado (Greeley), and the University of Wisconsin (Madison).

CURRICULUM AND CREDITS

Institute for Chemical Education (ICE) believes that attaining scientific literacy, a basic understanding of scientific principles and methods, is fundamental to the education of any student. During their summer workshops, teachers are assisted in overcoming some of the common obstacles faced in the effort to deliver first-rate science education. All workshops are geared toward helping teachers use more hands-on, interactive activities in their classrooms and laboratories. Workshop participants are treated as students by the hosting institution and may have the option of earning graduate credits.

THE INSTITUTION

ICE is a nationally recognized leader in science education devoted to the challenge of helping science teachers at all levels, from elementary to college, to improve and strengthen their teaching skills. More than 2,700 teachers have participated in ICE workshops over the past 12 summers. For more information about the individual college campuses, refer to a college directory or other reference.

THE ENVIRONMENT

Not applicable.

FACILITIES

Some programs are residential (Wisconsin and Colorado). Participants live in student dorms and use the chemistry department's classrooms and student laboratories. All chemistry and computer facilities are available to the workshop programs.

SUPPLIES NEEDED

No special supplies are required.

APPLICATIONS AND ADMISSIONS

Application forms for summer workshops are available in January. Contact ICE to receive one. Application deadlines are usually the first week in March.

Financial Aid: The ICE workshops are funded by the National Science Foundation and other similar organizations. ICE covers most of the cost of offering and attending the summer workshops. They ask that workshop participants raise supplemental funding of $100 a week from local sources such as school systems, local businesses, industry, or civic and professional organizations. ICE provides whatever assistance they can to raise local funds.

Costs: ICE will pay instructional costs, fees for academic credit through the host university, room and board, round-trip travel expenses to the ICE center for one person up to $250, and a stipend of approximately $300 per week. Availability of local funds has no bearing on acceptance to or participation in the program.

PIGEON LAKE FIELD STATION
University of Wisconsin–River Falls
River Falls, WI 54022
(715) 425-3256
Fax: (715) 425-0624
Contact: Barbara Audley, Director

SAMPLE COURSES

Courses include Aquatic Entomology, Ichthyology, Ornithology, Aquatic Ecology, Environmental Microbiology Workshop, Biology and Illustration, Environmental Ethics, Environmental Conservation, Field Studies in Northwestern Wisconsin Geology, Forest Climatology, and Applied Urban and Environmental Geography. Additional courses are offered in Business Administration, Education, Philosophy, Recreation, Physical Education, and Art.

CURRICULUM AND CREDITS

Because of its rural location and wooded setting, the Pigeon Lake Field Station (PLFS) has a unique academic atmosphere that is impossible to duplicate in a classroom setting. Consequently, the courses offered at the field station must be carefully selected; not every college course is suitable. Independent study is offered in several sessions. Normally, a student desiring independent study must make prior arrangements with the program director and instructor before registering.

Resident credits may be earned for successful work in system-sponsored courses at Pigeon Lake at any of the member campuses of the university system. The application of these credits toward a major for a degree program is governed by the campus at which a student seeks a degree. Students are urged to confer with their campus advisors concerning the acceptability of specified courses for satisfying degree requirements. One class constitutes a normal course load.

THE INSTITUTION

PLFS is located in Wisconsin's northwoods, 30 miles from the shore of Lake Superior, 30 miles north of the resort town of Hayward, and 6 miles east and south of the twin port cities of Superior, Wisconsin, and Duluth, Minnesota. The nearest village is Drummond, which is 4 miles to the east of Pigeon Lake on Highway 63.

Sponsored by the University of Wisconsin System, PLFS's summer session is a joint enterprise of 14 campuses of the system.

THE ENVIRONMENT

PLFS is located on the north shore of beautiful Pigeon Lake in the heart of the Chequamegon National Forest.

FACILITIES

Six well-equipped laboratories provide excellent instructional facilities during times when classes are not in session. Sixteen cabins are provided for student housing, with each cabin accommodating up to eight students. Students are given their cabin assignment upon arrival at the station. Facilities are rustic but heated, well lighted, and comfortable. Four bathhouses provide excellent shower facilities. Students eat family-style in a dining hall and are expected to reside and have their meals at the field station. It is the desire of the system to provide well-planned, balanced meals prepared by experienced cooks and served at a minimum cost to all students.

While the academic program has complete priority, there are recreational opportunities for such activities as swimming, volleyball, basketball, badminton, boating, horseshoe pitching, fishing, canoeing, and nature photography. Other features include evening movies, a TV, and indoor games in the recreation lodge. Expenses are covered by the activity fee.

SUPPLIES NEEDED

Neccessary supplies include informal clothing, beach wear, rain gear, warm clothing for cool evenings, sheets and pillowcases (pillows and blankets are provided), a flashlight, dissecting kit, and a study or desklamp. Course texts and other educational materials are available at the field station. Domestic pets are *not* allowed on the station grounds.

APPLICATIONS AND ADMISSIONS

Contact the institution at the above address for information on application and admission procedures.

Financial Aid: Financial assistance is handled on the same basis as on individual campuses. Students needing financial assistance should inquire or apply at their campus financial aid office.

Costs: A $70 nonrefundable deposit is due with the applicant's completed application form. Make checks payable to: University of Wisconsin–River Falls. Full payment of tuition, room, and board may be paid early to complete registration, but no later than two weeks prior to the participant's arrival at Pigeon Lake.

Some classes require a separate materials lab fee. Approximate course costs are listed below.

	Undergraduate	Graduate
Wisconsin Resident	$76 per credit	$131 per credit
Nonresident	$263 per credit	$428 per credit
Minnesota Reciprocity	$89 per credit	$132 per credit

Room and board costs are preset as a package based on the length of the course. Room for registered students is approximately $6 per day, and meals are an average of $13/day (for a 3-meal day). The activity fee is $1 per credit.

TREEHAVEN
University of Wisconsin–Stevens Point
2540 Pickerel Creek Road
Tomahawk, WI 54487
(715) 453-4106
Fax: (715) 453-4106
Computer modem/Fax: (715) 453-8616
Contact: June Everson, Office Manager and Registrar;
Dr. Corky McReynolds, Director; Bob Dall, Program Coordinator;
Anne Wilfahrt, Environmental Director

SAMPLE COURSES AND WORKSHOPS

Courses and workshops include Study of Wolves, Citizen Action in Environmental Education, and Facilitation Skills for Environmental Education. Some Elderhostel programs include Environmental Education Teaching Strategies, Leadership Development in Natural Resources, Snow Ecology and Winter Survival, Renewable Energy Workshop, Grand Weekend (grandparent-child nature study retreat), Family Nature Studies (summer naturalist programs), Voyageur Canoe Trips (in cooperation with Cleveland Metroparks), Outdoor Dinner and Concerts, and the Autumn Moon Festival.

CURRICULUM AND CREDITS

Many courses and workshops offer optional college credit. Natural Resources, University of Wisconsin–Stevens Point classes are for credit only. Treehaven is designed to be the hub of the College of Natural Resources summer session. During this time, majors in the College of Natural Resources attend one of two 6-week sessions, participating in field-oriented courses in wildlife, forestry, soils, and aquatics. In the autumn, winter, and spring, Treehaven hosts an array of public workshops, many of which offer optional college credit. Furthermore, both undergraduate and graduate courses for the College of Natural Resources are taught at Treehaven throughout the year, such as the Leadership Development Series for Natural Resources. In addition to workshops with available credit and credit courses, Treehaven serves as an interactive television site linked to the university system as well as local community colleges.

THE INSTITUTION

Located in northern Wisconsin, approximately 15 miles southwest of Rhinelander, Treehaven is owned and operated by the University of Wisconsin–Stevens Point. Treehaven's multipurpose, year-round design, flexible facilties, and location provide a beautiful and unique setting for public workshops, conferences, university courses, meetings, educationally oriented seminars and in-services, and school environmental programs.

THE ENVIRONMENT

Treehaven consists of 1,400 acres of northern forest. Buildings are situated on a glacial ridge overlooking Pine and Pickerel Creek Valleys, with the "Harrison hills" on the distant horizon. Treehaven's trails, which can be enjoyed throughout the year, lead to natural settings with an abundance of wildlife. Numerous lakes, streams, ski trails, and the Wisconsin River are located nearby.

FACILITIES

Treehaven is a complete residential facility. The main lodge includes a kitchen, dining room, library, and lounge areas. The classroom center is well equipped for conferences and includes several rooms that are adaptable to varying group sizes. Treehaven's buildings are located at the same elevation adjacent to each other and are connected by short walkways.

SUPPLIES NEEDED

Guests should come with clothing appropriate to the season. Biological study equipment, such as binoculars, may come in handy to study the variety of birds in this Great Lakes forest setting. Depending on the season, one may also wish to bring outdoor recreational equipment, such as cross-country skis and showshoes, although showshoes may be rented at Treehaven.

APPLICATIONS AND ADMISSIONS

For information on application and admission procedures, contact Treehaven at the above address and phone number.

Financial Aid: Contact Treehaven at the above address for the latest information on availability of financial aid.

Costs: Contact Treehaven for course/workshop class schedules and tuition/fees information.

WYOMING

LANDER LLAMA COMPANY
2024 Mortimore Lane
Lander, WY 82520-9771
(307) 332-5624
Fax: (307) 332-5624
Contact: Scott or Therese Woodruff

SAMPLE TRIPS
Three- to ten-day wilderness llama pack trips are offered to the Wind River–Absaroka Mountains region and the Red Desert region of western Wyoming.

CURRICULUM AND CREDITS
Lander Llama Company (LLC) offers a wide range of geographic destinations and trips. Each trip can be customized to fit the different needs and abilities of the participants. Llamas make great pack animals, as they are surefooted, easy to handle, and have the ability to make friendships for life. Credit may be available through independent or travel study.

THE INSTITUTION
LLC operates under a permit issued by the USFS Shoshone National Forest. They are licensed by the Wyoming Board of Outfitters and Professional Guides and are members of the Lander Chamber and International Llama Association.

THE ENVIRONMENT
The Wind River and Absaroka Mountains are special places, and with LLC's llamas and tour guides, trips are unforgettable.

FACILITIES
Llamas carry all gear and provisions, leaving the participants free of any heavy carrying. Meals are included, and any leftover freeze-dried food is left behind. Pack llamas bring fresh foods, produce, and Therese's special homemade desserts. Mouthwatering meals, complemented by delicious wines, enhance everyone's wilderness experience, and with a reservation for six, participants may choose their meals from a menu. LLC serves three meals per day except on the first and last days when two meals are served.

SUPPLIES NEEDED
Participants need only to bring personal clothing and toiletries. All other supplies are provided by LLC, including the highest quality backcountry equipment (i.e., tents, pads, sleeping bags, day packs, rain gear, and cooking gear) and first-aid equipment.

APPLICATIONS AND ADMISSIONS
Contact the above address for information on application and admission procedures.

Financial Aid: None available.

Costs: The Wind River and Absaroka Range trips are booked from mid-June through mid-September on a first-come, first-served basis. There is a three-day minimum with typical trips lasting five days. The Red Desert trips are three days long and run through the month of May, also on a first-come, first-served basis. A minimum of four people must apply in order to commence a new trip, and LLC reserves the right to mix groups of up to eight people per trip. Individuals and groups with less than four people may join any scheduled trips that have openings. Early reservations are highly recommended with LLC to receive desired time slots and travel arrangements. Upon early request, private customized trips can be arranged for larger groups. Approximate daily rates for guided trips are as follows:

three to five days—$135 (adults); $125 (children under 12).

six to ten days—$125 (adults); $115 (children under 12).

TETON SCIENCE SCHOOL
P.O. Box 68
Kelly, WY 83011
(307) 733-4765
Fax: (307) 739-9388
Contact: Registrar

SAMPLE COURSES AND PROGRAMS

Courses and programs are available for all age groups from elementary school through high school, and for adults from college age through Elderhostel.

Courses for young people include Teton Young Naturalists, Teton Junior Science School, Junior High Field Ecology, and High School Field Ecology. College courses include Birds of the Northern Rockies, Winter Ecology, and Wildlife Ecology. Teacher workshops include Increasing Environmental Literacy, Integrating Art and Science to Teach About the Environment, and Conflict Resolution.

Adult seminars include Yellowstone Bears, Animal Behavior, River Channels, Eagles and Hawks of the Greater Yellowstone Ecosystem, Interpreting Tracks and Sign, Geology of Jackson Hole, Wetland Identification, Ecology and Regulation, Wildflower Photography, Alpine Ecology, and the Night Sky. There is also a month-long Wilderness Emergency Medical Course.

CURRICULUM AND CREDITS

Teton Science School (TSS) offers year-round residential and nonresidential programs from one day to six weeks in length. Programs take students into the field for a hands-on approach to natural science learning that stresses basic concepts of ecology and specific aspects of the Greater Yellowstone Ecosystem.

TSS has cooperative agreements with the University of Wyoming, Central Wyoming College, Utah State University, and secondary schools to accredit many of the programs. Credit arrangements vary with each course, and specific information is included in registration materials. Costs for academic credit are not included in course fees except for Central Wyoming College credit, and must be paid separately. Contact the registrar for information regarding such financial arrangements and transferability of credit.

THE INSTITUTION

TSS is a nonprofit organization providing experiential educational opportunities in the natural sciences. The Greater Yellowstone region serves as an ecosystem model to foster understanding of ecology and appreciation for conservation practices. Program participants come from all over the United States and foreign countries.

THE ENVIRONMENT

TTS is located in Grand Teton National Park, Jackson Hole, Wyoming, at an elevation of 6,900 feet, and has a sub-alpine climate. The campus was once a dude ranch and retains much of its western charm. The campus is secluded and surrounded by mountain views, aspen forests, and open grasslands. Wildlife abounds on and around the campus.

FACILITIES

Students taking residential courses sleep in one of the dormitory-style log cabins. There is one for males and one for females. The dorms are heated and have modern bathrooms and showers. Students taking nonresidential courses at TSS can choose from a variety of accommodations in Jackson Hole, including motels, hotels, and campgrounds. For more specific information on lodging, contact the Jackson Hole Chamber of Commerce at (307) 733-3316.

SUPPLIES NEEDED

Clothing needs vary seasonally. Winter, in particular, requires specialized clothing. Participants taking a winter course at TSS are provided with a suggested list of clothing needs. During the rest of the year, clothing should be functional and casual. Good walking shoes are essential. Evenings are cool, even in the summer, so warm jackets are recommended. A hat is also recommended for protection from the sun in the summer and for warmth in the winter.

APPLICATIONS AND ADMISSIONS

Contact the registrar at the institution for information on application and admission procedures.

Financial Aid: Financial assistance is available and students with a genuine need are encouraged to apply. The scholarship fund includes a number of endowments, as well as special gifts provided by several families. There is also a Native American Fund supported by the Maki Foundation and the Wyoming State Department of Education. A travel scholarship for two TSS students has been established by Aspen Travel of Jackson Hole.

Costs: Contact the institution at the above address for information.

THE YELLOWSTONE INSTITUTE
P.O. Box 117
Yellowstone National Park, WY 82190
(307) 344-2294
Fax: (307) 344-2294
Contact: Don Nelson, Pam Gontz

SAMPLE COURSES

Courses include Waterfowl of Yellowstone; Wildlife Photography, Large Mammals of Yellowstone; Bears—Folklore & Biology; Yellowstone's Birds of Prey; Alpine Wildflowers; Wolves of Yellowstone; Ecology of Greater Yellowstone National Park; Fire, Ice, Fossil Forests; Geysers, Mudpots, Hotsprings; Geology Yellowstone Country; Mammal Tracking; Fly Fishing; Grizzly Bear Ecology and Management; Edible Plants and Medicinal Herbs; Learning Birds by Sound; Butterflies of Greater Yellowstone; John Colter—The Discovery of Yellowstone National Park; Lakes of Yellowstone by Canoe; Horsepacking—Springtime Flora and Fauna; Exploring the Yellowstone Ecosystem; Environmental Ethics; Family Days in the Thermal Basin; Hydrothermal Systems and the Yellowstone Caldera; Wildflowers of Yellowstone; Yellowstone's Wayside History; Yellowstone Before Tourists—Prehistoric People of the Park; Yellowstone Streams Through the Eyes of a Trout; Carnivores of the Greater Yellowstone Ecosystem; Episodic History of Yellowstone Lake; Introduction to Forest Ecology; Women and Yellowstone—A Historical Perspective; and How Mammals Survive Winter.

CURRICULUM AND CREDITS

Most courses are limited to 12–15 participants. Many, though not all, courses offer both graduate and undergraduate academic credit. Credit seekers may be required to take an exam, submit field notes, and/or complete a post-course project. Institutions that offer credit include the University of Montana, Montana State University, Idaho State University, Brigham Young University, Ricks College, and the University of Wyoming.

Many teachers enroll in Yellowstone Institute (YI) courses for recertification or professional growth credits. Certification of course completion listing the course title, hours of instruction, and the nature of the course is available upon request.

THE INSTITUTION

The YI is a private, nonprofit educational field program sponsored by the Yellowstone Association and operates on behalf of Yellowstone National Park. Approximately half of the institute's 80 courses take place at the historic Buffalo Ranch in the quiet, unpopulated Lamar Valley located in the northeast area of the park. Courses take place throughout the diverse ecosystem of Yellowstone National Park.

THE ENVIRONMENT

Yellowstone is a high plateau region that averages about 8,000 feet in elevation and is surrounded by 11,000–12,000-foot mountain peaks. Weather varies greatly, but summer days generally remain in the 70s to 80s, with nights cooling to the 40s and 50s. Precipitation ranges as well from very dry (12 inches of precipitation in the north) to more moist (25 to 30 inches of precipitation in the south). Vegetation is primarily evergreens with open sagebrush areas in the north.

FACILITIES

Most courses are conducted at the institute facility known as the Buffalo Ranch, an historic Park Service facility located in the Lamar Valley between the Northeast Entrance and Tower Junction. Classes meet there unless otherwise stated.

The main log building is heated and has two classrooms, with three bathrooms with showers and a kitchen where people do their own cooking. The facility, though clean and adequate, is quite simple. Unless otherwise specified, participants should provide their own food. There are stoves, refrigerators, and a small microwave for cooking. Space is limited so meals should be kept simple. Dishes, pots, pans, and cooking and eating utensils are provided.

There are 12 new multiple-occupancy log cabins, most of which have two or three single beds. They have no plumbing or electrical outlets but they are heated. Everyone must bring a warm sleeping bag. Cabin reservations should be made when registering for class. Space is limited, and cabin rental for family members of participants may be allowed if space is available. A copy of the institute's policy regarding family members and information about nearby lodging or camping facilities will be mailed on request.

For those who choose not to stay at the institute, other nearby sites in the park include campgrounds at Pebble Creek (9 miles east) and Slough Creek (7 miles west), or lodging at Mammoth Hotel (29 miles west), Roosevelt Lodge (11 miles west at Tower Junction), and Canyon Lodge (3 miles southwest). Motels outside the park can be found at Silver Gate, Montana (19 miles east), and Cooke City, Montana (23 miles east).

Participants should be in good general health for these courses because most courses require at least some walking at higher elevations. Classes that involve backpacking, horsepacking, canoeing, and fieldwork are more demanding.

SUPPLIES NEEDED

Much class time is spent outdoors. Participants should be prepared for a variety of mountain weather conditions and some cold temperatures. Rain gear and warm clothing are essential.

APPLICATIONS AND ADMISSIONS

Contact YI at the above address for their brochure and registration materials. Early registration is advised. Four weeks before class begins, each student will be mailed a course packet with course information, suggested study materials (if appropriate), and a park entrance fee waiver. Participants must provide their own health and accident insurance.

Financial Aid: None available.

Costs: Costs average $40–$45 a day, with a typical 3-day course costing approximately $125. Specific course costs are listed in the brochure which is usually available in early spring. Unless otherwise specified, charges do not include lodging, books, course materials, transportation, or university credit fees. Discounts are available for current members of the Yellowstone Association or for those who wish to join upon enrollment.

Section Two

INTERNATIONAL COURSES, PROGRAMS, AND EXPEDITIONS

AUSTRALIA

CAPE TRIBULATION TROPICAL RESEARCH STATION
Australian Tropical Research Foundation
Private Mail Bag 5
Cape Tribulation, Queensland
AUSTRALIA 4873
61 (0) 70-980-068/980
Fax: same as telephone
Contact: Dr. Hugh Spencer, Director

SAMPLE COURSES
While no formal courses are offered yet, courses in research ecology and natural history may be offered in the near future.

CURRICULUM AND CREDITS
Researchers considering projects in the Australian lowland wet tropics are invited to contact the station. The lack of lowland wet tropics research in the past means that plenty of opportunities are available for new researchers to start significant research programs and careers. Field laboratories such as the Cape Tribulation Tropical Research Station (CTTRS) can greatly enhance research efficiency, substantially reduce the cost of doing research in tropical climates, and serve as a meeting point with other researchers. Credit may be available through independent or travel study.

THE INSTITUTION
CTTRS is a research and educational facility on the Coral Coast, midway between Mossman and Cooktown in the Daintree area of far-north Queensland. Established in mid-1988, CTTRS encourages research in the Australian lowland wet tropics. The station is a member of the U.S.-based Organization of Biological Field Stations, and is informally affiliated with James Cook University in Townsville. The Bat House, a small rainforest environmental interpretation facility on Cape Tribulation Road, caters to tourist and backpacker traffic in the area, and also serves as a demonstration of appropriate technology (solar architecture, composting toilets, and photovoltaic power) for the area. The station is currently funded through user and visitor fees.

THE ENVIRONMENT
The research station is situated on regenerating pasture and rainforest land in the Mount Sorrow basin at the base of Cape Tribulation. Surrounded by Cape Tribulation National Park and by private land areas where long-term research can be carried out in a wide variety of habitats, the station lies within half a kilometer of the Coral Sea Coast and is adjacent to fringing reefs, mangrove, and Melaleuca communities.

FACILITIES
The station has laboratory and limited accommodation facilities plus a range of research equipment such as balances, spectrophotometer microscopes, radio-tracking

equipment, some biochemical and hit equipment, surveying gear, etc. Researchers at the field station have already initiated a number of long-term ecological research programs on aspects of the area's lowland tropical rainforest and its pollinators.

SUPPLIES NEEDED

The station provides linens, utensils, etc. Participants are encouraged to bring adequate sun-block, a wide-brimmed hat, and appropriate footwear. During the wet season plastic sandals are recommended for general work in the forest, and can be purchased through the station. A small personal first-aid kit is recommended. Medical assistance is 31 miles (50 kilometers) away, so be sure to bring any necessary prescriptions. While this may sound alarming to those new to the neotropics, snakes and other biting forest animals are few and far between. Because of the station's remoteness, sometimes articles from the United States can be hand-carried to the station (saving considerable time and costs in freight). Participants should contact the station a week or so before their departure date in case they have anything substantial that needs bringing over.

APPLICATIONS AND ADMISSIONS

A letter of interest together with a curriculum vitae, phone (home and work), fax, and e-mail contact numbers is required for both prospective researchers and volunteers. The station prefers volunteers who are at least 25 years old, unless compelling reasons dictate why a younger person should be accepted (extensive field experience, for example). Volunteers are expected to contribute wherever they are required. Although it is not always possible to provide volunteers with research experience during their visit, every effort is made to do so. Prospective researchers should outline their research programs (and their level of financial support) in sufficient detail to allow proper assessment by the station for their suitability to the available facilities and area. If they are not considered suitable, then modifications or an alternative venue will be suggested. Researchers, especially long-term ones, are requested to contribute labor toward the station's operation, and are asked to give talks to the general public on aspects of their research and interests.

Financial Aid: CTTRS offers two scholarships for postgraduate researchers to carry out research leading to MSc and Ph.D. qualifications in subject areas relevant to the aims of the station. Each scholarship provides one year of accommodation and bench fees at the station, which may be spread over a period of up to three years. When a person has a particular interest in a long-term project that is within the capacity of the station but cannot find adequate funding, the station director may consider providing free room and board, provided that the person is prepared to devote appoximately 40% of their time to station activities.

Costs: The research station depends upon user fees for its operation. Fees do fluctuate, so prospective visitors should inquire about these when writing to the station. To a certain degree, fees are levied on the applicant's ability to pay. The researcher's rate is approximately $45 a day (including bench fees), with student and assistant rates being $25 a day. Food is provided and the evening meal is catered. Volunteers are requested to pay approximately $75 per week to cover accommodation and food costs.

BERMUDA

BERMUDA BIOLOGICAL STATION FOR RESEARCH, INC.
17 Biological Station Lane
Ferry Reach, GE 01
BERMUDA
(809) 297-1880
Fax: (809) 297-8143
E-mail: biostation@bbsr.edu
Contact: Dr. Anthony H. Knap, Director;
Dr. Robert S. Jones, Deputy Director/Education Director

or

230 Park Avenue
Twentieth Floor
New York, NY 10169
(212) 207-1600

SAMPLE COURSES AND PROGRAMS

Courses and programs include Analysis of Marine Pollution, Marine Microbial Ecology, Zooplankton Ecology, Biology of Fishes, Global Environmental Change, Tropical Marine Invertebrates, Biological Oceanography, Marine Fish Culture—Short Course, Coral Reef Ecology, Analysis and Management of Marine Contaminants, and a Graduate Intern Program for dissertation research. Research Experiences for Undergraduates (REU) Program is National Science Foundation (NSF)–funded. An Elderhostel program educating senior citizens about environmental issues is offered.

CURRICULUM AND CREDITS

Bermuda Biological Station for Research, Inc. (BBSR) currently has education programs for high school, college, and graduate students. Between six and seven undergraduate and graduate-level courses in marine science are offered each summer.

As an independent, nonprofit international research facility, the station's mission is threefold: 1) to conduct research of the highest quality from the special perspective of a mid-ocean island; 2) to educate future scientists; and 3) to provide well-equipped facilities and responsive staff support for visiting scientists, faculty, and students from around the world. To fulfill this mission, a resident staff of scientists and technicians carry out projects based primarily in Bermuda. The station administers an internationally known program of summer courses in marine science and routinely hosts a diverse mix of visiting scientists and educational groups at all levels.

Visiting faculty generally set their own curricula, are in charge of group dynamics and discipline, and provide the bulk of instruction for their students. BBSR staff members are prepared to help with advance planning and can provide supplemental instruction on Bermuda's diverse environments.

The Bermuda Islands offer teachers many unique educational opportunities for field studies, allowing a wide range of topics that can be effectively taught, including oceanographic principles and techniques, the biology and geology of coral atolls, human interaction with an island ecology, and the special problems of an isolated island. BBSR provides educational groups with ideal laboratory and teaching facilities from which to conduct field studies. Credits to be awarded are determined by the student's home institution.

THE INSTITUTION

BBSR is located in Bermuda in the northwestern Sargasso Sea. The island's location offers unique opportunities for research. As the northernmost coral reef in the Atlantic, Bermuda provides a rich and varied biota within easy reach of academic institutions in the eastern United States with no continental shelf. There is easy access to the deep sea—more than 2 miles depth within 15 miles of the islands.

THE ENVIRONMENT

Bermuda is an isolated group of about 150 small islands in the western Atlantic Ocean, about 600 miles east of Cape Hatteras in the Atlantic time zone. Nearly 21 square miles in area, the principal islands are connected by bridges or causeways to form a 22-mile chain with a maximum width of 2 miles and maximum elevation of 259 feet. Its population is nearly 60,000.

Bermuda's warm-temperate, subtropical climate is influenced by the Gulf Stream to the west, which also supports its coral reefs, the northernmost in the Atlantic. The evenly distributed, average rainfall of 58 inches and an average humidity of 75%, favors the lush growth of most temperate and tropical plants, although the soil is thin.

These reef-protected islands are primarily aeolian limestone deposits perched on the southern rim of an extinct volcanic seamount. In addition to their marine environments, the islands also support coastal, upland, mangrove, marsh, and karst habitats.

FACILITIES

The heart of BBSR is Wright Hall, with a spacious lounge, dining facilities, and accommodations for visiting students and scientists. Most of the living quarters are dormitory-style doubles or singles, but six well-appointed apartments are also available. Additional accommodations for resident and visiting investigators, ranging from single-bedroom cottages to a four-apartment complex, are scattered about the 14-acre grounds.

Most laboratory facilities are in the Conklin Laboratory, attached to Wright Hall. Sixteen laboratories and several teaching laboratories serve resident staff and visitors. Recent NSF funding has provided for the construction of additional laboratory space for visitors.

The Redfield Building contains office space and a 100-seat lecture hall. The E. L. Mark Library contains over 16,000 volumes on all aspects of marine science, subscribes to more than 60 scientific journals, and exchanges with more than 300 research libraries around the world. A library microcomputer provides access through dialog to various abstracting services in the United States.

Research vessels include the *Weatherbird II*, a 115-foot former oil-rig supply ship converted for research and brought to BBSR in 1989; the *BBS II*, a 41-foot vessel designed for both shallow and deep-water research; and the *Pappa Pinky*, a 32-foot vessel for near-shore research.

SUPPLIES NEEDED

Necessary supplies are dependent on the type of research or group requirements. Contact the BBSR Education Office for information on available equipment and shipping procedures.

APPLICATIONS AND ADMISSIONS

Information on summer courses and other programs, application procedures, fees and funding, may be obtained by contacting the BBSR Education Office.

Financial Aid: Scholarships and partial funding for research is available. Visiting Ph.D. and graduate students may apply for BBSR grants to help with on-site costs for short term visits (typically 1–4 weeks). A visiting graduate intern program provides opportunities for long-term independent work. Graduate interns must be enrolled in recognized degree programs and serve as teaching assistants in BBSR's educational programs. A work-study program provides opportunities for graduate science students to gain practical scientific experience by working with a resident scientist. Room and board expenses are covered in exchange for performing other services.

Costs: The costs for accommodations, meals, lab use, courses, and vehicle and vessel use vary by program. Factors determining cost include number of participants in a group, length of stay, type of lab, type and usage of vessel, etc. Contact the BBSR Education Office at the above address for an up-to-date fee schedule.

CANADA

BAMFIELD MARINE STATION
Bamfield, British Columbia
CANADA VOR 180
(604) 728-3301
Fax: (604) 728-3452
Contact: Director

SAMPLE COURSES
Courses include Marine Invertebrate Zoology, Marine Phycology, Principles of Aquaculture, Salmonid Aquaculture, Marine Parasitology, Marine Ecology, and Biology of Fishes. Special Topics in Applied Aquacultural Science include Fish and Shellfish Health, Echinoderm Biology, Molluscan Aquaculture, Island Biogeography, Marine Biology for Teachers, Instruction to Marine Education, Biology of Marine Birds, Fisheries-Forestry Interactions, and Fossils of the Burges Shale.

CURRICULUM AND CREDITS
Field trips to Bamfield Marine Station (BMS) provide a unique educational experience for inquisitive people of all ages. The program is designed for school groups from intermediate level to 12th grade, college and university groups, extension education programs, natural history organizations, and various clubs. Each field trip is designed to meet the interests and needs of specific groups. The overall goal of BMS is to provide an exciting, hands-on introduction to marine biology.

THE INSTITUTION
BMS was established to fill a need for a permanent base for marine-oriented field operations on the west coast of Canada. A major criterion in choosing its location was that the laboratory be situated in an area subject to open-coast conditions to complement the protected water environments found at the government institutions, Department of Fisheries and Oceans Pacific Biological Station in Nanaimo, and the West Vancouver Laboratory. A number of locations were considered before the Bamfield area was chosen and the former site of the Pacific Cable Station was purchased from the Canadian Overseas Telecommunications Corporation in 1969.

In 1972 BMS was established by a consortium of five western Canadian universities and the Western Canadian Universities Marine Biological Society (WCUMBS) with support from the National Research Council. The members of WCUMBS include the University of Alberta, the University of British Columbia, the University of Calgary, Simon Fraser University, and the University of Victoria.

THE ENVIRONMENT
The marine station is located in the village of Bamfield on Barkley Sound on the west coast of Vancouver Island. Approximately 25 acres of the property are occupied by the facilities, leaving 160 acres of undeveloped primary and secondary forest. The Bamfield community, with a population of more than 200 residents, has little commercial development and minimal pollution.

International Courses, Programs, and Expeditions

Many of the major marine habitats common in temperate waters are represented in the vicinity of the laboratory. An unbroken exposure gradient stretches from Cape Beale on the exposed outer coast to the protected waters at the head of Alberni Canal. This coastline includes rocky shores, muddy bays, sandy areas, and gravel and boulder beaches.

The islands of the Deer and Broken Groups provide an array of shorelines. Beds of giant kelp, rocky pinnacles, reefs, walls, and shell-sand slopes support a diverse and abundant assemblage of subtidal organisms. The area has a total of 15 seabird nesting colonies on small islands. Gray whales, Steller's and California sea lions, and harbor seals are common in the area. There are also occasional sightings of harbor porpoises, elephant seals, and killer whales. Not only is Barkley Sound excellent for the study of the marine environment, but it is also a suitable place to study freshwater biology, maritime terrestrial botany and zoology, geology, oceanography, and archaeology.

FACILITIES

Accommodations are available in comfortable dormitories or bunkhouse rooms shared by 2 to 4 people. Linen is available upon request (small charge per issue) although most groups bring their own sleeping bags (pillow and pillowcase are provided). Food is served cafeteria-style in the dining hall. Prior notice is required for special diets.

The main laboratory facilities for research and teaching are housed in the former Bamfield Cable Station. The four floors of the building include the penthouse (administrative offices, library, lobby, and display area); first floor (teaching labs, storeroom, museum room, and computer room); second floor (research labs and photographic darkroom); and third floor (aquarium room and laboratory).

Adjacent buildings provide neurophysiology and environmental physiology laboratories and a workshop. The environmental physiology lab includes wet and dry labs, a radioisotope lab, aquarium room, and office space. Laboratories are supplied with basic analytical equipment as well as a scintillation counter, refrigerated centrifuge, microcentrifuge, freeze drier, research grade photomicroscopes, two swim tube respirometers, and neurophysiology equipment.

SUPPLIES NEEDED

The following list covers the essentials needed for all field trips: good rain gear, a jacket, pants and rubber boots, a flashlight, clothing suitable for cool moist climate with at least one change, hat and gloves, and a sleeping bag (unless linen is requested).

In general, participants find that the program takes up most of their time. A cassette tape recorder is available in the lounge, and cassettes (or musical instruments) are often brought along for leisure and social time. Cameras and/or binoculars are brought along by many visitors.

APPLICATIONS AND ADMISSIONS

Contact the institution at the above address for an application package.

Financial Aid: The Financial Assistance Program (with a fund totaling approximately $36,000) consists of undergraduate and graduate student awards.

Costs: Station charges include room and board and facility usage. The facility usage fee covers teaching and laboratory facilities, boat transportation, and station staff. Use of the station research vessel, the *M/V Alta*, is optional for field trip groups at an additional cost. Room and board fees are approximatley $820 for an 8-week course, and the course fee is approximately $250.

CHURCHILL NORTHERN STUDIES CENTER
Box 610
Churchill, Manitoba
CANADA R0B 0E0
(204) 675-2307 or (204) 675-2139
Contact: Staff

SAMPLE COURSES

Courses include Arctic Lifestyles and Survival, Birds of Churchill, Photography, Wildflowers of Churchill, Northern Mushrooms, Aurora Borealis and the Northern Sky, Circumpolar Ecosystems in Winter, Arctic Ecosystems, Edibles of the Arctic, Botany, Geology, Climatology, Ornithology, Cold Weather Testing, and Research.

CURRICULUM AND CREDITS

The Churchill Northern Studies Center (CNSC) is a nonprofit charitable organization with a mandate to facilitate Arctic research and education. A broad range of research has been conducted at CNSC. The center has been used by archaeologists, biologists (botany, ecology, genetics, ornithology, zoology), engineers, geographers, and linguists. CNSC provides logistical support for researchers working in the area.

All courses tend to run within a similar structure so a general overview will give participants an idea of what to expect. Mornings are often composed of one to two hours in the classroom or laboratory and then out in the field to put what the participants have learned in the classroom to real use. Even though no roads travel into Churchill, an extensive local road system allows good access to most areas that participants will be studying.

Most courses include a historical look at the Churchill community, and participants are given the opportunity to do some shopping and visit local attractions. The community offers most basic services and many unexpected ones for a community its size, including a Royal Bank of Canada, post office, health center, a library, swimming pool, bowling alley, a theater, two grocery stores, a convenience store, a liquor store, and many tours and hotels.

THE INSTITUTION

CNSC is located approximately 15 miles (24 kilometers) east of the Churchill community. Churchill can be reached either by plane or train. Participants should let the center know when and how they are arriving, and one of the staff members will come pick them up.

THE ENVIRONMENT

The Churchill region is located at the unique intersection of three biomes: coastal, boreal forest, and Arctic tundra. As one of the oldest settlements in Canada and as the focus of previous international scientific programs, anecdotal and scientific data relevant to several disciplines are available. Regular rail and air service make Churchill the most accessible area in the Canadian Arctic. Bears are mentioned here because most of the world knows Churchill as the "Polar Bear Capital." Bears start to come ashore in late July after the ice has melted and they are forced on land; however, sightings are rare until October and November when the bears congregate along the coast awaiting freeze-up. Viewing bears from all-terrain vehicles or helicopter is virtually guaranteed.

FACILITIES

The center consists of a large facility with dormitory-style accommodations, a kitchen, laboratories, classrooms, an observation dome, offices, a garage, herbarium, and library. During peak periods participants will most likely have two or more roommates. The rooms do not have a lot of storage space for gear. Nonetheless, there is plenty of bench space in the lab. The washroom facilities are centrally located with shower stalls (bring your own toiletries). The sleeping area is warm and comfortable with adjustable electric baseboard heaters in each room. There is a quiet lounge where participants can read or visit.

The kitchen provides wholesome cooking. With the high cost of transportation to Churchill one should not expect abundant quantities of fresh fruit or vegetables. Users of the center are expected to help with dishes and kitchen clean-up after every meal. This is usually done in rotating groups of four.

SUPPLIES NEEDED

The winter/spring period (October to June) is usually quite cold and wind chills can be severe. Therefore, bring a good parka, wind/ski pants, head gear, warm boots, mitts, a scarf, and several sweaters. Heavy snow storms are more likely in March and April. At this time of the year, extremely bright days are frequent and good UV protection sunglasses are a must. Bring clothes that can be layered and work well for this time of year. Nighttime temperatures can reach well below -20°C.

In late June to July the seasons change, and the whole of the lowlands becomes wet with patches of dry tundra. Wool socks with rubber boots or hip waders are necessary this time of the year. The mosquitoes and sand flies are out in full force so bring a high-deet bug repellent and/or headnet. Lastly, bring something light to wear as temperatures can get to +30°C, if only for a few days or a few hours. August and September are cooler months.

APPLICATIONS AND ADMISSIONS

Contact the institution at the above address for information regarding application and admission procedures.

Financial Aid: Inquire directly to CNSC regarding the availability of financial aid.

Costs: Since tuition and fees vary, interested persons should inquire directly with CNSC regarding costs for specific courses.

HUNTSMAN MARINE SCIENCE CENTER
Brandy Cove Road
St. Andrews, New Brunswick
CANADA EOG 2X0
(506) 529-1200
Fax: (506) 529-1212
Contact: Jamie Steel, Public Education;
Matt Litvak, Academic Programs

SAMPLE COURSES

Public education courses include High School–Level Marine Biology, Advanced Marine Biology and Marine Vertebrates, Marine Institute for Teachers, Marine Biology for Scuba Divers, and Bird Watching.

Academic courses include Marine Biology, Ecology and Behavior of Fishes, Marine Parasitology, Marine Aquaculture, Marine Developmental Biology, Coastal Marsh Plant Ecology, Scientific Diving for Marine Biologists, and Fisheries Resources.

CURRICULUM AND CREDITS

The Huntsman Marine Sciene Center (HMSC) stands unequaled in Canada for blending the interests and needs of academia, government, and industry, and providing opportunities in marine science research, education, training, information, and technology transfer. No other institution in Canada offers the unique combination of facilities, professional resources, and a broad spectrum of programs.

In support of enhancing knowledge in basic and applied marine science, HMSC offers a year-round teaching and research facility for undergraduate and graduate students, researchers, and those seeking continuing education. The public education department runs both on- and off-site programs for elementary, high school, and Elderhostel students, and also offers teacher training and curriculum development. The academic program coordinates university-accredited field courses on-site.

HMSC hosts workshops and seminars, and provides a service for the national and international scientific community in performing an abstracting indexing function for two major scientific publications—Aquatic Sciences and Fisheries Abstracts and the Canadian Journal of Fisheries and Aquatic Sciences.

THE INSTITUTION

In 1969, a group of eastern Canadian universities formed a consortium to establish a field station that would complement their marine biology and oceanography research programs. St. Andrews, located at the mouth of the Bay of Fundy, was the site of choice and the Huntsman Marine Laboratory was established on 100 acres adjacent to the federal department of Fisheries and Oceans Biological Station. In 1987 it was renamed the Huntsman Marine Science Center to reflect program diversity. A nonprofit organization, HMSC is currently supported by eight universities, four government departments, numerous corporations, and the general public.

THE ENVIRONMENT

HMSC is located on the shores of the St. Croix Estuary, next to one of the world's most diverse marine regions. The extremely high tides from the Bay of Fundy make this an ideal area for studying a wide range of marine creatures and habitats.

FACILITIES

Access to a variety of environments, freshwater and saltwater holding facilities, laboratories, boats, scientific equipment, and a supply of live specimens make HMSC an ideal location for marine studies.

Visitors may be accommodated in housekeeping apartments or in one of two dormitory facilities. A cafeteria is located in the Anderson House residence. Exhibits, tours, guided beach walks, and interpretive programs at the aquarium/museum allow visitors to explore the marine life of Canada's Atlantic coastal region and gain an understanding of our relationship to and dependence upon the marine environment. Live exhibits feature harbour seals, wolffish, lumpfish, lobsters, and a touching pool. A special exhibit of unusual and little-known deep-sea marine life contains a unique assortment of life-size models and larger-than-life paintings of deep-ocean-dwelling animals of Atlantic Canada. A gift shop carries marine and environment-oriented merchandise.

SUPPLIES NEEDED

Supplies are provided and included in course fees.

APPLICATIONS AND ADMISSIONS

Contact HMSC at the above address for further information on application and admission procedures.

Financial Aid: Themadel Bursaries of $300 each are awarded to 30 participants annually. Three Huntsman Graduate Research Fellowships of $2,500 per participant are also available each year.

Costs: All costs include tuition, dormitory accommodation, meals, supplies, and equipment. Academic course costs range from approximately $875 to $1,600, and from $550 to $850 for public education courses.

MEANOOK BIOLOGICAL RESEARCH STATION
c/o Department of Biological Sciences
University of Alberta
Edmonton, Alberta
CANADA T6G 2E9
(403) 492-5497 or (403) 675-4934
Fax: (403) 492-9234 or (403) 675-3228
Contact: Dr. Ellie Prepas, Director

SAMPLE PROGRAMS

No formal courses are being offered as of yet, but credit may be given for research as independent or travel study programs.

CURRICULUM AND CREDITS

Meanook Biological Research Station (MBRS) is primarily a research station, with nonresearch activities restricted to field trips and tours at this time.

Researchers are welcome at MBRS throughout the year. During peak field season (April to September), research takes precedence at the station. Fees are reasonable and allocated on a cost-recovery basis. From September to April, MBRS is available for groups and classes who wish to use the facility for field trips or retreats. If space is available, small groups may be accommodated during the field season. Travel study or summer research opportunitites are not always available for credit.

THE INSTITUTION

MBRS is a permanent research facility located approximately 84 miles (135 kilometers) north of Edmonton and 9 miles (15 kilometers) south of Athabasca, Alberta. MBRS has been operating since 1983 and is part of the Department of Biological Sciences at the University of Alberta.

THE ENVIRONMENT

MBRS provides a unique opportunity for aquatic and terrestrial research in both the western boreal mixed-wood forest and aspen parkland ecoregions of Alberta. Users of MBRS have ready access to excellent, diverse field sites, a common pool of equipment, and well-equipped laboratories year-round.

MBRS is located in a sparsely populated area with a wide range of terrestrial, aquatic, and wetland habitats nearby. The station is situated on a 528-acre National Wildlife Area (NWA) at the southern boundary of the western boreal mixed-wood forest with the aspen parkland ecoregion. NWA consists of 143 acres of cultivated land, a 18.5-acre building site, and 367 acres of woodlands dominated by aspen, balsam, poplar, and paper birch.

THE FACILITIES

Twelve permanent buildings and two large ATCO trailer complexes are currently located on the area. Facilities include living accommodation for up to 56 researchers, four laboratories, four prototype experimental ponds, workshop, a black-and-white darkroom, small reference library, and storage facilities for field gear. Sleeping accommodations are divided between two houses and the two trailer complexes (33 rooms total). A central kitchen is staffed by a cook from May to August (and on an "as-needed" basis throughout the rest of the year). There are also two satellite kitchens. Recreational facilities include a lounge with a TV and VCR; volleyball, basketball, and badminton courts; a fire pit; and 5 miles (8 kilometers) of trails for jogging, biking, and cross-country skiing.

Research facilities are distributed between four buildings. Equipment and facilities available to researchers include a flume for flowing water experiments, an aquatic facility with holding tanks and aquaria for fish observations, a general laboratory stocked with microscopes and standard laboratory glassware, a large chemical laboratory equipped with gas, oxygen, vacuum, distilled deionized water, drying ovens, pH meters, refrigerator/freezer space, computers, autoclaves, balances, fume hoods, and specialized limnological equipment. MBRS also has an area for the storage of scuba tanks and gear, a collection of boats and trailers ranging from 8 to 22 feet, outboard motors, field sampling equipment (terrestrial and aquatic), ATVs, a 4 x 4 truck, and a fleet of various vehicles rented from the University of Alberta.

SUPPLIES NEEDED

Researchers and other station users are required to bring bedding, toiletries, and clothing suitable for the remote location of MBRS. Researchers requiring highly specialized equipment will need to make arrangements with the director or station manager for laboratory space and availability of equipment.

APPLICATIONS AND ADMISSIONS

Students interested in independent travel-study programs or summer research opportunities should send a résumé and cover letter to the director of MBRS.

Only researchers with strong research programs or the potential for strong research programs are encouraged and offered space to work at MBRS. First placement goes to applicants from the University of Alberta. MBRS is committed to developing collaborative programs with scientists from other universities, government agencies, and the private sector. Groups interested in using MBRS as a retreat or a site for a field trip should contact the above address.

Financial Aid: None available.

Costs: Approximate costs for use of MBRS are $17 per day for a short-term research program (under one month), $230 per month for a long-term research program (with chores), $460 per month for a long-term research program (without chores); $15 per student for a day-use-only field trip, and $17 per day per student for overnight field trips.

MINGAN ISLAND CETACEAN STUDY
285 Green Street
St. Lambert, Québec
CANADA J4P 1T3
(514) 465-9176
Fax: (418) 949-2845

or

106 Bord de La Mer
Longue-Pointe-de-Mingan
Québec, CANADA G0G 1V0
(514) 465-9176
Fax: (418) 949-2845
Contact: Richard Sears, Director

SAMPLE EXPEDITIONS
Five- and ten-day expeditions and research sessions are offered in whale/marine mammal biology, education, and conservation.

CURRICULUM AND CREDITS
Mingan Island Cetacean Study (MICS) operates a research station from May to November in the Mingan Island region of the Québec North Shore. MICS offers educational programs (research expeditions) to the public from June to October, for the purpose of helping to finance the research and enhance the public awareness of marine mammals. MICS expanded its research effort to the Sea of Cortes, Baja California (Mexico), in 1983 in order to broaden the existing knowledge on marine mammals. Here, as in the Gulf of St. Lawrence, public educational research programs oriented toward marine mammals are offered. Credit is available through independent or travel study.

THE INSTITUTION
MICS is a nonprofit research organization involved in the study, education, and conservation of marine mammals along the North Shore of the Gulf of St. Lawrence, Québec, in the region of the Mingan Islands. Whales, dolphins, and seals abound near the islands making the area an ideal site for study.

MICS is best known as the first organization in the world to have carried out long-term studies of the blue whale and other marine mammals in the region. The research specifically focuses on the local populations of blue, humpback, finback, and minke whales, with complementary studies of the North Atlantic white-sided dolphin and white-beaked dolphin.

THE ENVIRONMENT

The main educational programs are week-long summer sessions, during which time nature enthusiasts can join the research teams and observe the world's largest animals. For seven or ten days, participants live in the coastal village of Longue Pointe de Mingan, the Gateway to the Mingan Islands. Now a National Park Reserve, these islands are located within three miles of shore in an area renowned for its distinctive limestone rock formations. Participants get introduced to the many rookeries of sea birds, such as puffins, Arctic terns, murres, and eider ducks, as well as the unique geology and flora of this archipelago.

SUPPLIES NEEDED

When packing for an expedition, keep in mind that it can be cool on the water and in the evenings. Wool sweaters, socks, hats, gloves, and a well-lined jacket are recommended. Rain gear, rubber boots, and a good pair of sunglasses are also recommended.

APPLICATIONS AND ADMISSIONS

Contact the institution for information on application and admission procedures.

Financial Aid: None available.

Costs: Approximately $155 a day per person. All MICS live-in expeditions include room and board.

UNIVERSITY FIELD STATION (DELTA MARSH)
Box 38, RR. #2
Portage la Prairie, Manitoba
CANADA R1N 3A2
(204) 857-8637
Fax: (204) 857-4683
Contact: Dr. Gordon G. C. Robinson

or

The University of Manitoba
230 Machray Hall
Winnipeg, Manitoba
CANADA R3T 2N2
(204) 474-9297
Fax: (204) 275-3147
Contact: Dr. Gordon G. C. Robinson

SAMPLE COURSES

Courses include Principles of Ecology, Vascular Flora of Manitoba, Community Ecology, Population Ecology, Field Ecology, Ornithology, Wetland Ecology, and Waterfowl Management.

CURRICULUM AND CREDITS

The primary purpose of the station is to increase understanding of the dynamics of wetland ecosystems through a long-range research program. The station is operational year-round and offers a unique opportunity for winter ecology. It provides a resource for study at the postgraduate, undergraduate, and high school levels, in addition to serving other educational purposes. Areas of study include population dynamics of birds, mammals, and fish, parasitology, freshwater algae and invertebrate ecology, toxicological studies, and population and community studies of marsh and terrestrial plants.

In addition to undergraduate courses offered, school groups and environmental organizations are encouraged to make use of the field station programs and facility. A variety of exercises suited to wetland and intercommunity relationships are offered for all ages and interests, primarily from September to early May. A brochure listing educational exercises may be obtained from campus or the field station offices.

THE INSTITUTION

The University Field Station was established as a research and teaching facility in 1966 by Dr. Jennifer Shay. The 5,400-acre (2,187-hectare) Delta Marsh, situated behind the south shore of Lake Manitoba, is one of the largest and most investigated marshes in North America. Representing one of the few remaining extensive marshes in North America, it presents a wide and unique diversity of habitats and biota for research. Mallard Lodge, built in 1932 on the 2,301-acre (932-hectare) estate of Winnipeg businessman Donald Bain, remains one of the finest lodges on the marsh. Originally used as a hunting lodge, it now houses the station office, provides accommodation, and serves as the primary meeting place at the field station.

The University Field Station property is part of a gamebird refuge and wildlife protection area. Most of the property was designated in 1987 as an ecologically significant area. With permission, researchers have been allowed access to the adjoining 20-acre (8-hectare) property owned by the Portage Country Club. The station is operated through the Faculty of Science at the University of Manitoba and is a member of the Organization of Biological Field Stations.

THE ENVIRONMENT

The station is located on the forested dune ridge separating Lake Manitoba and the marsh, which has dense beds of submerged aquatics, emergent reedbeds, and shallow wetlands bordered by willows. Rich agricultural land borders the southern edge of the marsh, but vestiges of prairie and remnants of aspen parkland also exist.

Researchers and students in the fields of biology, geology, geography, and archaeology are invited to utilize the field station and surrounding areas. Riding Mountain National Park and the Carberry Sandhills are within driving distance and offer opportunities for specialized projects.

FACILITIES

The field station has six independent laboratories equipped with hot and cold water. Refrigerator and freezer space is available for those who require it. Laboratory space is assigned according to the researcher's specific requirements. Researchers are expected to provide their own specialized equipment.

The station has two half-ton trucks, ten canoes, boats with 20-horsepower motors, and a snowmobile for use on a rental basis. IBM and Macintosh computers, a laser printer, photocopier, and IBM typewriter are available for researchers. As well, there is a fully equipped workshop for the construction of scientific field apparatus, a library with 500 volumes and a reprint collection, a herbarium containing 1,000 plant specimens collected from areas in and around Delta Marsh, and a representative insect and invertebrate collection. Bird and mammal skins are also available for studying and teaching purposes.

A bibliography of research papers resulting from research conducted at the University of Manitoba Field Station (Delta Marsh) is available upon request to the director.

SUPPLIES NEEDED

Users are requested to provide their own specialized research equipment. Residents must provide their own towels and toiletries (linens are provided).

APPLICATIONS AND ADMISSIONS

Persons wishing to register for any summer credit courses offered at the University Field Station should contact the Admissions Office, 424 University Center, University of Manitoba, Winnipeg, Manitoba, Canada R3T 2N2 for application and registration materials. Researchers wishing to conduct their own research projects at the field station should contact either the campus or field station offices for information.

Financial Aid: None available.

Costs: Contact the institution for information on tuition rates for specific courses. Accommodation rates, including meals, range from approximately $16 to $23 a day per person, or from approximately $105 to $149 a week per person. Apartments and cottages are also available, ranging from approximately $129 to $356 per month (not including meals). Special group rates are also available.

COSTA RICA

ORGANIZATION FOR TROPICAL STUDIES
La Selva Biological Station
Apartado 676
2050 San Pedro De Montes De Oca
COSTA RICA
(506) 240-6696
Fax: (506) 240-6783

or

(North American Headquarters)
P.O. Box 90630
Duke Station
Durham, NC 27708-0630
(919) 684-5774
Fax: (919) 684-5661
E-mail: nao@acpub.duke.edu
Contact: Dr. Shaun Bennett

SAMPLE COURSES
Courses include Tropical Biology—An Ecological Approach, Tropical Managed Ecosystems, Environmental Concerns in Tropical Countries, Tropical Diversity and Conservation, Tropical Forestry, Tropical Plant Systematics, and Agroecologia.

CURRICULUM AND CREDITS
These courses carry formal university credit the number of credits being commensurate with course length (generally 3 to 8 credits). Research and thesis internships are also available.

THE INSTITUTION
The Organization for Tropical Studies (OTS) is a consortium of 44 academic institutions from Costa Rica, the United States, and Puerto Rico. The goals of this nonprofit organization are to promote education and research in tropical biology, and to link these activities to rational and sustainable uses of natural resources. In Costa Rica, OTS maintains three field stations, of which La Selva is the largest and most active.

The station serves as an education center for a broad variety of courses in different aspects of tropical biology. It is also one of the most active ecological research sites in the world.

THE ENVIRONMENT
La Selva encompasses a variety of ecosystems characteristic of the wet lowland tropics. The protected area adjoins the Braulio Carrillo National Park. Within La Selva exist virgin tropical wet forests, logged-over forests, secondary forests of different ages, agricultural habitats such as plantations and pastures, as well as swamps, creeks, and rivers. Annual precipitation is 4,000 millimeters with an average of more than 100

millimeters every month; a drier period, locally called "el verano," occurs between January and May. Biological diversity is very high and includes approximately 2,000 species of higher plants, 400 species of birds, and thousands of insect species.

FACILITIES
Most courses are conducted in Costa Rica where OTS maintains several field stations. For information on the availability of specific facilities, contact OTS at the above address.

SUPPLIES NEEDED
Each course requires different supplies. Inquire with OTS for specifics.

APPLICATIONS AND ADMISSIONS
Contact OTS at the above address for application materials. In addition to the completed application form, the following materials are requested: a curriculum vitae, graduate and undergraduate transcripts, three reference letters from the applicant's professors, an application fee (currently $25), an endorsement from an OTS board member (for students applying from OTS-member institutions), and a letter describing the applicant's interests, plans, and reasons for wanting to join the course. Each course has its own application deadline date, so interested persons should contact OTS as early as possible.

Financial Aid: Inquire with OTS directly; some fellowships are available.

Costs: Tuition varies depending on the course selected but generally ranges from approximately $1,000 to $1,550 for students from OTS-member institutions and from $2,600 to $6,000 for students from nonmember institutions.

RANCHO NATURALISTA
Apdo. 364-1002
San Jose
COSTA RICA

or

Costa Rica Gateway
Department 1425
Box 025216
Miami, FL 33102-5216
Phone/Fax: (506) 267-7138
Contact: John W. Erb

SAMPLE PROGRAMS
Programs include Nature Study, Bird Watching, Local Flora and Fauna Study, and Ecotourism.

CURRICULUM AND CREDITS
A variety of standard and custom-designed tours are available at moderate additional cost to resident guests. An example of one might be a 2-day, 1-night birding tour

International Courses, Programs, and Expeditions

in San Gerardo de Dota to see quetzals and other high-elevation birds. Credit is available through independent or travel study.

THE INSTITUTION

Rancho Naturalista became a nature lodge in February 1987. Although the first guests were collecting lepidopterists, the majority of the guests present were bird watchers. Resident birding guides who are conversant with other aspects of nature are available.

THE ENVIRONMENT

The 125-acre ranch lies in a transitional, premontane rainforest in the Caribbean zone. Three hundred eighty-six species of birds have been recorded in the area. The extensive trail system reveals various species of toucans, motmots, tanagers, parrots and parakeets, hummingbirds, trogans, etc. Near the lodge, several species of *Morphos* and a large variety of *Hesperidae, Nymphalidae, Pieridae* and *Papilionidae* can be seen. More than 12,000 species of moths are found in Costa Rica, a large percentage of which can be found around the lodge.

The ultimate vacation for birders, lepidopterists, entomologists, botanists, ornithologists, and nature photographers. Daytime temperatures remain consistently in the 70s while the nights are mildly cool in the mid-60s. Rain can be expected in the afternoons from May to November. The flower-surrounded lodge affords a 22-mile panoramic view of the volcanos Irazu and Turrialba.

FACILITIES

The lodge has six comfortable bedrooms and four baths reserved for guests. A one-bedroom, one-bath cottage and a duplex cottage with one bedroom and one bath for each side is also provided. Each bathroom has a hot-water shower. Telephones are available in the local villages. Balanced, nutritious meals are served in one or both dining rooms, and a variety of fresh fruits and vegetables are provided year-round.

SUPPLIES NEEDED

Bring light, comfortable clothing, a sun hat and lotion, water-resistant walking shoes or boots, binoculars, a camera with lots of film, a swimsuit, and rain gear. Dress is casual and comfortable.

APPLICATIONS AND ADMISSIONS

Reservations may be made by writing, phoning, or faxing John W. Erb, c/o Rancho Naturalista at the address above. A security deposit of approximately $200 per person is required. A group leader of eight or more persons is free of charge.

Financial Aid: None available.

Costs: From November to April, rates per person are approximately $603 per week. This cost includes all transportation, meals, lodging, laundry, local tours, and taxes. A 3-day minimum is required to receive free transportation. When available, horseback riding is also included. From May to October, the weekly rates are approximately $499 per week.

NEW ZEALAND

CREATIVE VENTURES
100 Hawke Street
P.O. Box 18-681
Christchurch
NEW ZEALAND
Phone/Fax: 64-3-388-0154
Contact: Alan L. Edelmann

SAMPLE PROGRAMS

Programs include 6-, 8-, 12-, and 20-day discovery tours of New Zealand; Sacred Journey of Aotearoa—A Focus on Maori and Farming Culture; plus Nature and Adventure.

CURRICULUM AND CREDITS

Participants are given the opportunity to learn about some of New Zealand's natural and exotic inhabitants. The native flora and fauna are diverse, beautiful, and quite unique. Variations in natural environments from rainforest and desert to submarine and alpine are all nearby. Bush walks and some overnight camping in huts is part of the itinerary.

Workshops and seminars are part of the itinerary for each tour. Learn from local qualified tutors about the finer points of their knowledge and experience. Participate in experiential sessions to develop skills—whether it be a craft, wildlife studies, outdoor skills, ecological balance or inner/spiritual challenges. Credit may be available—check with Creative Ventures (CV). Opportunities for independent and travel study are always available.

THE INSTITUTION

CV operates internationally from Australia, New Zealand, Hawaii, Europe, and the U.S. mainland.

THE ENVIRONMENT

National parks, state forests, and reserves abound in New Zealand. Experience the magic and majesty of these Southern Hemisphere mountains, lakes, forests, beaches, bays, and rivers. Walk some of the well-known trails as well as visit some of the lesser-known, though no less special, places. Get to know the locals as well as the native birds of New Zealand like the bellbird, tui, fantail, and kea. Learn about the different forests such as podocarp, hardwood, broadleaf, kauri, and beech. Smell the succulent nectar of the many flowers and watch the bees work the honey dew droplets on aphid-covered beech trees. Visit sheep and deer farms, watch the shearers and sheep dogs working, and learn about New Zealand's developing horticultural industry.

FACILITIES

The discovery tours described in the CV brochure include all accommodations, internal transportation, airport transfers, two meals a day, personal guides, seminars, workshops and tutors, a scenic flight, a white-water rafting trip, and a boat excursion.

Many other optional extra adventures and excursions are also available. Free time is given for such choices.

SUPPLIES NEEDED

Personal gear for walking and adventuring is necessary, including layers of clothing for a variety of different temperatures.

APPLICATIONS AND ADMISSIONS

Advance bookings are required. Credit cards are accepted (please add 5%). All holidays are subject to minimum and maximum numbers as well as variations due to unforeseen circumstances. CV is not liable for any losses or damages incurred during travel, although all due caution will be observed. Private travel insurance is recommended. Interested participants who book directly with CV will receive a 10% discount, or they may book with a U.S. travel agent "Down Under Answers." Call (800) 788-6685.

Financial Aid: None available.

Costs: A 6-day tour is approximately $1,395, an 8-day tour $1,790, and a 12-day tour $2,595. Other costs for custom programs are given a price quote.

VIRGIN ISLANDS

VIRGIN ISLANDS ENVIRONMENTAL RESOURCE STATION
P.O. Box 250
St. John
USVI 00831
(809) 776-6721
Fax: (809) 776-6645
E-mail: cgrippa@uvi.edu
Contact: Cynthia A Grippaldi, Research Facility Supervisor

SAMPLE PROGRAMS
The Virgin Islands Environmental Resource Station (VIERS) serves the local community and visiting groups through on-site, year-round environmental education programs and activities. Seashore explorations, mangrove walks, demonstrations in plant or animal identification and snorkeling allow visitors of all ages to discover the local environment. Training sessions and hands-on activities for teachers and others involved in environmental education take advantage of the diversity of ecosystems and isolation of the facility.

CURRICULUM AND CREDITS
Credit may be obtained through independent study, particularly with the internship program. Contact VIERS for further information.

THE INSTITUTION
VIERS is the field station of the University of the Virgin Islands under the direction of the Eastern Caribbean Center. Since 1966 VIERS has offered unique learning experiences for students and scientists interested in environmental education, training, and research of terrestrial, coastal, and marine communities of small tropical islands. VIERS has hosted or worked cooperataively with marine biology and/or ecology programs from numerous institutions and organizations.

THE ENVIRONMENT
VIERS is located on the remote southeastern shore of St. John at Lameshur Bay, within the boundaries of the Virgin Islands National Park and the UNESCO Biosphere Reserve, which offer protection for the various pristine habitats. To protect the environment and resources that make VIERS so valuable, all research and study activities within the park require approved permits from the Virgin Islands National Park. Cruz Bay, the main community of St. John, is accessible by ferry from St. Thomas and is a 40-minute drive from VIERS. The main campsite is located in a lowland tropical dry forest at the base of Bordeaux Mountain. Two sheltered bays with coral reefs and seagrass beds bordered by mangroves are located directly to the south of the main campsite. In the late 1960s, the easternmost side of the bay was the site of the internationally significant Tektite I and Tektite II underwater habitat programs.

FACILITIES

The field station is a remote and rustic camp in a coastal tropical setting, consisting of five dormitory-style cabins and two efficiency research cabins, as well as a classroom, library, office, restroom, and shower facilities. Maximum occupancy is 40 people. The kitchen staff provides three meals a day in the dining hall for overnight groups. All visitors share in cleaning responsibilties.

To supplement the natural marine and terrestrial laboratories, VIERS provides modest diving facilities for marine operations and laboratory space with two circulating seawater tables.

SUPPLIES NEEDED

VIERS provides participants with a "What to Bring" list. It is also advisable to bring any special biological study equipment and supplies one may need. A limited amount of equipment is available at the lab. Contact VIERS at the above address for more details.

APPLICATIONS AND ADMISSIONS

Contact VIERS at the above address for application forms and additional information.

Financial Aid: No financial aid is available; however, participants in the internship program will work at VIERS for 20 hours per week in lieu of lodging fees.

Costs: The fee for lodging in the dormitory cabins is approximately $40 per person per night, and includes lab space, three meals per day, and bed linens. The lodging fee for research cabins is $25 per person per night for the first person and $15 for each additional person, or a monthly rate of approximately $400 for the first person and $100 for each additional person (since these cabins have kitchens, meals are not included in the fee). There are also reasonable fees for boat and scuba tank usage.

SECTION THREE

NATIONAL SCIENCE FOUNDATION TEACHER ENHANCEMENT PROGRAM: U.S. COURSES AND WORKSHOPS

NATIONAL SCIENCE FOUNDATION TEACHER ENHANCEMENT PROGRAM

The National Science Foundation (NSF) sponsors numerous summer workshops for teachers at the elementary, middle, and senior high school levels. Most workshops involve academic year follow-up activities. Workshops are offered in all the biological and physical sciences as well as mathematics. Almost all workshops provide stipends as well as college credit.

Although the actual workshops change periodically—some end while new ones are added—the following list includes most of the workshops that were offered in the summer of 1995 and the academic year follow-up activities. While many of the listed workshops will terminate eventually, and new workshops will be added, it should be understood that the purpose of this listing is twofold:

- To inform teachers that these workshops exist and provide information so that teachers may obtain applications.
- To give teachers an idea of the scope of the workshops that are offered.

Not all workshops are open to all teachers; some are offered exclusively to teachers in a particular locale (city, town, or county). Others are offered exclusively to teachers in a particular state or region. Many workshops, however, are offered at the national level. Space in these workshops is limited and competition can be very keen.

This listing does not provide all the details about each workshop; the intention is to list the names of the workshops given by state, as well as the names and addresses of the workshop coordinators (principal investigators). For more information on a particular workshop, interested teachers should contact the workshop coordinators. In addition, teachers should contact the NSF Teacher Enhancement Program at the following address to receive a listing of the most current workshop offerings:

National Science Foundation
Teacher Enhancement Program
4201 Wilson Boulevard
Arlington, VA 22230
(703) 306-1613

The NSF offers many other programs in addition to the Teacher Enhancement Program workshops. Information on such programs can be found in the *Guide to Programs—National Science Foundation*, which is available from Forms and Publications, National Science Foundation (at the above address). Interested individuals may wish to request a copy of the *NSF Bulletin*, which is also available from the same address. Direct any inquiries to the editor, *NSF Bulletin*.

ALABAMA

PRINCIPAL INVESTIGATOR: Gladiola Dale
INSTITUTION: Jacksonville State University, 700 Pelham Road North, Jacksonville, AL 36265-9962; (205) 265-0511
DATES: January 1, 1993–June 30, 1996
TITLE: An Integrated Mathematics/Science Enhancement Program for Middle School Teachers

PRINCIPAL INVESTIGATOR: Tommy Smith
INSTITUTION: University of Alabama–Birmingham, UAB Station, Birmingham, AL 35294; (205) 934-4011
DATES: September 1, 1992–February 29, 1996
TITLE: Improving Mathematics Teaching in Grades 6–9 Through the Integration of Content, Technology, and Manipulatives

PRINCIPAL INVESTIGATOR: Lee Summerlin
INSTITUTION: University of Alabama–Birmingham, UAB Station, Birmingham, AL 35294; (205) 934-4011
DATES: November 15, 1992–April 30, 1997
TITLE: Training Laboratory Managers: A Comprehensive Experience for High School Chemistry Teachers

PRINCIPAL INVESTIGATOR: John Wright
INSTITUTION: University of Alabama–Huntsville, Huntsville, AL 35899; (205) 895-6295
DATES: May 1, 1993–October 31, 1995
TITLE: Huntsville Elementary Science Program

ARIZONA

PRINCIPAL INVESTIGATOR: Mark Bauer
INSTITUTION: Navajo Community College, Box 67, Tsaile, AZ 86556; (602) 724-3311
DATES: September 1, 1991–February 29, 1996
TITLE: Science Consultant Program for Navajos in Northwest New Mexico

PRINCIPAL INVESTIGATOR: David Gay
INSTITUTION: University of Arizona, Tucson, AZ 85721-0007; (602) 621-2211
DATES: September 1, 1992–February 28, 1997
TITLE: Making Everybody Count—Transforming the Middle School Mathematics Classroom

PRINCIPAL INVESTIGATOR: Richard Greenberg
INSTITUTION: University of Arizona, Tucson, AZ 85721-0007; (602) 621-3237
DATES: October 1, 1992–March 31, 1996
TITLE: Image Processing for Teaching: Development for National Dissemination

PRINCIPAL INVESTIGATOR: David Hestenes
INSTITUTION: Arizona State University, Tempe, AZ 85287-9804; (602) 965-9011
DATES: January 1, 1994–May 31, 1999
TITLE: Modeling Instruction in High School Physics

PRINCIPAL INVESTIGATOR: Martha Narro
INSTITUTION: University of Arizona, Tucson, AZ 85721-0007; (602) 621-2211
DATES: September 1, 1992–February 28, 1998
TITLE: University of Arizona Biology Teaching

PRINCIPAL INVESTIGATOR: T. Lon Owen
INSTITUTION: Northern Arizona University, Flagstaff, AZ 86011; (602) 523-9011
DATES: September 15, 1992–February 28, 1998
TITLE: Western Regional Program for Precollege Biological Science Education

PRINCIPAL INVESTIGATOR: Susan Sprague
INSTITUTION: Mesa Foundation for Educational Excellence, 549 North Stapley Drive, Mesa, AZ 85203; (602) 898-7700
DATES: August l, 1993–July 31, 1995
TITLE: An Advanced Elementary Science Leadership Institute

PRINCIPAL INVESTIGATOR: Elias Toubassi
INSTITUTION: University of Arizona, Tucson, AZ 85721-0007; (602) 621-2211
DATES: July 1,1993–December 31, 1995
TITLE: Project PRIME (Promoting Reform in Mathematics Education)

ARKANSAS

PRINCIPAL INVESTIGATOR: Gaylord Northrop
INSTITUTION: University of Arkansas—Little Rock, 2801 South University, Little Rock, AR 72204; (501) 569-3000
DATES: March 1, 1993–August 31, 1996
TITLE: Arkansas STRIVE—A Joint Venture for Math/Science Teacher Enhancement Through Involvement in Research

CALIFORNIA

PRINCIPAL INVESTIGATOR: Bruce Alberts
INSTITUTION: University of California–San Francisco, 500 Parnassus, San Francisco, CA 94143; (415) 476-4986
DATES: July 15, 1991–June 30, 1995
TITLE: UC San Francisco Science Institute for Elementary Teachers

PRINCIPAL INVESTIGATOR: Donald Anderson
INSTITUTION: University of California–San Diego, 9500 Gilman Drive, La Jolla, CA 92093; (619) 534-6523
DATES: January 1, 1993–June 30, 1996
TITLE: Supercomputer Teacher Enhancement Project (STEP)

PRINCIPAL INVESTIGATOR: Jacqueline Barber
INSTITUTION: University of California–Berkeley, Berkeley, CA 94720; (510) 642-2000
DATES: January 1, 1993–December 31, 1996
TITLE: Primary Leadership Institute in Science and Mathematics (PRISM)

PRINCIPAL INVESTIGATOR: Harvey Barnett
INSTITUTION: Cupertino Union School District, 10301 Vista Drive, Cupertino, CA

95014; (408) 252-3000
DATES: September 1, 1992–February 29,1996
TITLE: ACOT (Apple Classrooms of Tomorrow) Teacher Development Center

PRINCIPAL INVESTIGATOR: Katharine Barrett
INSTITUTION: University of California–Berkeley, Berkeley, CA 94720; (510) 642-2000
DATES: May 15, 1994–March 31, 1996
TITLE: Marine Activities, Resource and Education—A Teacher Enhancement Program

PRINCIPAL INVESTIGATOR: Jean Beard
INSTITUTION: San Jose State University Foundation, One Washington Square, San Jose, CA 95192; (408) 924-1000
DATES: May 1, 1992–June 30, 1997
TITLE: Evolution and the Nature of Science

PRINCIPAL INVESTIGATOR: Joanne Becker
INSTITUTION: San Jose State University Foundation, One Washington Square, San Jose, CA 95192; (408) 924-1000
DATES: April 15, 1992–September 30, 1996
TITLE: San Jose Mathematics Leadership Project

PRINCIPAL INVESTIGATOR: Anne Bouie
INSTITUTION: Interface Institute, 8500 A Street, Oakland, CA 94621; (510) 635-1755
DATES: April 15, 1992–September 30, 1995
TITLE: Science Enrichment Collaborative

PRINCIPAL INVESTIGATOR: James Bower
INSTITUTION: California Institute of Technology, 1201 E. California Blvd. Pasadena, CA 91125; (818) 356-6811
DATES: December 15, 1992–November 30, 1995
TITLE: Hands-On Science in Pasadena—Middle School Extension

PRINCIPAL INVESTIGATOR: Jane Bower
INSTITUTION: Mills College, 5000 MacArthur Boulevard, Oakland, CA 94613; (510) 430-2255
DATES: September 15, 1993–February 28, 1999
TITLE: Leadership Institute for Teaching Elementary Science (LITES)

PRINCIPAL INVESTIGATOR: Phyllis Brady
INSTITUTION: Office of Santa Barbara County Superintendents of Schools, 4400 Cathedral Oaks Road, Santa Barbara, CA 93110; (805) 969-4711
DATES: July 15, 1992–December 31, 1995
TITLE: Early Equity in Science and Mathematics

PRINCIPAL INVESTIGATOR: Klaus Brasch
INSTITUTION: California State University–San Bernardino Foundation, 5500 University Parkway, San Bernardino, CA 92407-2397; (714) 880-5000
DATES: August 15, 1992–January 31, 1996
TITLE: A Model System for the Science Education of Diverse Populations

PRINCIPAL INVESTIGATOR: Chris Craney
INSTITUTION: Occidental College, 1600 Campus Road, Los Angeles, CA 90041; (213) 259-2500
DATES: August 1, 1991–January 31, 1997
TITLE: Teachers + Occidental = Partnership in Science (TOPS)

PRINCIPAL INVESTIGATOR: David Deamer
INSTITUTION: University of California–Davis, Davis, CA 95616-8678; (916) 752-1011
DATES: December 1, 1992–March 31, 1996
TITLE: Science Institute for Elementary School Teachers

PRINCIPAL INVESTIGATOR: Janice Eckmier
INSTITUTION: California State University–Northridge, 18111 Nordhoff Street, Northridge, CA 91330; (818) 885-1200
DATES: June 15, 1993–November 30, 1996
TITLE: Functions and Transformations—Higher Order Mathematics (FATHOM)

PRINCIPAL INVESTIGATOR: Judith Fritz
INSTITUTION: Tech Museum of Innovation, 145 West San Carlos, San Jose, CA 95113; (408) 279-7150
DATES: May 15, 1992–October 31, 1995
TITLE: Extending Science Education—Teaching with and About Technology

PRINCIPAL INVESTIGATOR: William Hamner
INSTITUTION: University of California–Los Angeles, 405 Hilgard Avenue, Los Angeles, CA 90024; (310) 825-4321
DATES: February 1, 1992–July 31, 1995
TITLE: A Novel Interdisciplinary Science Teacher Education Program for the Los Angeles Unified School District with a Marine Science Thematic Approach

PRINCIPAL INVESTIGATOR: Chris Hasegawa
INSTITUTION: Sacramento City Educational Foundation, 520 Capitol Mall, Sacramento, CA 95814; (916) 264-4300
DATES: September 1, 1993–February 29, 1996
TITLE: Jaime Escalante Math Program (JEMP)

PRINCIPAL INVESTIGATOR: Theresa Hernandez-Heinz
INSTITUTION: San Francisco Unified School District, 135 Van Ness Avenue, San Francisco, CA 94102; (415) 241-6000
DATES: June 1, 1994–September 30, 1997
TITLE: Teaching with 4D—Diversity, Dialogue, Dimensions, and Design

PRINCIPAL INVESTIGATOR: Kimi Hosoume
INSTITUTION: University of California–Berkeley, Berkeley, CA 94720; (510) 642-2000
DATES: April 1, 1994–March 31, 1998
TITLE: Bridging Preschool and Kindergarten Through Teacher Enhancement in Science and Mathematics

PRINCIPAL INVESTIGATOR: Linda Huetinck
INSTITUTION: California State University–Northridge Foundation, 18111 Nordhoff Street, Northridge, CA 91330; (818) 885-1200

DATES: May 1, 1993–October 31, 1995
TITLE: Teacher Institute for Using Computer Visualization for Teaching Mathematics

PRINCIPAL INVESTIGATOR: Barbara Huntington
INSTITUTION: Long Beach Unified School District, 701 Locust Avenue, Long Beach, CA 90813; (310) 436-9931
DATES: June 1, 1992–November 30, 1997
TITLE: Scientists in the Making

PRINCIPAL INVESTIGATOR: Raymond Ingersoll
INSTITUTION: University of California–Los Angeles, 405 Hilgard Avenue, Los Angeles, CA 90024; (310) 825-4321
DATES: February 1, 1993–January 31, 1996
TITLE: Interdisciplinary System for the Study of Urban Environmental Science (ISSUES)

PRINCIPAL INVESTIGATOR: John Jewett
INSTITUTION: California Poly Pomona Foundation Inc., California State Polytechnic University–Pomona, 3801 West Temple Avenue, Pomona, CA 91768; (909) 869-2000
DATES: April 15, 1993–September 30, 1996
TITLE: Alliance of Mentors for Physics Instruction—A Teacher Leadership Institute

PRINCIPAL INVESTIGATOR: Ralph Kanning
INSTITUTION: Foundation for Advancements in Science & Education, 4801 Wilshire Boulevard, Los Angeles, CA 90010; (213) 937-9911
DATES: April 1, 1993–September 30, 1995
TITLE: Teacher Enhancement

PRINCIPAL INVESTIGATOR: Kurt Kreith
INSTITUTION: University of California–Davis, Davis, CA 95616-8678; (916) 752-1011
DATES: May 1, 1993–August 31, 1995
TITLE: Building a Mathematical Base for Environmental Studies Curricula

PRINCIPAL INVESTIGATOR: Eunice Krinsky
INSTITUTION: California State University–Dominguez Hills, 1000 East Victoria Street, Carson, CA 90747; (213) 516-3300
DATES: June 1, 1994–November 30, 1997
TITLE: Math Teacher Institute (MTI)

PRINCIPAL INVESTIGATOR: Thomas Lester
INSTITUTION: California State Department of Education, Sacramento, CA 94244; (916) 657-2451
DATES: February 15, 1994–June 30, 1999
TITLE: Math Matters

PRINCIPAL INVESTIGATOR: Yvonne Lux
INSTITUTION: Poway Unified School District, 13626 Twin Peaks Road, Poway, CA 92064; (619) 748-0010
DATES: January 1, 1994–June 30, 1997
TITLE: Making Science Real

PRINCIPAL INVESTIGATOR: George Madrid
INSTITUTION: East Los Angeles College, 1301 Brooklyn Avenue, Monterey Park, CA 91754; (213) 265-8650
DATES: August 1, 1992–January 31, 1996
TITLE: Jaime Escalante Math and Science Program

PRINCIPAL INVESTIGATOR: Ellen Metzger
INSTITUTION: San Jose State University, One Washington Square, San Jose, CA 95192; (408) 924-1000
DATES: April 1, 1993–August 31, 1996
TITLE: The California Earth Science Academy

PRINCIPAL INVESTIGATOR: Carl Naegele
INSTITUTION: University of San Francisco, 2130 Fulton Street, San Francisco, CA 94117-1080; (415) 666-6292
DATES: June 1, 1994–November 30, 1997
TITLE: Microcomputer-Based Laboratory Tools for High School Physics

PRINCIPAL INVESTIGATOR: Steven Oppenheimer
INSTITUTION: California State University–Northridge, 1811 Nordhoff Street, Northridge, CA 91330; (818) 885-1200
DATES: May 1, 1992–October 31, 1997
TITLE: Institutionalizing Student Biology Research Projects

PRINCIPAL INVESTIGATOR: David Pagni
INSTITUTION: California State University–Fullerton Foundation, Fullerton, CA 92634; (714) 773-2011
DATES: August 1, 1992–January 31, 1996
TITLE: Language and Mathematics Projects (LAMP)

PRINCIPAL INVESTIGATOR: Donald Paulson
INSTITUTION: California State L.A. University Auxiliary Services Inc., 5151 State University Drive, Los Angeles, CA 90032; (213) 343-2531
DATES: May 15, 1992–October 31, 1995
TITLE: Hands-on Physical Science Workshops for Elementary Teachers

PRINCIPAL INVESTIGATOR: Jack Price
INSTITUTION: California Poly Pomona Foundation Inc., California State Polytechnic University–Pomona, 3801 West Temple Avenue, Pomona, CA 91768; (909)869-2000
DATES: May 15, 1992–August 31, 1995
TITLE: Integrating Science and Mathematics Teaching for the Middle School Underrepresented Student

PRINCIPAL INVESTIGATOR: Paul Saltman
INSTITUTION: University of California–San Diego, 9500 Gilman Drive, La Jolla, CA 92093; (619) 534-2230
DATES: March 15, 1994–December 31, 1995
TITLE: Science and Technology Enhancement and Enrichment Project (STEEP)

PRINCIPAL INVESTIGATOR: Robert Semper
INSTITUTION: Exploratorium, Marina Boulevard and Lyon Street, San Francisco, CA 94123 (415) 561-0360
DATES: December 1, 1993–November 30, 1995
TITLE: Planning for the National Center for Teacher Education

PRINCIPAL INVESTIGATOR: Richard Shavelson
INSTITUTION: University of California–Santa Barbara, Santa Barbara, CA 93106; (805) 893-2485
DATES: March 15, 1991–February 29, 1996
TITLE: Transferring New Assessment Technologies

PRINCIPAL INVESTIGATOR: Harris Shultz
INSTITUTION: Orange County Superintendent of Schools Office, 200 Kalmur Drive, Fullerton, CA 92631; (714) 966-4001
DATES: October 1, 1993–October 31, 1997
TITLE: C3—The Next Steps

PRINCIPAL INVESTIGATOR: Cary Sneider
INSTITUTION: University of California–Berkeley, Berkeley, CA 94720; (415) 642-6000
DATES: August 15, 1992–July 31, 1995
TITLE: Summer Institutes for Teacher—Leaders in Global Systems Science

PRINCIPAL INVESTIGATOR: Judith Sowder
INSTITUTION: San Diego State University Foundation, 5300 Campanile, San Diego, CA 92182-0771; (619) 594-5200
DATES: July 1, 1994–November 30, 1997
TITLE: Reforming the Preparation and Professional Development of Elementary and Middle School Mathematics Teachers

PRINCIPAL INVESTIGATOR: Mare Taagepera
INSTITUTION: University of California–Irvine, Irvine, CA 92717; (714) 856-6345
DATES: January 1, 1994–December 31, 1998
TITLE: Orange County Science, Technology, and Society Network

PRINCIPAL INVESTIGATOR: Dorothy Terman
INSTITUTION: Irvine Unified School District, 5050 Barranca Parkway, Irvine, CA 92714; (714) 651-0444
DATES: April 15, 1992–January 31, 1996
TITLE: Irvine–McDonnell Douglas Science Partnership

COLORADO

PRINCIPAL INVESTIGATOR: William Blubaugh
INSTITUTION: University of Northern Colorado, Greeley, CO 80639; (970) 351-1890
DATES: September 1, 1994–February 28, 1998
TITLE: Rocky Mountain Secondary Teacher Enhancement Initiative in Mathematics

PRINCIPAL INVESTIGATOR: James Ellis
INSTITUTION: Biological Sciences Curriculum Study, 5415 Mark Dabling Boulevard, Colorado Springs, CO 80918; (719) 531-5550

DATES: February 15, 1993–July 31, 1996
TITLE: Teacher Development Modules for Elementary School Science

PRINCIPAL INVESTIGATOR: James Ellis
INSTITUTION: Biological Sciences Curriculum Study, 5415 Mark Dabling Boulevard, Colorado Springs, CO 80918; (719) 531-5550
DATES: June 1, 1992–November 30, 1996
TITLE: Colorado Science Teacher Enhancement Program (COSTEP)

PRINCIPAL INVESTIGATOR: James Giese
INSTITUTION: Social Science Education Consortium Inc., 3300 Mitchell Lane, Suite 240, Boulder, CO 80301-2272; (303) 492-8154
DATES: September 1, 1992–August 31, 1995
TITLE: Leadership Training Program for Secondary School Teachers in the History and Nature of Science and Technology

PRINCIPAL INVESTIGATOR: John Hoover
INSTITUTION: American Indian Science and Engineering Society (AISES), 1630 30th Street, Suite 301, Boulder, CO 80301; (303) 492-8658
DATES: June 1, 1993–November 30, 1996
TITLE: AISES Math/Science Teacher Enhancement Project

PRINCIPAL INVESTIGATOR: Kenneth Klingenstein
INSTITUTION: University of Colorado–Boulder, Regent Drive, Boulder, CO 80309; (303) 492-1411
DATES: December 1, 1992–May 31, 1996
TITLE: A Comprehensive Approach to Using Internet Resources to Enhance K–12 Education

PRINCIPAL INVESTIGATOR: Paul Kuerbis
INSTITUTION: Colorado College, 14 East Cache La Poudre, Colorado Springs, CO 80903; (719) 389-6000
DATES: June 1, 1994–November 30, 1996
TITLE: Colorado College Integrated Science Teacher Enhancement Program (CCISTEP)

PRINCIPAL INVESTIGATOR: James Schreck
INSTITUTION: University of Northern Colorado, Greeley, CO 80639; (970) 351-1890
DATES: September 1, 1993–June 30, 1995
TITLE: Chemistry and Physics Fundamentals for Pre-High School Teachers

PRINCIPAL INVESTIGATOR: Ronald Schukar
INSTITUTION: Social Science Education Consortium, Inc., 3300 Mitchell Lane, Suite 240, Boulder, CO 80301-2272; (303) 492-8154
DATES: October 1, 1992–March 31, 1996
TITLE: Enhancing Middle School Science Through Community Service

PRINCIPAL INVESTIGATOR: Fredrick Stein
INSTITUTION: Colorado State University, Fort Collins, CO 80523; (970) 491-1101
DATES: April 15, 1992–September 30, 1995
TITLE: Small Scale Science Teachers as Researchers (S^3TAR)

PRINCIPAL INVESTIGATOR: Sallie Watkins
INSTITUTION: University of Southern Colorado, 2200 Bonforte Boulevard, Pueblo, CO 81001; (719) 549-2100
DATES: March 15, 1992–August 31, 1995
TITLE: The Pueblo Project

CONNECTICUT

PRINCIPAL INVESTIGATOR: William Brown
INSTITUTION: Eli Whitney Museum, Inc., 915 Whitney Avenue, Hamden, CT 06517; (203) 777-1833
DATES: September 15, 1992–February 29, 1996
TITLE: Water Learning Lab

PRINCIPAL INVESTIGATOR: Daniel Dolan
INSTITUTION: Wesleyan University, Middletown, CT 06457; (203) 347-9411
DATES: February 15, 1993–July 31, 1996
TITLE: Mathematics Technology Institute

PRINCIPAL INVESTIGATOR: Babu George
INSTITUTION: Sacred Heart University, 5151 Park Avenue, Fairfield, CT 06432-1023; (203) 371-7999
DATES: October 1, 1993–March 31, 1997
TITLE: SMARTNET 2000—A Teacher Enhancement Program for Precollege Science and Mathematics Education

PRINCIPAL INVESTIGATOR: Hank Gruner
INSTITUTION: Science Museum of Connecticut, 950 Trout brook Drive, West Hartford, CT 06119; (203) 236-6339
DATES: January 1, 1994–June 30, 1999
TITLE: Project Search—Statewide Teacher Enhancement in Connecticut

PRINCIPAL INVESTIGATOR: Donald LaSalle
INSTITUTION: Talcott Mt. Science Center for Student Involvement, Avon, CT 06001; (203) 677-0035
DATES: April 1, 1993–September 30, 1996
TITLE: Resource and Training Network for Science Teachers in Urban Middle Schools of Connecticut

PRINCIPAL INVESTIGATOR: J. Gregory McHone
INSTITUTION: Wesleyan University, Middletown, CT 06457; (203) 347-9411
DATES: June 1, 1994–November 30, 1996
TITLE: Field Science Institute for Teachers

PRINCIPAL INVESTIGATOR: Marilyn Schaffer
INSTITUTION: University of Hartford, 200 Bloomfield Avenue, West Hartford, CT 06117; (203) 768-4100
DATES: June 1, 1992–November 30, 1995
TITLE: Teachers, Technology, and Environmental Concerns—Formula for Real Science in the Elementary School

PRINCIPAL INVESTIGATOR: Albert Snow
INSTITUTION: Discovery Museum, 4450 Park Avenue, Bridgeport, CT 06604; (203) 372-3520
DATES: October 1, 1993–January 31, 1997
TITLE: The Connecticut Museum Collaborative for Science Education

PRINCIPAL INVESTIGATOR: Jane Tedder
INSTITUTION: Rescue Inc., 355 Goshen Road, Litchfield, CT 06759; (203) 567-0863
DATES: May 1, 1994–October 31, 1997
TITLE: Western Connecticut Middle Grades Math and Science Teacher Leadership Project

DELAWARE

PRINCIPAL INVESTIGATOR: Ronald Wenger
INSTITUTION: University of Delaware, Newark, DE 19716; (302) 451-2000
DATES: April 1, 1992–February 29, 1996
TITLE: The Delaware Teacher Enhancement Partnership—A Model for Implementing the National Council of Teachers of Mathematics (NCTM) Standards

DISTRICT OF COLUMBIA

PRINCIPAL INVESTIGATOR: Bill Aldridge
INSTITUTION: National Science Teachers Association, 1742 Connecticut Avenue, N.W., Washington, D.C. 20009-1171; (202) 328-5800
DATES: March 15, 1994–August 31, 1996
TITLE: A National Teacher Enhancement/Implementation and Evaluation Project for Grades 9-10—Scope, Sequence, and Coordination in Science

PRINCIPAL INVESTIGATOR: Andrea Anderson
INSTITUTION: Association of Science-Technology Centers, 1025 Vermont Avenue, N.W., Suite 500, Washington, D.C. 20005; (202) 783-7200
DATES: August 1, 1990–July 31, 1995
TITLE: Institute for Teacher Educators at Science Museums

PRINCIPAL INVESTIGATOR: W. Austin
INSTITUTION: Howard University, 2400 Sixth Street, N.W., Washington, D.C. 20059; (202) 636-6100
DATES: June 15, 1994–November 30, 1996
TITLE: Project SCORE

PRINCIPAL INVESTIGATOR: Jerry Bell
INSTITUTION: American Association for Advancement Science, 1333 H Street, N.W., Washington D.C. 20005; (202) 326-6400
DATES: June 1, 1994–November 30, 1996
TITLE: Integrated Environmental Science and Technology Education for Middle Grade Teachers

PRINCIPAL INVESTIGATOR: A. M. Benbow
INSTITUTION: American Chemical Society (ACS), 1155 16th Street, N.W., Washington, D.C. 20036; (202) 872-4600

DATES: November 1, 1993–April 30, 1997
TITLE: Operation Chemistry—Phase II

PRINCIPAL INVESTIGATOR: Diane Bunce
INSTITUTION: Catholic University of America, 620 Michigan Avenue, Washington, D.C. 20064; (202) 635-5305
DATES: March 15, 1992–August 31, 1995
TITLE: ICE Fundamentals Program for Minority Teachers and Teachers of Minority Students

PRINCIPAL INVESTIGATOR: Jane Dillehay
INSTITUTION: Gallaudet University, 800 Florida Avenue, N.E., Washington, D.C. 20002; (202) 651-5000
DATES: February 1, 1993–July 31 1996
TITLE: Summer Institute for Middle School and High School Teachers of the Deaf in Life and Environmental Sciences

PRINCIPAL INVESTIGATOR: A. Graham Down
INSTITUTION: Council for Basic Education, 725 15th Street, N.W., Washington, D.C. 20005; (202) 347-4171
DATES: September 1, 1992–February 29, 1996
TITLE: Independent Study in the Sciences and Humanities Fellowship Program

PRINCIPAL INVESTIGATOR: Frances Haley
INSTITUTION: National Council for the Social Studies, 3501 Newark Street, N.W., Washington, D.C. 20016; (202) 966-7840
DATES: May 1, 1992–October 31, 1995
TITLE: The Interdisciplinary Study of Urbanism in Middle School—Mathematical Association of America

PRINCIPAL INVESTIGATOR: William Anthony Hawkins
INSTITUTION: Mathematical Association of America, 1529 18th Street, N.W., Washington, D.C. 20036; (202) 387-5200
DATES: February 15, 1992–July 31, 1995
TITLE: Strengthening Underrepresented Minority Mathematics Achievement Through a Consortium of Middle School and High School Intervention Projects (SUMMAC)

PRINCIPAL INVESTIGATOR: Mary Hemenway
INSTITUTION: American Astronomical Society, 2000 Florida Avenue, N.W., Suite 300, Washington, D.C. 20009-1231; (202) 328-2010
DATES: February 1, 1994–May 31, 1997
TITLE: American Astronomical Society Teacher Resource Agents (AASTRA)

PRINCIPAL INVESTIGATOR: Karen Hollweg
INSTITUTION: North American Association for Environmental Education, 1255 23rd Street, N.W., Suite 400, Washington, D.C. 20037; (202) 862-1991
DATES: March 15, 1994–May 31, 1997
TITLE: VINE Follow-Through—Developing Strategies and Materials for Promoting More Meaningful Classroom Follow-up to Informal Hands-on Investigations

PRINCIPAL INVESTIGATOR: Douglas Lapp
INSTITUTION: National Academy of Sciences, 2101 Constitution Avenue, N.W., Washington, D.C. 20418; (202) 334-2138
DATES: August 1, 1991–July 31, 1996
TITLE: National Elementary Science Leadership Initiative

PRINCIPAL INVESTIGATOR: Robert Lewis
INSTITUTION: National Science Teachers Association, 1742 Connecticut Avenue, N.W., Washington, D.C. 20009-1171; (202) 328-5800
DATES: August 15, 1991–July 31, 1995
TITLE: Inservice Institutes for Junior/Middle School Science Teachers with Presidential Awardees as Instructional Mentors

PRINCIPAL INVESTIGATOR: Shirley McBay
INSTITUTION: Quality Education for Minorities Network, 1818 N Street, N.W., Suite 350, Washington, D.C. 20036; (202) 659-1818
DATES: July 1, 1994–November 30, 1995
TITLE: A Conference to Discuss the Mathematics and Science Teacher Preparation and Enhancement Programs at Predominantly Minority Institutions

PRINCIPAL INVESTIGATOR: James Sandefur
INSTITUTION: Georgetown University, 37th and O Street, N.W., Washington, D.C. 20057; (202) 687-5055
DATES: July 15, 1992–December 31, 1996
TITLE: Leadership Training Institute in Dynamical Modeling

PRINCIPAL INVESTIGATOR: Harold Sharlin
INSTITUTION: Emeritus Foundation, 1614 20th Street, N.W., Washington, D.C. 20009; (202) 232-0863
DATES: August 15, 1992–February 29, 1996
TITLE: Elementary Students Doing Science with Real Scientists

PRINCIPAL INVESTIGATOR Maxine Singer
INSTITUTION: Carnegie Institution of Washington, 1530 P Street, N.W., Washington, D.C. 20005; (202) 387-6400
DATES: December 15, 1993–May 31, 1999
TITLE: Carnegie Academy for Science Education

PRINCIPAL INVESTIGATOR: Arnold Strassenburg
INSTITUTION: National Science Teachers Association, 1742 Connecticut Avenue, N.W., Washington, D.C. 20009-1171; (202) 328-5800
DATES: April 1, 1994–September 30, 1996
TITLE: Teacher Enhancement in Support of Higher Standards

PRINCIPAL INVESTIGATOR: Sylvia Ware
INSTITUTION: American Chemical Society (ACS), 1155 16th Street, N.W., Washington, D.C. 20036; (202) 872-4600
DATES: May 15, 1994–October 31, 1995
TITLE: Travel Grants to the 13th International Conference on Chemical Education

FLORIDA

PRINCIPAL INVESTIGATOR: Judy Chen
INSTITUTION: Miami Museum of Science Inc., 3280 South Miami Avenue, Miami, FL 33129; (305) 854-4247
DATES: May 1, 1993–October 31, 1995
TITLE: InTech National Dissemination

PRINCIPAL INVESTIGATOR: Angelo Collins
INSTITUTION: Florida State University, Tallahassee, FL 32306-1009; (904) 644-6200
DATES: December 1, 1992–November 30, 1995
TITLE: Program for Learning and Research in Science for Middle School Teachers

PRINCIPAL INVESTIGATOR: Donald Hall
INSTITUTION: University of Florida, Gainesville, FL 32611; (904) 392-3261
DATES: January 1, 1993–June 30, 1995
TITLE: Insect Field Biology for Middle School Teachers

PRINCIPAL INVESTIGATOR: Michael Hynes
INSTITUTION: University of Central Florida, 4000 Central Florida Boulevard, Orlando, FL 32816; (407) 823-3000
DATES: July 1, 1992–June 30, 1996
TITLE: An Industrial Partnership to Improve Mathematics and Science Education in Central Florida

PRINCIPAL INVESTIGATOR: Leonard Lipkin
INSTITUTION: University of North Florida, Jacksonville, FL 32216; (904) 646-2666
DATES: July 1, 1994–June 30, 1996
TITLE: Technology, Discovery, and Communication in Secondary School Mathematics

PRINCIPAL INVESTIGATOR: Thomas Marcinkowski
INSTITUTION: Florida Institute of Technology, 150 West University Boulevard, Melbourne, FL 32901-6988; (407) 768-8000
DATES: May 15, 1994–October 31, 1998
TITLE: The Central and South Florida Middle School Partnership Program

GEORGIA

PRINCIPAL INVESTIGATOR: Wyatt Anderson
INSTITUTION: University of Georgia, Athens, GA 30602; (706) 542-3000
DATES: September 15, 1993–December 31, 1997
TITLE: Leadership Resource Teams to Implement Interdisciplinary Middle School Science

PRINCIPAL INVESTIGATOR: Larry Hatfield
INSTITUTION: University of Georgia Research Foundation, Inc., Athens, GA 30602; (706) 542-3000
DATES: May 1, 1990–August 31, 1996
TITLE: Leadership Infusion of Technology in Mathematics and Its Use in Society (LITMUS)

HAWAII

PRINCIPAL INVESTIGATOR: James Anderson
INSTITUTION: University of Hawaii–Manoa, 2530 Dole Street #C-200, Honolulu, HI 96822; (808) 956-8975
DATES: March 1, 1994–February 28, 1997
TITLE: Volcanology for Earth Science Teachers

PRINCIPAL INVESTIGATOR: Edward Boughton
INSTITUTION: Maui Economic Development Board Inc., 590 Lipoa Parkway, Kihei, HI 96753; (808) 875-2300
DATES: February 1, 1993–July 31, 1997
TITLE: Hands-on Science for Maui—Today's Children for Tomorrow's World

ILLINOIS

PRINCIPAL INVESTIGATOR: John Baldwin
INSTITUTION: University of Illinois at Chicago, Chicago, IL 60680; (312) 996-7000
DATES: April 1, 1993–September 30, 1996
TITLE: College Preparatory Mathematics Project

PRINCIPAL INVESTIGATOR: Samuel Bowen
INSTITUTION: Argonne National Laboratory, 9700 South Cass Avenue, Argonne, IL 60439; (708) 252-2000
DATES: September 1, 1993–August 31, 1997
TITLE: Partial Support for the Department of Energy National Teacher Enhancement Project

PRINCIPAL INVESTIGATOR: Jon Johnson
INSTITUTION: Elmhurst College, 190 Prospect, Elmhurst, IL 60126-3296; (708) 617-3500
DATES: August 1, 1993–January 31, 1997
TITLE: A Mentoring Network for Increasing Technology-Based Mathematical Instruction

PRINCIPAL INVESTIGATOR: Michael Koenig
INSTITUTION: Belleville Public Schools District #118, 105 W.A. Belleville, Belleville, IL 62220; (618) 233-2830
DATES: July 1, 1994–November 30, 1997
TITLE: Developing Elementary and Middle School Mathematics Professionals

PRINCIPAL INVESTIGATOR: Zafra Lerman
INSTITUTION: Columbia College, 600 South Michigan Avenue, Chicago, IL 60605-1996; (312) 663-1600
DATES: November 1, 1992–April 30, 1996
TITLE: Workshop Utilizing an Innovative Approach to the Teaching of Science in the Middle School Level

PRINCIPAL INVESTIGATOR: Jennifer Lewis
INSTITUTION: University of Illinois at Urbana-Champaign, 506 South Wright Street, Urbana, IL 61801; (217) 333-1000
DATES: April 1, 1993–September 30, 1996
TITLE: Materials Technology Workshop for High School Science Teachers

PRINCIPAL INVESTIGATOR: Robert Panoff
INSTITUTION: University of Illinois at Urbana-Champaign, 506 South Wright Street, Urbana, IL 61801; (217) 333-1000
DATES: January 15, 1994–May 31, 1996
TITLE: Resource for Science Education—An Infrastructure for High Performance Computing and Communications in Education

PRINCIPAL INVESTIGATOR: Thomas Rossing
INSTITUTION: Northern Illinois University, De Kalb, IL 60115-2854; (815) 753-1000
DATES: June 1, 1993–November 30, 1995
TITLE: Institute for Teacher Enhancement in Physics

PRINCIPAL INVESTIGATOR: David Winnett
INSTITUTION: Educational Service Center, Region 16, 500 Wilshire Drive, Belleville, IL 62223; (618) 398-5280
DATES: June 1, 1993–November 30, 1996
TITLE: Turning on the LITES (Leaders in Teaching Elementary Science)

PRINCIPAL INVESTIGATOR: Fred Yaffe
INSTITUTION: Eastern Illinois University, Charleston, IL 61920-3099; (217) 581-5000
DATES: June 1, 1993–November 30, 1996
TITLE: Formation of a Psychology Institute (PsyIns) to Provide High School Psychology Teachers with Interactive, Hands-on Lab Experiences to Teach Psychology as a Scientific Endeavor

INDIANA

PRINCIPAL INVESTIGATOR: Lawrence Braile
INSTITUTION: Purdue University Research Foundation, West Lafayette, IN 47907; (317) 494-4600
DATES: May 1, 1994–October 31, 1998
TITLE: Earth Processes Education Program for Teachers (Grades 5–9)

PRINCIPAL INVESTIGATOR: William Dando
INSTITUTION: Indiana State University, 217 North Sixth Street, Terre Haute, IN 47809; (812) 237-2121
DATES: January 15, 1993–June 30, 1995
TITLE: In-Service Program in Physical Geography—Introductory, Advanced, and Outreach Models

PRINCIPAL INVESTIGATOR: Daniel Maki
INSTITUTION: Indiana University, 300 North Jordan Avenue, Bloomington, IN 47401; (812) 855-0848
DATES: January 1, 1993–June 30, 1996
TITLE: Implementing the Standards on Mathematical Modeling

PRINCIPAL INVESTIGATOR: Harry Morrison
INSTITUTION: Purdue University, West Lafayette, IN 47907; (317) 494-4600
DATES: August 15, 1993–January 31, 1996
TITLE: Purdue Instrument Van Project—A University/High School Collaboration for Enhancing Learning in the Laboratory

PRINCIPAL INVESTIGATOR: Justin Price
INSTITUTION: Purdue University, West Lafayette IN 47907; (317) 494-4600
DATES: July 1, 1991–June 30, 1995
TITLE: Enhancing Teachers' Ability to Teach Mathematics as Communication

PRINCIPAL INVESTIGATOR: Daniel Shepardson
INSTITUTION: Purdue University, West Lafayette, IN 47907; (317) 494-4600
DATES: June 1, 1992–November 30, 1995
TITLE: Integrating Laboratory Instruction and Assessment (INLAB)

IOWA

PRINCIPAL INVESTIGATOR: James Shaymansky
INSTITUTION: University of Iowa, 107 Calvin Hall, Iowa City, IA 52242-1396; (319) 335-3500
DATES: January 15, 1994–May 31, 1998
TITLE: Science, Parents and Literature—The Science Pals Project

PRINCIPAL INVESTIGATOR: Robert Yager
INSTITUTION: University of Iowa, 107 Calvin Hall, Iowa City, IA 52242-1396; (319) 335-3500
DATES: May 1, 1994–September 30, 1996
TITLE: Iowa Scope, Sequence, and Coordination, Grades 6–10

KANSAS

PRINCIPAL INVESTIGATOR: Judith Roitman
INSTITUTION: University of Kansas, Main Campus, Lawrence, KS 66045; (913) 864-2700
DATES: April 15, 1992–September 30, 1995
TITLE: Northeast Kansas Elementary School Mathematics Dissemination Project

PRINCIPAL INVESTIGATOR: Richard Welton
INSTITUTION: Kansas State University, Manhattan, KS 66506; (913) 532-6318
DATES: May 1, 1992–October 31, 1995
TITLE: The Development of an Innovative Model to Enhance the Knowledge and Skill Levels in Basic Sciences for Secondary Agriscience Teachers

PRINCIPAL INVESTIGATOR: Elizabeth Yanik
INSTITUTION: Emporia State University, 1200 Commercial, Emporia, KS 66801; (316) 341-1200
DATES: March 15, 1992–August 31, 1995
TITLE: A Collaborative Partnership Between High School and University Mathematics Faculty

KENTUCKY

PRINCIPAL INVESTIGATOR: William Bush
INSTITUTION: University of Kentucky Research Foundation, Lexington, KY 40506; (606) 257-2000

DATES: December 1, 1992–May 31, 1996
TITLE: The Kentucky Middle Grades Mathematics Teacher Network

LOUISIANA

PRINCIPAL INVESTIGATOR: Sheila Pirkle
INSTITUTION: Louisiana State University–Baton Rouge, Baton Rouge, LA 70803-2750; (504) 388-3202
DATES: April 15, 1994–September 30, 1997
TITLE: LSU SEPUP Implementation Center

PRINCIPAL INVESTIGATOR: Stearns Rogers
INSTITUTION: McNeese State University, Lake Charles, LA 70609-2004; (318) 475-5000
DATES: July 1, 1992–December 31, 1995
TITLE: Leadership Program for High School Biology, Chemistry, and Physical Science Teachers

PRINCIPAL INVESTIGATOR: Lola Soileau
INSTITUTION: East Baton Rouge Parish School Board, 1050 South Foster Drive, Baton Rouge, LA 70806; (504) 922-5400
DATES: August 1, 1993–December 31, 1998
TITLE: Primarily Physical Science

PRINCIPAL INVESTIGATOR: Carolyn Talton
INSTITUTION: Louisiana Tech University, Tech Station, Ruston, LA 71272; (318) 257-0211
DATES: December 15, 1991–May 31, 1996
TITLE: Middle Grades Math/Science Project

MARYLAND

PRINCIPAL INVESTIGATOR: John August
INSTITUTION: Mount Saint Mary's College and Seminary, Emmitsburg, MD 21727-7796; (301) 447-6122
DATES: September 1, 1993–June 30, 1997
TITLE: Mathematical Studies in Modeling at Mount Saint Mary's (MSM-2)

PRINCIPAL INVESTIGATOR: Richard Berg
INSTITUTION: University of Maryland College Park, College Park, MD 20742; (301) 405-1000
DATES: February 1, 1993–July 31, 1995
TITLE: Physics Workshop for the Middle School

PRINCIPAL INVESTIGATOR: Bo Ann Bohman
INSTITUTION: Carroll County Public Schools Education, 55 North Court Street, Westminster, MD 21157; (410) 848-8280
DATES: July 1, 1992–December 31, 1995
TITLE: Kindergarten Science—Foundations for Understanding

PRINCIPAL INVESTIGATOR: Valerie Chase
INSTITUTION: National Aquarium in Baltimore, 501 East Pratt Street, Baltimore, MD 21202; (410) 576-3800

DATES: March 15, 1993–August 31, 1998
TITLE: Aquatic Science Teacher Institute for Master Teachers of "Living in Water"

PRINCIPAL INVESTIGATOR: John Fowler
INSTITUTION: Triangle Coalition for Science and Technology Education, 5112 Berwyn Road, Third Floor, College Park, MD 20740; (301) 220-0872
DATES: February 15, 1993–July 31, 1996
TITLE: Summer Industrial Fellowships for Teachers—An Expanded Program

PRINCIPAL INVESTIGATOR: Teodoro Halpern
INSTITUTION: American Association of Physics Teachers, 5112 Berwyn Road, College Park, MD 20740; (301) 345-4200
DATES: June 15, 1994–November 30, 1996
TITLE: Building Bridges for Cooperation in Physics Education

PRINCIPAL INVESTIGATOR: Charles Hancock
INSTITUTION: American Society for Biochemistry and Molecular Biology, 9650 Rockville Pike, Bethesda, MD 20814; (301) 530-7145
DATES: May 15, 1992–October 31, 1995
TITLE: High School Teacher Summer Research Fellowships

PRINCIPAL INVESTIGATOR: Marsha Matyas
INSTITUTION: American Physiological Society, 9650 Rockville Pike, Bethesda, MD 20814; (301) 530-7164
DATES: August 1, 1994–November 30, 1996
TITLE: Frontiers in Physiology—An Enhancement Program for Teachers

PRINCIPAL INVESTIGATOR: Richard McCuen
INSTITUTION: University of Maryland College Park, College Park, MD 20742; (301) 405-1000
DATES: March 15, 1993–August 31, 1995
TITLE: Engineering-Mathematics Training Institute

PRINCIPAL INVESTIGATOR: L. Odom
INSTITUTION: Montgomery County Public Schools, 850 Hungerford Drive, Rockville, MD 20850; (301) 279-3000
DATES: February 15, 1994–July 31, 1998
TITLE: Mathematics Content/Connections

PRINCIPAL INVESTIGATOR: Robert Ridky
INSTITUTION: University of Maryland College Park, College Park, MD 20742; (301) 405-1000
DATES: September 1, 1992–February 29, 1996
TITLE: Development of Teacher Competence in Classroom Use of Scientific Data Sets

PRINCIPAL INVESTIGATOR: E. Wendy Saul
INSTITUTION: University of Maryland Baltimore County, Baltimore, MD 21228; (301) 455-1000
DATES: December 1, 1992–May 31, 1997
TITLE: Interactive Bibliographic Database Resources for Elementary School Science

PRINCIPAL INVESTIGATOR: E. Wendy Saul
INSTITUTION: University of Maryland–Baltimore County, Baltimore, MD 21228; (301) 455-1000
DATES: October 1, 1993–March 31, 1998
TITLE: Integrating Science Across the Elementary and Middle School Curriculum

PRINCIPAL INVESTIGATOR: Leon Ukens
INSTITUTION: Towson State University, Towson, MD 21204-7097; (301) 830-2000
DATES: May 1, 1990–October 31, 1995
TITLE: Baltimore Elementary Science Teaching Project

PRINCIPAL INVESTIGATOR: Dean Wood
INSTITUTION: Hood College, Frederick, MD 21701-9988; (301) 663-3131
DATES: June 1, 1994–November 30, 1997
TITLE: The Development of Teacher Enhancement Activities Based Upon Indicators of Institutionalization of an Exemplary Science Curriculum

MASSACHUSETTS

PRINCIPAL INVESTIGATOR: James Amara
INSTITUTION: Minuteman Regional Vocational Technical School, Marrett Road, Lexington, MA 02173; (617) 861-6500
DATES: August 15, 1991–January 31, 1996
TITLE: Math/Science Enhanced Manufacturing Center

PRINCIPAL INVESTIGATOR: Robert Boutilier
INSTITUTION: Bridgewater State College, Gates House, Bridgewater, MA 02325; (508) 697-1200
DATES: July 15, 1992–November 30, 1995
TITLE: Southeastern Massachusetts Outdoor Elementary Science Education Project

PRINCIPAL INVESTIGATOR: Prassede Calabi
INSTITUTION: TERC, 2067 Massachusetts Avenue, Cambridge, MA 02140; (617) 547-0430
DATES: February 15, 1993–July 31, 1996
TITLE: Teacher Enhancement in Pedagogy and Ecology

PRINCIPAL INVESTIGATOR: Richard Carter
INSTITUTION: Bolt, Beranek, and Newman, Inc., 150 Cambridge Park, Cambridge, MA 02138; (617) 873-2000
DATES: November 1, 1991–April 30, 1996
TITLE: Empowering Teachers—Mathematical Inquiry Through Technology

PRINCIPAL INVESTIGATOR: Richard Carter
INSTITUTION: BBN Systems & Technologies Corporation, 150 Cambridge Park, Cambridge, MA 02140; (617) 873-2000
DATES: April 1, 1994–August 31, 1996
TITLE: The Mathematical Inquiry Videotapes—Tools for Professional Growth

PRINCIPAL INVESTIGATOR: Leroy Cook
INSTITUTION: University of Massachusetts–Amherst, Whitmore Building, Amherst, MA 01003; (413) 545-0111

DATES: February 15, 1993–July 31, 1996
TITLE: University Physics Departments and Alliance for Teacher Enhancement (UPDATE)

PRINCIPAL INVESTIGATOR: Mark Driscoll
INSTITUTION: Education Development Center, 55 Chapel Street, Newton, MA 02158; (617) 969-7100
DATES: July 1, 1994–November 30, 1996
TITLE: Leadership for Urban Mathematics Reform

PRINCIPAL INVESTIGATOR: Ira Geer
INSTITUTION: American Meteorological Society, 45 Beacon Street, Boston, MA 02108; (617) 227-2425
DATES: January 1, 1994–December 31, 1997
TITLE: The Maury Project: Exploring the Physical Foundations of Oceanography

PRINCIPAL INVESTIGATOR: Richard Hallgren
INSTITUTION: American Meteorological Society, 45 Beacon Street, Boston, MA 02108; (617) 227-2425
DATES: September 1, 1991–February 29, 1996
TITLE: Project ATMOSPHERE—Providing the Nation's Precollege Teachers of Grades 5–9 with Instructional Resource Materials and Learning Experiences in the Atmospheric Sciences

PRINCIPAL INVESTIGATOR: Howard Hiatt
INSTITUTION: American Academy of Arts and Sciences, Norton's Woods, 136 Irving Street, Cambridge, MA 02138; (617) 492-8800
DATES: April 1, 1994–September 30, 1995
TITLE: Exploring for Consensus on Major Problems in Education

PRINCIPAL INVESTIGATOR: John Jahoda
INSTITUTION: Bridgewater State College Foundation, Gates House, Bridgewater, MA 02325; (508) 697-1200
DATES: May 1, 1992–October 31, 1995
TITLE: A Cooperative Program to Enhance the Teaching of Science Using Marine Mammal Research for Grade 5–8 Teachers

PRINCIPAL INVESTIGATOR: Paul Joyce
INSTITUTION: Sea Education Association, P.O. Box 6, Woods Hole, MA 02543; (508) 540-3954
DATES: February 15, 1993–July 31, 1995
TITLE: Sea Experience—Theoretical and Practical Summer Programs of Teacher Enhancement in Marine Science

PRINCIPAL INVESTIGATOR: Grace Kelemanik
INSTITUTION: Education Development Center, 55 Chapel Street, Newton, MA 02158; (617) 969-7100
DATES: August 1, 1994–September 30, 1995
TITLE: Dissemination Plan for the Industry Volunteer Model

PRINCIPAL INVESTIGATOR: Margaret Kenney
INSTITUTION: Boston College, Chestnut Hill, MA 02167; (617) 552-8000

DATES: May 1, 1992–October 31, 1995
TITLE: Implementation of the National Council of Teachers of Mathematics Standard in Discrete Mathematics

PRINCIPAL INVESTIGATOR: Robert Moses
INSTITUTION: Algebra Project, Inc., 99 Bishop R.C.H. Aln. Drive, Cambridge, MA 02139; (617) 491-0200
DATES: February 15, 1994–July 31, 1995
TITLE: The Algebra Project in Mississippi—Evaluation and Implementation Activities

PRINCIPAL INVESTIGATOR: Barbara Nelson
INSTITUTION: Education Development Center, 55 Chapel Street, Newton, MA 02158; (617) 969-7100
DATES: August 1, 1993–November 30, 1996
TITLE: Mathematics for Tomorrow

PRINCIPAL INVESTIGATOR: Timothy O'Sullivan
INSTITUTION: University of Massachusetts–Dartmouth, North Dartmouth, MA 02747-2300; (508) 999-8000
DATES: February 1, 1993–July 31, 1996
TITLE: Buzzards Bay Rim Project

PRINCIPAL INVESTIGATOR: Robert Prigo
INSTITUTION: Network, Inc., 300 Brickstone Square, Andover, MA 01810; (508) 470-1080
DATES: April 15, 1990–September 30, 1995
TITLE: Velmont Elementary Science Project

PRINCIPAL INVESTIGATOR: Nancy Roberts
INSTITUTION: Lesley College, 29 Everett Street, Cambridge, MA 02138-2790; (617) 868-9600
DATES: September 1, 1991–February 29, 1996
TITLE: Creating Lasting Links

PRINCIPAL INVESTIGATOR: Faye Ruopp
INSTITUTION: Education Development Center, 55 Chapel Street, Newton, MA 02158; (617) 969-7100
DATES: September 1, 1992–February 29, 1996
TITLE: Teachers, Time, and Transformation—A Grassroots Model for Reform in Practice and Curriculum

PRINCIPAL INVESTIGATOR: Deborah Schifter
INSTITUTION: Education Development Center, Mount Holyoke College, South Hadley, MA 01075-1488; (413) 538-2023
DATES: August 1, 1993–November 30, 1996
TITLE: Teaching to the Big Ideas

PRINCIPAL INVESTIGATOR: Irwin Shapiro
INSTITUTION: Harvard University, Byerly Hall, 8 Garden Street, Cambridge, MA 02138; (617) 495-1000
DATES: July 1, 1992–December 31, 1995
TITLE: Misconception Videos Project (MVP)

PRINCIPAL INVESTIGATOR: Irwin Shapiro
INSTITUTION: Harvard University, Byerly Hall, 8 Garden Street, Cambridge, MA 02138; (617) 495-1000
DATES: July 1, 1992–December 31, 1995
TITLE: Support Program for Instructional Competency in Astronomy (Project SPICA)

PRINCIPAL INVESTIGATOR: Michael Silevitch
INSTITUTION: Northeastern University, 360 Huntington Avenue, Boston, MA 02115; (617) 437-2000
DATES: September 15, 1992–December 31, 1996
TITLE: Training Leadership Teachers to Enhance Science Education Through Experiments and Demonstrations (SEED)

PRINCIPAL INVESTIGATOR: Michael Silevitch
INSTITUTION: Northeastern University, 360 Huntington Avenue, Boston, MA 02115; (617) 437-2000
DATES: April 1, 1994–August 31, 1998
TITLE: Statewide Implementation Program (SIP)—A Cesame Extension Dissemination and Implementation of Exemplary Science and Mathematics Programs in Massachusetts

PRINCIPAL INVESTIGATOR: Sandra Spooner
INSTITUTION: Cambridge School Department, 850 Cambridge Street, Cambridge, MA 02141; (617) 349-6400
DATES: June 1, 1994–September 30, 1997
TITLE: Habits of Mind—Science in Cambridge

PRINCIPAL INVESTIGATOR: H. Stanley
INSTITUTION: Boston University, 121 Bay State Road, Boston, MA 02215; (617) 353-2000
DATES: September 1, 1993–February 28, 1997
TITLE: Patterns in Nature—A New Approach to Interdisciplinary Science

PRINCIPAL INVESTIGATOR: Morton Sternheim
INSTITUTION: Five Colleges, Inc., 97 Spring Street, Amherst, MA 01002; (413) 256-8316
DATES: March 1, 1992–August 31, 1995
TITLE: The 5C/5E Project—The Five College Education in the Earth's Environment, Ecology, and Energy Project

PRINCIPAL INVESTIGATOR: Douglas Zook
INSTITUTION: Boston University, 121 Bay State Road, Boston, MA 02215; (617) 353-2000
DATES: April 1, 1992–September 30, 1995
TITLE: Exploring the Microcosms—Microlife as a Dynamic Learning Tool in Middle and Secondary Classrooms

PRINCIPAL INVESTIGATOR: Bernard Zubrowski
INSTITUTION: Education Development Center, 55 Chapel Street, Newton, MA 02158; (617) 969-7100
DATES: May 1, 1994–April 30, 1996
TITLE: Looking at Students' Interactions with Materials and Phenomena—A Collection of Video and Print Resources for Teachers

MICHIGAN

PRINCIPAL INVESTIGATOR: Howard Hagerman
INSTITUTION: Michigan State University, East Lansing, MI 48824-1046; (517) 355-1855
DATES: May 1, 1992–October 31, 1995
TITLE: Operation Toolbox—A Program in Environmental and Behavioral Biology for Science Teachers

PRINCIPAL INVESTIGATOR: Donald Herbert
INSTITUTION: Mr. Wizard Foundation, 44800 Helm Street, Plymouth, MI 48170; (800) 992-8388
DATES: June 15, 1992–May 31, 1996
TITLE: Mr. Wizard TV Science Workshops

PRINCIPAL INVESTIGATOR: Christian Hirsch
INSTITUTION: Western Michigan University, Kalamazoo, MI 49008; (616) 387-1000
DATES: June 15, 1994–November 30, 1997
TITLE: Mathematical Sciences Sequential Summer Institute for High School Mathematics Teachers

PRINCIPAL INVESTIGATOR: P. Douglas Kindschi
INSTITUTION: Grand Valley State University, Allendale, MI 49401; (616) 895-6611
DATES: September 1, 1991–February 29, 1996
TITLE: Teachers in Industry Strategy

PRINCIPAL INVESTIGATOR: Joseph Krajcik
INSTITUTION: University of Michigan–Ann Arbor, 515 Jefferson, Ann Arbor, MI 48104-2210; (313) 764-1817
DATES: September 1, 1991–August 31, 1995
TITLE: Enhancing the Teaching of Project-Based Science

PRINCIPAL INVESTIGATOR: Penelope Peterson
INSTITUTION: Michigan State University, East Lansing, MI 48824-1046; (517) 355-1855
DATES: February 15, 1992–July 31, 1996
TITLE: Teachers' Learning from Reform—The Case of Mathematics Instruction in California

PRINCIPAL INVESTIGATOR: William Stapp
INSTITUTION: University of Michigan–Ann Arbor, 515 Jefferson, Ann Arbor, MI 48104-2210; (313) 764-1817
DATES: February 15, 1993–January 31, 1996
TITLE: Global Rivers Environmental Education Network (Project GREEN)—A Teacher Enhancement Program

PRINCIPAL INVESTIGATOR: Mary Whitmore
INSTITUTION: University of Michigan–Ann Arbor, 515 Jefferson, Ann Arbor, MI 48104-2210; (313) 764-1817
DATES: July 1, 1991–June 30, 1995
TITLE: A Special Summer Institute for Science Teachers (ASSIST)

MINNESOTA

PRINCIPAL INVESTIGATOR: Richard Allen
INSTITUTION: Saint Olaf College, 1520 Saint Olaf Avenue, Northfield, MN 55057-1098; (507) 646-2222
DATES: May 1, 1994–April 30, 1998
TITLE: Teachers Empowering Teachers—Vertically Integrated, Inquiry-Based Geometry in School Classrooms

PRINCIPAL INVESTIGATOR: John Frey
INSTITUTION: Mankato State University, Mankato, MN 56002; (507) 389-6767
DATES: January 1, 1992–June 30 1995
TITLE: Teacher Enhancement in Applied Ecology

PRINCIPAL INVESTIGATOR: Naum Kipnis
INSTITUTION: Bakken Library of Electricity in Life, 3537 Zenith Avenue South, Minneapolis, MN 55416; (612) 927-6508
DATES: July 1, 1992–June 30, 1995
TITLE: Science Teachers Discover Physics

PRINCIPAL INVESTIGATOR: Geneva Middleton
INSTITUTION: Minnesota Educational Cooperative Service Unit Association, 1600 Madison Street, Mankato, MN 56001; (507) 345-7500
DATES: January 15, 1992–June 30, 1995
TITLE: Project Activity-Centered Science (PACS)

PRINCIPAL INVESTIGATOR: Mary Roberts
INSTITUTION: Intermediate District 287, Hennepin Technical College, 1820 Xenium Lane, North Plymouth, MN 55441; (612) 559-3535
DATES: July 15, 1993–December 31, 1997
TITLE: PriMath II—Developing Teacher Leaders to Foster Mathematics Talent in K–4 Students

MISSISSIPPI

PRINCIPAL INVESTIGATOR: John Bedenbaugh
INSTITUTION: University of Southern Mississippi, Box 5011 Southern Station, Hattiesburg, MS 39406; (601) 266-7011
DATES: January 1, 1993–June 30, 1996
TITLE: A Model for Secondary Teacher In-Service Science Instruction and Leadership Development

PRINCIPAL INVESTIGATOR: Rosalina Hairston
INSTITUTION: University of Southern Mississippi, Box 5011 Southern Station, Hattiesburg, MS 39406; (601) 266-7011
DATES: January 1, 1993–June 30, 1996
TITLE: Building Leadership to Enhance the Teaching of Secondary School Biology in Mississippi

MISSOURI

PRINCIPAL INVESTIGATOR: Shirley Hill
INSTITUTION: University of Missouri–Kansas City, Kansas City, MO 64110-2944; (816) 235-1000
DATES: June 1, 1994–October 31, 1996
TITLE: Enhancing the Teacher's Role in Assessment (EXTRA)

PRINCIPAL INVESTIGATOR: Paul Markovits
INSTITUTION: Cooperating School District of St. Louis, 1460 Craig Road, St. Louis, MO 63146-4842; (314) 872-8282
DATES: September 15, 1992–February 29, 1996
TITLE: Biotechnology Advocacy and Science Education (BASE) Program in Teacher Enhancement for Grades 6–8

MONTANA

PRINCIPAL INVESTIGATOR: Gil Alexander
INSTITUTION: Canyon Ferry Limnological Institute Inc., 7653 Canyon Ferry Road, Helena, MT 59601; (406) 475-3638
DATES: June 15, 1992–November 30, 1995
TITLE: Missouri River Water Quality Network

PRINCIPAL INVESTIGATOR: Arnold Craig
INSTITUTION: Montana State University Bozeman, MT 59717; (406) 994-0211
DATES: July 1, 1993–April 30, 1997
TITLE: Chemistry Concept Workshops

PRINCIPAL INVESTIGATOR: Robert Madsen
INSTITUTION: Little Big Horn College, P.O. Box 370, Crow Agency, MT 59022; (406) 638-2228
DATES: February 15, 1993–July 31, 1996
TITLE: Field-Based Instruction for Native American Elementary Teachers (FINEST)

PRINCIPAL INVESTIGATOR: Lee Metzgar
INSTITUTION: University of Montana, Missoula, MT 59812; (406) 243-0211
DATES: February 1, 1992–July 31, 1995
TITLE: Conservation Biology Workshop

PRINCIPAL INVESTIGATOR: Gerard Vandeberg
INSTITUTION: Blackfeet Community College, P.O. Box 819, Browning, MT 59417; (406) 338-5421
DATES: September 1, 1991–February 29, 1996
TITLE: Blackfeet Mathematics and Science Education Improvement Project

PRINCIPAL INVESTIGATOR: Gerald Wheeler
INSTITUTION: Montana State University, Bozeman, MT 59717; (406) 994-0211
DATES: March 1, 1993–August 31, 1996
TITLE: A National Science Teachers Network

NEBRASKA

PRINCIPAL INVESTIGATOR: James Marlin
INSTITUTION: University of Nebraska-Lincoln, 14th and R Streets, Lincoln, NE 68588; (402) 472-7211
DATES: June 1, 1993-November 30, 1995
TITLE: An Electronic Economics Tutor for Teachers

PRINCIPAL INVESTIGATOR: James Marlin
INSTITUTION: University of Nebraska-Lincoln, 14th and R Streets, Lincoln, NE 68588; (402) 472-7211
DATES: May 1, 1993-October 31, 1996
TITLE: Nebraska Economics Fellows Institute for Secondary School Teachers

PRINCIPAL INVESTIGATOR: Bruce Mattson
INSTITUTION: Creighton University, 2500 California, Omaha, NE 68178; (402) 280-2700
DATES: December 1, 1992-May 31, 1997
TITLE: High School Chemistry Teacher Demonstration Workshop—Fast-Track Skills Building for Underprepared Chemistry Teachers

NEVADA

PRINCIPAL INVESTIGATOR: P. Kay Carl
INSTITUTION: Clark County School District, 2832 East Flamingo Road, Las Vegas, NV 89121; (702) 799-5011
DATES: June 15, 1992-May 31, 1996
TITLE: Mathematics and Science Enhancement

NEW HAMPSHIRE

PRINCIPAL INVESTIGATOR: Judith Kull
INSTITUTION: University of New Hampshire-Durham, Durham, NH 03824; (603) 862-1234
DATES: September 1, 1992-February 28, 1997
TITLE: Middle School Mathematics and Science Collaborative

PRINCIPAL INVESTIGATOR: Carol Muller
INSTITUTION: Dartmouth College, Hanover, NH 03755; (603) 646-1110
DATES: January 1, 1993-December 31, 1996
TITLE: Engineering Concepts for the High School Classroom

NEW JERSEY

PRINCIPAL INVESTIGATOR: Ted Chittenden
INSTITUTION: Educational Testing Service, Rosedale Road, Princeton, NJ 08540; (609) 921-9000
DATES: July 15, 1992-December 31, 1995
TITLE: Documenting and Understanding Young Children's Science Learning

PRINCIPAL INVESTIGATOR: Angela Cristini
INSTITUTION: Ramapo College of New Jersey, 505 Ramapo Valley Road, Mahwah, NJ

07430; (201) 529-7500
DATES: June 15, 1994–November 30, 1997
TITLE: Revitalizing Science Teaching Using Remote Sensing Technologies (RST²)

PRINCIPAL INVESTIGATOR: George Daniel
INSTITUTION: Somerset/Hunterdon Business Education Partnership, Inc., 64 West End Avenue, Somerville, NJ 08876; (908) 725-6032
DATES: September 1, 1993–February 28, 1998
TITLE: Science Alliance 2

PRINCIPAL INVESTIGATOR: Edward Friedman
INSTITUTION: Stevens Institute of Technology, Castle Point on the Hudson, Hoboken, NJ 07030; (201) 216-5000
DATES: December 15, 1992–May 31, 1996
TITLE: Enhancing Mathematics Instruction Through Computer-Oriented Active Learning Environments

PRINCIPAL INVESTIGATOR: Dale Koepp
INSTITUTION: Woodrow Wilson National Fellowship Foundation, Box 642, Princeton, NJ 08542; (609) 924-4666
DATES: May 1, 1992–June 30, 1995
TITLE: Biology Institutes—National Science and Mathematics Leadership Program

PRINCIPAL INVESTIGATOR: Roberta Moldow
INSTITUTION: Seton Hall University, 400 South Orange Avenue, South Orange, NJ 07079-2689; (201) 761-9000
DATES: September 1, 1992–February 29, 1996
TITLE: Development of Hands-on, Inquiry-Based Instruction in Secondary School Biology

PRINCIPAL INVESTIGATOR: Joseph Rosenstein
INSTITUTION: Rutgers University New Brunswick, New Brunswick, NJ 08903; (908) 932-1766
DATES: March 15, 1992–August 31, 1995
TITLE: Leadership Program in Discrete Mathematics—Phase II

NEW YORK

PRINCIPAL INVESTIGATOR: Gary Benenson
INSTITUTION: CUNY City College, Convent Avenue and 138th Street, New York, NY 10031; (212) 650-7000
DATES: January 1, 1992–November 30, 1995
TITLE: The Urban Environment as the Vehicle for Elementary School Science Teaching

PRINCIPAL INVESTIGATOR: Annette Berkovits
INSTITUTION: New York Zoological Society, Bronx River Parkway and Fordham Road, Bronx, NY 10458; (718) 367-1010
DATES: February 1, 1992–July 31, 1996
TITLE: Summer Seminars for Secondary School Teachers—Instruction in the Use of Zoological Collections in Teaching Science

PRINCIPAL INVESTIGATOR: Alan Berkowitz
INSTITUTION: Institute of Ecosystem Studies, P.O. Box AB, Millbrook, NY 12545; (914) 677-5343
DATES: February 1, 1994–July 31, 1996
TITLE: Schoolyard Ecology for Elementary School Teachers (SYEFEST)

PRINCIPAL INVESTIGATOR: Pierre-Yves Bouthyette
INSTITUTION: Elmira College, Park Place, Elmira, NY 14901; (607) 735-1800
DATES: January 15, 1993–December 31, 1996
TITLE: In-Service Teacher Enhancement Program in Biology

PRINCIPAL INVESTIGATOR: Bonnie Brownstein
INSTITUTION: CUNY Graduate School University Center, 33 West 42nd Street, New York, NY 10036; (212) 642-1600
DATES: July 15, 1992–June 30, 1996
TITLE: Action Physics—Science and Mathematics Education Through the Physics of Movement

PRINCIPAL INVESTIGATOR: Arthur Camins
INSTITUTION: New York City Board of Education, Community School District #16, 1010 Lafayette Avenue, Brooklyn, NY 11221; (718) 919-4112
DATES: November 15, 1992–February 29, 1996
TITLE: Science in the Seamless Day—An Interdisciplinary, Urban, and Multicultural Enhancement Program for Elementary School Teachers

PRINCIPAL INVESTIGATOR: Glenn Crosby*
INSTITUTION: Division of Chemical Education, Inc., New Rochelle, NY
DATES: August 15, 1993–January 31, 1997
TITLE: A Regional Teacher Enhancement Program for High School Teachers of Chemistry at the 13th Biennial Conference on Chemical Education
*Contact Dr. Glenn Crosby, Washington State University, Pullman, WA 99163; (509) 335-5605.

PRINCIPAL INVESTIGATOR: Vincent Cusimano
INSTITUTION: New York City Board of Education, 110 Livingston Street, Brooklyn, NY 11201; (718) 935-2000
DATES: September 1, 1991–February 29, 1996
TITLE: A Collaborative Approach to Improving Science Instruction Through Technology—Grades 7–9

PRINCIPAL INVESTIGATOR: Rodney Doran
INSTITUTION: SUNY at Buffalo, Buffalo, NY 14260; (716) 645-2000
DATES: September 1, 1991–August 31, 1995
TITLE: Science for the Handicapped

PRINCIPAL INVESTIGATOR: Peter Dow
INSTITUTION: Buffalo Society of Natural Sciences, 1020 Humboldt Parkway, Buffalo, NY 14211; (716) 896-5200
DATES: July 1, 1991–June 30, 1995
TITLE: Project TEAM (Teacher Education At the Museum)

PRINCIPAL INVESTIGATOR: Lauren Farber
INSTITUTION: Community School District #6, New York City School System, 665 West 182nd Street, New York, NY 10033
DATES: July 15, 1992-June 30, 1997
TITLE: School Based Elementary Science Restructuring Program

PRINCIPAL INVESTIGATOR: Alan Friedman
INSTITUTION: New York Hall of Science, 4701 111th Street, Corona, NY 11368; (718) 699-0675
DATES: July l, 1994-December 31, 1997
TITLE: The Science Discovery Lab System—Sustained Enhancement for In-service Teachers

PRINCIPAL INVESTIGATOR: Edward Goldman
INSTITUTION: Brooklyn Tech Research Foundation Inc., Brooklyn Technical High School, 29 Fort Green Place, Brooklyn, NY 11217; (718) 858-5150
DATES: May 1, 1993-October 31, 1996
TITLE: Urban Mathematics, Science, and Technology Leadership Project

PRINCIPAL INVESTIGATOR: William Halligan
INSTITUTION: New York State Education Department, Cultural Education Center, Albany, NY 12234; (518) 474-3852
DATES: September l, 1991-August 31, 1995
TITLE: Increasing Hands-on Elementary Science in the Classroom with the Use of Video Technology for Teacher Inservice

PRINCIPAL INVESTIGATOR: Robert Highsmith
INSTITUTION: National Council on Economic Education, 432 Park Avenue South, New York, NY 10016; (212) 730-7007
DATES: March 15, 1992-August 31, 1995
TITLE: Enhancement of Analytic Thinking Through Advanced Economic Education in Secondary Schools

PRINCIPAL INVESTIGATOR: David Knee
INSTITUTION: Hofstra University, Hempstead, NY 11550; (516) 463-6600
DATES: June 15, 1992-November 30, 1996
TITLE: Leadership in Middle Grade Mathematics—A Teacher-Enhancement Program

PRINCIPAL INVESTIGATOR: Thomas Liao
INSTITUTION: SUNY at Stony Brook, Stony Brook, NY 11794; (516) 689-6000
DATES: April 1, 1992-June 30, 1995
TITLE: Teacher In-Service Program in Technological Literacy and Engineering Concepts

PRINCIPAL INVESTIGATOR: Martin Marin
INSTITUTION: CUNY City College, Convent Avenue and 138th Street, New York, NY 10031; (212) 650-7000
DATES: January 1, 1993-June 30, 1996
TITLE: The Aerospace Science Leadership Institute

PRINCIPAL INVESTIGATOR: Martin Marin
INSTITUTION: CUNY City College, Convent Avenue and 138th Street, New York, NY 10031; (212) 650-7000
DATES: December 15, 1993–May 31, 1997
TITLE: The Weather Watch Leadership Network

PRINCIPAL INVESTIGATOR: David Micklos
INSTITUTION: Cold Spring Harbor Lab Quantitative Biology, Bungtown Road, Cold Spring Harbor, NY 11724; (516) 367-8397
DATES: April 1, 1993–September 30, 1996
TITLE: A Two-Piece Program to Develop and Support a Nationwide Corps of Human and Molecular Genetics Resource Teachers at the Secondary Level

PRINCIPAL INVESTIGATOR: John Niman
INSTITUTION: CUNY Hunter College, 695 Park Avenue, New York, NY 10021; (212) 772-4000
DATES: September 15, 1992–February 29, 1996
TITLE: Project ET—Energizing Teachers of Mathematics, Science, and Technology in Grades 4–9

PRINCIPAL INVESTIGATOR: Theron Rockhill
INSTITUTION: SUNY College at Brockport, Brockport, NY 14420; (716) 395-2211
DATES: January 15, 1993–December 31, 1995
TITLE: Applications and Modeling in the Secondary Mathematics Curriculum

PRINCIPAL INVESTIGATOR: Peter Seligmann
INSTITUTION: Ithaca College, 953 Danby Road, Ithaca, NY 14850; (607) 274-3013
DATES: April 1, 1993–September 30, 1996
TITLE: Leadership Institutes to Promote Effective Computer Usage in Middle and Secondary School Laboratories

PRINCIPAL INVESTIGATOR: Carl Stannard
INSTITUTION: SUNY at Binghamton, P.O. Box 6000, Binghamton, NY 13902-6000; (607) 777-2000
DATES: April 15, 1992–January 31, 1996
TITLE: Statewide Training for Educators in Physical Sciences—STEPS K–12 Leadership Program

PRINCIPAL INVESTIGATOR: Patricia Tinto
INSTITUTION: Syracuse University, 201 Administration Building, Syracuse, NY 13244; (315) 443-1870
DATES: December 15, 1992–May 31, 1997
TITLE: Mathematics Teacher/Researchers Collaborating for Collaboration in the Classroom (MTRC^3)

PRINCIPAL INVESTIGATOR: Dana Packman
INSTITUTION: Norman Howard School Research Development and Outreach, Rochester, NY 14618; (716) 461-1600
DATES: January 15, 1992–June 30, 1995
TITLE: Supporting Middle School Learning Disabled Students in the Mainstream Mathematics Classroom

PRINCIPAL INVESTIGATOR: Stephen Pryor
INSTITUTION: SUNY College at Old Westbury, P.O. Box 210, Old Westbury, NY 11568-0210; (516) 876-3000
DATES: December 15, 1992–November 30, 1995
TITLE: Science Educators Enhancement and Development Program

PRINCIPAL INVESTIGATOR: Gilbert Turchin
INSTITUTION: Community School District #3, 300 West 96th Street, New York, NY 10025; (212) 678-2000
DATES: May 15, 1994–June 30, 1995
TITLE: Teacher Enhancement Planning Project—New York City Community School Districts 3 and 5

PRINCIPAL INVESTIGATOR: Martin Weiss
INSTITUTION: New York Hall of Science, 4701 111th Street, Corona, NY 11368; (718) 699-0675
DATES: August 15, 1992–January 31, 1996
TITLE: MICROLAB Institute

PRINCIPAL INVESTIGATOR: Susan Zakaluk
INSTITUTION: New York City Public Schools, 110 Livingston Street, Brooklyn, NY 11201; (718) 935-2000
DATES: May 1, 1994–October 31, 1995
TITLE: Real World Investigations

NORTH CAROLINA

PRINCIPAL INVESTIGATOR: George Brett
INSTITUTION: Microelectronics Center of North Carolina, 2520 Tri-Center Boulevard, Durham, NC 27713; (919) 685-9977
DATES: August 1, 1994–June 30, 1995
TITLE: Presidential Awardees in Communication Using the Internet

PRINCIPAL INVESTIGATOR: George Bright
INSTITUTION: University of North Carolina–Greensboro, Greensboro, NC 27412-5001; (919) 334-5000
DATES: September 1, 1992–June 30, 1995
TITLE: Calculator Institute for Middle School Mathematics Teachers

PRINCIPAL INVESTIGATOR: Dorothy Doyle
INSTITUTION: North Carolina School of Science & Mathematics, 1219 Broad Street, Durham, NC 27705; (919) 286-3366
DATES: December 15, 1992–May 31, 1997
TITLE: Contemporary Calculus and Precalculus Lead Teacher Development

PRINCIPAL INVESTIGATOR: David Haase
INSTITUTION: North Carolina State University at Raleigh, Raleigh, NC 27695-7103; (919) 737-2011
DATES: April 1, 1993–September 30, 1996
TITLE: Team Science

PRINCIPAL INVESTIGATOR: Gerald Meisner
INSTITUTION: University of North Carolina-Greensboro, Greensboro, NC 27412-5001; (919) 334-5000
DATES: May 1, 1994–October 31, 1996
TITLE: Technology Tools for Science and Mathematics Learning

PRINCIPAL INVESTIGATOR: John Risley
INSTITUTION: North Carolina State University-Raleigh, Raleigh, NC 27695-7103; (919) 737-2011
DATES: September 1, 1992–February 29, 1996
TITLE: Physics Courseware Evaluation Project—Courseware Evaluation and PCEP Teacher Institute

PRINCIPAL INVESTIGATOR: Russell Rowlett
INSTITUTION: University of North Carolina-Chapel Hill, Chapel Hill, NC 27514; (919) 962-2211
DATES: June 1, 1994–November 30, 1998
TITLE: North Carolina Leadership Network for Earth Science Teachers

PRINCIPAL INVESTIGATOR: Georgiana Searles
INSTITUTION: North Carolina Museum of Life and Science, 433 Murray Avenue, Durham, NC 27704; (919) 220-5429
DATES: April 15, 1992–September 30, 1995
TITLE: Project Scientifica

PRINCIPAL INVESTIGATOR: Norma Sermon-Boyd
INSTITUTION: Jones County Schools, Trenton, NC 28585; (919) 448-2531
DATES: July 15, 1994–December 31, 1995
TITLE: Jones County Reaching for Learning Mathematics

PRINCIPAL INVESTIGATOR: Carole Smith
INSTITUTION: Camden County Schools, Board of Education, Camden, NC 27921; (919) 335-0831
DATES: September 15, 1993–February 28, 1997
TITLE: Computational Training for Teacher Enhancement, Action, and Motivation

OHIO

PRINCIPAL INVESTIGATOR: Lawrence Badar
INSTITUTION: Case Western Reserve University, Cleveland, OH 44106; (216) 368-2000
DATES: September 1, 1993–August 31, 1996
TITLE: Engineering Awareness for High School Teachers

PRINCIPAL INVESTIGATOR: Jnanendra Bhattacharjee
INSTITUTION: Miami University, Oxford, OH 45056; (513) 529-1809
DATES: May 15. 1992–October 31, 1995
TITLE: Teacher Enhancement Molecular Biology and Recombinant DNA Technology

PRINCIPAL INVESTIGATOR: Aaron Burke
INSTITUTION: Dayton City School District, 348 First Street, Dayton, OH 45402;

(513) 461-3002
DATES: February 15, 1994–June 30, 1996
TITLE: Project Grow—The Development of Hands-on, Inquiry-Based Middle School Mathematics and Science Teachers

PRINCIPAL INVESTIGATOR: Franklin Demana
INSTITUTION: Ohio State University Research Foundation, 1210 Lincoln Tower, 1800 Cannon Drive, Columbus, OH 43210-1200; (614) 292-OHIO
DATES: March 1, 1990–June 30, 1995
TITLE: Technology Reform and Network Specialist Inservice Training (TRANSIT) Project

PRINCIPAL INVESTIGATOR: Claudia Khourey-Bowers
INSTITUTION: Canton City Schools, 617 McKinley Avenue, S.W., Canton, OH 44707; (216) 438-2500
DATES: February 1, 1994–July 31, 1998
TITLE: Grassroots Science Leadership Institute

PRINCIPAL INVESTIGATOR: Barbara Patterson
INSTITUTION: Cleveland Education Fund, Hanna Building, Cleveland, OH 44115; (216) 566-1136
DATES: September 15, 1990–August 31, 1995
TITLE: Teacher-Student-Industry Model Math

PRINCIPAL INVESTIGATOR: Arlyne Sarquis
INSTITUTION: Miami University, 4200 East University Boulevard, Middletown, OH 45042; (513) 424-4444
DATES: May 1, 1994–October 31, 1996
TITLE: Teaching Science with Toys—Cultivating Advancements in Physical Science (TOYS–CAPS)

OKLAHOMA

PRINCIPAL INVESTIGATOR: Robert Howard
INSTITUTION: University of Tulsa, 600 South College Avenue, Tulsa, OK 74104; (918) 631-2000
DATES: June 15, 1992–November 30, 1995
TITLE: Program to Improve the Science Curriculum in Elementary School (PISCES)—Workshops to Develop Oklahoma Teachers

PRINCIPAL INVESTIGATOR: Ken Crawford
INSTITUTION: University of Oklahoma Norman Campus, Norman, OK 73019; (405) 325-2151
DATES: June 15, 1992–November 30, 1995
TITLE: Earth-System Education for Science Teachers Using the Oklahoma Regional Mesonetwork (EARTHSTORM)

OREGON

PRINCIPAL INVESTIGATOR: Juliet Baxter
INSTITUTION: Eugene School District 4J, 200 North Monroe Street, Eugene, OR 97402 (503) 687-3123

DATES: May 15, 1994–September 30, 1996
TITLE: Integrating Science Concepts

PRINCIPAL INVESTIGATOR: Christie Borgford
INSTITUTION: Portland State University, P.O. Box 751, Portland, OR 97207-0751; (503) 725-4433
DATES: December 15, 1992–May 31, 1996
TITLE: The Role of the Laboratory in Learning Chemistry in the 1990s

PRINCIPAL INVESTIGATOR: Thomas Dick
INSTITUTION: Oregon State University, Corvallis, OR 97331; (503) 737-0123
DATES: March 1, 1993–August 31, 1996
TITLE: National Dissemination of Calculus Reform in High Schools by the Oregon State University Calculus Curriculum Project

PRINCIPAL INVESTIGATOR: Diana Fisher
INSTITUTION: Multnomah County School District #1, 501 Dixon, Portland, OR 97227; (503) 249-2000
DATES: May 1, 1993–October 31, 1996
TITLE: Cross-Curricular Systems Thinking and Dynamic Using STELLA (Project CC-STADUS)

PRINCIPAL INVESTIGATOR: David Heil
INSTITUTION: Oregon Museum of Science and Industry, 1945 S.E. Water Avenue, Portland, OR 97214; (503) 797-4000
DATES: July 1, 1990–March 31, 1996
TITLE: National Science and Technology Week—Teacher Training and Materials Dissemination Network

PRINCIPAL INVESTIGATOR: Lowell Herr
INSTITUTION: Catlin Gabel School, 8825 S.W. Barnes Road, Portland, OR 97225; (503) 297-1894
DATES: June 1, 1993–May 31, 1997
TITLE: Project PHYSlab

PRINCIPAL INVESTIGATOR: Vicki Osis
INSTITUTION: Oregon State University, Corvallis, OR 97331; (503) 737-0123
DATES: April 1, 1993–September 30, 1996
TITLE: Translating Current Global Environmental Change Research for Middle School

PRINCIPAL INVESTIGATOR: Gail Whitney
INSTITUTION: Oregon Graduate Institute of Science & Technology, 20000 N.W. Walker Road, Beaverton, OR 97006; (503) 690-1121
DATES: March 15, 1992–August 31, 1996
TITLE: Apprenticeships in Science and Engineering for Rural and Remote Areas

PENNSYLVANIA

PRINCIPAL INVESTIGATOR: Samuel Cameron
INSTITUTION: Beaver College, Easton and Church Roads, Glenside, PA 19038; (215) 572-2900

DATES: March 1, 1992–August 31, 1995
TITLE: Project in Natural Science Psychology for High School Psychology Teachers

PRINCIPAL INVESTIGATOR: Arnold George
INSTITUTION: Mansfield University of Pennsylvania, Mansfield, PA 16933; (717) 662-4000
DATES: June 1, 1992–November 30, 1995
TITLE: Chemistry for Children—A Program for Elementary and Middle School Teachers Precollege Chemistry

PRINCIPAL INVESTIGATOR: M. Kathleen Heid
INSTITUTION: Pennsylvania State University–University Park, University Park, PA 16802; (814) 865-4700
DATES: February 15, 1992–January 31, 1996
TITLE: Empowering Mathematics Teachers in Computer-Intensive Environments

PRINCIPAL INVESTIGATOR: Roseanne Hofmann
INSTITUTION: Montgomery County Community College, 340 DeKalb Pike, Blue Bell, PA 19422-0758; (215) 641-6550
DATES: January 15, 1994–December 31, 1995
TITLE: Graphics Calculators and Internet Coalition Conference

PRINCIPAL INVESTIGATOR: Curtis Howard
INSTITUTION: PATHS/PRISM, 7 Benjamin Franklin Parkway, Philadelphia, PA 19103; (215) 665-1400
DATES: March 15, 1992–August 31, 1995
TITLE: Philadelphia Science Resource Leaders for the Middle Grades

PRINCIPAL INVESTIGATOR: John Madden
INSTITUTION: Pennsylvania State University–University Park, University Park, PA 16802; (814) 865-4700
DATES: September 1, 1991–February 29, 1996
TITLE: Mathematics Opportunities in Engineering, Science, and Technology (MOEST)

PRINCIPAL INVESTIGATOR: Donald Mitchell
INSTITUTION: Juniata College, Huntingdon, PA 16652-2119; (814) 643-4310
DATES: September 1, 1992–February 29, 1996
TITLE: Juniata College Science Outreach Program

PRINCIPAL INVESTIGATOR: Teresa Pica
INSTITUTION: University of Pennsylvania, Philadelphia, PA 19104; (215) 898-5000
DATES: July 1, 1994–December 31, 1998
TITLE: Penn-Merck Collaborative for the Enhancement of Science Education

PRINCIPAL INVESTIGATOR: Peter Rubba
INSTITUTION: Pennsylvania State University–University Park, University Park, PA 16802; (814) 865-4700
DATES: August 15, 1991–July 31, 1995
TITLE: Teacher Development and Research in STS Education for Rural Middle/Junior High School Science Teachers from Central Pennsylvania and Northern West Virginia

PRINCIPAL INVESTIGATOR: Kenneth Schroder
INSTITUTION: Franklin Institute Science Museum, 20th and Benjamin Franklin Parkway, Philadelphia, PA 19103; (215) 448-1200
DATES: May 1, 1994–October 31, 1997
TITLE: Commonwealth Excellence in Science Teaching Alliance (CESTA)

PRINCIPAL INVESTIGATOR: Jatnes Taubler
INSTITUTION: Saint Vincent College, Latrobe, PA 15650-2690; (412) 539-9761
DATES: January 1, 1993–June 30, 1997
TITLE: Building Relationships with Industry for Delivering and Generating Educational Support (BRIDGES)

PRINCIPAL INVESTIGATOR: Allen Wolfe
INSTITUTION: Lebanon Valley College, Annville PA 17003; (717) 867-6100
DATES: April 1, 1994–June 30, 1998
TITLE: Science Education Partnership for South Central Pennsylvania

RHODE ISLAND

PRINCIPAL INVESTIGATOR: Sharon Lloyd Clark
INSTITUTION: Brown University, 45 Prospect Street, Box 1876, Providence, RI 02912; (401) 863-1000
DATES: January 1, 1994–December 31, 1997
TITLE: Zooscope—Focus on Middle School Teaching

PRINCIPAL INVESTIGATOR: Mary Hibert
INSTITUTION: Brown University, 45 Prospect Street, Box 1876, Providence, RI 02912; (401) 863-1000
DATES: March 15, 1993–August 31, 1997
TITLE: Math/Science Fellows—Restructuring Mathematics and Science in Essential Schools

SOUTH CAROLINA

PRINCIPAL INVESTIGATOR: Celia Adair
INSTITUTION: University of South Carolina–Spartanburg, Spartanburg, SC 29303; (800) 599-2000
DATES: June 1, 1992–November 30, 1996
TITLE: Partnership for Excellence—A Model Program for Professional Development of Middle and Secondary School Mathematics Teachers

PRINCIPAL INVESTIGATOR: Patty Smith
INSTITUTION: School District of Pickens County, SC, 1348 Griffin Road, Pickens, SC 29671; (803) 855-8150
DATES: February 15, 1993–July 31, 1997
TITLE: SALT—Specialists and Lead Teachers in Elementary Mathematics

SOUTH DAKOTA

PRINCIPAL INVESTIGATOR: Leland Bordeaux

INSTITUTION: Sinte Gleska College Center, Mission, SD 57555; (605) 856-4891
DATES: February 1, 1994–May 31, 1996
TITLE: Native American Mathematics and Science Education Leadership

TENNESSEE

PRINCIPAL INVESTIGATOR: Duane Giannangelo
INSTITUTION: Memphis State University, Memphis, TN 38152; (901) 678-2000
DATES: January 1, 1994–June 30, 1998
TITLE: West Tennessee Geography Project

PRINCIPAL INVESTIGATOR: Don Kellogg
INSTITUTION: University of Tennessee–Martin, Martin, TN 38238; (901) 587-7777
DATES: July 15, 1993–December 31, 1995
TITLE: Planning Project for Statewide Improvement of Elementary Science in Tennessee

PRINCIPAL INVESTIGATOR: Jack Rhoton
INSTITUTION: East Tennessee State University, Johnson City, TN 37614-0002; (615) 929-4112
DATES: February 1, 1992–January 31, 1996
TITLE: Reaching for Excellence in Secondary School Science

TEXAS

PRINCIPAL INVESTIGATOR: Robert Clark
INSTITUTION: Texas Engineering Experiment Station, 301 Wisenbaker Engineering Research Center, Texas A&M University, College Station, TX 77843-3126; (401) 845-3211
DATES: June 1, 1992–November 30, 1995
TITLE: Texas Regional Enhancement Program for Underprepared Physics Teachers

PRINCIPAL INVESTIGATOR: Robert Clark
INSTITUTION: Texas Engineering Experiment Station, 301 Wisenbaker Engineering Research Center, Texas A&M University, College Station, TX 77843-3126; (401) 845-3211
DATES April 1, 1993–July 31, 1996
TITLE: Texas Regional Enhancement Program for Underprepared Physical Science Teachers

PRINCIPAL INVESTIGATOR: Linda Crow
INSTITUTION: Baylor University College of Medicine, One Baylor Plaza, 1200 Moursund Street, Houston, TX 77030; (713) 798-4951
DATES: May 1, 1994–April 30, 1997
TITLE: Science Classroom Assessment and Teaching Strategies

PRINCIPAL INVESTIGATOR: Elnora Harcombe
INSTITUTION: William Marsh Rice University, P.O. Box 1892, Houston, TX 77251; (713) 527-8101
DATES: July 1, 1992–June 30, 1995
TITLE: Rice University/HISD Science Partners for Houston Project

PRINCIPAL INVESTIGATOR: Hugh Hudson
INSTITUTION: University of Houston, Houston, TX 77204-2161; (713) 749-1101
DATES: July 1, 1993–March 31, 1996
TITLE: Enhancement Program for Physical Science Teachers

PRINCIPAL INVESTIGATOR: Robert James
INSTITUTION: Texas A&M University Research Foundation, College Station, TX 77843-3126; (409) 845-3211
DATES: December 15, 1992–November 30, 1995
TITLE: Texas Biotechnology Teacher Enhancement Project

PRINCIPAL INVESTIGATOR: Richard Kasschau
INSTITUTION: University of Houston, Houston, TX 77204-2161; (713) 749-1101
DATES: May 1, 1993–July 31, 1996
TITLE: High School Psychology Teacher Workshop—A Network Approach

PRINCIPAL INVESTIGATOR: Mary Long
INSTITUTION: Austin Independent School District, 1111 West 6th Street, Austin, TX 78703; (512) 414-1700
DATES: January 1, 1991–June 30, 1995
TITLE: Austin Science and Math Consortium—A Private Sector School Partnership for Tomorrow's World

PRINCIPAL INVESTIGATOR: Kathleen Martin
INSTITUTION: Texas Christian University, Fort Worth, TX 76129; (817) 921-7000
DATES: November 15, 1992–April 30, 1997
TITLE: A Professional Development School Model of Teacher Enhancement in Elementary School Mathematics and Science

PRINCIPAL INVESTIGATOR: Richard Olenick
INSTITUTION: University of Dallas, 1845 East Northgate Drive, Irving, TX 75062-4799; (214) 721-5000
DATES: June 15, 1993–November 30, 1997
TITLE: Comprehensive Conceptual Curriculum for Physics (C^3P)

PRINCIPAL INVESTIGATOR: Carol Stuessy
INSTITUTION: Texas A&M University Main Campus, College Station, TX 77843-1265; (409) 845-3211
DATES: January 1, 1993–December 31, 1996
TITLE: Teachers as Research Partners—Testing a Problem-Solving Curriculum Model That Integrates Mathematics and Science

UTAH

PRINCIPAL INVESTIGATOR: C. Clements
INSTITUTION: University of Utah, 110 Park, Salt Lake City, UT 84112; (801) 581-7200
DATES: August 1, 1992–July 31, 1995
TITLE: Elementary Mathematics Through Teacher Partnership

PRINCIPAL INVESTIGATOR: LaMont Jensen
INSTITUTION: Davis County, Davis County Private Industry Council, Farmington, UT

84025; (801) 451-3236
DATES: September 1, 1991–February 29, 1996
TITLE: Davis County Private Sector Partnerships for Math/Science Improvement (Davis County PSP)

VERMONT

PRINCIPAL INVESTIGATOR: Arthur Hessler
INSTITUTION: Saint Michael's College, Winooski Park, Colchester, VT 05439; (802) 654-2000
DATES: December 15, 1993–May 31, 1999
TITLE: Vermont Rivers Teacher Enhancement Project

PRINCIPAL INVESTIGATOR: J. Parsons
INSTITUTION: National Gardening Association, 180 Flynn Avenue, Burlington, VT 05401; (802) 863-1308
DATES: July 1, 1993–December 31, 1995
TITLE: Growing Science Inquiry

VIRGINIA

PRINCIPAL INVESTIGATOR: Mary Bellamy
INSTITUTION: National Association of Biology Teachers, 11250 Roger Bacon Drive, Reston, VA 22090; (703) 471-1134
DATES: September 1, 1992–February 28, 1998
TITLE: Encouraging High School Student Research in Biology Through Teacher-Scientist Partnerships

PRINCIPAL INVESTIGATOR: Carlton Brown
INSTITUTION: Hampton University, Hampton, VA 23669; (804) 727-5000
DATES: August 1, 1991–July 31, 1995
TITLE: Virginia HBCU Consortium for Science Education

PRINCIPAL INVESTIGATOR: Preston Prather
INSTITUTION: University of Virginia Main Campus, University Station, Charlottesville, VA 22903; (804) 924-0311
DATES: June 1, 1992–May 31, 1996
TITLE: Integrated Physical Science for Elementary Teachers (IPSET)

PRINCIPAL INVESTIGATOR: Marcia Tharp
INSTITUTION: Old Dominion University Research Foundation, Hampton Boulevard, Norfolk, VA 23529-0050; (804) 683-3637
DATES: March 1, 1993–August 31, 1996
TITLE: VANT Outreach Program

PRINCIPAL INVESTIGATOR: Jeffrey Witmer
INSTITUTION: American Statistical Association, 1429 Duke Street, Alexandria, VA 22314; (703) 684-1221
DATES: June 1, 1994–November 30, 1996
TITLE: Science Education and Quantitative Literacy

WASHINGTON

PRINCIPAL INVESTIGATOR: Nancy Angello
INSTITUTION: Highline School District, 15675 Ambaum Boulevard, S.W., Seattle, WA 98146; (206) 433-0111
DATES: July 1, 1993–December 31, 1996
TITLE: Science is BASIC (Bridging Assessment into Science Instruction and Curriculum)

PRINCIPAL INVESTIGATOR: Dianne Barr-Cole
INSTITUTION: Educational Service District 112, 2500 N.E. 65th Avenue, Vancouver, WA 98661; (360) 750-7500
DATES: August 15, 1992–January 31, 1996
TITLE: The Gorge, the River, the Valley, and the Ocean

PRINCIPAL INVESTIGATOR: Glenn Crosby
INSTITUTION: Washington State University, Pullman, WA 99164-1036; (509) 335-3564
DATES: January 1, 1991–December 31, 1995
TITLE: A Master's in Chemistry Program for Out-of-Field Teachers

PRINCIPAL INVESTIGATOR: Robert Gibbs
INSTITUTION: Eastern Washington University, Cheney, WA 99004; (509) 458-6200
DATES: June 15, 1992–November 30, 1997
TITLE: Restructuring Elementary School Science

PRINCIPAL INVESTIGATOR: Carole Kobota
INSTITUTION: University of Washington, 1400 N.E. Campus Parkway, Seattle, WA 98195; (206) 543-2100
DATES: March 15, 1994–August 31, 1997
TITLE: Washington Initiative in Science Education—Science Teacher Enhancement Project

PRINCIPAL INVESTIGATOR: James Stewart
INSTITUTION: Western Washington University, 516 High Street, Bellingham, WA 98225-9009; (206) 650-3000
DATES: June 15, 1994–October 31, 1997
TITLE: Operation Physics Outreach

PRINCIPAL INVESTIGATOR: Robert Watts
INSTITUTION: University of Washington, 1400 N.E. Campus Parkway, Seattle, WA 98195; (206) 543-2100
DATES: June 15, 1993–November 30, 1996
TITLE: Outreach Program for Junior High Science Teachers of American Indian and Native Alaskan Students in the Pacific Northwest

PRINCIPAL INVESTIGATOR: Richard Zollars
INSTITUTION: Washington State University, Pullman, WA 99164-1036; (509) 335-3564
DATES: August 1, 1993–January 31, 1997
TITLE: Teacher Institute for Science/Mathematics Education Through Engineering Experiences

WEST VIRGINIA
PRINCIPAL INVESTIGATOR: Hobart King
INSTITUTION: West Virginia Geological & Economic Survey, P.O. Box 879, Morgantown, WV 26507; (304) 291-4251
DATES: August 1, 1992–January 31, 1996
TITLE: Earth Science in West Virginia for the 21st Century

WISCONSIN
PRINCIPAL INVESTIGATOR: Marilyn Duerst
INSTITUTION: University of Wisconsin–River Falls, River Falls, WI 54022; (304) 291-4251
DATES: May 1, 1994–April 30, 1998
TITLE: Physical Science Institutes for K–3 Teachers

PRINCIPAL INVESTIGATOR: Raymond Kessel
INSTITUTION: University of Wisconsin–Madison, 750 University Avenue, Madison, WI 53706; (608) 262-1234
DATES: March 15, 1992–August 31, 1995
TITLE: Summer Institute Core, Outreach, and Multiplier Program for Genetics Education

PRINCIPAL INVESTIGATOR: Karen Klyczek
INSTITUTION: University of Wisconsin–River Falls, River Falls, WI 54022; (715) 425-3911
DATES: July 1, 1994–November 30, 1997
TITLE: Inservice Program in Biotechnology for Secondary Life Science and Agriculture Education Teachers

PRINCIPAL INVESTIGATOR: Leroy Lee
INSTITUTION: Wisconsin Academy of Sciences, Arts & Letters, 1922 University Avenue, Madison, WI 53705; (608) 263-1692
DATES: April 15, 1992–September 30, 1995
TITLE: Leadership Development—Earth Science Resource Associates

PRINCIPAL INVESTIGATOR: Leroy Lee
INSTITUTION: Wisconsin Academy of Sciences, Arts & Letters, 1922 University Avenue, Madison, WI 53705; (608) 263-1692
DATES: November 1, 1993–April 30, 1998
TITLE: Field Institutes for Elementary School Teachers

PRINCIPAL INVESTIGATOR: John Moore
INSTITUTION: University of Wisconsin–Madison, 750 University Avenue, Madison, WI 53706; (608) 262-1234
DATES: June 1, 1992–November 30, 1995
TITLE: Empowering Teachers to Enhance Science Education

PRINCIPAL INVESTIGATOR: John Moore
INSTITUTION: University of Wisconsin–Madison, 750 University Avenue, Madison, WI 53706; (608) 262-1234
DATES: June 15, 1994–May 31, 1996
TITLE: Chemistry Fundamentals for Middle School Teachers—Maintaining the ICE Network

PRINCIPAL INVESTIGATOR: Molly Murray
INSTITUTION: University of Wisconsin–Madison, 750 University Avenue, Madison, WI 53706; (608) 262-1234
DATES: January 15, 1994–June 30, 1997
TITLE: Earthkeeping—Restoration-Based Teacher Training Institutes

PRINCIPAL INVESTIGATOR: James Stewart
INSTITUTION: University of Wisconsin–Madison, 750 University Avenue, Madison, WI 53706; (608) 262-1234
DATES: August 15, 1992–July 31, 1995
TITLE: Site-Specific Environmental Education

PRINCIPAL INVESTIGATOR: James Stewart
INSTITUTION: University of Wisconsin–Madison, 750 University Avenue, Madison, WI 53706; (608) 262-1234
DATES: September 1, 1992–August 31, 1995
TITLE: Enhancement of Minority Student Achievement in the Science Classroom

PRINCIPAL INVESTIGATOR: John Tonnis
INSTITUTION: University of Wisconsin–La Crosse, 1725 State Street, La Crosse, WI 54601; (608) 785-8000
DATES: May 1, 1992–October 31, 1996
TITLE: Certification and Qualification Program for Underprepared Secondary Chemistry Teachers

PRINCIPAL INVESTIGATOR: Richard Wilke
INSTITUTION: University of Wisconsin–Stevens Point, Stevens Point, WI 54481; (715) 346-0123
DATES: November 1, 1992–April 30, 1996
TITLE: In-Service Teacher Training in Environmental Education

PRINCIPAL INVESTIGATOR: Paul Williams
INSTITUTION: University of Wisconsin–Madison, 750 University Avenue, Madison, WI 53706; (608) 262-1234
DATES: December 15, 1992–November 30, 1995
TITLE: Dissemination Through Wisconsin Fast Plants Master Leader Workshop

PRINCIPAL INVESTIGATOR: Donald Woolston
INSTITUTION: University of Wisconsin–Madison, 750 University Avenue, Madison, WI 53706; (608) 262-1234
DATES: September 1, 1992–August 31, 1995
TITLE: Project X—Exchange of Information on Technical Careers

WYOMING

PRINCIPAL INVESTIGATOR: A. Duane Porter
INSTITUTION: University of Wyoming, Laramie, WY 82071; (307) 766-1121
DATES: December 1, 1993–May 31, 1998
TITLE: Model Master's Degree Program

AFTERWORD

This directory lists over 200 institutions, companies, and agencies that offer workshops, seminars, field courses, programs, safaris, and expeditions in the natural sciences. Questionnaires were mailed to approximately 3,500 institutions and other entries came from ads, newspaper articles, and word-of-mouth. This list is, however, not exhaustive.

All the institutions I contacted were delighted to provide information for inclusion in this book. There were a few, however, that did not respond. Perhaps these institutions are often overbooked and did not want additional publicity for courses or programs that are always filled to capacity.

If you, the reader, know of additional institutions, programs, or agencies that are not described here and that you feel would be appropriate for inclusion in any future editions, please send me their address. You may direct your correspondence to:

Dr. Jack Edelman
P.O. Box 400737
Brooklyn, NY 11240-0737

My philosophy is that any travel experience is a learning experience and an educational accomplishment. "Learning" does not begin in elementary school nor does it "end" in graduate school; rather, it is a continuum on this mega-school we call Earth.

ABOUT THE AUTHOR

Jack R. Edelman, Ph.D., has been teaching biology in the New York City Public School System for 18 years, and has served as an adjunct professor of biology at several New York City area colleges and universities. He received his bachelor's degree in biology from Brooklyn College, master's degrees in biology from Long Island University and Saint John's University, and master's degree and professional diploma in Educational Administration from Pace University. In 1990 he received his doctorate in biological sciences from Saint John's University, specializing in cytogenetics and chromosome research. To date, Dr. Edelman has published over one dozen papers on chromosome research in scientific journals throughout the world. He has also served as an item writer for the Regents' Biology Examinations, New York State Education Department.

Some of his pastimes include gardening and music; he is an avid record collector and has performed as a radio disk jockey. He is also a member of the American Federation of Television and Radio Artists, the Knights of Pythias, and the Science Teachers Association of New York State.